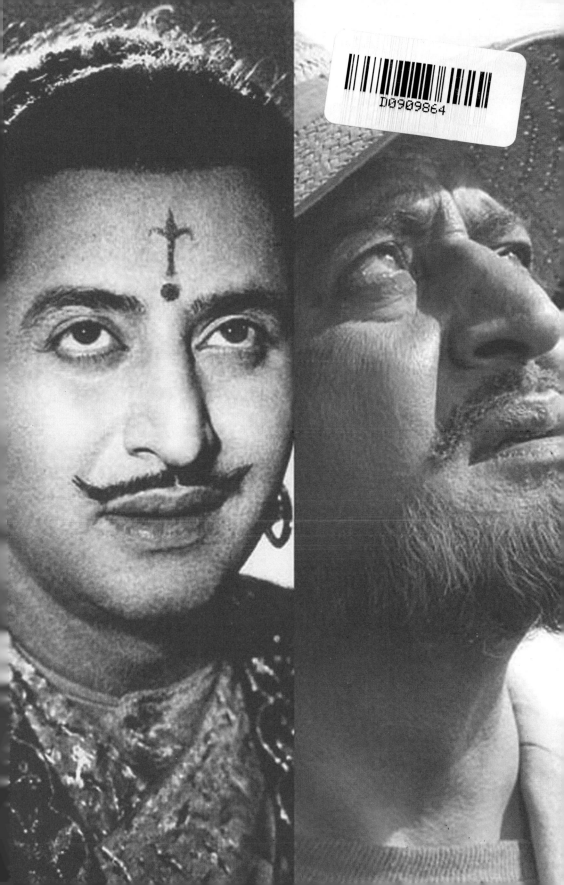

...and
PRAN
A BIOGRAPHY

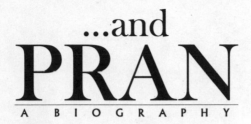

...and
PRAN
A BIOGRAPHY

Bunny Reuben

HarperCollins *Publishers* India
a joint venture with

THE
INDIA
TODAY
GROUP

New Delhi

First published in India in 2005 by
HarperCollins *Publishers* India
a joint venture with
The India Today Group

Copyright © Arvind Sikand 2005

Bunny Reuben asserts the moral
right to be identified as the author of this work.

HarperCollins *Publishers*
1A Hamilton House Connaught Place, New Delhi 110001, India
77-85 Fulham Palace Road, London W6 8JB, United Kingdom
Hazelton Lanes, 55 Avenue Road, Suite 2900, Toronto, Ontario M5R 3L2
and 1995 Markham Road, Scarborough, Ontario M1B 5M8, Canada
25 Ryde Road, Pymble, Sydney, NSW 2073, Australia
31 View Road, Glenfield, Auckland 10, New Zealand
10 East 53rd Street, New York NY 10022, USA

Typeset in 11.5/14 Weiss
Atelier Typecraft

Printed and bound at
Thomson Press (India) Ltd.

Contents

Amitabh Bachchan

'Pratiksha', 10th North-South Road, Juhu-Parle Scheme, Bombay 400 049.

Some actors aren't just artistes we admire, or chessmen in a strange game. They are us, expressing our brightest and darkest thoughts, enacting a gamut of roles ranging from the psychologically complicated to the absolutely simple. They are a bigger 'us'.

Actors are our friends, figures who loom in our lives larger than our actual acquaintances. Pran *Saab* has been one such colossus, his presence affecting myriad generations of film viewers. In fact, for nearly five decades there was a mysterious, almost magical, interaction between him and the audience.

Pran means 'life'. And he has given cinema just that with his seamless artistry. He struck terror in the heart of the audiences, assuaging them finally with the moral — 'ladies and gentlemen, evil does not win'.

Screen villainy is a thankless job which Pran *Saab* accepted and carried out with such a degree of perfection that he became the actor the entire nation loved to hate. That indeed was the measure of his extraordinary success. Parents did not want their children to meet him. Occasionally, he would even be feared and dreaded at public gatherings.

Evidently, he came to terms with that, bemused with the power of cinema to influence the audience in a way that sketches only a thin line between the real and the reel. Subsequently, the thespian turned the tables with a marvellous sleight of hand. He donned the mantle of a character artiste with equal skill and felicity. Versatility became his imprimatur.

Circa 1960, I caught my first glimpse of Pran *Saab*. In the course of a fleeting visit to Mumbai, I had requested some family friends to take me to a film shooting. At the R.K. Studios, Pran *Saab* was sitting inconspicuously on a chair, close to a tin shed. He was polite and courteous; he posed for a photograph with us. I returned home with his autograph, a bit disoriented. Like others, I asked myself: 'How can a villain be so good and hospitable?'

Now, of course, I know better than to mix up the actor with the human being. Ironically perhaps, the shooting at the R.K. Studios that day was for *Chhalia*, the debut film of Manmohan Desai with whom I went on to do quite a few of my most memorable films.

Some years later when I came to Mumbai to seek a film career, I often met Pran *Saab's* son Sunil '*Tunni*' Sikand, a close friend of my brother Ajitabh. As an actor trying to find a foothold, my first interface with Pran *Saab* was on the sets of *Zanjeer*. By that time, he had made an effortless transition from villainy to character roles following his superb performance in *Upkar*. He had asserted, as it were, that a villain does not have to remain a villain. He had set a significant precedent: Shatrughan Sinha and Vinod Khanna, who began with negative roles, went on to become superheroes.

On the very first day of the *Zanjeer* schedule, we shot the police station sequence in which I am rude to Sher Khan. I lose my cool and hurl terrible invectives at him. I did feel a bit hesitant to break into a tirade but when I saw him I felt reassured. After all, it was largely because of Pran *Saab* that I had been cast in *Zanjeer*. Om Prakashjee who had good words for my performance in *Parwana* had generously recommended me to producers in Chennai and also to Pran *Saab*. In turn, Pran *Saab* backed me to the hilt when the cast of *Zanjeer* was being finalized.

This was my first film with Prakash Mehra and Salim-Javed. I was relatively new to the film industry, I did feel apprehensive. Pran *Saab* was very helpful, he set me at ease. In fact, he was the biggest selling point of the film. I marvelled at the manner in which he took tremendous care over his looks. Right from the hennaed wig and beard to his costume and make-up, he ensured that every element was flawless.

All my scenes in *Zanjeer* with him were tough. Often during the action sequences, I kept hoping I wouldn't miss my punch cue and end up hurting him. For one of the sequences, we had to climb up a wall with a rope. He was the first man up. Irrespective of the long and arduous process of getting into his make-up and costumes, he was also the first one on the set. Invariably. Infallibly.

Even if his shot was over, he would remain on the set, watching the proceedings with a keen eye. Certainly one of the high points of the film was the '*Yaari Hai Imaan…*' set piece which he performed with incomparable agility and vigour.

Pran *Saab* never interfered with anyone's work. He never argued with anyone, he never asked for alterations in the dialogue or a situation in the script and he never once lost his temper. He would complete a day's work diligently and leave.

Subsequently, I gleaned a little known facet of his during the outdoor shooting spell of *Ganga Ki Saugandh* in Rishikesh, Hardwar and Jaipur. Pran *Saab* is hugely fond of Urdu poetry and literature. He keeps abreast of all sports events to this day. At one point, he was fond of *shikaar*. He has an encylopaedic knowledge of *sher-o-shairee*, folk tales and ribald humour. At get-togethers in the evening, he would enthrall the unit with risqué jokes and recitations of couplets.

He would be delightful company after the shoots. He would enjoy his evening Scotch. And he would smoke cigarettes with such a distinctive style that it became his trademark trait, on as well as off screen. Anyone who has seen his performances can deduce that he has given every role a special quality, detailing every character with imaginative little touches. Like the way he rubbed his neck knowing his character of the dacoit would be hanged at the end of *Jis Desh Mein Ganga Behti Hai.*

Throughout an estimable career, he used his eyes, voice, diction, facial mobility and body language to powerful effect. He could memorize reams of dialogue just by glancing at the sheets of paper handed over to him on the sets, more often than not a minute before the call of lights, action, camera. He never made a mistake, the lines flowing smoothly from a photographic memory.

Whether he was playing a Christian like the endearing Michael in *Majboor*, the Pathan Sher Khan flicking his hair back in *Zanjeer*, the street-smart fun person displaying amazing comic synergy with Dadamoni Ashok Kumar in *Victoria No: 203*, the volatile convict in the black-and-white *Shaheed* or the upper-crust father in *Bobby*, it was evident that he took great pains to differentiate every one of his characters, thus giving them a new and always credible edge. Even if he was saddled with a stereotyped role, like all actors are on occasion, the part received a fresh interpretation and impetus.

I had the privilege of working with Pran *Saab* in several films including *Amar Akbar Anthony*, *Kasauti*, *Majboor*, *Don*, *Kaalia*, *Naseeb*, *Nastik*, *Sharabi*, *Andha Kanoon* and *Inquilab*. For the climax of *Naseeb*, located in a revolving restaurant, he went through training in sword fencing. He had 'swashbuckled' expertly before in the movies but being a stickler for doing the right thing, he insisted on a fortnight of retraining. The last time we worked together was for *Mrityudaataa*, in which he graciously assented to play a cameo part.

Through all the films we worked on, it was clear that he is a man of principles. If there was a particular line of dialogue or a situation in any script, bordering on the crude or which was socially and morally objectionable, he would comment on that immediately. He wouldn't get into an unresolvable conflict with the writer or the director but use fair reason and logic to stress his point of view. That is why every film maker knew that Pran *Saab* would go this far and no further; he had demarcated a boundary for himself, whereby he would not do anything that was vulgar or unaesthetic...

Pran *Saab* is extremely shy, opening up essentially when he knows he is among friends and like-minded colleagues. He has been one of my kindest guides and masters. On the films we did together, if he ever felt that I could improve upon a take, very apologetically he would murmur: 'Don't misunderstand me...but why don't you try it that way?' If he was pleased with my take, he would never fail to compliment me.

Curiously, Pran *Saab* would never see his own films. It was nearly twenty years after the release of *Zanjeer* that he saw the film accidentally. He called me to say: 'I liked your performance.' It felt wonderful even if his compliment came two decades later.

That Pran *Saab* was an astute counterpoise to the great stalwart actors is apparent to any film aficionado. Chameleon-like, he could change his demeanour and outlook by simply wearing a thick pair of glasses or donning jodhpurs and leather boots in the vintage entertainers, while representing a supreme challenge to the widely idolized heroes. As the tormentor of Dilip Kumar *Saab* in *Ram Aur Shyam* and the hurdle in the way of Dev Anand *Saab* in the black-and-white *Jab Pyar Kisise Hota Hai*, Pran *Saab* held his own right till the finale when he may have lost the battle but triumphed immeasurably as an actor.

From him, I have learnt that professionalism is an actor's main qualification and strength. There was never a day when he reported late, never a day he cancelled a shoot because he was feeling under the weather. One day, he was on the sets, exceptionally reserved and uncommunicative. After hours when he continued to be in a shell, the director asked him if something was wrong. Pran *Saab* very quietly said that he had just lost his brother but he didn't want to cancel the shoot because life must go on.

Among his closest friends were the late Satish Bhalla and Yash Johar. Not given to flamboyant tastes, Pran *Saab* has led a life of self-respect and dignity. I have never heard him asking for a favour. Rather, he has been a man and actor of strong convictions and values. His appeal has transcended fads and trends. Regrettably, he has not received an iota of the recognition which he deserves in abundance.

Needless to emphasize, the longevity of his tenure and his abiding dedication merit official honours and awards which have largely been denied to him. As they have said of so many grand character actors in the West, they don't make them like him any more. An artiste of his stature would have been lionized in the US, Europe, wherever. Alas, here acknowledgement has been grudged to him. Inexplicably.

This book chronicling his life and career is a heartfelt hosanna for Pran *Saab*. I am proud to be associated with the endeavour and wish Arvind, Sunil and Pinky [Pran *Saab*'s children] the best for honouring their father in this valuable and much-needed manner.

Cinema may change both in content and technique. But nothing can take away from Pran *Saab's* boundless contribution to Indian cinema. Whenever he had to climb up a wall, he left us, another generation, behind. He was always up first.

Sir, thank you for giving us all so much of yourself, without ever getting anything from us in return. You are our inspiration, our Pran *Saab*.

12 July 2004

Acknowledgements

I wish to thank my daughter Lakshmi Reuben-Gopali for her invaluable help in the writing of this biography.

I would also like to thank Pran *Saab's* daughter Pinky Bhalla for her meticulous work with cataloguing and selecting photographs and coordinating family interviews.

Pinky also suggested the title of this book. When she was asked: 'Why "... *and Pran*"?', she produced an email written by a fan who thought Pran's name was 'and Pran', since in all his films, he used to be the last one listed in the line-up of the cast!

Thanks are due also to Pran *Saab's* elder son Arvind Sikand for conceiving this biography and for his anecdotes, inputs, invaluable help and patience during the writing of this biography, and to Pran *Saab's* younger son Sunil Sikand for his help in editing the book as well as remembering many anecdotes and incidents, some even at the last minute!

The publishers have extended the maximum cooperation in the production of this book, for which I thank them.

The following friends and well-wishers are also thanked for their valuable contributions to this book: First and foremost, thanks go to Dinshaw Mehta, Pran's long-time admirer-turned-friend who collected and preserved much information about Pran in huge volumes and has even videotaped many of Pran's old films, from television channels that telecast vintage movies, for Pran's personal collection.

I thank Dr (Mrs) Sushila Rani Patel and Suryakant Patel, wife and the eldest son of the late Baburao Patel of *Filmindia;* Rajendra Ojha of Screen World Publications; Shashikant Kinikar of Pune; Dr Padmanabh Joshi of Ahmedabad; Harish Raghuvanshi of Surat; Aparna Phadke, retired librarian of the Film & Television Institute of India in Pune. I would also like to thank the following newspapers and magazines: *Screen, Cine Advance* (the Bombay edition of the Calcutta weekly newspaper), *The Telegraph, Sakal* (Pune), *Loksatta,* the *Times of India, Filmfare, Cine Blitz, Stardust, Star & Style, Sunday Mid-Day, Trade Guide* and *Sportsworld.*

Thanks also to my ex-secretary Vanita for painstakingly entering into the computer every last bit of research and creating order in the deluge of information unearthed for this biography and to Ram Kumarjee, Pran's secretary, who kindly and patiently did numerous things that were of help and went out of his way to unearth extra facts for the Filmography.

Thanks also to the many friends, family members and film folk who gave their time and shared their memories of Pran *Saab,* all of which have contributed to making this book a 'must-buy' for all admirers and fans of Pran.

1 August 2004   Bunny Reuben

Prologue

The theatre has been darkened – the only light comes from the images illuminating the screen. Silence reigns as the audience watches the film unfold.

Suddenly, the scene changes and it is soon obvious that one of those ubiquitous song-and-dance sequences, thought to be a necessary ingredient of the potboilers churned out by Bollywood, will start. The reality, of course, is that audiences make use of these musical interruptions to the story to have a quick smoke or to answer nature's call. Cigarette songs or loo songs, they are called.

This time, though, things are different. The atmosphere is now charged and the audience seems to sit up as though gearing up for something special.

Soon it is clear what that something special is...

The music starts.

The actor starts singing: *'Raaz Ki Baat Keh Doon Toh, Jaane Mehfil Mein Phir Kya Ho?'*[1]

---

[1] From S. K. Kapoor's film, titled *Dharma* (1973). The singers are Mohammed Rafi and Asha Bhonsle. The music by Sonik Omi had lyrics penned by Varma Malik, which when translated mean: 'If I reveal the secret now, I wonder what will be its effect on the gathering here.'

The audience goes mad! They whistle and scream and clap to the beat of the *qawwali*.[2] Some even dance in the aisles! And as the *qawwali* draws to a close, the audience is in a frenzy!

Their reaction is so spontaneous and enthusiastic that one takes it for granted that the actor in question is a popular hero of the time. But no, instead of a popular hero, the one triggering off such a reaction is none other than Pran – hero-villain-character actor – who has captivated the audience to the extent that even the escapist cigarettes and nature's calls are forgotten!

How did Pran, who for years had been typecast as villain, and who switched to doing character actor roles only in the late 1960s, arouse this kind of adulation and mass hysteria on a par with the popular heroes of the time?

Especially when others of his generation have either been eased out of the scene or have compromised and are seen in roles that no actor worth his salt would want to do, how has Pran gone from one significant role to another, and from one milestone to another in a career spanning several decades? A career sixty years' long?

Pran himself prefers to think that his longevity as an in-demand actor has been due to the fact that he has always observed three principles in life which were instilled in him by his father.

First, his father advised him that while climbing the stairs to success, one should always wish well those on the way down. This is because if in the future you are on the way down, you may find that those very people may be ascending the stairs again. They will recall your good grace and little gestures and will wish you well in return.

Secondly, his father said that one should always have two drinks at home before leaving for a party where liquor is to be served. This is so that one may not overdrink at one's host's house and get labelled 'greedy' or 'cheap'. This principle has also helped him not to take advantage of the producers for whom he worked, even when many contemporaries thought nothing of doing so.

---

2   A *qawwali* originally represents a style of Sufi devotional singing. However, the *qawwalis* in Hindi films *usually* depict a poetic clash between a man and a woman and are marked by a catchy rhythm.

Finally, his father asked him always to take a stand from which he would not have to back down, and to maintain a position which he would not have to forsake.

Over the years, Pran has faithfully followed his father's advice. He believes that these are the principles which have helped him gain the reputation of the 'gentleman villain' and be successful in life.

When and where did this amazing journey begin? The reality is no less mind-boggling than the most fantastic piece of fiction...

PART ONE

ONE

Destiny Lingers at the *Paan* Shop

1

Pre-Partition Lahore was an exhilarating place in which to be. The city pulsated with a life of its own.

Several lives, in fact.

Lives lived at different tempos, at different times and in all corners of this northwestern hub of undivided India.

Lahore's Heera Mandi attracted lovers of beauty, *sher-o-shairee* [1] and music to its hedonistic and decadent self. Anyone who came here was drawn into the heady fragrance of its warm bosom where a strange but pleasing cacophony of melody and percussion, of *ghazals* [2] and *thumris*,[3]

---

[1] Couplets and poetic verse.
[2] A form of Urdu/Persian poetry, usually romantic. A *ghazal* can be recited or sung.
[3] A *thumri* is a song sung in Hindustani classical music where the emphasis is on the mood created by the lyrics.

of *ghunghroos* [4] and '*waah!-waahs!*' [5] assaulted the ear, and enticing voices held promise of coming pleasures.

Equally tantalizing was the conglomeration of unique smells – typical nighttime smells – smells one could always associate with Heera Mandi. The aroma of mouth-watering kebabs being barbecued over the charcoal fire mingling with scent of jasmine, wafted on the gentle breezes blowing through Heera Mandi, while the heavier perfumes of *ittar*[6] settled down for the evening among the seekers of unlimited pleasur in the *kothas*[7] there.

On the streets, however, were the men soaking in the atmosphere of the place in anticipation of various enjoyments, or having just relished some of them, were single-mindedly looking for the next source of gratification.

That was Heera Mandi. A place of pleasure. Pleasure upon pleasure. Some of the most delicious North-West Frontier food could also be had here, and since no meal in India is considered complete without *paan*, those folded triangles of betel leaves loaded with a variety of delightful fillings, so too the Heera Mandi experience was not really complete without eating one of the variety of *paans* which gave the senses one last treat of a pleasure-filled evening.

Of course, since these *paan* shops had stiff competition in the form of the various other delights of Heera Mandi, they had perfected the art of making unusual and different kinds of *paan*. And so their fame spread, ensuring that many others, even those who did not normally frequent Heera Mandi, came here to try out their magnificent *paans*.

One winter's evening, a group of three or four friends went to a *paan* shop on Mysalyore Road, placing an after-dinner order for a round of *paans*. One of them, a bright young photographer's assistant, was clearly the focal point of this group. Being young and away from his family, he had soon made many friends. Certainly, earning as he did a fair amount of money, he found that making many friends was no big deal.

---

[4]   Light brass bells strung together or stitched onto a pad of cloth and tied around the ankles of dancers in the houses of ill-repute.

[5]   Exclamations of appreciation.

[6]   Oil-based fragrances extracted from various sources, like flowers or resinous woods.

[7]   Houses of ill-repute or brothels.

Pran, the young photographer's assistant, did not know it then, but that night in Lahore in 1939 was going to turn out to be memorable. Destiny was on the prowl that night.

Just by ordering their *paans* at the shop of that colourful character named Ram Lubhaya in Heera Mandi a totally new chapter in Pran's life was going to open. His life was going to take a dramatic turn. Four words would launch him on a most amazing voyage of discovery and experience.

Four words. 'What is your name?'

As each one of the friends had ordered a special variety of *paan* for himself, the order was taking some time. Some had had theirs made and had already stuffed it into their mouth, while others were waiting patiently for theirs. Suddenly, Pran noticed a middle-aged man giving him the once-over. The man looked jovial and convivial. Obviously, here was a man who enjoyed his drinks. And what was more, the man was sizing him up from head to foot.

With the conceit that belongs to young manhood, Pran ignored him. After a while however, the man couldn't contain himself. He approached Pran and asked: 'What is your name?'

'By then,' Pran related, 'I was not only slightly drunk, but I was also irritated at the way he had been looking me up and down. So I retorted: "What's it got to do with you?"

'"No! No!" the man quickly replied, his tone placatory. "Please do not misunderstand me. My name is Wali Mohammed Wali..."

'"...and so?" I interrupted, not recognizing the name.

'"I'm a writer and Dalsukh M. Pancholi, the famous film producer purchased one of my stories. That film is already made and released. I am now writing another subject for him."

'"So?"

'"The name of the film is *Yamla Jat* which is to be made in Punjabi, and what I want to say is this...I have been observing the way you have been chewing your *paan*. There is a certain menace to it. Your looks match the looks of one of the characters in the script I've written. Will you be interested in acting in the film?"'

Pran stared at him suspiciously. This offer had come as a shock to him. Eventually, he replied: 'No.'

The stranger was not deterred by this rebuff. He insisted that Pran drop in at the film studio the following day. More to get rid of the man than anything else, Pran agreed.

'Alright then. Here's my card. Come to Pancholi Art Studios tomorrow at ten in the morning.'

In spite of his reluctance, Pran accepted the card.

'By then,' Pran continued, 'my friends and I had almost finished the *paans*, so we went away.'

The next morning dawned clear and bright, and Pran, remembering the stranger of the night before, mentally dismissed him as well as his unusual offer.

Why?

The stranger had offered Pran a part in a film being made by Dalsukh M. Pancholi, who happened to own what were possibly the best-equipped studios in Lahore, the capital of pre-Partition Punjab!

And the only films worth talking about in Lahore were those being made by Dalsukh M. Pancholi. So, reasoned Pran, for Wali Mohammed Wali to have offered a 'nobody', a stranger on the street, a chance to *act* in one of the great man's films *had* to have been the result of him having imbibed a little too freely.

By way of explanation Pran later said: 'It was *quite obvious* that the man had been high when we met at the *paan* shop. And when you are high, you make all kinds of empty promises, even to a stranger who is also a little high!

'I thought that the movie offer too was one such promise and decided not to waste my time pursuing it. So, putting the stranger out of my mind, I dashed off to my shop.'

There was no way that this stranger named Wali Mohammed Wali could trace the handsome young man of the previous night, since he did not know where he lived.

But Destiny had not stopped to catch its breath at that *paan* shop, just so that a tipsy film*wallah* could make an acting offer to a total stranger, an offer the young man may or may not take seriously.

No. Destiny had lingered there for quite a while. And although Pran had dismissed the offer made by the stranger of the previous night, Destiny had still bigger things in store for the young man and it was going to stay on the prowl.

2

'The following Saturday,' Pran continued, 'when I went to see a movie at the Plaza Cinema, I bumped into Wali *Saab* there! He recognized me immediately and, right there in the foyer, in front of strangers all around us, he gave me the firing of my life, freely using the choicest abuses in Punjabi!

'"Shame on you! I offered you – a total stranger – the chance of a lifetime! And you did not turn up! You made my position before Pancholi *Saab* very awkward! I told him that I had found the perfect boy for our film and then you let us down very badly!"'

Pran had to placate him, and apologizing profusely, agreed to go wherever Wali wanted.

But obviously Wali *Saab* was sceptical. So, he insisted on taking Pran's address and going there personally to make sure that the young lad actually came to the studios!

Things went smoothly after that.

Wali *Saab* escorted the young man to Pancholi Art Studios where arrangements for his screen test had already been made.

In this context, Pran recalled: 'The moment we reached there, they began work on my screen test. First, Moti B. Gidwani did my make-up. I came to know later that he was the director of this film.

'Along with my screen test, they also took my photographs and prints were made immediately. I also saw those photographs.

'*Thinking back in later years, I remember vividly that this is how I felt...since those first photographs of mine, thousands of my stills have been taken. But what there was in those first photographs could never be seen in any of the photographs taken ever since!*

'It wasn't just because my make-up had been done very well, or that the photographer was an expert, or...that I was a very handsome man!

'No. The real difference was this – I wasn't an *actor* at that time! *I was living my real life, an ordinary life, no different from that of millions of others.*

'But after becoming an actor, I have become many different personalities and lived many different lives. I have donned a variety of costumes, expensive and otherwise, I have donned a number of wigs, different beards and moustaches.

'Still, *nothing*, no character, no costume, no wig, could compare to that look of an ordinary, real-life man! Not even the most expensive and sophisticated camera could capture a *truer* me than those first photographs had done!

'Both Gidwani *Saab* and Pancholi *Saab* saw the photographs and liked them. And that's how I got the role which Wali *Saab* was so anxious I should get.'

It is to Pran's credit as a young man living away from his family that even then, he was hesitant. His family ties were so strong that he pleaded: 'Please, Sir. Please, just once, let me ask my family about all this. After all, I am leaving one profession and going into a totally different one – the film line!'

Pran knew that his family would have something to say about this sudden turn in his life. In fact, they would probably have quite a lot to say! The prejudice against being in films in those early decades of the twentieth century was very strong.

It was infra dig to be a film*wallah*. There was considerable justification for this prejudice because in those early years of Indian cinema, heroines were sought in *kothas*. Singing girls, dancing girls, semi-prostitutes and girls of dubious morality were plucked away from the Heera Mandis of the land and hustled into the big, bad world of the movies, and also into the beds of the men who had 'found' them! And somehow none of it really ever mattered to the 'found' ones! But girls from respectable families dared not even allow the thought of becoming a film actress creep into their minds!

Dalsukh Pancholi made it obvious that he did not like the young man's hesitation, howsoever justified it may have been from Pran's point of view. His tone changed as he uttered words which virtually amounted to a 'take-it-or-leave-it' ultimatum. He said curtly:

'Young man, day in and day out we are flooded with offers from scores of young men, all wanting to become screen heroes! Consider yourself lucky that, in your case, Wali *Saab* has liked your personality and recommended you to me. So, if you're ready, you'll have to fill up our studio form *now* – and sign it!'

What was really worrying Pran was this: he had been offered fifty rupees per month to work in the film. But Pran was already earning two hundred rupees a month at the photography shop! He voiced his problem to Pancholi.

Pancholi immediately responded: 'Alright, continue to work in the shop. We'll call you for shooting as and when we need you.'

Destiny, which had lingered first at that *paan* shop, and had prowled around long enough, was now crouching behind Pancholi *Saab* and gesticulating frantically to the young man:

'*Say yes!*'

'*Sign now!*'

'*Don't lose this golden opportunity!*'

'*The gates which these fifty rupees open for you will lead to many millions in the future.*'

Perhaps Destiny's urgings seeped into the young man's mind by some silent osmosis. Or perhaps the right hand of God nudged him in the ribs right then. Or perhaps...anything.

'Alright, Sir. I'll sign now, Sir!'

Moments later, Pran had signed the form. He was now a valid employee, an actor-to-be at Dalsukh M. Pancholi's huge studios, then the Hollywood of Lahore in undivided India.

The spirit of adventure which compelled him to embark on a career in still photography, when everyone else in his family were making more conventional career choices, now also made him, with more zeal than ever, enter the new and exciting profession of an actor.

Any doubts about how his family would react were brushed aside. Endless and thrilling possibilities lay before him and he was not going to turn his back on them.

Not now.

TWO

The Beginning...

1

Pran Krishen Sikand was born on 12 February 1920[1] in Ballimaran, Old Delhi, in the lap of luxury. The Sikands were a traditional and a prosperous family whose ancestral lineage went back several generations, making them respected, even revered, by their community. Pran recalled:

---

[1] Pran remembers an incident that set right a mix-up regarding his date of birth. When Pran applied for a driving licence, he was asked to fill out a form. Since he did not remember his exact date of birth, he wrote '22 February 1920' in the appropriate column, since he vaguely recalled his father's sister having once told him that he had been born in the third week of February in 1920. Thus, '22 February 1920' became his official date of birth. Interestingly, soon after, Pran received a letter from an individual residing in Ballimaran, who told him of an article he had read in which Pran's date of birth was given as '22 February 1920'. The writer of the letter explained that he was an employee of the municipality and could produce evidence to prove that Pran had actually been born on *12 February 1920*. All the Ballimaran resident requested was for Pran to write back. Pran obliged and duly received the promised documents establishing his true birth date!

'The locality in which our home was situated was a crowded suburb of Delhi, full of narrow lanes, though the houses were large and spacious.

'My father's name was Lala Keval Krishen Sikand. My mother's name was Rameshwari. We were four brothers and three sisters in all. The eldest were my two sisters Pramila, then Karuna. Then came Prem Krishen. Following was another sister Rajinder, whom we always called by her pet name Jindo. After her came Raj Krishen, then me, Pran Krishen, and finally Kripal Krishen.

'Basically, our native place was Punjab. We were a Hindu joint family and we owned several *bighas*[2] of land in our village. Our village was named Bharowal, near the city of Hoshiarpur. We had to get down at Sailakhurd Station to reach Bharowal, a small village. From Sailakhurd, we either walked the full seven miles to our village, or we took a bullock cart.

'My father was a civil engineer, with a well-established government contract business, who specialized in building roads and bridges.... Because of his highly specialized skills, he was frequently transferred to places where roads and bridges needed to be built. This meant that, as our family grew, we had to move house every two to three years. As a result, we never put down roots in any one place.

'Our address changes from Kapurthala, to Unnao, then Meerut, Dehradun and Rampur, meant that we had to change schools quite often as well. During one of these transfers, I passed my Matriculation examination from the Raza High School in Rampur State (formerly a state, it became part of the United Provinces under the British).'[3]

Although it may have been unsettling in many ways for the Sikand family to have to move so often, it appears that the young Pran actually benefited from seeing so many different places and coming into contact with so many different people in this vast subcontinent that is India.

He did not know it then, but there were certain physiognomies seeping into his subconscious; they would surface one day in the future when the time came for him as an actor to create new faces, new looks for each of the characters he would one day depict.

---

[2] A *bigha* is 1.6 acres.

[3] Kapurthala is now in Punjab, while Unnao and Meerut are now in Uttar Pradesh and Dehradun and Rampur are in Uttaranchal.

2

'As a child, Pran could be just as mischievous as the boy next door!'
Pran's oldest *bhabhi*, Kuldeep, said. Sister-in-law Kuldeep, who was married
to Pran's eldest brother, had many interesting personal anecdotes going
back into the 1940s. Repeating family lore, Kuldeep continued:[4]

'I am talking of those days when *Baujee*[5] used to stay in Unnao. At
that time Pran was in school. Pran was very fond of watching and learning
anything he saw. He would put forth his best efforts for that. *Baujee* used
to travel by his car. When he would go, Pran would stare unblinkingly
at the manner in which he would start the car and drive it away.

'One day, when *Baujee* came for lunch, Pran took his car, started it
the way he had seen *Baujee* do and drove away. After a while, when *Baujee*
was still having lunch, Pran came and stood near him and started
stammering, "the car...the car...." *Baujee* got angry and said: "What are
you stammering about?" Then *Matajee*[6] asked him: "What has happened?"

'Pran replied: "The car has fallen into the
pond."

'When asked the reason for his mischief,
Pran said: "I watched *Baujee* start the vehicle,
but I had not seen him turning right or left
or stopping. So, when I saw the pond ahead
of me, I opened the door and jumped out and
saved my life, but...but...the car fell into the
pond!" '

The incident not only highlighted Pran's
mischievous tendencies as a boy, but also
provided a glimpse into the future with regard
to his powers of observation and how he
would effectively use what he saw!

A rare photograph of
Pran as a boy.

---

4   Kuldeep Prem Krishen Sikand passed away in December 2002, some months after
she shared these reminiscences for this biography.
5   *Baujee* or *Babujee* referred to her father-in-law, Pran's father, Lala Keval Krishen Sikand.
6   *Matajee* or mother.

3

As a student, Pran recalled that he was by and large obedient – at least he was when *in* the school – but he was not greatly interested in studies. During the early years, he recollects that he used to write on a slate, since notebooks were then a rarity. He learnt Urdu up to his Matriculation. This knowledge later helped him in discovering a phenomenal range of Urdu poets, whose works he can spontaneously reel off, all from memory. Due to his father's frequent transfers, the rhythm of his studies was disturbed. Consequently, he did not perform any great academic feats.

Pran got through his years in high school, finally reaching that first important stage of life that every growing boy reaches – a stage where the initial significant decisions are made, decisions which are frequently far-reaching and which often determine futures, careers, in fact, life itself.

Soon after Pran passed his Matriculation examinations, his father summoned him and asked whether he had any plans about the college he would join.

Pran was quick to inform his father that it would be pointless (from his point of view) to try and study further in view of the fact that he had only managed to scrape through high school! And, since the subject had been brought up, what he really had in mind was not academics, but a career in photography!

Young Pran had done his homework well! He wanted to become a professional photographer, so he specifically asked that he be trained by his father's friend who owned a shop, A. Das & Company, Photographers, situated at Connaught Place, Delhi. It is likely that Pran understood that by asking to be trained by his father's friend, he would be allaying any fears that his family would undoubtedly have had at the thought of letting Pran move out from under its protective care.

Lala Keval Krishen Sikand gave deep thought to this matter for a while and then felt it wiser to give his son a free rein. Besides, he would be under the tutelage of his friend in Delhi itself, where most of the family was based. So he decided to let the boy do something he had set his heart on.

So Pran joined A. Das & Company as an apprentice. 'I learnt developing and printing there,' he later divulged.

That happened during the mid-to-late 1930s, when the British still ruled the undivided land. During the hot summer months that sear North India, the British would move to the Himalayan foothills, to Simla (now Shimla), their summer capital. So, in an unusually canny move with an eye to doing business throughout the year, A. Das & Company (Delhi) *followed* their customers to Simla for the summer!

Naturally, therefore, along with the establishment, the young teenager Pran also went to Simla, where he became more proficient in photography and learned the tricks of the trade.

Interestingly, it was during the period there that Pran's acting 'career' began, when he participated in the annual Ram Leela festival playing Sita to Madan Puri's Ram![7] Ironically, like Pran, Madan Puri too went on to join the Indian film industry, more often than not playing the villain's role rather than the hero's.

The young lad did not know it then, but circumstances and the apparently directionless twists and turns, which Destiny causes in every human being's life, were about to engineer one more such apparently reasonless move in his life.

'After opening a branch in Simla,' Pran said, 'A. Das & Company opened their new branch in Lahore, to which I was sent along with one of its partners. There I kept improving my knowledge of still photography and doing all the work in the shop. Because of this, I had even started earning a salary at A. Das & Company and shortly thereafter went on to become the top man with them.'

We can now perceive that Destiny had worked out a pattern, a master plan, a step-by-step graph in which this bright and energetic young man was to move.

Destiny's master plan had brought Pran, a youth on the threshold of his twenties, to Lahore, which was then a major film-producing city of undivided India.

'This was my first entry into Lahore...'

And it was the city of Lahore that was going to plant Pran's feet on the road which would take his life and his future on to a far more glorious path than his then limited ambition to become a good still photographer could ever have taken him.

---

[7] In the epic Ramayana, Sita is Ram's wife.

THREE

Lahore: A Star Career Begins

1

So it was that a few months after arriving in Lahore,[1] Pran, the nineteen-year-old photographer's assistant, suddenly found himself placed on a new career path – that of an actor's.

Had there been any award given to casting directors then, it is certain that Wali Mohammed Wali would have won it hands down! To assign someone an important role, purely on the basis of his looks and the hint of menace that came through in the way he chewed his *paan*, should be indicative of the man's capacity to visualize the character while he wrote the villain's part for *Yamla Jat*, which was to be made in Punjabi.

---

[1] According to old friend, V. N. Nayyar, when Pran first came to Lahore he stayed with Chander of Chandermal Inderkumar Film Distribution Office, as arranged by his sister's husband, Raizada Narendra Kumar, who was their general manager in Calcutta. Since Chander also had business dealings with the Karnavis of Calcutta and had a branch office in Lahore, it was arranged that Pran would stay with him for a while.

What is amazing is that Wali *Saab* was slightly inebriated when he saw Pran at Ram Lubhaya's *paan* shop! This, and the fact that he had no way of making sure that this chance encounter would result in the young man accepting his offer, made Pran feel that Destiny had played a big part in his entering films and that whatever happened was nothing short of a miracle!

It was almost as if Destiny had actually taken him by the hand and made him switch tracks from behind the camera to in front of it. Ever since that incident took place, Pran Krishen Sikand has never been behind the camera!

However, the experience he gained from working with A. Das & Company would help him in this new career of his. He had a good working knowledge of composition, camera angles, light and shade and make-up, and this aspect would surely make things much easier for him.

2

Yamla Jat, Pran's very first starring vehicle, was to be made in the Punjabi language. Although born into a Punjabi family, Pran had spent his formative years in Delhi and the United Provinces, and so could not speak Punjabi like a native, with the diction, rhythm and cadences that were distinct to the language. Reminiscing about this setback, Pran said:

'After working before the camera for the first two days – I was assigned the villain's role in *Yamla Jat* – I became aware of murmurings starting to float around that "he doesn't speak Punjabi with the proper accent."

'Because I was his "find", Wali *Saab* was gentleman enough to ensure that someone whom he had recommended to Pancholi *Saab* should not prove to be a let-down,' Pran added.

'Wali *Saab* reassured Pancholi *Saab*, saying: "Please sir, do not worry. I'll make him speak Punjabi like a born and bred Punjabi in the next few days!" Then Wali *Saab* put his brother Nazim Panipati on the job of polishing my Punjabi diction.'

'And it was hard work, but I was soon able to speak *thaite* Punjabi,'[2] recalled Pran, 'and even able to use the choicest of words like Wali *Saab* had used in the foyer of Plaza Cinema!'

---

[2]   *Thaite* Punjabi is the language as the native Punjabi, bred in that area, would speak it.

Pran and Anjana in a scene from *Yamla Jat* (1940).

Evidently, Pran did a good job with his diction, for due to his role in *Yamla Jat*, he got offers to work in some *more* Punjabi films! As a result, in the first decade of his career, Pran acted in quite a few Punjabi 'socials'. But he took care not to get stuck in one groove, preferring to accept films both in Punjabi and the more widely used Hindustani (or Hindi) films. As an upshot of this, Pran would be seen in films released nationwide.

With regard to how he initially felt about his role in *Yamla Jat* and a career in films, Pran confessed: 'To begin with, I had no interest whatsoever in wanting to join films. In fact, I felt my role in the film was a bit silly.'

But the switch had been made and Pran wholeheartedly threw himself into giving his best to his new profession. Regarding his early experiences in the studios, he recollected:

'The director used to tell me: "Speak your dialogue like this – or like that." So that's what I did. I just followed as I was directed – and it all came out very natural! I was very relieved to see the rushes! Until then I had been somewhat nervous but I never allowed anybody to notice that!

'I had never even taken part in stage plays during my school years, so it wasn't as if I had this urge to act since childhood. But I guess the audience liked what I did, because I was not "acting", I was just being myself!' Pran reminisced.

Even though Pran himself had felt that his role in his first film *Yamla Jat* was a trifle ridiculous, the fact remains that he did very well in it, for Pancholi Studios went on to sign him as a villain for yet another film in Punjabi, this one titled *Chaudhry*, which was also a big hit.

After *Chaudhry*, Pran was signed to do a small walk-on role in *Khazanchi*, which was Pancholi's foray into Hindi-language films, which even then constituted the national market. It was adapted from a Hollywood film called *The Way of All Flesh*[3] and was released in theatres long before the original film was released in India. So when the distributors of that film announced its release, they billed it as 'the English *Khazanchi*'!

The success of *Khazanchi* was largely due to its excellent music score by Ghulam Haider. Pancholi was so encouraged by the success of this film that he immediately launched another film, *Khandaan* for the national market.

This time though, Pancholi had decided to do something different – he decided to cast Pran for the first time as the romantic *hero* opposite the teenaged Noorjehan, who had earlier worked as Baby Noorjehan with him in *Yamla Jat* and *Chaudhry*.

Although Pran and Noorjehan got on well in *Khandaan*, he was not at ease singing the romantic duets required by the script. He elaborated: 'As the hero, I had to sing a duet with Baby Noorjehan. I was very happy that I had got such a big chance, but after seeing the film, I didn't like myself in the songs. So I decided to take such films in which there were either no songs, or where there were fewer songs to be picturized on me. Besides, running around the trees after my heroine was something I was never comfortable with. In fact, every time I had to run after my heroine, I'd run away!'

---

[3] Remade from the Emil Jannings' 1927 film, *The Way of All Flesh* was released in 1940. Directed by Louis King, it starred Akim Tamiroff and Gladys George, among others.

Despite Pran's discomfiture with regard to the songs, however, *Khandaan* went on to become a silver jubilee superhit. Even its songs, composed by the highly talented and by then already famous Ghulam Haider, were all very popular, and are heard and sung even today.

There was no better springboard for being catapulted to stardom than to be groomed and presented by Pancholi Art Pictures and Studios, which was a colossus in the film-producing fraternity. All four films were successful in a row!

3

While today's Hindi film audiences will vividly remember Pran's 'villain' look or his 'character-actor' look, there is good reason to have a clear picture of what Pran looked like as a young man, since it was his 'look' that had caught the attention of Wali Mohammed Wali.

Kamini Kaushal, who lived and was educated in Lahore, recently said: 'Pran had that certain style about him, about which *everyone* talked.'

The famous Urdu writer Saadat Hasan Manto best described how Pran looked in the early 1940s: 'He was a handsome man, and a popular

Pran riding his *tonga* in Lahore.

figure in Lahore because of his impeccable clothes and the most elegant *tonga*[4] in the city which in those days he used for joyrides in the evenings.'

The late Satish Bhalla, who eventually became Pran's *samdhi*, remembered him from the time when he himself lived in Lahore:[5]

'I was about thirteen years old, and at that time Pranjee was our hero. We were his fans. He used to drive past us in his *tonga*. We would admire him. He, of course, never noticed us!'

Yes, Pran was hero material alright, always nattily dressed in smart suits, silk ties, with silk handkerchiefs and that Errol Flynn moustache! Not surprisingly, Pran himself confessed: 'In those days I was only fond of games and flashy American way of dressing and my father's indulgence encouraged me to cultivate these [tastes].'[6]

In spite of the worldly-wise way of life, there was a certain innocence about him which was apparent to a discerning minority. Interestingly, Manto offered a perceptive one-line reading of Pran's character in his book:[7] 'I had met Pran earlier through Shyam[8] and we had become friends immediately *as he was a man without anything up his sleeve.*' That early friendship with Manto, which developed in Lahore, would stand Pran in good stead just a few years down the line.

Flashbacking about his life in the northern part of undivided India, to pre-Partition Lahore, Pran said:

'Life in Lahore was carefree and without any hassles. Lahore was a thriving film centre in pre-Partition India. It was also a city that kept abreast in men's fashions.

'You could see our Indian men in smart English style suits and after every furlong[9] there was a bar! Lahore was one place where you could get a glass of whisky even after midnight at the railway canteen!

---

4   Horse carriage.
5   Satish Bhalla passed away during the writing of this biography. His son, Vivek, is married to Pran's daughter, Pinky. A *samdhi* is the daughter's or son's father-in-law.
6   In *Screen*, 18 January 1952.
7   *Stars from Another Sky – The Bombay Film World of the 1940s* (Penguin, New Delhi, 1998).
8   Shyam was a top-rank, tall and very handsome leading man who literally died with his boots on. He passed away tragically after falling off horseback during the shooting of Filmistan's *Shabistan*.
9   201.2 metres.

'And then of course, there was the Heera Mandi, the entertainment and cultural centre of the town – that's where all the young men flocked to hear and watch beautiful girls sing and dance!'

Dalsukh M. Pancholi added his own special memories about Pran when interviewed in the late 1950s:

'My memories of Lahore would be incomplete without saying something about Pran, the famous "bad man" of the Indian screen.

'I met Pran in a curious way. One day I had seen a young man cycling recklessly down the Mall, the fashionable thoroughfare of Lahore, a camera slung over his shoulder. His recklessness impressed me. Then to my surprise, Wali *Saab* brought that very boy to meet me!'

Pran was an outstanding young man, attracting people's attention without quite knowing it. That is why he was probably not even aware that Pancholi had already seen him cycling down the street!

Pancholi also recalled Pran smile meaningfully and say that he would come to the studios as Pancholi had asked, but only if the heroine would allow him to take her pictures!

Pancholi had grown very fond of Pran and was like a father figure to him. He recalled another very interesting anecdote involving Pran and himself in Lahore.

At the time of the incident, Pran had probably graduated from reckless bicycling to reckless motorcycle riding. It was not long before he got involved in a motorcycle accident and summons were issued, calling on him to present himself before the honorary magistrate.

For quite a long time Pran evaded the summons. The police commissioner then phoned Pancholi, who provided an escort for his favourite actor to be taken to the magistrate's court. Efforts were made on Pran's behalf with some higher-ups to get the matter dismissed. Even cash incentives proved futile!

Charged on four counts, Pran was fined Rs 25 on each count. Pran's escort then pleaded with the magistrate that Pran, being a 'poor' man, could not pay such a big fine! The fine was then reduced to Rs 20 for each count. During the proceedings, the magistrate who had been observing Pran carefully, suddenly did something very unusual.

Leaning forward, he made very complimentary references to the young actor's good looks – especially his eyes – those very eyes that would later 'seduce' countless heroines and young women and yet instill fear and trepidation in the hearts of mothers the world over! Inevitably therefore, and in view of the fact that this was a first offence, the magistrate reduced the fine to a nominal Rs 5!

It appears that Pran Krishen Sikand's overall personality dominated by his eyes evidently accomplished what (and this was to the magistrate's credit) even cash incentives could not!

Lahore, in those days was also the fashion capital of Punjab, and because of earning quite well from his job at A. Das & Company, Pran was able to happily indulge his sartorial inclinations and tastes!

'In one of my early films,' Pran said, 'I enacted the role of a city person. During its shooting, I changed a number of suits. All these suits were my personal ones. You can therefore imagine my annoyance when one evening, while going out in one of my best suits, I came across a group of college boys walking behind me and commenting loudly: "Look at his audacity! See how he's showing off! He is walking so arrogantly – but he's actually only wearing the company's suit!" '

'You'd be surprised,' Pran still chuckles at the memory, 'I had been earning 200 rupees a month as a photographer, and in those days that was big money! Yet I didn't hesitate when Wali *Saab* made that offer. I chucked the photographer's job to become a mere 50-rupees-a-month actor!'

Looking at the bright side of things, Pran recalled that the other advantage he seemed to have gained after the release of the film *Yamla Jat* was that people, who until then used to consider him a loafer, now started considering him an actor!

4

Pancholi Art Pictures and Studios were not only responsible for propelling Pran towards near-instantaneous stardom, but working with them also afforded Pran the opportunity to make friendships that would stand the test of time.

A few years before Pran was being groomed for his role in the Punjabi-language *Yamla Jat*, events began to unfold which would lead up to meeting one such friend.

Dalsukh M. Pancholi had also given another total newcomer, a little girl, her big break in films. Pancholi had 'discovered' her when she arrived at his doorstep.

In an early interview, Pancholi recalled: 'One morning, a ten-year-old girl was standing at the entrance of my Pancholi Studios. As my car stopped for the gates to open, I got out. Immediately that little girl came close to me – and began to sing!

'Her singing lacked polish and her movements were clumsy but her voice had a rare charm; it held my attention. I took her on and cast her in my film, *Gul Bakavali* which I made in 1932.'

That girl was Baby Noorjehan, who went on to become very famous as a singing star, and came to be known as the Nightingale of the Punjab and later the *Mallika-e-Tarrannum* (the Queen of Melody) of Pakistan!

When Pancholi cast her in *Yamla Jat* in 1939, which was Pran's debut-film as villain, Baby Noorjehan was still just a teenager. Pran says, 'I met Noorjehan for the first time during the making of *Yamla Jat*, when she was still known as Baby Noorjehan. I played the villain and she acted the role of the younger sister of the heroine, Anjana!'

Their next significant film together was *Khandaan*, released in 1942. And it was during the making of this film that young Noorjehan fell in love… no, not with her hero, but with her *director*, Syed Shaukat Hussein Rizvi, and eloped with him!

But we shall come back to Noorjehan later.

5

Another good friend Pran made on his way up the stairs to success, during the early part of his career in Lahore, was V. N. Nayyar.

Nayyar, a film journalist in Lahore, had launched his own English-language monthly *Film Critic* in 1940. Knowing that friendships with film land's famous personalities was crucial to its success, he lost no time in getting acquainted with Wali *Saab*, his wife Mumtaz Shanti,[10] Pancholi and others.

---

[10] Mumtaz Shanti was a leading film heroine in the 1930s and 1940s.

A rare poster of *Khandaan* (1942).

'It was Wali *Saab* who brought him [Pran] to my office,' Nayyar said. 'That was my first meeting with Pran and we quickly became close friends.'

Nayyar was instrumental in getting Pran at least one film assignment. Apparently, Nayyar had a friend named Dr Anand Prakash Parkar. This Dr Parkar had evidently and rapidly made a substantial fortune by advertising and marketing sex potency and everlasting youth medication! According to Nayyar, this friend of his used to earn about Rs 30,000 to Rs 40,000 rupees a month, which was a huge amount in those days.

Excess and idle money and the lure of films have a potent mutual attraction. So when Nayyar recommended that the worthy Dr Parkar produce a film, he got an easy 'yes' out of the man. Naturally, since film making was a totally alien field for Dr Parkar, he left the entire business of setting up the project and casting the film to Nayyar.

'Who should we take for hero?' Dr Parkar asked Nayyar.

'Pran of course!' Nayyar said emphatically. 'Didn't you see how good he was in *Khandaan* and *Kaise Kahun*? He's well known to me and you'll have no trouble with him!'

And so Dr Parkar launched himself as a producer of a film titled *Pardesi Balam*, a Punjabi-language film. Nayyar particularly remembered that Pran got his first car from the money he earned from that film.

Although it is not known of what make that particular car was, it probably kindled in Pran the desire to own unusual and unique cars, reflecting his distinctive style, the same as his manner of dressing did.

6

The bouquet of more than twenty films in which Pran acted in the late-1940s in Lahore chalks him up as a young man who could perform both hero's roles as well as villain's roles with equal ease.

Additionally, his breezy demeanour, his fashionable style of dressing as well as his love of the good things of life appeared to effortlessly attract other people's attention — even the attentions of those whose own attentions were much sought after by others! This further strengthened his star status in Lahore. Pran's films were so popular that his *Shahi Lutera* was reported to have still been running to full houses in Pakistan during the 1960s.

The films had kept coming and along with them came success. Simultaneously, beneath the façade of a kind of normalcy, discontent and political discord were simmering just beneath the surface.

One of Pran's films, *Buth Taraash* (The Sculptor of Idols), directed by J. P. Advani, with music by popular music director, Ghulam Haider, was released during troublesome times…1947.

That was the year in which the Indian subcontinent, home to a variety of people belonging to a multiplicity of religions, was arbitrarily sword-slashed into two nations — primarily on the basis of religion — into Pakistan and India.

FOUR

Marriage...
and a New Chapter of Life

1

The years preceding 1947 were momentous ones when the history of the subcontinent was being written. Every event was history being made.

Even as Pran's career was taking off in Lahore, events on the family front would have a bearing on how his life would eventually turn out.

Pran had gone right ahead and, without consulting his father, made his decision to become an actor, in spite of his initial misgivings about becoming one. He knew that his father really doted on him. Pran explained why, saying: 'My mother had died in the early 1930s shortly after the youngest in the family, Kripal, was born. I was a mere eleven- or twelve-year-old boy at that time. Naturally, I began to seek my father's love and approval in whatever I did. We became very close. I was my father's favourite. In fact, my three brothers and three sisters were quite disgusted with me!'

It had been this same indulgence that had enabled Pran to cleverly convince his father about letting him discontinue his studies and take up photography instead. He said: 'When I expressed my desire to learn still-photography, my father too thought it wise to let me go and apprentice with his friend in Delhi.' So Pran, confident that his father would indulge yet another decision of his, took that first step and entered films.

Yet, somewhere in his mind the doubt niggled that his father would not be pleased. So, even after the success of *Yamla Jat*, Pran could not summon the courage to reveal to his father that he had begun working in films. When the news eventually broke, it came as a huge shock to Lala Keval Krishen Sikand.

Providing some background information to what happened next, Pran disclosed: 'After the release of my first few films, it became evident that my father was not really happy with this new decision of mine. He summoned me home to Delhi and asked me to join some other profession.

'But by now, I had completely given up my job at A. Das & Company and become quite involved with my new career. Although I knew it was not considered a respectable career, I wanted to go back to it, to Lahore and my independence. Yet, out of respect and love for my father, I stayed. This time however, I went to work with his friend Kuldip Singh who had factories in Ambala and Panipat.' [1]

Pran's eldest *bhabhi*, Kuldeep, who, after the death of her mother-in-law, took the place of mother in the family, put things quite simply, 'Pran did start working with *Baujee's* friend but his heart was just not there.'

In the best Indian tradition, where marriage is thought to be the panacea for all woes, even curing a person of insanity, Pran's father decided that he would find a suitable match for his son. Perhaps if he were married to a girl from Delhi itself, he would be 'cured' of this insanity – films – and not go back to Lahore!

Pran's father did what any widower would do: he left the task of finding a suitable girl to the female members of his family.

And find a suitable girl they did! A girl called Shukla Ahluwalia.

---

[1]   Ambala and Panipat are now in the state of Haryana.

A proposal for marriage was quickly sent to the Ahluwalia family. Discussions began.

The close relations between the two families and the girl's own good qualities meant that Pran's father soon approved of the young, beautiful and graceful Shukla as a prospective wife for his son.

2

Unfortunately, Lala Keval Krishen Sikand did not live long enough to see them married. Neither did he live to see his unusual son re-enter the film line and go on to achieve such heights of popularity.

Pran put it succinctly: 'My father died in 1944 of a heart attack in Delhi.'

However, Kuldeep, spoke in detail about how, after a short break during which time he worked in his father's friend's factory in Ambala, Pran went back to a career in films. She said: 'My *sasurjee*[2] died quite suddenly in his sleep one afternoon.'

'After all the rituals and customs were over, the family members found that Pran had become very silent. He could not concentrate on any work and looked worried. So his elders thought that perhaps it would be better to let him do as he pleased. So, Pran went back to Lahore in 1944 and began his acting career again,' she added.

Interestingly, when Pran himself was asked about the circumstances which led him to return to Lahore, he added some more details: 'Actually, I had been given a small role in one of Pancholi's pictures before I answered my father's summons. Then Pancholi called me back to reshoot *one* scene.' Smiling wickedly, Pran continued: 'That was *just* the opportunity I was waiting for. So I went back to Lahore, did the one scene...and did not return to Delhi!'

Not until later, anyway. Because, as Kuldeep put it: 'When the topic of marriage was raised again, Pran said he *would* marry the girl whom *Baujee* had fixed.'

And to do that, he would have to go back to Delhi.

---

[2] Father-in-law.

Despite having the family's seal of approval, however, the marriage proposal had run into some opposition. Interestingly, Shukla said that while the other members of her family did not really oppose the marriage, her *behnoi*,[3] Ajit Walia, who is married to Shukla's elder sister Pushpa, did do so.

The main reason, of course, was Pran's choice of profession. Films were not considered a suitable career, especially since the male members from both sides were either serving under the old princely states in pre-independent India, or were in business, or were in the armed forces. Pran's mother's family was from Kapurthala. His maternal uncle, Rai Bahadur Mathuradas, used to be the prime minister of Kapurthala, while Shukla's father's eldest brother, her *badé taujee*, had been the prime minister in Indore, formerly known as the Holkar State.[4]

Even though working in films was not thought to be a respectable profession, Shukla seemed to have no qualms about marrying a film person. She said: 'Due to our families being related, I had met *him* well before our marriage. Our family had gone to see *his* films. Although we used to live in Rawalpindi, when *his* first film *Yamla Jat* was released, the whole family went to see it in Lahore!'

Ajit's objections were soon brushed aside and the marriage arrangements went on as planned.

Pran too admitted that the marriage was partly a love marriage and partly an arranged one: 'You see, our families were not only related, but our families were good friends as well. Shukla and I had met each other off and on at our relatives' place, and we both liked each other. So you can say it was both a love marriage as well as an arranged one!'

'Thus, barely a year after my father expired,' Pran said, 'I got married to a most noble and graceful girl named Shukla in Delhi on 18 April 1945.'

---

[3] *Behnoi* is one's sister's husband.
[4] Indore is now in the state of Madhya Pradesh.

3

Pran, who had gone back to Lahore and films, came all the way to Delhi to marry Shukla, *baraat, baraatis* and all.[5]

Continuing her reminiscences, Shukla said: 'After my *badé taujee* retired, he settled down in Delhi. My father had died by that time. I had no mother too, but I did have a good stepmother. Still, my *badé taujee* undertook the responsibility of my marriage.

'That is how *he* [6] and I were married in Delhi at my *bade taujee's* huge *kothi* [7] on 18 April 1945 when I was nearly twenty-one years of age.'

As expected, the wedding was a grand affair since not one wedding, but two weddings, took place within two days of each other. Shukla's older cousin, the daughter of her *badé taujee*, was scheduled to marry two days before Pran and Shukla got married, because according to tradition, it was always the elder one who should be married first.

When Pran's *baraat* came to Delhi for the wedding, it was Pran's eldest brother and sister-in-law who fulfilled the role of parents, performing all the rituals that are part of elaborate Punjabi weddings. 'Since Pran's mother had passed away much earlier, and being the eldest *bhabhi*,' Kuldeep said, 'I performed all those rituals for Pran and Shukla which a mother performs during a wedding, such as, *pani bharna, muh dikhai, kangana khilana*.'[8]

---

[5] The *baraat* is the traditional manner in which the bridegroom, seated on a mare, is escorted in a procession of relatives and friends, all exuberantly dancing to the accompaniment of music, drums and fireworks, as they make their way to the bride's home for the wedding ceremony.

[6] Traditionally, out of respect, an Indian wife does not take her husband's name. Hence, all through this biography, Shukla Sikand refers to her husband in the third person.

[7] Mansion.

[8] Literally, 'filling water' (a ritual which signifies that the bride will bring good fortune and plenty to her new family), 'looking at the face' (a gift in cash or kind given when the bride's veil is lifted), and 'putting on the bangles' (a ritual where the ladies of the bridegroom's family put special, usually heavy, bangles on the bride's wrists, which denote she is now bound to her new family). All these rituals and customs are meant to welcome the bride into her new family by showing her how valued she is.

Pran with wife Shukla.

Speaking about the affection she has for them both, Kuldeep went on to reveal that thereafter whenever she met Pran and Shukla, she would always hold out her arms to welcome and embrace both of them simultaneously, so that neither of them would feel that she had embraced the other first.

Ajit and Pushpa Walia have their own memories to share. They said: 'We have known Pran since 1939–40, much before his marriage to Shukla. After their wedding, Pran and Shukla went to Mussoorie on their honeymoon. Although we had been married four years earlier, we went along with them! Actually, my friend had a place in Mussoorie, which we had arranged to have for a few weeks...'

Honeymoon over, the young couple settled down to married life in their own house in Lahore.

When they got married in 1945, Pran already had at least six films to his credit, a good many of them having had a successful run at the box office.

Shukla adds: '*His* father didn't like him working in films. So, to please his father, *he* left the film line for a while. *He* had hidden the truth from his father and had worked in those films, that is why my father-in-law was so upset. But what my father-in-law did not know then was that *he* would go on to achieve so much in this line. *He* resumed his work as an actor only after his father's death and within the year, he had so many offers pouring in that he was well into films at the time of our marriage.'

And when he signed more films after marriage, many concurred that his wife Shukla had brought him good fortune.

4

As was the custom, a few months after the wedding, Shukla returned to her family in Delhi. When it was time to return to Lahore, Shukla brought along a German shepherd from her uncle's house, which her cousin had gifted her to keep her company during the long hours when Pran was away at work. Dogs had always been part of his and her growing up years and continued to be so after their marriage.

By the time the twenty-five-year old Pran and the nearly twenty-one-year-old Shukla got married, both had already been shaped by their family background and individual experiences.

Shukla was born on 1 October 1924. Although her mother had died early, Shukla was raised in a cocoon of love and trust by a very good stepmother and a large joint family. The good values inculcated early in life have always remained with her and have proved to be the rock-like foundation on which she was able to raise her own family.

Coming as she did from a very well-to-do family, Shukla was brought up in comfort, not having to do the usual chores which people from lower income groups would have to do.

Shukla recalled those early years saying: 'Initially I had some problems in handling the house because I had never been put into that habit from childhood. But after marriage we had servants, so that helped.'

Seven months after the wedding day, Shukla found herself pregnant with their first child.

5

The years 1945, 1946 and 1947 saw the demand for independence from the foreign rulers being stepped up. The signs were clear. The British Empire was definitely on its way out.

Underneath the veneer of sanity, wherein national leaders were thinking of ways in which the handover of power could be accomplished to their satisfaction, the masses were also being churned up for the eventuality that was on the secret agenda of some individuals.

The transfer of power would afford those people the opportunity to carve out portions of the land for themselves, over which they could exercise a not very different kind of dominion from what had, over the past centuries, been exercised over the largely uneducated masses of the subcontinent.

Soon, every man, woman and child would be affected by the turmoil which was to envelop the land.

For Pran, however, these things did not hold much meaning. More important than the fact that his films were doing well and that his career was now well established, was anticipation of the arrival of their first child.

On 11 August 1946, Arvind made his entry onto the centre stage of his parents' lives. Little Arvind, who quickly got nicknamed *Bubboo*, was the apple of his parents' eyes and in the days to come would unknowingly 'save' his father's life.

FIVE

Destination: Bombay

1

August 1947.
Bombay...[1]
The *city of dreams* where everybody who aspires to hit the headlines fantasizes about seeing his or her name glow in gigantic neon lights on cinema theatre marquees.

Bombay...the Hollywood of India.

Of course, films were being made in Calcutta and Madras and other cities of India, but they were regional-language films – Bengali films, Tamil films, Telugu films, Marathi films, Kannada films, Punjabi films, Malayalam films and Gujarati films.[2] The regional-language film industry had its own group of directors and actors. But they were seldom able to make the crossover from one language to another.

---

[1] Now called Mumbai.
[2] While regional-language films were being made in different centres during the 1930s and 1940s, a few films were also made in the English language – like J.B.H. Wadia's *Court Dancer*. This movie was made in Hindi and Bengali as *Raj Nartaki*.

But Bombay, even in the mid-1940s, was different. Bombay was then, as it is now, the big time. And if you had to make it big, you simply had to become a star in the national language (Hindi) films produced in Bombay — India's magic city of cinema, the only city whose heyday wasn't far off, when many more Hindi-language films would be made *here* per year than English-language films would be made in Hollywood.[3]

In the years before that fateful date in 1947, Hindustani films and Punjabi films were already being made in Lahore, then one of the motion-picture centres of undivided India.[4]

Pran, who had married and started a family, would probably have made Lahore his home for life had Partition not happened.

But Partition did happen.

And although Pran and his family were spared the actual horrors that were perpetrated as there was a massive exodus of people from one part of the subcontinent to the other, evidently Partition had cut deep wounds into his psyche. He had felt compelled to leave the land he so dearly loved, knowing he probably could never return.

Referring to that time now long past, Pran asked: 'Do you know why I never ever went back to Lahore? Not even *once* in all these years, though there have been so many invitations?'

Answering his own questions, he said emphatically: 'Because I never wanted to go back to the place from which we had been forced to leave!'

Elaborating on the turn of events, Pran went on to say: 'My eldest son Arvind, whom we call *Bubboo*, was born on 11 August 1946. The political situation in Lahore had been steadily worsening and increasingly, rumours and speculation about a probable partition of the country were spreading.

'Then unrest and rioting began in Lahore. Fearing for my safety, as every other person feared for his, I began to carry a Rampuri knife on my person. Things were so uncertain that I quickly sent my wife, Shukla and little *Bubboo* to Indore, to my sister-in-law Pushpa Walia's home.

---

[3] Although classified as Hindi films, the language used was Hindustani, which is derived from the Urdu and Hindi languages.
[4] The other main cinema-producing centres in India were Bombay, Madras, Calcutta and Hyderabad.

"After all," I thought, "if it comes to a quick getaway, a single person can do so more easily than one with a wife and child to protect."

'I remained alone in Lahore and continued to work there even though the situation began to worsen due to the riots. Then I got a call from Shukla asking me to come to Indore to celebrate *Bubboo's* first birthday which fell on 11 August 1947.

'"I can't make it," I said.

'" In that case, we won't celebrate the birthday at all," is what my wife promptly replied.'

Pran's initial reaction, one of irritation, was only momentary. He loved his wife and son dearly and he did not fail to perceive her sentiments in wanting her husband and father of their child to be present at the celebration of their son's first birthday.

Not wanting to disappoint his wife Shukla, Pran packed only for a week. But he put in some of his smartest, most fashionable suits, and hurried off to Indore to be in time for his firstborn's first big day.

Shukla's insistence would soon prove providential.

'I too did not like the idea of our first son's first birthday passing uncelebrated, unnoticed,' Pran continued. 'So, on 10 August 1947, I arrived in Indore. With the situation in the country being so tense, we tuned to a radio station the following morning and heard that Lahore was being bathed in blood. People were being massacred and everyone seemed to have gone mad. We looked up into the heavens and uttered a silent prayer. I had been saved by my wife's stubborn determination that I be present for my firstborn's first birthday.'

Willing himself to continue, Pran said: 'There I was, in Indore, in our relative's home, with a young wife and child and no place to call our own. I couldn't very well return to Lahore — because suddenly "home" was in another country!'

Yes, Pakistan had been formed on 14 August 1947, and the very next day, 15 August, India too gained Independence.

So, borrowing some money from a close friend, Pran brought his family to Bombay. Pran knew that after Lahore, being an actor in Bombay was a career in the big time. He was confident of being able to pick up in Bombay a well-established acting career that had been left off in Lahore. After all, he was no novice, having acted in over twenty films between his first *Yamla Jat* (1940) and *Birhan* (released in 1948).[5]

As he later said: 'I had already starred in both hero's and as well as villain's roles in many films back in Lahore, even other than those which I had done for Pancholi. Surely, I would have no difficulty breaking into the film world in Bombay.'

His first entry into films in Lahore was nothing short of a miracle. Even today he calls it 'Destiny'. Even his safe arrival into India was a result of a fortunate turn of events. But would there be another miracle? Would he be able to get work in Bombay as easily as he had reckoned?

2

The optimistic twenty-seven-year-old arrived in Bombay on 14 August 1947 with nothing...nothing but his talent, his wife and his son.

And his wife? All that she carried were her silent prayers that the Almighty should make her husband's dreams come true.

Pran knew the glorious days of stardom in Lahore were in the past. He was in Bombay now. Still, buoyed by self-confidence, Pran took his small family and checked in at the Taj Mahal Hotel.

The Taj Mahal Hotel in Bombay, was, even in the 1940s, the classiest in town. The Taj Mahal Hotel and the Gateway of India, both of which stand virtually facing each other, are to this day two immortal landmarks of India's premier city.

Chuckling reminiscently at the prices charged by the Taj way back in 1947, Pran revealed that for a princely sum of fifty-five rupees a day, one could get an entire suite consisting of two large rooms and a balcony! And, it came with morning tea and bananas, followed by breakfast, then lunch followed by evening tea and biscuits – and all rounded off with an excellent dinner! All that for just fifty-five rupees! Today, you have to pay more than that just to have a cup of tea there!

---

[5] Some of Pran's films made before 1947 had their theatrical release after Partition. Among these were *Barsaat Ki Ek Raat, Nek Dil, Chunaria* and *Birhan*, all of which were released in 1948.

Shukla's memories filled in some more detail: 'They would take one or two rupees extra for the child. I had brought my maidservant along with me to help me with *Bubboo*. In fact, there was so much food that even our maidservant could eat from the food that came for us!'

But work was not easy to come by. Pran recalled that time: 'Anyway, I did not get film assignments right away, like I had thought I would. Some people like Wali *Saab* had come earlier than us from Lahore to Bombay. He had married the actress Mumtaz Shanti and they had taken an office in Famous Studios at Mahalaxmi.[6] Gradually others, like actor Om Prakash and film maker B. R. Chopra, had followed suit. So I too thought that getting work should not be that difficult.

'The great Urdu writer Saadat Hasan Manto, a dear friend of mine who was employed at Bombay Talkies, then one of the leading film companies in the country, took me to Malad[7] in an effort to get me some work. However, at that time nothing happened.'

The search for film assignments that had begun with a great deal of sanguinity had, for some odd reason, become one long, dreary, unsuccessful and hopeless grind. All that the actor from Lahore, with more than twenty films under his belt, heard was...

'No.'

'No. Sorry.'

'Sorry, nothing for now.'

The negatives clanged raucously like a cruel refrain in his brain. They were like body blows delivered by some ruthless boxer.

Yet, Pran asserted: 'The feeling was strong in me that a lucky period was now about to begin. But...we had no money!'

3

Sure, the young actor and his wife had come to Bombay with high hopes. But those high hopes began to crash in slow motion. And the downward spiral began.

---

[6]   An area in central Bombay, well known for its racecourse, temple and the Famous Studios.

[7]   A suburb of Bombay.

They went from one hotel to another – from the most expensive Taj Mahal, downwards to a cheaper hotel at half rates – at twenty-five rupees per day with food.

And the young actor was out all day, seeking work.

It wasn't long before even twenty-five rupees a day became unaffordable. So, the young couple moved to a still cheaper hotel – the Strand Hotel which was near the Radio Club.[8]

Foreseeing that the struggle to re-establish their lives would perhaps take longer than anticipated, Pran and his wife Shukla decided that *Bubboo* should not have to endure the difficult period, and that he should be sent to his maternal aunt in Indore. Temporarily entrusting her precious one to her sister, Pushpa Walia, Shukla was soon back at her husband's side.

Other than wanting to stretch their money, Shukla revealed one important reason for moving out of the Strand Hotel: 'Although it was cheaper, we didn't like the food, so we shifted to Hotel Fredricks. It also had big rooms like at the Taj. But there the food was basically European – quite bland, stew and all that, which was not to *his* taste, so sometimes we used to order food from the Coronation Darbar Restaurant at Grant Road.[9] We stayed at Fredricks for some five to six months.'

Soon, they found that they would have to shift from Hotel Fredricks as well.

Shukla, remembering those times with the in-built stoicism present in women of her generation, said: 'My *maama*[10] used to stay nearby, at a walking distance from Fredericks Hotel. His son-in-law was in the Navy and they used to live in the naval base nearby.[11] We used to meet the family often. I used to visit them when Pran was out searching for work. They offered that we stay along with them. We went there for a few days but we felt a bit awkward there, so we shifted over to Delamar Hotel on Marine Drive. The atmosphere was good there and I used to cook my child's food in the room. They didn't object. They were very nice –

---

8   Situated on the southern end of the promenade that extends from the Radio Club to the Gateway of India, both in Colaba, south Bombay.
9   A restaurant in central Bombay which serves excellent Mughlai dishes.
10 Mother's brother.
11 At the southern tip of Bombay.

people. So we stayed there much longer than at the other hotels – about ten months,' Shukla said.

The end was not far off.

They had to pay their hotel bills at the end of each week. Inevitably, the time came when they hit rock bottom. At the end of one particular week they found themselves facing the worst scenario of their lives.

Destiny had turned its face away from them. There was no money.

Husband and wife looked in each other's eyes.

Silence.

What could either of them say to the other? Was this really the end of the road?

Turning away slightly from him, so he should not see what she was doing, Shukla took off her gold bangles.

'Here,' she turned, offering them to him. 'This will help us through these bad times.'

'No!' he was close to anger – not at her, at his own helplessness.

'Use these now,' she urged her husband. She could not bear to see the expression on his face.

'No!'. The anger was evident now.

So she added quickly: 'After all, these things are made so that they may be of use at just such a time. They are only gold bangles, after all. They are given traditionally at weddings just for such hardships.'

'No!' he shouted.

But her quiet calm conquered his anger. She knew that his pride was hurting. Hurting badly.

'Take them now – and go.'

Her finality decided the issue.

'I was new in Bombay and didn't know whom to meet, where to go,' Pran said, the pain of remembered moments flitting across his face.

'So I asked a casual acquaintance, an assistant at a film company,' Pran continued, 'to take me to the proper place where I could get money for my wife's bangles.'

Even today Pran cannot forget those moments when Shukla's eyes met his as he held out the money to her. It seemed as though the entire world had come crashing down upon them.

He had just done what he felt was the worst possible thing to do – pawned his wife's gold bangles. Knocking at so many doors in film land had yielded nothing. Right then, a bleak future was all that he could see.

'I cursed *Murliwalé*[12] for having heaped such humiliation on our heads,' Pran said, eyes moistening with the memory of that bitter time.

And even as he railed and ranted against divine injustice, Pran's *Murliwalé* must surely have been smiling inscrutably down at him.

Pran didn't know it then, when exhausted and bitter, he collapsed on the bed, refusing even his wife's solace and sympathy...

No, neither Shukla nor Pran knew it then, but Destiny suddenly decided to take a look at their plight. And, in as many hours as it takes one day to become the next day, Destiny took a hand in connecting a career interrupted in Lahore to a career about to begin in Bombay. Destiny did what Pran believes is the unheard-of third miracle.

---

[12] Literally, 'flute player'; Pran refers to Lord Krishna as *Murliwalé*.

SIX

Pran's 'Tryst' with Destiny

1

On the eve of India's Independence, that is, on 14 August 1947, India's first prime minister, Jawaharlal Nehru, addressed the fledgling nation with his (now-immortal) speech: 'Long years ago, we made a tryst with Destiny. . . .' And as India kept her tryst with Destiny, Pran too, would keep his own.

After relentlessly struggling for almost eight months, the tide had to change for the young Sikand family. It began to slowly flow forward now. Destiny had begun to look benevolently at them and was even beginning to smile.

That 'smile' came in the form of a telephone call, sometime in early 1948. It was from the Bombay Talkies Studios in the distant suburb of Malad.

'Come to our studio. We may have something for you.'

After eight months of unemployment those were the sweetest words he had ever heard! Pran went, determined to say 'yes' to whatever he got.

He was in such dire straits that he left for Malad very early in the morning so that he would able to travel 'ticketless' on the suburban train!

The production manager came at ten in the morning. The ensuing conversation made it clear that for the time being the amount of remuneration was the most important consideration.

'We have a role for you,' the production manager announced.

'How much?' Pran promptly asked.

'Five hundred rupees. That's fixed.'

It appears that the recommendations given by the famous Urdu writer Saadat Hasan Manto, actor Shyam, and dancer-actress Cuckoo had finally worked.

Pran had worked with Cuckoo in some films in Lahore before he came to Bombay. So when he met her again in the foyer of the Taj Mahal Hotel, she had put in a word for him at Bombay Talkies.

Shyam's putting in more than a few good words for Pran came after Manto's recommendation, which had only got him as far as an interview. Shyam had requested the bosses at Bombay Talkies to take Pran's screen test rather than rejecting him outright without knowing how he came across on screen.

They did, and Pran was called for this role.

When Pran was told that his remuneration would be five hundred rupees and not a penny more, Pran was actually overjoyed, but after a small pause he said: 'Alright, but on one condition . . .'

'What's that?'

'I want a hundred rupees in advance.'

Pran smiled as he remembered this exchange, then continued to speak: 'They were happy that I had agreed so easily for what was actually a small amount. So they gave me the advance.

'I came home and told Shukla: "Dress up, we're going out!"

'We then went straight to the Ambassador Hotel. We both ate — rather Shukla ate and I drank — before eating, of course! And needless to say, I blew the entire hundred rupees there itself!'

Of course it was another matter that they had to go back to the inexpensive hotel that was home to them until things got better.

The role he had been offered by Bombay Talkies was for *Ziddi*, in which the romantic leads were to be played by the debonair Dev Anand and the graceful Kamini Kaushal. That was the first assignment.

Destiny seems to have gone into overdrive right then, because when a gloriously tipsy Pran and wife Shukla returned to their small hotel, there was a message waiting for him.

The night duty attendant told Pran: 'Some man named Navalkar[1] had come for you. He left a message. He said to tell you that he is coming tomorrow at ten.'

'The following morning, the man named Navalkar did arrive,' recalled Pran, 'and I was taken to the well-known producer Baburao Pai's office at Famous Studios, Cadell Road.[2] I was introduced here to *Saheb Mama*[3] who, besides being an art director, was also one of the partners of Prabhat Studios, Poona.'

Pran kept silent, listening to both Navalkar and *Saheb Mama* conversing. They were obviously talking about him. The man to whom Pran had been introduced must also have been a portraitist because he kept asking Pran questions – and sketching – at the same time!

The conversation between Navalkar and *Saheb Mama* was in Marathi which Pran could not understand. Being so obviously the subject of their conversation, Pran enquired about what they were talking.

Navalkar told him that *Saheb Mama* was commenting on how beautifully expressive Pran's eyes were.

Now when Pran heard Navalkar say that *Saheb Mama* had commented favourably about his eyes, he instinctively knew that he was going to get this film as well.

'I was asked to come to Poona the following day,' said Pran. 'So I went. The train expenses and stay in Poona had all been paid for. Then we talked about money.

'*Saheb Mama* asked: "How much will you take for acting in a film?"

'"How much will you give?"

'"We cannot give you more than five hundred rupees at the moment."

---

[1]   Navalkar was a cameraman at Prabhat Studios, Poona, and also a producer-partner of K. Amarnath.

[2]   Cadell Road is the former name of Veer Savarkar Marg, the westernmost road linking Prabhadevi and Mahim in central Mumbai. The Famous Studios were demolished many decades ago, making way for residential buildings.

[3]   The form of respectful address people used while talking about or to Shree Fatehlal.

'I thought: *"I've already asked Bombay Talkies yesterday for five hundred rupees. So for the next film, even if it is only marginally increased, it should be for more."* So, pretending to get up, I said: "It's not enough. I need to be paid more."

'They got the shock of their lives!

'"When we are paying our hero, Ram Singh, five hundred rupees a month, how can we pay you more?'

'"*Per month? Good God!"* I thought — I was under the impression it was five hundred rupees for the *full film* — but no, it was five hundred rupees *per month!*'

But, shaping rapidly as he was into a good actor, Pran kept all surprise away from his face. Looking cool and self-assured, he continued to bargain! And they did capitulate!

'"Alright! Alright!" they grumbled. "We'll pay you six hundred rupees per month, but ..." they pleaded with me, "please do not let our hero learn about this."'

Thus, the second film Pran signed right after *Ziddi* was Prabhat Pictures' *Apradhi*. And the hapless hero never got to know that he was being given a hundred rupees less than the villain Pran!

As it turned out, Navalkar's and *Saheb Mama's* decision to give Pran the very powerful role of a young revolutionary at a salary higher than that of the hero's proved to be a good one.

Just prior to the commencement of filming Pran heard on the grapevine that during casting for this film, someone had suggested to *Saheb Mama* that Pran, his choice of actor for the role of the revolutionary, was not up to the mark. *Saheb Mama* had gotten very angry and counterquestioned the objection saying: 'Why do you not look beneath the surface? His beautiful eyes will tell you he is right for the role.'

His role was certainly not inconsequential; *Saheb Mama* had assigned him a positive role and the parallel lead in *Apradhi*.[4] The character had been developed by combining the political lives of well-known national leaders, Achhutrao Patwardhan and Jayprakash Narayan, and the story used quite a few of their experiences while they were 'underground'.

---

4   Released on 25 February 1949, *Apradhi* was directed by Yeshwant Pethkar, with music by Sudhir Phadke and starred Ram Singh, Madhubala, Leela Pande and Pran.

This film is one of the earliest in which Pran attempted to create a get-up for the character he was to play. Pran admitted that praise from such a veteran had not just flattered him but had also spurred him to get on with the task of proving the dissenters wrong.

Buoyed by Shree Fatehlal's faith in his acting ability, he gave an inspired performance in the film and indisputably proved that he was capable of doing good work despite lacunae in the other areas of the film.

About *Apradhi*, Pran felt: 'It was a great role and I felt particularly happy when the legendary Baburao Patel showered me with high praise in his review of that film.'[5]

Baburao Patel was known never to mince his words. His reviews used to contain trenchant and scathing comments about whatever he found negative in the film. One could be sure that no film worthy of censure escaped his fiery pen! Regarding *Apradhi*, Baburao Patel had headlined his review: 'APRADHI, POOR STORY WITH POORER DIRECTION!'

Despite such a forceful headline dismissing the film, Baburao's comments about Pran are worth quoting: '*Pran looks quite like Achhutrao Patwardhan in his revolutionary patriot's role and as such gives a pretty intelligent performance.*'[6]

This praise was indeed more than generous, considering that Baburao Patel had, in just the previous sentence of the same paragraph, trashed the hero's performance, saying: 'Ram Singh plays the athletic stud bull and not even in a single shot does he betray any pretensions for screen acting.' While praising Madhubala's versatile performance and Pran's intelligent one, the review, on the whole, knocked down the film. Baburao sealed its fate with these words: 'The picture fails to appeal.'

The elation brought on by his successful meeting with Shree Fatehlal and Navalkar of Prabhat Studios goaded Pran to press on with his efforts to resume his career that had been cut short in Lahore by Partition.

So Pran next went to meet Wali Mohammed Wali, the man who had discovered him at Ram Lubhaya's *paan* shop in Lahore. Wali *Saab* too had

---

[5]   Baburao Patel was editor-proprietor of India's earliest and most influential film magazine, *Filmindia*. After its heyday, he changed its name to *Mother India*.

[6]   *Filmindia*, April 1949.

come to India after Partition and had started a production office in Famous Studios at Mahalaxmi.

The moment he entered Wali *Saab's* office, Wali *Saab* blessed him with the words that spontaneously come out of an Indian heart — '*Tumhari lambi umar hogi!*'[7]

Apparently, Wali *Saab* had at that very moment been talking about Pran since he was in the process of selecting the cast for his new film *Putli.*[8] Wali was a master at casting the right person for the right role. He felt that Pran was just the person to play the villain in *Putli*, and was about to search for him.

He offered Pran one thousand rupees per month for the film.

Pran was speechless! The man who had played such a crucial role in the miraculous way in which Pran was 'discovered' was apparently still around to play a significant part in the revival of Pran's career. What more could he say other than give his assent?

After finalizing the deal with Wali Mohammed Wali, Pran visited the office of his friend, S. M. Yusuf, which was located nearby. Yusuf told him that he had a role for Pran in his new film *Grahasti.*[9] He was asked if he would do the film for the monthly remuneration of one thousand rupees.

Over four consecutive days, immediately on the heels of signing *Ziddi*, and in an almost miraculous way, Pran had signed three more films — *Apradhi*, *Putli* and *Grahasti*.

Grahasti went on to become a golden jubilee hit all over India, running in one particular cinema for an astounding fifty-four weeks! Its stupendous success turned the spotlight on Pran, who had played a 'good man's' role in it.

---

[7] Loosely translated: 'You will live long!'

[8] Produced under the banner of Punjab Film Corporation, *Putli* (1950) starred Wali's own wife, Mumtaz Shanti, in the title role of the woman-revolutionary Putlibai, and Pran, as the bad man, headed the cast which included Yakub, Husn Banu, Majnu (a comedian, whose real name was Harold Lewis) and others.

[9] Aina Pictures' *Grahasti* (released in 1948) was produced and directed by S. M. Yusuf. It co-starred Sulochana Chatterjee opposite Masood Parvez, a leading man who had a very brief career. The supporting cast was headed by Kuldip Kaur, a famous vamp of the 1940s and 1950s, who made a successful screen teaming with Pran. The film also included Lalita Pawar, Shyama, Yakub, Mirza Musharraf and Sharda.

However, with the number of 'bad man' roles that Pran had done since *Yamla Jat*, he seemed to have gotten under the skin of negative characterizations. Also, the 'good man' roles coming his way were not that many.

Interestingly, with regard to the effect playing bad man in all these films had on Pran, Firoze Rangoonwalla wrote in an article on him in *Screen*: 'The only scar all this [playing bad man in film after film] left on Pran was an unconscious habit of narrowing one eye and enlarging the other. I still remember that even when he was playing lovey-dovey with his little heroine Sharda in *Grahasti* and singing a duet *"Tere naaz uthane ko jee chahta hai"*[10] with her, the expressions on his face suggested that his intentions towards the lady were not exactly honourable!' [11]

However, one film that Pran signed during this period was to set the tone of his career for the next nearly two decades, a film which placed Pran firmly on the road to on-screen villainy.

That film was *Badi Bahen*.

2

It is generally agreed that it was D. D. Kashyap's *Badi Bahen*,[12] which established Pran as the villain to watch out for.

By the time Pran was signed for *Badi Bahen*, he had consciously begun to infuse into his roles that certain something, which would ensure that each character he played would turn out unlike any other.

In *Badi Bahen*, Pran adopted a 'trademark' action. Remembering his role in the film, Pran revealed that he decided to use his ability to blow perfect smoke rings while smoking his cigarettes to establish the 'style' of the character.

Pran recalls: 'The director was so impressed with my smoke rings that at the point where I am supposed to come into the story, he changed

---

[10] Loosely translated: 'My love for you makes me want to indulge all your coquettish demands.'

[11] In its issue dated 25 November, 1988.

[12] Released in 1949, Famous Pictures' *Badi Bahen* was directed by D.D. Kashyap, a well-known film maker of the 1940s and 1950s. The film had Geeta Bali, Suraiya and Rehman in lead roles.

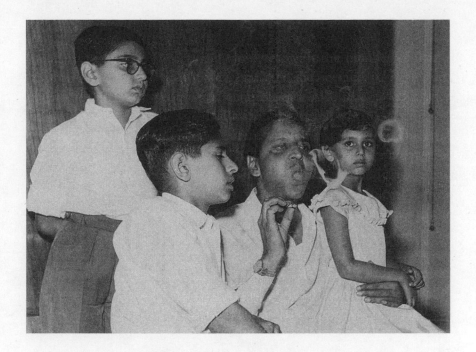

Pran demonstrating his ability to blow smoke rings to his children
Sunil, Arvind and Pinky.

the scene so that it would begin without actually showing me. He had
me blow a perfect smoke ring and shot it wafting into the frame, hitting
Geeta Bali and her being startled by it. Then the camera moved slowly
to bring me in close-up, to introduce my character in the film.'[13]

This was an utterly original way to create a palpable tension in the
audience, an expectation, anticipating the entry of a key character – the
story's 'bad' factor.

The unusual way in which the scene was picturized had the desired
effect. The moment the audience saw the smoke rings they immediately
knew that Pran was on the prowl.

Badi Bahen was a box office superhit with fabulous songs composed
by Husnlal Bhagatram that are remembered even to this day. It won the
Best Picture Award at the very first Annual *Veni* Film Awards function.

---

[13] In *Badi Bahen*, Suraiya played the role of Geeta Bali's elder sister, who works as a
maid-servant in order to give her younger sister a good education. Pran played Ajit,
a scoundrel, who, while promising to marry Geeta Bali, seduces her and then
abandons her.

These earliest film awards were started by the then famous Gujarati film journalist and magazine editor-proprietor Badri Kachwala, whose opinionated *Veni* was a very popular Gujarati-language film magazine of the 1930s and 1940s.

Badi Bahen's winning an award provided Pran the needed boost at the right time. Well known is the fact that producers suddenly begin to flock to sign up an artiste only because his or her last film has become a big hit. Apart from a film becoming a hit, getting a good review was, and still is, another factor which contributed to the artiste's climb up the ladder. With reference to *Badi Bahen*, *Filmfare* declared that this film had 'established him [Pran] as Indian cinema's no. 1 baddie', determining for Pran what course his career would take.[14]

3

Studio gates that were once clanged shut, now began to open. Pran had begun to sign film after film. There was no looking back.

For Pran, Lahore would eventually be relegated to the sepia-toned past. His only links with it were some of his friends from there, who had made their way to India, and the experiences they held in common. And these had proved to be real friends.

And during this early period as Pran slowly began to get work in Bombay, he formed some enduring friendships with his fellow actors, among whom were Ashok Kumar and Dev Anand.

'I met Ashok Kumar for the first time in Bombay Talkies,' Pran reminisced. 'However, initially I was more friendly with Dev Anand. The special thing about both Dev and Dadamoni [Ashok Kumar] was that they never talked *against* anybody.'

These friendships were cemented during the train rides to and from the Bombay Talkies studios in Malad. Pran talked about those days when Bombay was not as overcrowded as it is today. So it was no big deal for film actors and budding stars to board a local train – they could do so without fear of being mobbed.

---

[14] In April 1997.

Referring to his days of struggle in 1948, Pran observed: 'We artistes used to board the train at Churchgate, Dev Anand, Kamini Kaushal and myself, and get down at Malad, then walk to the studio. In the evening too, we used to return together up to Churchgate station and then go to our individual homes. This helped us become good friends, and we developed very friendly relationships with each other. In the train, you see, we got the time to chat, and the chance to get to know each other better.'

4

When Pran got that unforgettable call from Bombay Talkies, he and his wife were still staying in Hotel Delamar at Marine Drive, just a few blocks away from the Churchgate station.

However, in 1948 itself, once some money began to come in from the movies he had signed in quick succession, little *Bubboo*, who until then had been with his aunt Pushpa Walia in Indore, was by this time reunited with his parents in Bombay.

As things began to stabilize, Pran, wife Shukla and their child Arvind moved – first to one of Shukla's cousin's house and then to another relative's place.

Moving from place to place during those early years and facing hardships was perhaps something that Shukla had never dreamt she would have to deal with. But deal with it she did, with grit and a determination that could only have been born out of a deep love for, and faith in, her husband's abilities to provide for the young family.

For a few months they even stayed with producer-director S.M. Yusuf and his wife at their home in Worli, before finally finding rented accommodation in a building called Mazagaon Terrace, in Mazagaon, a part of Byculla.[15]

Narrating how they came to reside in that rented flat, Shukla revealed: 'My cousin, that is, *maama's* son, was in the Army and we used to meet him often. He had a friend who was Anglo-Indian. His family had left

---

[15] Byculla is an area in central Mumbai.

India in 1947 and had gone to London. This man was staying alone in the flat. So he suggested we stay with him as paying guests. We stayed there for two years. Mr Stanley was a good old man. He had given us the use of his entire flat except for one bedroom, which he retained for his own use.

'Old Mr Stanley sometimes used to eat with us. Even after we moved away, the old man used to come and visit us. But after some time, he just didn't turn up; maybe he had died or had left to live with his family,' Shukla conjectured.

The slicing of the subcontinent by Partition had such a devastating impact that it had left both sides bleeding for years to come. For some, the emotional wounds would never heal. It was understandable for anyone to feel pressurized by the situation. But Shukla never once regretted her decision to come to Bombay with her husband and be there for him while he re-established his career.

'I willingly supported him. I never felt overwhelmed by all the problems nor did he ever give me reason to feel that way,' Shukla averred. 'The reason I was able to cope was because our family background was strong and sound. I knew that if the difficulties ever crossed the limit, we could always turn to our relatives who would surely help us, and some of them even did so.

'And by the time we finally settled down in Mazagaon, I had managed to get across our old cook from Lahore, who used to serve us from my father's time. I had kept a maid as well to help me with *Bubboo*. These two were a great help to me,' said Shukla gratefully.

For by the beginning of 1949, Shukla was pregnant again.

The future, both on his professional and personal fronts, looked promising once again.

The bad period had finally ended. *Murliwalé* had turned his attention to the young star from Lahore who had lost everything that he had built up there due to the impact of Partition.

PART TWO

SEVEN

The Fabulous Fifties

1

After the maelstrom of Partition, Pran had miraculously managed to land on his feet in Bombay's cinema world. The ensuing struggle to re-establish himself in the latter half of the 1940s made him determined of one thing: He would never allow such difficulties to come upon his family again.

And this he would do by trying to ensure that his career, now restarted, should take off like never before — and stay up.

By combining talent with strategy, he would plan for a long innings in his chosen profession. He would work hard, he would slog, he would put in long hours. He would do all he could to ensure that the usually rare second chance, which he had been given, would now be sustained and built up by the sheer dint of his hard work.

Initially, Pran had taken the route that every other villain at that time had. He had 'done what he was told' and given his 'villainy' the only 'colour' required by the script and his directors — black! The films made during this period had called for only one dimension, and Pran had given it all he had. Thus, the first half of the 1950s saw Pran make great strides towards achieving a screen persona that would long continue to be associated with him — that of villain.

By 1954, five years into the second decade of his film career, Pran had acted in some thirty-three films. This was more than the entire number of films in which he had acted during the first decade of his career![1]

Pran acted in approximately seventy-three films in the second decade of his career. Some of the finest assignments and the most coveted roles came flooding into Pran's career throughout the 1950s. It was during this decade that Pran also began to accept roles that allowed him to explore different genres of the cinema medium, other than the 'social' genre that required an obvious, completely 'rotten-to-the-core' villain.

Pran acted in several costume dramas, some of which are *Sheesh Mahal*, *Aan Baan*, *Halaku* and *Raj Tilak*. Then he also tried his hand at fantasy films, such as *Sindbad the Sailor*, *Aleef Laila* and *Daughter of Sindbad*.

Nimmi and Pran in the fantasy film *Aleef Laila*.

---

[1] According to the information available, Pran acted in at least thirty films during the first decade of his film career — from 1940 to 1949. There were more films in which Pran acted. However, the records of those films have been lost during Partition.

Pran essaying the role of Sindbad the sailor.

These films, however, were just highly exaggerated versions of the 'social' films being made at this time; the only difference being that these were fantastical stories with elaborate costumes and special effects, and, of course, the ubiquitous 'all-bad' villain, which somewhat limited the range of Pran's talent.

The action flick was another genre with which Pran experimented. *Toofan, Do Gunde* and *Madam XYZ* were some of the films he did within this genre.

Kundan, based on Victor Hugo's classical story, *Les Miserables,* and retold in inimitable style by the great Sohrab Modi, was yet another type of movie in which Pran acted.

The thriller-suspense genre also found a place in Pran's line-up of films in the 1950s. Other than *Madhumati,* he also worked in *Moti Mahal,* and *Guesthouse.*

During this exciting period of experimentation with different genres, Pran also decided to try his hand at comedy. *Chham Chhama Chham, Pilpili*

Shyama and Pran in a sequence from *Pilpili Saheb*.

Saheb, Hum Sab Chor Hain and *Ek Jhalak* were among some of the films from this genre. These were precursors to some of Pran's most famous comic characterizations yet in the future.

Pilpili Saheb garnered praise for both the film and Pran's work in it. *Filmfare* headlined its review: 'PILPILI SAHEB GAY ROLLICKING COMEDY'. Among other things, the reviewer wrote: 'A gay, crazy romantic comedy…planned and produced only to entertain, *Pilpili Saheb* succeeds very well on that score…*Pran as the (heroine's) husband and Kuldip as his extramarital interest put over good portrayals, Pran's being another of his poised roles.*'

With regard to *Asha*, *Screen's* headline read: 'ASHA MAKES FAST ENTERTAINER.' The reviewer commented: '*Pran as the villain Raj has some good moments of acting and gives an uninhibited performance… he is quite effective.*'

No doubt, his effectiveness as an actor able also to perform in comic roles is due to an ability he has which was revealed by yesteryear's top actress and today's TV producer, director and character artiste, Asha Parekh, who had first met him when she worked as a young actress on the sets of *Asha*, in the 1950s. Mentioning that she had subsequently worked with Pran in a number of films, Asha said she had been able to observe him closely. She then also disclosed something about Pran of which not many people are aware: *'Pran has got a great sense of humour.'*

It is this *'great sense of humour'* or an innate sense of comic timing which has contributed in no small measure to his success in the comic genre, from the 1950s onwards.

Actually, all these 'comedies' made in this decade too belonged to the 'social' genre, but their makers had wisely added generous doses of comedy, romance and sometimes, even suspense, drama and crime-filled mystery to their stories, so that there was something in the film for everyone. The moderate-to-good success of these films had further aided the development of Pran's career.

Indeed, it was as if the spotlight had suddenly been switched on and was focused upon the new actor who had compelling eyes and a fiery personality. And the films in which Pran had acted thus far saw him investing his screen roles with an artistry so convincing that it made him 'almost there' as film land's most sought-after villain.

Vyjayanthimala and Pran as they appeared in *Asha*.

2

'Film assignments began to come in regularly by now, and each in its own way was big for me at that time!' Pran reflected with a smile, as he spoke of the 1950s. 'The great Sohrab Modi of Minerva Movietone Studios offered me a good role in an already star-studded film *Sheesh Mahal...*'[2] Given the pomp and pageantry of Sohrab Modi's films and the star-studded cast, this film became a huge hit.

Talking about another one of his early successes, Pran acknowledged: 'In retrospect, I may say that it was B. R. Chopra's *Afsana*[3] which can be counted as my first really b-i-g picture in Bombay. Ashok Kumar, whom I'd met earlier in Bombay Talkies, and the regal Veena were in that film.'

Pran's role in *Afsana* was an important one, which depicted him having an affair with the wife of one of the two characters played by Ashok Kumar. The movie was a hit, completing twenty-five weeks in theatres. In reviewing *Afsana*, which was B. R. Chopra's first film, the tabloid-weekly *Movie Times* observed: *'Pran provides some excellent villainy.'*

Referring to Pran's performance in another one of his successful films during this decade, the review of AVM's *Bahar* in *Movie Times*, under the headline 'BAHAR: ENTERTAINMENT PAR EXCELLENCE', made this comment: 'Pran the "typed" villain goes through his *Badi Bahen* routine with his usual verve and gusto...*he plays the perfect villain.'*

There were more such reviews, all underscoring the fact that Pran's performance had in some, not inconsiderable, measure contributed to the film's success.

However, what is interesting is the fact that, even though some of the other films in which Pran had acted, drew negative comments in themselves,

---

2   *Sheesh Mahal* (released in 1950) was produced and directed by Sohrab Modi, who also acted in it. The cast included other big names such as Naseem Banu, Pushpa Hans, Nigar Sultana, Mubarak, Amarnath, Jawahar Kaul, Leela Misra and Pran.

3   Produced under the banner of Shri Gopal Pictures, *Afsana* (released in 1951), was directed by B. R. Chopra and had music by Husnlal-Bhagatram. It starred Ashok Kumar in a very striking double role opposite Veena. Playing important supporting roles were Pran, Kuldip Kaur, Jeevan, Cuckoo, Baby Tabassum, Ratan Kumar and Chaman Puri. B. R. Chopra later remade this film (in 1972) under his own banner of B.R. Films, with the title *Dastaan*, which starred Dilip Kumar, Sharmila Tagore, Bindu, and Prem Chopra, who played the role Pran had earlier done.

his performances used to be praised — or at any rate, the reason for his having given a less-than-perfect performance was attributed to a poorly etched role, a badly written script or an absolutely unbelievable storyline.

Thus, with regard to *Bahu*,[4] *Filmfare's* review was one of the few in which Pran received the rare negative comment: '*...Pran, too (like Shashikala the vamp) is ill at ease in his poorly written villain's role.*'

Filmfare went a step further when it reviewed *Asha*,[5] and commented on Pran's performance thus: '*Pran as the villain turns in another of his suave, polished performances whenever the not-so-polished direction allows him to do so.*'

And while the same magazine headlined its review of *Lakeeren*[6] as 'POOR FILM DESPITE FIRST-RATE PORTRAYALS', it went on to devote a full paragraph to Pran's role and performance:

'... Pran as the young rake who has desired Asha (Nalini Jaywant) from childhood and marries her from a perverted passion for revenge which he indulges with callous brutality, *gives a performance which is histrionically superb and completely convincing.*'[7]

Pran was assessing his career graph by observing and listening to *what* the media said. Where most other artistes would look only at the accolades, Pran preferred to pay close attention to even the *slightest* negative statement.

When the *Movie Times'* review of *Malkin*[8] was headlined, 'MALKIN HAS ALL THE REQUISITES OF A GOOD FILM', and praised '*the consummate artistry of Pran*', it could have been easy

Pran holding visitor Geeta Bali's head on the sets of *Malkin*, while Nutan looks on amusedly.

---

4 *Bahu* (1955), directed by Shakti Samanta, co-starred Usha Kiron, Karan Dewan and Pran.
5 Producer-director M. V. Raman's *Asha* (released in 1957), starred Kishore Kumar, Vyjayanthimala and Pran.
6 *Lakeeren* (1954), had a big star cast headed by Ashok Kumar and Nalini Jaywant.
7 *Filmfare*, 14 May 1954.
8 Gope Productions' *Malkin* (released in 1953), starred Nutan, Sajjan, Purnima and Pran.

for him to relax and breathe easy. But the review had also commented that his performance was 'slightly marred by his very unnatural and odd hairstyle'.

If nothing else, the reviews caused him to understand the importance of the 'look' of the character he was to play and how that 'look' would contribute to the overall impact of his role.

Hence he began to cultivate close relationships with the make-up men, the beard- and wig-makers, the costume designers, the fight composers, the choreographers — all those behind-the-scenes technicians including the most important technician whom all leading men and women, no matter how important, befriend and hold in high esteem — the cinematographer.

In addition to the reviews, Pran knew that he would need to keep his finger on the pulse of audience reaction to his performances. This, he felt, would be the best gauge of his work. So Pran began to use all the feedback he could get, good or even if slightly bad, to his advantage by bettering his work in film after film.

And such close associations began to pay dividends, as shall be seen in further chapters.

When some of those films became box-office hits, it was not long before the 'big' offers began to roll in. Offers for exciting roles opposite top-notch stars now began to come to him more and more frequently.

Pran made up for lost time by signing many of the films he was offered. He also began to concentrate on the films in which he had something substantial to do, that is, on those roles that would allow him the *freedom* to broaden and round out the character he was given to play. So, little by little, Pran began to invest something 'extra' into these roles, subtly adding dimensions to them, transforming them from mere roles to characterizations.

Among the more noteworthy roles, which came to Pran during the 1950s, was the Bimal Roy directed *Biraj Bahu*.[9] It was a social melodrama in which Pran played the wicked village *zamindar* who covets Biraj and tries to enjoy her at any cost. For all practical purposes, it was yet another unidimensional villain's role, but Pran brought many subtle shades to his

---

[9] Hiten Chaudhary Productions' *Biraj Bahu* (released in 1954) was directed by Bimal Roy and had Kamini Kaushal and Abhi Bhattacharya in the lead.

interpretation of the character; these were among his first steps towards establishing himself as a 'thinking' villain.

Bimal Roy's *Madhumati*,[10] with its theme of reincarnation, starring Dilip Kumar and Vyjayanthimala in lead roles, came next in the line-up of noteworthy roles.

Once again playing the covetous local *zamindar*, Raja Ugra Narain, who hankers after the tribal girl, Madhumati, Pran played it differently to what he had done thus far, bringing refinement to his villainy and adding spice to the delineation of the character.

Reviewing *Madhumati*, the newspaper *Cine Advance* commented: 'The supporting cast is particularly good with Pran, Jayant and Tiwari coming through with splendid performances.'

In contrast, *Filmfare* pointed out that 'Pran has a role which gives him no opportunities…. The scene in which Pran is apprehended with the aid of an unearthly visitor takes the cake for incredibility.'

Although the story appeared implausible and the scope of Pran's role in it was limited, the fact still remains that Pran had injected into Ugra Narain's characterization shades that discerning eyes could see, especially how he portrayed the lust the character feels for the girl, and the thin veneer of congeniality that conceals his evil intentions.

Pran's other 1958 release was *Adalat*.[11] This hugely successful melodrama brought Pran much recognition, and also got him outstanding critical acclaim.

In its review, *Filmfare* remarked: '*Pran very nearly steals the show with his impeccable performance in one of the most villainous villain roles seen in many a year. The different guises he adopts reveal his versatility, and he shares top acting honours with Nargis* [the heroine].'

In fact, in his concluding remarks the reviewer even went so far as to say: '*Adalat* is a picture as stale as yesterday's newspaper, still it is worth seeing because of the good performances' – one of which was Pran's.

Interestingly, Pran himself counts *Adalat* and *Halaku* as two of the most interesting and satisfying performances of his career[12] – *Adalat*,

---

[10] Released in 1958.

[11] Kwatra Films' *Adalat* co-starred Nargis with Pradeep Kumar and Pran.

[12] Among his other interesting films, Pran makes special mention also of *Jis Desh Mein Ganga Behti Hai* (1960), *Shaheed* (1965) and *Upkar* (1967).

because he got the chance not only to use a variety of disguises but also an array of accents as the villain who finds ways to unremittingly harass the heroine and *Halaku* because here was a role of a lifetime!

3

In most of Pran's interviews during the 1950s (and thereafter), he has singled out the *Halaku* for special mention.[13] Why did Pran hold this film so close to his heart?

For one, Pran was selected to play the title role in a exciting new genre – the historical costume drama. And although the film was more fiction than fact, Pran was not going to let the golden opportunity to gain maximum mileage from this assignment pass him by. He knew he would have to put a lot of thought into his role and the way he would present and portray Halaku.[14]

Another reason why Pran holds this role close to his heart is that this film was different! For once, here was a film named after the villain! And Pran was always interested in things that were different.

And a third, and possibly the most important reason, was that Pran was going to have to don make-up and wear a costume, which was completely different to anything he had done until that point.

In most of his get-ups in his films until then, the character Pran played was 'essentially Pran', in that he was easily recognized as the actor Pran playing a particular character. Whereas in *Halaku*, the entire look and get-up did not allow even an iota of Pran the actor to come through. The moment Pran donned his make-up and costume, it was as if Halaku, Il Khan himself, the grandson of the Great Mongol Ghenghis Khan, was visiting the sets that day!

Speaking for this biography, Nadira, a contemporary of Pran, recently said: 'Pran has lived every moment of his role of *Halaku*! He was magnificent in it! You give him something different to act and he takes it up as a challenge.'

---

[13] P.N. Arora's historical costume drama, *Halaku* (released in 1956), directed by D. D. Kashyap, starred Pran (in the title role) with Meena Kumari, Ajit and Veena.

[14] Also known as Hulagu, grandson of Ghenghis Khan, leader of the Mongol and Tatar tribes.

Pran or Halaku?

That, in essence, is Pran – a man who loves everything that is different from the usual and a man who cannot resist a challenge!

Talking about *Halaku*, Pran said: 'This was not his [Kashyap's] first film. I had the title role in it. Meena Kumari was the heroine and Ajit *Saab* was the hero.

'When Kashyap *Saab* went to Meena Kumari to tie her in for the film, she wanted to know who was doing the role of Halaku. When he said "Pran *Saab*", she made a face showing her disappointment in his choice. But when she saw my get-up and a few rushes, she was very happy and told Kashyap: "Your choice is good." I felt encouraged that such a big artiste had commended me. My joy knew no bounds.'

Apparently, Pran had viewed the role as a once-in-a-lifetime role and was prepared to make any amount of sacrifices for it, even to the point of altering his basic appearance.

For most men on the Indian subcontinent, their well-tended moustache is the undisputed symbol of masculinity and male pride. So what Pran did for his role in *Halaku* reveals how much he prized that role and to what extent he was willing to go. In order to create an authentic 'look' for the character, he shaved off his famous moustache!

Character actress Shammi, who played 'first maid' to the heroine Meena Kumari in *Halaku*, recalled an interesting incident that happened during its filming, which serves to illustrate how seriously Pran took his role as Halaku.

Kashyap was directing the shot which Rajendra Malone, the cinematographer, had conceived. The sets that were built were massive. That particular shot was to be taken in a long corridor that had doors on one side, which was supposed to be the part of the palace where Pran, who played the great Mongol warlord, had kept Meena Kumari captive.

The scene had to start with the camera showing Pran and the full length of the corridor in a long shot. Pran, with his retinue of officials and servants behind him, had to then start walking briskly from the far end of the corridor, past door after door, coming towards the last door (which was Meena Kumari's room) and the camera, which was positioned near it. Pran would turn into this last door and go up to Meena Kumari and start talking to her in an attempt to coerce her into giving in to his desires.

Since the shot was lengthy, it would best be effective only if done in one smooth and fluid 'panning take'. The obvious thing to do was what Pran had decided. He was going to do his best to make sure that there were no endless retakes of this tiring shot. He would stride purposefully towards Meena Kumari's door and in one smooth motion swing into her room and get on with the task of intimidating her.

Now Kashyap and Malone were both rather smitten with Meena Kumari's acting talent and looks. So they used to focus both their attentions – and their camera – on her! It did not matter much to them that the other stars in the cast had noticed their 'weakness', and that their preoccupation with their heroine was making them the butt of many jokes, besides which a certain lack of concentration on the part of the other artistes had crept into the proceedings.

Shammi recalls that walk and trying to keep pace with Pran. 'I used to be full of fun in those days and was always wanting to play mischief. So, just before the third door from the camera,' she says gleefully, 'I dug him in the ribs from behind to see if he would falter in his regal and purposeful stride. Although he almost faltered, he quickly recovered and kept up his pace, completing the shot as planned.

'When the director shouted "cut!" and the shot was over, Pran turned to me and with a seriousness that came as a surprise, since he knew that I had only done it in fun, said: "Don't ever do that again! Or else, I'll kill you!"

'Being quite young, I tried to deny it, but he knew it was me. He went up to Rajendra Malone, who was the cameraman and asked him as well as Kashyap how the shot had turned out and if he could do a retake since he did not feel satisfied with what he had done. But Kashyap and Malone both said the shot was perfect and that nothing needed to be done to better it. In fact, when they later played back the scene, we found that there was no break in his stride at all!

'Pran's dedication to his work struck me then. I realized then that no matter whether the film's focus was on you or not, one must give each scene the best we have. That will keep us focused and only then will our work be appreciated.'

The *Filmfare* review of *Halaku* must have pleased Pran because it vindicated his conviction, even before the shooting had started, that here was a role – a central role – of a lifetime. Headlined 'HALAKU: WELL-ACTED STORY OF GRANDSON OF GHENGHIS KHAN', the reviewer commented:

'Among the stars, *Pran dominates the picture in the title role of Halaku. His is a full-blooded performance alive with the brooding passion of the Hun and his sudden excesses of violence.* It is not his fault if, in his case, action is not in keeping with the character sought to be presented. *What is in the actor's hands he does, and does well, bringing to what must be the best role of his career, a power and finesse which dominate the picture.'*

In fact, Pran's performance as the ruthless Mongol warlord was so chilling and power-packed that he cornered a large chunk of the votes for Best Actor in the *Filmfare* Awards that year.

The truth of these statements was strikingly brought home in the year 2003, after this film, first released in 1956, was telecast on a popular television channel, which regularly shows vintage Hindi films. Not only does Pran unconsciously dominate the scenes in which he appears, he also succeeds in eliciting a response that only a rare master-actor can do – a sense of pity for an otherwise hateful character and a vague feeling of empathy towards someone who has loved, even lusted, in vain.

4

The growing urge in Pran to try out different genres and his success in doing so encouraged him to keep on striving to inject something new into all the roles he performed, regardless of what the critics had to say about them.

Even though some of the roles offered to him were the usual, run-of-the-mill variety, which left him with little room to improvise and experiment, Pran put his heart into the preparation of each role, making every effort to rise above the mediocre script and produce a performance that was both skilful and believable.

By and large, however, no matter what hateful deeds Pran committed on screen, and no matter that some of his films lacked in terms of the script and characterizations, his own work and talent were recognized by the fourth estate.[15]

In the latter half of the 1950s, as the decade began to wind down, the releases of Pran's films were on the rise. And some of these were 'big-banner' films. In the avalanche of reviews that appeared during this time, Pran's performance was almost always noticed and appreciated, further consolidating his position as a villain. The comparatively small number of uncomplimentary reviews out of a total of seventy-three releases in the 1950s certainly reflects an outstanding record for any actor.

---

[15] The fourth estate was originally any group regarded as having power in the land; it now specifically refers to the press.

Although one of his important films, *Chori Chori* [16] did not impress *Filmfare*'s critic, he did name Pran along with some of the other veteran character artistes as making 'brief and excellent appearances', but said that they were 'wasted in perfunctory parts'.

Munimji, [17] on the other hand, fared generally well with the critics. *Filmfare* headlined its review as: 'POWERFUL STORY AND GOOD PERFORMANCES HIGHLIGHT *MUNIMJI*' and went on to say: '...An action-filled story which sizzles with adventure and romance and is studded with gay songs and dance numbers to say nothing of the sparkling dialogue and performances which are excellent...*Pran, as the arch villain, contributes powerfully to the drama. His is a poorly written role but Pran makes it realistic and baneful by the sheer power of his acting.*'

Tumsa Nahin Dekha[18] earned Pran this one line from the *Filmfare* critic: '*Pran does full justice to his villain's role.*'

Critical acclaim continued to follow Pran from 1957 through 1958, in which year the now immortal producer S. S. Vasan of Gemini Studios of Madras signed up Pran for the big star cast of *Raj Tilak*. Headlined 'GEMINI'S *RAJ TILAK* IS AN ENGROSSING ADVENTURE ROMANCE,' the *Filmfare* review emphasized that the film was '...a lavish production; it holds the attention of the audience right up to the final fade-out...the plot is a gripping one and the story moves at such a fast pace that the audience is given no time to know whether the happenings are credible.'

The reviewer also added: 'The portrayals of the principal artistes are uniformly good, *Pran putting over a dominating performance. The tall and dynamic "villain" strides with complete self-confidence through his entire footage and steals the show.*'

Headlining its review as '*CHANDAN*[19] HAS EXCELLENT MASS APPEAL' the weekly *Screen* noted: '*It is Pran as the sinister Moti and Shyama as the spouse*

---

[16] AVM's *Chori Chori* (released in 1956) was directed by Anant Thakur, with Raj Kapoor, Nargis and Pran in leading roles.

[17] *Munimji* (released in 1955) was directed by Subodh Mukerji and starred Dev Anand, Nalini Jaywant, Nirupa Roy and Pran.

[18] Filmistan's *Tumsa Nahin Dekha* (released in 1957) was directed by Nasir Hussain and had Shammi Kapoor, Ameeta and Pran in the lead.

[19] Cameraman Fali Mistry's *Chandan* (released in 1958), directed by M. V. Raman, starred Nutan, Shyama, Kishore Kumar, Mala Sinha, Karan Dewan and Pran.

who leave a more lasting impression on the audience with excellent performances.' For its part, *Filmfare* in its review paid him this compliment: *'Pran, as the libertine, turns in another of his polished portrayals...'*

The reviews only corroborated the message Pran sent out, loud and clear, during the decade of the 1950s: Here was an actor who could be counted on to consistently turn in a noteworthy performance, even when there were several things lacking in a script.

5

For an actor, who played hero in the beginning of his career and had the chance to continue as hero, to accept more and more roles as villain may seem puzzling. Especially when everyone around him seemed to gravitate to a film career only so as to play hero, it appeared strange that Pran not only gladly accepted villains' roles, but also put his heart and soul into doing an excellent job of them.

Pran was the kind of person who right from the very beginning of his mature life had wanted to be different from the rest in whatever he did — whether that had to do with his career choice (he had chosen to be a still photographer rather than conventionally follow his father's footsteps and become a civil engineer) or his switch-over to films (choosing a new medium over the 'security' of a two-hundred-rupee job).

So now, rather than accepting any of the insipid hero's roles that were the order of the day and fizzling out early in his career, as had happened to so many of his contemporaries, playing villain and being good at it was yet another expression of what Pran had always naturally done — chosen to be different!

Shubha Khote worked for the first time with Pran in *Champakali*.[20] Speaking about Pran, she disclosed: 'Pran is a very down-to-earth person. I never felt I was working with a great actor and a big star whom I had seen in school and college days in films like *Munimji*. I used to think "he is such a handsome man, why does he do villains' roles, why doesn't

---

[20] Filmistan's *Champakali* (released in 1957) was directed by hit-maker Nandlal Jaswantlal, famous in movie circles as 'a heroine's director', starred Bengal's leading actress Suchitra Sen opposite Bharat Bhushan.

he become the hero?" *But come to think of it, the villain has to be very handsome if he has to compete with the hero!*'

Kamini Kaushal, when recently interviewed for this book, made a very interesting observation about how a villain should look: 'I think that to be a hero you can be mild, good-looking and pleasant, *but to be a villain you've got to be a nasty guy, and yet, people, especially the heroine, must find you very attractive and irresistible.*'

And that is precisely the image which Pran had spontaneously cultivated. It was not phony or put-on, but had developed entirely unconsciously, since Pran has always been stylish and has somehow always managed to attract the opposite sex. This was a big 'plus' when playing the villain. So, rather than play hero, with his obvious magnetism, Pran gladly played villain, since he felt that without the villain there could be no story at all!

In fact, he very clearly stated in the 18 January 1952 issue of *Screen*: 'I do not *want* to be a goody-goody hero.'

On another occasion Pran confessed why he never wanted to be the hero: 'Somehow I always felt *terribly* shy singing those romantic, lover-boy type of songs. *Apne ko jamta nahin tha bhai* [21] I was no good at it!'

He went on to say that every time he had to romance Baby Noorjehan in *Khandaan*, he would find reasons to run away from the sets! He expressed his feeling quite frankly: 'The hero invariably makes a fool of himself when he says all those things he is forced to say while singing a love duet. No, I always preferred being the villain with something to do.'

Hence, since running-around-the-trees and song-and-dance sequences are part and parcel of Indian cinema, he decided to stick to on-screen villainy!

Speaking to a film newspaper in 1957,[22] Pran had made some worthwhile observations: 'What is the difference between a film hero and a villain? I shall explain. After all, the villain is also one of the aspirants to the leading lady's love but his means are meagre and the hero snatches away the girl from him. The only loss to me in my present

---

[21] Loosely translated: 'I was not cut out for such things, my friend!'
[22] *Cine Advance*, 20 June 1957.

capacity is that I get a couple of thousand rupees *less* than the leading man. Well, that loss could be written off in favour of dramatic art.'

In spite of the 'loss', the fact remains that during the 1950s Pran's career really took off and he used to like to say: 'Villainy may not pay in the next world! But it certainly does in this! Celluloid villainy, that is!'

However, pondering awhile, he summed up his attitude to his roles and to his work, saying: '*I still have a chance to take off this mask of villainy, but then I shall stop making any progress.*'

And the progress could not stop. He would not let it.

While Pran's career graph was registering a steady rise, he could not forget that troublous times were not so far back in the safety of the past.

Besides, there had been a steady growth on the family front too.

EIGHT

The Family Grows…

1

In early 1949, while they were still staying as paying guests at Mazagaon Terrace, Pran's wife Shukla became pregnant again.

Pran recalls those days: 'We didn't know of any nursing home in which to admit Shukla. So Mumtaz Shanti, Wali *Saab's* wife, herself an important leading lady, got Shukla booked at the D'Silva Nursing Home at Bandra. Today it is called the Holy Family Hospital. I remember the doctor, he was a very fine man.'

At around this time, Shukla began to explore the spiritual side to her nature. A young woman who had just come through some rough times, made rougher because she just could not allow her husband to know how it had been affecting her, a young wife and mother finding herself in a new city and experiencing a whole new gamut of feelings and emotions because the only constant in her life right then was change – surely it was natural to want to seek a spiritual anchor for some inner stability.

That was when producer-director P. L. Santoshi's wife introduced her to Kammo Baba, a holy personage who himself was a follower of

Shirdi Sai Baba,[1] and who lived a little further away from Filmistan Studios in Goregaon, a suburb of western Bombay.

Kammo Baba proved to be a benefactor to both Shukla and Pran. Her faith in Kammo Baba would help Shukla through her difficult times.

'I started frequenting his place, once in 10 or 15 days, or whenever the urge came. Baba used to call me *beti* and he treated me as one,' Shukla said fondly. 'Others had to stand in queue to meet him but for me there was no restriction. Occasionally, if I dropped in there during lunch time, and Baba was about to have lunch, he would ask me to join him. I feel that your love grows for the person who loves you in return. He loved me a lot, he would always ask about the welfare of his son-in-law, that is my husband, and my child.'

In 1949, in the hours before her second delivery, Shukla was suffering a great deal in hospital. Unable to see his wife suffer the throes of labour, Pran went to meet Kammo Baba as soon as Shukla told him to.

Pran recalled the whole incident as if it had happened only yesterday: 'I borrowed a friend's car and reached Goregaon only to find that the *fakir*[2] was about to leave for another destination. When I told him of Shukla's pain, Kammo Baba gave me a locket and a wad of cotton dipped in *attar*.[3] He asked me to keep them near Shukla's ears. And before letting me go, he embraced me for two minutes and then said: "Go to her soon."'

'Actually,' Pran continued with a degree of amazement, 'the moment he embraced me and held me like that, I found out later that it was at *that* precise moment my wife delivered the baby!

'Thus, our second son, Sunil, whom we affectionately call *Tunni*, was born on 19 September 1949.

'When I returned to Shukla's side I placed the wad of cotton behind one of her ears,' Pran related, 'and Shukla's pain that had carried on even after the birth, miraculously subsided!

'Although everybody was happy to inform me that a boy had been born, secretly I was just a little disappointed for I had wanted a girl. I

---

[1]   Shirdi Sai Baba is not to be confused with Satya Sai Baba. Shirdi Sai Baba lived simply, believed in one Almighty unseen Creator and repudiated idol worship.
[2]   Holy man.
[3]   Oil-based, heavy perfume.

had reasoned that we already had a boy, and a girl would have made our family complete. But then everything is in God's hands...' Pran's voice trailed off.

Pran was especially very keen on having a little girl who would be daddy's little girl. 'We tried once more, with the hope that this time it would be a girl. And to prevent disappointment, we thought to ourselves, *"even if we don't get a girl this time, we'll at least have three bahus* [daughters-in-law] *to bring into the house!"*

'But by the grace of God, this time we *did* get a girl! *Murliwalé* had heard my prayers!' said Pran with a smile. For on 8 November 1952, Pran and Shukla became the proud parents of a much-awaited baby girl. Delighted with this pretty little 'gift', they named her Pinky.

The family had grown in the seven years, from *'hum do'* [4] in 1945, to *'hum paanch'* [5] in 1952.

2

'We had stayed on at Mazagaon till 1950,' Pran recollected. 'Then I started getting much better offers, so when *Tunni* was a young child, we shifted to a better flat in Pali Hill. Nice though Mr Stanley was, the cistern in his toilet always leaked!'

By then, the film industry and the big studios had, by and large, shifted to north Bombay and Pran, like most film people, realized that rather than staying in south or central Bombay,[6] it would be more advantageous if they relocated to the suburbs. So he rented a ground floor, two-bedroom flat at No. 2, Pali Hill.

'It was a much better and bigger place, with a lot of garden space, where the landlord, Shantilal Bajaj, would even grow cucumbers!'

Explaining why a larger living area and garden space was a consideration in their choice of a home, Pran revealed:

---

[4] Loosely translated: 'The two of us'.
[5] Loosely translated: 'The five of us.'
[6] Any area south of Bandra is designated central and south Bombay. In those days, Bandra was the official beginning of the suburbs.

'Let me go back a little.... One of the most precious things in my life which I lost after Partition were my dogs. My father was as fond of them as I was and we'd had many dogs right from my childhood.... After Shukla and I married and set up home in Lahore, we had an Alsatian dog that was given to us by Shukla's cousin, General Daulat Singh. Regretfully, we had to leave the dog behind during Partition.

'Looking back on my life, I may say that I have never stayed without dogs throughout my life. It was only during that bad period when we had to stay in various hotels that I couldn't afford to keep a dog. But the moment we shifted into the Pali Hill flat, the first thing I did was to buy a dog! His name was Bonzo and he was a lovely Golden Retriever.'

At about the same time as Pinky's birth, Shantilal Bajaj, who owned large portions of land in Pali Hill, decided to develop the property as a colony of bungalows for the rich and famous, named Union Park.[7] Naturally, he first looked to the film industry for potential buyers. Seeing the Sikand family grow, he invited Pran to book a house there too.

'Mr Bajaj was kind enough to agree to take the payment in instalments. It was a good scheme. So I booked two plots there after Pinky's birth — one for the bungalow and the other for a garden. I have always been used to a lot of space,' Pran explained, 'and this gave me the opportunity to finally have my own garden where I could grow my cacti and roses, and where we could finally have many more dogs, which could roam free.'

'We shifted into the bungalow around the middle of 1955 and almost the first thing we did was to get more dogs! There were Bullet, an Alsatian, as well as Whisky and Soda, a white Pomeranian and a black cocker spaniel, respectively. At that time Arvind was nine and already at boarding school, Sunil was six, and Pinky was just three! But we still hung on to No. 2, Pali Hill, giving up that house only much later,' recounted Pran.

Perhaps the pain of losing one's home and possessions and the uncertainties that they went through after their arrival in India were still fresh.

---

[7] Union Park is on the north side and at the bottom of Pali Hill, Bandra, and the edge of Khar, in Bombay.

3

Due to Bajaj's film world connections, many other film people had also
bought bungalows in Union Park. These included leading film personalities
such as producers-directors Bhagwandas Varma, Amiya Chakraborty,
M. Sadiq and Nanabhai Bhat, leading men Ranjan and Sajjan, who also
did villain and character-actor roles, the vamp Shashikala and her producer-
husband Om Prakash Saigal, well-known comedian Gope and his wife,
the actress Latika, music director Ghulam Mohammed and many others.
That one square mile in Bandra soon had more film people living there
than in any other part of Bombay, giving it the sobriquet – the Beverly
Hills of Bombay

'But strangely enough,' Pran reminisced, 'soon after the film crowd
moved into the Union Park bungalows, misfortune – or even worse –
befell them. Gope fell from popularity, became insolvent and died.
Bhagwandas Varma, Sadiq Babu and Nanabhai Bhat sold their houses and
left. Ranjan shifted to Malad, became insane, jumped out of his window
and died soon thereafter.

'At the club, of which Shukla had become a member, the ladies began
whispering to her that the colony was ill-omened. They suggested that
it was better to sell off that house and move into an apartment. It had
the desired effect. One day, Shukla came and suggested to me that we
sell this house and buy a house in some other place. That sort of
frightened me a little: *"What could be the matter?"* I thought.

'By then I realized that somebody had talked her into it. So I said:
"It may take some time to find a new house and if we buy a flat, then
we can't have the dogs. Of course, we can sell this house and buy another
one, but there's one condition – you will have to stop going to Kammo
Baba."

'"Why?" Shukla asked me.

'"Remember?" I said, "The foundation of our house was laid by
Kammo Baba. If you feel that we'll be safe here, then okay, we'll remain
here, otherwise we'll leave."

'Because of her faith in Kammo Baba, Shukla agreed to stay on, and
by the grace of Kammo Baba and *Murliwalé*, our home was kept safe. He
was a great man!'

It may seem strange that a worldly-wise person such as Pran would put faith in a *fakir*. There was one instance that occurred in Pran's own life that must have made him believe that Kammo Baba had supernatural powers. What happened was this:

The Rampuri knife that Pran had secretly carried for his protection during the pre-Partition days of violence and uncertainty in Lahore still remained with him even into the 1950s. He was so much in the habit of carrying the knife everywhere he went, that it also went with him on one of his trips abroad – to Singapore.

'While in Singapore,' said Sunil Sikand, 'it appears that a brawl erupted in the pub where Dad was having a drink, and during the ensuing fight, he whipped out his knife. I don't think he really used it, but yes, the knife was there and also, it appears, the readiness to use it if necessary. This incident was not reported in the press.

'When Dad returned from Singapore, he went to meet Kammo Baba, who asked him why he depended on a knife for safety. Dad was speechless. Kammo Baba then told him to put away that knife forever and never rely on it again to keep him safe.'

Kammo Baba died about twenty years ago, but even now people of all religious faiths go to his *mazaar* [8] and spread a special *chaadar* [9] on it to pay their respects. Shukla too goes there regularly.

The uncanny manner in which faith and fulfilment have played cause and effect in Pran's life and career, taking him gradually but steadily upwards, is something worth pondering over.

4

The Pran and Shukla Sikand family, now complete with two sons and a daughter, entered a new phase in Bandra.

Shukla harked back to those times, saying: 'Finally we were settled in our own bungalow. *He* was doing quite well in films here. Then, when the South boom began, he also started going South for shooting. But

---

[8]   Grave or mausoleum.
[9]   A sheet made of flowers which is customarily spread on the grave of a person.

it was quite a job for him to organize his dates. He had never expected me to get involved with his career, so I wisely stayed out of it. When we were at Mazagaon Terrace he used to handle his work himself and continued to do so until we got properly settled in Bandra. Then he got a secretary to handle things.'

With Pran away at work so much, it was only natural for Shukla to find herself at a loose end. 'I liked playing cards. Since *he* had placed no restrictions or bounds on me, and I had spare time, I joined the CCI [Cricket Club of India] around 1953. I used to go there daily to play. Even now, I play cards for some two to three hours, but I go to a nearby club,' Shukla said.

She recalled those early years saying: 'Having been brought up in the lap of luxury, I did not have the training needed to handle the cooking, raise the children or manage the servants. Our servants, who were mostly Garhwalis and one was a Christian, brought up the children. The children, *Bubboo* and *Tunni*, used to go to and return from school or tuitions. So I never had to do much work. The servants used to handle everything. But I was needed to oversee what was going on.'

However, playing cards was only to pass her time. Some years earlier itself, Shukla's pious nature and deep faith in God had given her life depth as well as stability that was sorely needed by her as she fulfilled her role of wife and mother.

With Pran very busy, Shukla got on with her routine and the kids carried on with theirs: school, tuitions and play.

With so many film folk residing in the same area, it was but natural that their kids get together with Pran's three kids for some fun and games. For a few years, Arvind and Sunil played together with the other children in the locality, but in 1953 the twosome was broken up.

Pran and Shukla had attempted to provide their children with the best available education in the land, to ensure that if their children studied well, then the world of films would be – not the *only* option – but *just one* of the many options they could pursue for a career.

Since Arvind has been the most academically inclined of their three children, in 1953, Pran got his seven-year-old enrolled in Lawrence School, Sanawar, and personally went with him to help him settle in. Arvind used to come home for the holidays and the family would become whole again.

With Arvind already studying at Sanawar, it was only natural to assume that Sunil would follow. But he did so only in 1958, and stayed on there for only four years before missing Bombay terribly, returning and joining the Cathedral and John Connon School!

Since Sunil spent more time in Bombay than his brother, he had more memories of his childhood and the time he spent playing with his friends! As he puts it, 'I was too busy enjoying myself as a kid.'

Sunil remembers his father's enthusiasm when he and his friends used to play cricket: 'When we were kids, there was no traffic. We all used to play cricket on the street and he'd join in with us. We used to play in the garden or in the streets ahead. When we played *chor-police*,[10] our boundaries used to be Danda village on the one side and Khar gymkhana on the other side.

'We used to roam about everywhere. There were not many people around. There were a few bungalows and the rest was the golf links down to Carter Road. There was no road as such, just a walking path. If you wanted to cycle all the way to Carter Road, then at one point you had to get down. There was lots of greenery and wide-open spaces. So the area in which we kids rambled was quite wide!'

'Dad used to join us when we played cricket. All the boys of the colony used to come to our place in the evenings. All the screaming and the "not out's!" were there. It was part and parcel of our daily cricket. Dad would also indulge in the shouting. He'd bat and then go, forget the fielding! A lot of the boys who used to come over to play were mostly film people's sons. There was Sadiq *Saab*'s son Mehmood, then there was Purnima*jee*'s son Anwar, Sajjan *Saab*'s two sons, music director Ghulam Mohammed's son, Aziz, and Mumtaz and others. Every evening, there were lots of kids all around, so we played cricket and in the monsoon, we'd go to the golf links and play football,' reminisced Sunil about those special days of childhood.

The family had grown...

Pran's career, which towards the end of the 1940s had just about begun to pick up speed, got a fresh impetus from 1950 itself, due to the entry of new players in the film production arena – the rich and well-organized South Indians.

---

[10] Cops and robbers.

NINE

Bollywood and the South

1

In late 1949, Indian cinema was poised for a very major and exciting leap forward, a long jump that would add a fascinating chapter to its history. Nobody was at that time prepared for it, but when it came, it came as a harbinger of wonderful times ahead. The South Indian film industry was about to invade and take over Hindi cinema and its stars, both big and small.

The film industry in the South, which had always been far more disciplined and better organized than its counterpart in Bombay, had, by the late 1940s, made its first major move into the production of Hindi-language films for the national market.

In the late 1940s–early 1950s, the pioneers who made this move were the film tycoons of the South – especially studio owners S. S. Vasan of Gemini Studios (Madras); A. V. Meiyappan Chettiar of AVM Studios (Madras); S. M. S. Naidu of Pakshiraja Studios (Coimbatore); 'Venus' Krishnamurthy; and much later, in 1967, B. Nagi Reddy of Vijaya-Vauhini Studios (Madras).

In fact, the first film that came from the South was S. S. Vasan's spectacularly mounted *Chandralekha* in 1948. This venture recorded fantastic box-office returns and soon all the big names in the South were scrambling to make films with big-name film stars from Bombay.

The moment they entered the all-India arena of commercial Hindi film making, there was, naturally, much interest shown by the Bombay film fraternity to bag the more lucrative acting assignments being offered by Madras tycoons.

Soon, every big name both on the screen and behind the screen in the Bollywood of the 1950s began to spend more time in Madras than in Bombay.

Amongst the many film personalities who worked in a stream of films from the South were Ashok Kumar, Dilip Kumar, Rajendra Kumar, Sunil Dutt, Pran, Om Prakash, Nirupa Roy, Nutan, Waheeda Rehman, Mala Sinha, Kishore Kumar, Dharmendra, Sanjeev Kumar, Johnny Walker, Mukri and music directors C. Ramchandra and Chitragupt.

There are innumerable anecdotes of how the South Indian film magnates functioned and of their relationships with the big stars from Bombay as compared to the way the Bollywood-based producers flattered and fawned upon the stars even though they were paying them huge sums of money.

First of all, the South Indian film tycoons never negotiated directly with the Bombay stars. They had a hierarchy of executives and controllers of production whose job it was to liaise with the film stars, character artistes, music directors and others from Bombay, and to coordinate the business of settling their terms and conditions apart from handling logistics such as their mode of travel, their stay at the top-class Madras hotels and other such administrative matters.

Bargaining was never a problem. The South Indian executives, who frequently visited Bombay, always knew the current price of each in-demand actor and actress and, instead of paying more, they were available for the same price, or even less, because the money was paid out in an unusually short period of time. Eventually, a few of these South Indian gentlemen who represented the Madras-based studio-owning tycoons became so friendly with the stars that they went on to become producers themselves!

2

Pran was amongst the most in-demand Bombay stars for the 'made-in-South-India' variety of Hindi films. Speaking about *Bahar*, his very first film assignment in Madras, Pran made the following observations: 'A. V. Meiyappan Chettiar, the owner of AVM Studios and the producer of many superhit Tamil films, sent his emissary to sign me up for *Bahar* which was to be directed by M. V. Raman.

'Raman had already made many superhit films in Tamil but this was his first directorial assignment in a Hindi film. This was also the first Hindi film assignment in Madras for Vyjayanthimala, Karan Dewan, Om Prakash and Rajinder Krishen.[1]

'All of us became popular very rapidly with both the Tamil film producers as well as the entire hierarchy of their workers. We were well liked, well paid and well looked after. We were given a lot of respect and in return we also gave them a lot of respect.

'This is basically what made a small group of us very popular in Madras, especially Om Prakash, Rajinder Krishen, C. Ramchandra, myself and a few others.'

A typical day in the life of these actors working in the South was as follows:

In the morning, the studio car would be waiting punctually at the appointed hour in the five-star hotel portico. The production executive who was allotted to a particular star would first ring from downstairs, then go up and escort the star to his car. They would leave punctually for the studios and go on the sets with full costume and make-up, *on the dot*. And, also on the dot, the producer, the big man himself, used to be waiting at the entrance to the studio floor and, with a polite *namasté*,[2] would escort his star to the set, sit around till the first shot of the day was taken, then proceed to his office to attend to his own work, leaving the star and the director to do theirs.

---

[1] Vyjayanthimala, a renowned South Indian classical danseuse, went on to star in several Bollywood hits; Karan Dewan was known for his memorable role in *Ratan*; Om Prakash went on to earn kudos as a comedian and character actor; and Rajinder Krishen was a renowned lyricist and dialogue writer.

[2] A gesture of greeting, with the arms folded at the elbows and palms joined together, fingertip to fingertip.

A full eight-hour shift was the norm in Madras. No visitors were allowed entry – nobody could loiter around and chit-chat with the stars. For them, film making was a serious business, a multimillion-rupee industry, and it was treated with that same dignity.

And during off-duty hours, Bombay's film stars were treated with all the comforts to which they were accustomed.

Because of this rigid discipline, because the South Indian magnates made their films methodically and released them on schedule, and because they knew how to stage-manage simultaneous, multiple, nationwide releases, almost every Hindi film which came out of South India in that era turned out to be a superhit all over the country.

Pran remembered *Bahar* with a certain degree of affection and gratitude: 'This film was more or less like the trademark of the entry of us Bombay stars into Madras.'

With regard to the working conditions in Madras and elsewhere down South, Pran noted: 'Everybody was totally work-oriented. Much more work was accomplished day-to-day in Madras than was ever being done back here in Bombay. They were serious about film making; the South Indians used to work more and gossip less. We learnt discipline from them and learnt to be punctual also.'

3

In early 1950s Pran career was on the upswing. More and more offers were coming his way which would help him provide not just the necessities for his growing family, but also some of the luxuries that the young couple could afford before the madness of Partition had swept everything away.

Other than moving to the more quiet and up-market area of Pali Hill in Bandra, Pran and Shukla also bought a car, a Hillman from Shukla's cousin, General Daulat Singh. This car was used not just by Pran but also by the family, especially when Pran had to go to the South for shooting or had a free day at home.

Referring to the adventure that involved their car during this period, Pran recounted: 'I must tell you a very interesting incident which occurred when *Bahar* was near completion and the time to organize its Bombay premiere was almost at hand. This was in 1951...

'Since we had just shifted to No. 2, Pali Hill, we did not yet have a telephone. I knew that Shantilal Bajaj's family, staying on the second floor, had a phone. So I had requested them to allow me to give their number to a few people.

'One day, while I was home alone, a man suddenly came saying, "there's a call for you, please come upstairs". After climbing the stairs I found that it was a phone call from my wife. They had had an accident and the children, *Bubboo* (Arvind) and *Tunni* (Sunil) were with her.

'"Are you all alright?" I asked, thinking that they may have got injured or something.

'"Yes. We are all safe but the car is badly damaged," she said.

'Hearing this, I felt relieved. But at the same time annoyance got the better of me, and I just blurted out: "Why did you make me climb all the way to the second floor? You could just have rung up the police, reported the matter and then come home!"

'When she returned, she was very angry. She scolded me saying: "We had an accident and you were not even concerned! And to make matters worse, you're asking – 'why did you call me up to the second floor?'"

'I placated her as much as was possible and then quietly turned the topic to the smashed-up Hillman. I said: "Maybe *Murliwalé* who gave us our first car did not want us to have it any more. Maybe He means that our second car should be a bigger and better one."

'The premiere of *Bahar* was not far off. I had already made up my mind that we would go in for a bigger car. I had never taken Shukla for any film premiere until then and when I told her that I would take her for this premiere, she too said: "In that case, we should go in a bigger car."

'What she didn't know was that I was already bargaining with a man for a bigger car! Perhaps if I had bargained more strongly, the man may have reduced the price. But I needed that car badly – *before* the premiere of *Bahar*. And thanks to *Murliwalé*, I got it, even though I paid some five thousand rupees more for that car – which was a Chrysler!

'It was a fashion in those days to hold premieres for new films, especially for big films. It was one of film land's most important social events and everybody looked forward to attending premieres and to the lavish dinner parties that invariably followed. So I was glad that we had bought this new car, a purchase made necessary by my wife's smashing up the Hillman!'

Attending the premiere of *Bahar* was important because, firstly, it was Pran's first South film and, secondly, being seen in a car with attitude, a car that nobody else had, was in keeping with the suave villain image he had at the time.

Bahar went on to become a superhit all over India and Pran signed a whole bunch of big new films, which turned out to be big hits too.

With *Bahar* turning out to be such a grosser at the turnstiles, Pran was signed up to play villain in a number of films. Between 1950 and 1955, he signed, on an average, six films per year – South films, that is. The number of his assignments in Bombay was correspondingly on the rise.

Thus, Pran spent a great part of his time commuting between Bombay and Madras. Although he was given five-star treatment in five-star hotels in Madras, it was but natural that he would crave home-made Punjabi food during his long sojourns in South India.

One very providential happening was when his younger brother Kirpal's employers transferred him to Madras.[3] Kirpal recalled those days with warmth and pride: 'He used to come home very often. He loved home-made food and used to bring big stars like Dilip [Kumar] *Saab*, Manoj [Kumar] *Saab*, who liked *mah makhni*, *keema kabab* and *parathas*.[4]

4

In the period between 1951 (when *Bahar* was released) and 1955 (when the song-studded *Azaad* would be released) Pran signed over two dozen films. Some of the major assignments among these were *Sabz Baagh*, which co-starred Nimmi, Suraiya and Shekhar, P.L. Santoshi's *Chham Chhama Chham*, which co-starred Rehana and Kishore Kumar, V. M. Vyas's *Sanskar*, Wali Mohammed Wali's *Zamane Ki Hawa* and K. Amarnath's *Aleef Laila*.

---

[3] Kirpal Sikand used to work as a sales manager for Ramesh Khosla's Khosla Fans in Madras.

[4] *Mah makhni* is black-skinned lentils well cooked in butter, *keema kababs* are kebabs made of minced meat and *parathas* are layered Indian flat bread, with or without stuffing.

One very significant film that Pran signed during this period was Raj Kapoor's *Aah*, with Nargis and Raj Kapoor in lead roles. In this movie Raj Kapoor did something out of the ordinary in that he gave Pran a good man's role. Wearing glasses for the character, that of a doctor, Pran projected a subdued personality in this movie.

When asked why Raj Kapoor had chosen to give him a good man's role at a time Pran was strengthening his position as a villain, Pran answered: 'My role in *Aah* was to be done by the late Motilal. But there was some problem of dates, so Raj *Saab* selected me. He had faith in my talent, so he did not care about my strong image as a villain.'

Going on to talk about his role as the good doctor in *Aah*, Pran pointed out: 'During the shots, he [Raj Kapoor] would observe me very closely and say: "Cut! Cut!" I would ask what happened. He would say: "One of your eyes was smaller than the other!" He would cut out that scene if any of my villainous expressions crept in – which would happen quite unconsciously! He would not let me react like a villain!'

His other big films, however, strengthened his negative screen persona. These included Hiten Chaudhary's *Biraj Bahu*, directed by Bimal Roy and based on a novel by the eminent Bengali writer Sarat Chandra Chatterjee.

Another significant film in which Pran starred as a 'bad man' during this decade was Pakshiraja Studios' *Azaad*. The Coimbatore-based S. M. Sriramulu Naidu had signed up very big names for both on-screen and behind-the-screen work for his film. On-screen were Dilip Kumar, Meena Kumari, Om Prakash, Achala Sachdev, Subbulaxmi and Pran. And for the songs, which also became very popular, he had signed up Rajinder Krishen to write the lyrics and C. Ramchandra to compose the music.

Azaad was a start-to-finish project to be completed within a period of three months. This was apparently one of the conditions to which all those who had signed up for the film had agreed. Some perceptively observed that in an all-out effort to ensure that the Bombay stars stayed put for the entire three months of the proposed shooting schedule, the moment the Bombay*wallahs* arrived in Coimbatore, their return tickets were put away for safe-keeping until stipulated three months were over. Instructions were apparently given that if anyone turned up at the airport to buy another ticket for a short hop to Bombay and back, they should not be issued one!

It appears that due to the undivided attention that was given to it, *Azaad* went on to become a superhit all over India. *Filmfare*, in its review headlined 'PAKSHIRAJA STUDIOS' *AZAAD* IS DELIGHTFUL ADVENTURE ROMANCE', commented about the 'bad man': 'Pran as a villain is suave.'

5

As Pran began to sign an increasing number of films in Bombay and later also in Madras, he knew that he would have to do things differently if he was to, not just earn a living, but also hold his own against the formidable array of villains then competing for work.

Pran was also cynically aware that the gamut of villainy then portrayed in Hindi cinema was pretty unidimensional – the villain was always completely 'black', with little or no shades of grey. A look at his films of the late 1940s and early 1950s will illustrate this point.

Although initially, and wisely at that, Pran contented himself with doing what everybody else was doing – playing the overpronounced, obvious villain – it was to his credit that even while so doing, he used his brains rather than only his striking looks and personality. He decided to consciously infuse into his roles that certain something, which would ensure that each character he played would turn out to be different.

However, Pran realized that achieving this objective would require that he give the matter due forethought and preparation, so that the kind of negative roles he had been doing in almost all of his films since *Badi Bahen*, could be made more interesting and credible. Perhaps, without treading on anybody's toes, he could inject into his character some defining shades of grey! This factor, more than anything else, he was convinced, would determine how much staying power he would have in the days to come.

To achieve this objective, Pran decided to add subtle nuances to his character, and to do so without antagonizing anybody – within the framework of the unwritten rules present in the film industry. 'So,' disclosed Pran, 'in collaboration with the director and the writer, I tried to add something new to the role. All that I was concerned about was: what is the scope of my character in the script, how much can I help the script, and how much will the script help me?'

This approach ensured him a place in the ranks of sought-after villains.

Therefore, in spite of many instances where Pran acted in more than one film directed by the same director, each performance was significantly different from the other. He had subtly inserted a variety of nuances and shades to the hitherto standardized interpretation of villainy.

The outcome of this strategy was plain enough for all – the audiences, the reviewers and, thankfully, the film makers themselves – to see.

Which is why the noted film historian, Raju Bharatan, in his article for the *Patrika Sunday Magazine*, dated 25 February 1990, could justifiably remark: 'Thus, both in *Biraj Bahu* and *Madhumati*, though the director (Bimal Roy) was the same, the villain was "different" even though it was the same personality: Pran!'

Reviewing *Biraj Bahu, Filmfare* (15 October 1954) commented: 'Pran's suave villain is a histrionic gem, smooth, easy, slick, utterly hateful in a degree which is a measure of his art.'

However, even as Pran was working to add dimensions to his characterizations of the 'bad men' he had to portray in film after film, he decided it was time to explore the possibility of extending his repertoire. He was convinced that he had the ability to perform in a variety of roles and genres.

Speaking for *Filmfare* way back in 1952, Pran had stated: '*Although I enjoy doing villainous roles like the ones I did in Afsana, Sheesh Mahal, Biwi and Bahar, because they offer a great deal of scope to show one's acting ability, I would like to do comedies and sympathetic roles also.* I would especially like to act a character like Stephen Fox in *The Foxes of Harrow*.'

Pran's next comment revealed how much, deep inside, he would have liked a change of image, to be appreciated in a 'good man's' role: 'Of course, whether I get to do "good men's" roles or character roles depends on how my fans and moviegoers accept my "goodness" in *Aah*. If they do, then perhaps women will accept me with less fright in their eyes, and the shouts of the crowds whether at premieres, cinemas, football grounds or outside studios will include a few compliments also, instead of the usual *Chaar Sau Bees Pran* and *Cheediemaar*.'[5] Then Pran added wistfully: 'And who knows, like my two sons, there might even be other

---

[5] Both these are derogatory and abusive terms.

little boys who will feel quite sad when a dagger or bullet goes through my back.'

Coming back to reality, he declared: 'I am an actor. When the lights are on, the camera starts running and the director shouts, "Action!" then all I know is that I am a character speaking and expressing what the film demands. I take equal pleasure in playing good or bad characters.'

Other than Kwatra Films' *Pilpili Saheb*, a romantic comedy, and *Sheeshe Ki Deewar* (both released in 1954), in both of which Pran played a hero, and Subhash Pictures' *Chhalia*, where he played an Afghan bandit with a heart of gold, and Raj Kapoor's *Aah*, Pran would have to wait till 1965 before he would bag a full-fledged sympathetic role in Manoj Kumar's *Shaheed*.

That was because, according to Pran: 'The roles for villains kept pouring in and I kept on doing them. It is strange, but right in the middle of all these villain's roles, in 1953, Raj Kapoor had given me a good man's role in *Aah*. But unfortunately, that film didn't do well. After that no other producer dared to give me a good man's role. Although *Filmfare* in its review of *Aah* made a positive comment about me, saying "Pran as Raj's friend, is good in the supporting role," I did not get any more good men's roles for quite a while more.'

In spite of being typecast as villain, the 'invasion' from the South had brought good fortune to Pran professionally – both in the South as well as in Bombay. Yes, the 1950s had indeed been fabulous. But the coming decades would be even more exciting.

But before taking a leap into the 1960s, let us take a close look at what was happening with Pran's career planning and growth...

TEN

Pran and 'The Big Three'

1

Pran Krishen Sikand had begun his career in 1939 in Lahore long before the names of Dev Anand, Raj Kapoor or Dilip Kumar hit the marquee.[1]

Having established himself in villainous roles early on in his career and having developed a good professional rapport with his co-actors, Pran was often the preferred choice to fill many of the 'bad men's' roles from the 1950s onwards. Some of his most successful films were with the original 'evergreen actor', Ashok Kumar,[2] and with 'The Big Three'.[3]

---

[1] Dilip Kumar started out in 1944, a couple of years before Dev Anand, with Bombay Talkies' *Jwar Bhata*. Dev Anand 's first picture as a hero was Prabhat's *Hum Ek Hain* in 1946 and although Raj Kapoor worked as a child artiste way back in 1936, his first adult role was in Bhalji Pendharkar's *Valmiki* in 1946 and as hero in Kidar Sharma's *Neel Kamal* in 1947.

[2] More information on Pran's professional association and friendship with Ashok Kumar is dealt with in Chapter 21.

[3] During the 1940s and 1950s, generally regarded as the golden era of Indian cinema, the three romantic heroes, Dev Anand, Dilip Kumar and Raj Kapoor came to be known as 'The Big Three'. Interestingly, the trio never worked together in any film.

A warm handshake – Pran and Dev Anand.

Therefore, it was not long before Pran developed a rapport with all three of them. However, his equation with each of them was different.

Pran apparently shared a special rapport with Dev Anand, who was born in 1923. This special bond developed when Dev Anand and Pran worked together for the first time in Bombay Talkies' *Ziddi*.[4] This was the film which finally overturned the lean period that had somehow got prolonged after Pran's arrival in Bombay in 1947.

Pran's excellent command over Urdu is relevant here. He has learnt not only how to read and write the language, but was (and is) also a great lover of *sher-o-shairee*.[5] This ability enabled him to use that language to his advantage in his Lahore films. But as far as Hindi was concerned, he was still not quite comfortable with the language and found it difficult to cope with lengthy dialogues.

Ziddi was one of Dev Anand's earlier pictures (his sixth) and since he had more skill with the language, Pran took his help with certain Hindi

---

[4] Ziddi starred Dev Anand, Kamini Kaushal, Veera, Nawab, Kuldip Kaur, Pran, Pratima Devi, Indu, Mohsin, Chandabai, Amir Banu and Shivraj.
[5] Couplets and poetic verse.

words in the dialogue, getting Dev to pronounce the words, while he would transliterate them into Urdu.

Pran never forgot that early kindness and, consequently, during their equally long careers, co-starred with Dev Anand in nine films, sometimes as villain, sometimes character actor and once even as his father – in *Warrant* (1975)!

After *Ziddi*, Pran and Dev Anand acted together in Filmistan's *Munimji* in which Nalini Jaywant was the heroine. This film was a hit. Then came Shivaji Productions' *Amardeep*, directed by T. Prakash Rao in 1958 in which there were three heroines Padmini, Vyjayanthimala and Ragini. This film also did well.

This film was followed by Nasir Hussain's *Jab Pyar Kisise Hota Hai*, which also starred Asha Parekh and once again was a hit! It is no wonder that in many quarters, Pran and Dev Anand were considered a lucky combination.

The 1970s saw Pran and Dev Anand doing *Johny Mera Naam*, *Yeh Gulistan Hamara*, *Joshila*, *Warrant*, and *Des Pardes*. Most of these films did good business at the box office.

At one point in this 'hit' relationship, Pran even suggested to Prakash Mehra that he make *Zanjeer* with his friend Dev Anand as hero. However, it appears that Dev was not ready to experiment with his established image and lost out on the role that ultimately sent Amitabh Bachchan's till then struggling career zooming to incredible heights.[6]

However, their friendship extended beyond the studios. Having worked in so many films together, Pran was in a good position to observe firsthand whether stardom had changed his friend Dev Anand or not. In this context, Pran affirmed: 'Even after working in so many films, Dev is just the same as he was in the beginning. His behaviour hasn't changed at all. He never talks against anybody.'

Pran is lavish in his praise of Dev Anand and his attitude to life, work and friends. 'Hats off to that man!' exclaims Pran. 'Dev came to me one day to offer me a villain's role in one of his films. I said that I wouldn't refuse him anything, but that if I did the role the audience would not accept me in it, since I had just switched over to doing character roles. It didn't

---

6 For further details, see Chapter 23.

take him even a minute to make up his mind and say: "All right. I understand." The whole meeting was over in two minutes.'

What particularly struck Pran was how Dev did not let the former's refusal come in the way of a future project. In this project, he was able to offer Pran a role more in keeping with the kind he was then accepting. That film was *Des Pardes* in which Pran played the role of Dev Anand's elder brother. So it is not without reason that Pran warmly says about Dev: 'That man is genuinely wonderful!'

Commenting on Dev Anand, on another occasion Pran remarked: 'He is one person who has never entered into any film politics. Although I must say that all of us, Dev, Goldie,[7] myself, Danny[8] and Shatrughan Sinha[9] among others, did participate in a rally on 13 March 1977, during which we spoke up against the repressive policies of the then minister for information and broadcasting, Mr Vidya Charan Shukla, who had clamped down on the industry during the Emergency.'

Marvelling at Dev's energy, Pran says: 'All his life he has been "fast" in everything he does. He works fast, walks fast, talks fast. He is always on the go.' Even though Dev Anand is as busy as ever and may not get the time to keep up with 'old' friends, Pran understands his friend's need to immerse himself in work.

2

Pran's association with Dilip Kumar[10] has stood the test of time. He and Dilip, the second actor of the triumvirate, have come a long way together.

Firstly, both of them shared a common bond: both came from the northwestern area of the Indian subcontinent, Dilip being born and raised in Peshawar and Pran living in Lahore.

---

7 'Goldie' was Vijay Anand's nickname. Goldie was Dev Anand's younger brother. He passed away in February 2004.
8 Danny Denzongpa started off in minor roles in the early 1970s and later established himself as a villain.
9 Shatrughan Sinha has played villain and hero. He later became a Union minister in Prime Minister Atal Bihari Vajpayee's cabinet.
10 Dilip Kumar was born on 11 December 1922.

There were other commonalities too: both of them love the Urdu language and its beautiful poetry, both enjoy music and both of them relish the good things of life. Added to that, both of them love cinema.

However, it was quite a few years after Pran established himself in Bombay that Dilip Kumar and he got a chance to act together. Undoubtedly, this opportunity allowed them to get to know each other better and their friendship flourished.

The first film that Pran did with Dilip Kumar was *Azaad*.[11] Intending to make the film in three months at a stretch, in Coimbatore, Tamil Nadu, S.M. Sriramulu Naidu did not allow the actors to leave the city even for a short while. So the actors found themselves spending most of their free time in each other's company because of the linguistic and cultural differences between the North and the South.

Many such film land friendships started and grew on the sets of films made in the South or on outdoor location shooting schedules.

Next came the classic *Devdas*, produced and directed by Bimal Roy, starring Dilip Kumar, Vyjayanthimala, Suchitra Sen, Motilal and Pran. Pran only had a small guest role in this film.

Bimal Roy's *Madhumati* was released next, with haunting music by Salil Chaudhary. It starred Dilip Kumar, Vyjayanthimala, Pran and Johnny Walker. The interaction between the characters played by Dilip Kumar and Pran was somewhat limited, but in the few scenes together, the latent rivalry they had to convey came through.

In Dilip Kumar and Pran's next film together, *Dil Diya Dard Liya*,[12] they had to interact much more. This was one of the strongest 'bad man's' roles Pran played throughout his career. The story and screenplay of this film were by Dilip Kumar and although the film's producer, A. R. Kardar, was supposed to have directed it, it is a fairly well-known fact that Dilip's creative inputs often exceeded those of the credited director. Speaking of his role in the film, Pran went on to say: 'Even though the film didn't do very well, I had an outstanding negative role in it; it remains one of my best performances and one of my favourite films to date.'

---

[11] For more details, see Chapter 9.
[12] Producer-director A. R. Kardar's *Dil Diya Dard Liya* (1966) co-starred Dilip Kumar, Waheeda Rehman, Rehman and Pran.

Pran makes it a point to emphasize the fact that 'in *Dil Diya Dard Liya*, my performance was very good only because of Dilip *Saab*.' Elaborating on how the good quality of his performance could be attributed to Dilip, Pran said: 'In most films, I never laugh loudly. But in *Dil Diya Dard Liya* the role demanded it. This was the only film in which I used malicious laughter to heighten the villainy and Dilip Kumar helped me a lot with my performance. Dilip *Saab* was always of the opinion that "the scene should stand in its entirety, only then will it come off good. Until *all* the artistes in the scene have not given their best, the scene cannot come off well." Because of this, he never used to overwhelm a scene or the other actors working with him in a scene. He never used to object to retakes, even if the other artiste was calling for it to improve his or her own work. Dilip *Saab* has always been a real master of his profession.'

Speaking about Pran, Manoj Kumar recently said: 'After he did the shooting of *Dil Diya Dard Liya*, Pran *Saab* told me, "Dilip *Saab* did the make-up with his own hands – and what a performance he gave! What beautiful dialogue he wrote for me!" Pran never said, "*I* delivered the dialogue so beautifully!" Instead, being modest, what Pran would say was: "How nicely Dilip extracted the work from me!" '

But any creative process is one of give and take. When Pran used to get into the flow of work, he was impressive. And just as Pran said he had benefited from Dilip's help, Dilip too benefited from Pran's mastery of the medium. So complete was Pran's grasp over the medium that during the shooting of *Dil Diya Dard Liya*, after giving a particular shot, Dilip Kumar would look at Pran to ascertain whether he [Dilip] had done the scene perfectly!

3

There are several interesting incidents that took place during the shooting of *Dil Diya Dard Liya* in western Madhya Pradesh.

An inaccessible palace in Mandu, the capital of the erstwhile principality of Malwa, was chosen to provide an excellent backdrop for *Dil Diya Dard Liya*. The building, converted by the early 1960s into a modern guesthouse, was part of the Jahaz Mahal, where the local king,

Baaz Bahadur, lived many centuries ago. And not far away from this spot, so the legend goes, one may still see Baaz Bahadur's beloved Rani Roopmati dancing. [13]

Producer-director A. R. Kardar spent about a month in Mandu with an eighty-member strong unit to film *Dil Diya Dard Liya*. Pran was also there and as usual, when the cameras were not running, he was very witty, keeping everybody in splits of laughter.

Pran remembers telling a group of journalists that when A. R. Kardar (he was referred to as *Mianjee*) arrived on location, strange things happened! During his first night in Mandu, *Mianjee* saw Roopmati dance in his dreams. So the next morning he was all poetry – and sang like a nightingale. But he was suddenly silent the day after. The very witty reason Pran gave for this was that the previous night *Mianjee* had seen Baaz Bahadur stride into his dreams!

With such witticisms, Pran made the long and weary days of shooting on location more cheerful for the unit members.

Speaking about another memorable role, this one in B. Nagi Reddy's *Ram Aur Shyam*, Pran recalled: 'Dilip *Saab* used to do the actual work even though the name as director was somebody else's. And he used to help all co-artistes with their work. As a man, I've had a deep and affectionate friendship with him.'

In *Ram Aur Shyam*, Dilip Kumar (in a double role) plays the twins Ram and Shyam, who try to withstand the machinations of their brother-in-law, Gajendra, a role very ably played by Pran.[14] The story was such that Pran and Dilip had many scenes together.

The fights between Dilip and Pran were brilliantly conceived and the scenes where Gajendra whips Ram were so well done that audiences everywhere would wince at every whiplash. Years later (in February 2000), Shenaz Walji (a fan), in an email to Pran, would confess: 'I loved all your movies, but the one I remember the most is *Ram Aur Shyam*. That

---

[13] In early times, Madhya Pradesh was known as Malwa. Its history can be traced right back to Emperor Ashok [third century B.C.E]. Between the twelfth and sixteenth centuries C.E, the fortified city of Mandu was often the scene of battle. In 1561, the last ruler, Baaz Bahadur fled Mandu rather than face Akbar the Great's advancing armies, leaving the beautiful Roopmati to choose *jauhar*, death over dishonour.

[14] The twins' sister's role was played by Nirupa Roy.

is the movie in which you really scared me. I can still remember the fear I felt for Dilip Kumar when you brought your whip to beat him.'

Pran succeeded in striking terror and evoking hatred in the hearts of viewers to such an extent that when Dilip Kumar (as Shyam) retaliates and whips the daylights out of Gajendra, the audience would applaud.

Their next film together was S. V. Films' *Aadmi*, directed by A. Bhim Singh. This film co-starred Manoj Kumar and had Waheeda Rehman and Simi as the leading ladies.

Aadmi dealt with a grim theme – the extent to which a young man, who has been the recipient of a millionaire's largesse, goes to repay that generosity and kindness, even at the cost of his own happiness. The role that was eventually played by Manoj Kumar was to have been played by Dharmendra. But he had backed out at the last minute.

Manoj Kumar acknowledges even today that he is an unabashed fan of Dilip Kumar's, and that Dilip Kumar *himself* had urged him to do that role in *Aadmi*. Although acting with The Thespian would be a privilege beyond compare, Manoj Kumar knew fully well that he could easily be overshadowed by his idol, who was the very reason why he had joined films in the first place. However, Dilip Kumar's urgings were not the stimulus for doing that parallel role.

No, the real reason Manoj Kumar acted in *Aadmi* is that Pran asked him to do so!

What had happened was that Pran had helped out the film's producer, Veerappa, to get together the original cast of the film, which had Dharmendra playing the parallel lead. But suddenly, without giving any reason, Dharmendra withdrew from the cast. Pran felt embarrassed since he was the one who had recommended Dharam's name. To solve the producer's problem, Pran told Manoj: 'I want you to do this picture.'

Thus, Manoj came to join the cast of *Aadmi*.

4

Pran's association with Dilip Kumar had always been an intimate one. Living as they did, just about half a kilometre away from each other, Dilip Kumar, also known as Yusuf Khan, and three of his sisters, Akhtar, Sayeeda and Farida, used to go over to Pran's place fairly regularly. Being single then, Yusuf used to find more time to spend with friends and family.

Sunil Sikand recalled that the atmosphere at those impromptu parties used to be so informal that in between all the chatting and laughing, they would also play 'dumb charade', the entire family getting into the spirit of the game. Two teams would be formed and all of them – Dilip Kumar, Pran and Shukla included – used to participate! He remembers how Dilip Kumar would give them some really difficult names of films to mime! Like once he gave the opposing team the title *Pffft*, which he probably made up. But Dilip Kumar insisted that there was a film by that name; it was the sound made by a silencer-fitted gun going off!

And of course, Pran's large-heartedness would ensure that there would be alcohol and good food as a fitting end to a pleasure-filled family evening!

Dilip Kumar's wedding was a really big occasion for all his friends, because he had been avoiding matrimony for quite a long time and had become almost adept at side-stepping the overtures of any determined girl or her parents!

But then he said 'yes' to Naseem Banu's proposal for him to marry her daughter Saira Banu, and the two got engaged on 2 October 1966, at Saira's home on Pali Hill. Pran too was among the close friends who were there on that occasion.

The wedding was fixed in a hurry – for 11 October 1966!

That close friends made every effort to attend the wedding is evidenced by what happened to Pran that day: 'I remember the day when Dilip was to get married,' he reminisced. 'I was in Kashmir and it was pouring, but this was one wedding which I had to attend. Flights were being cancelled and suddenly I got a call from him saying, "I am getting married and you have to come!" '

Coming to Bombay from Kashmir to attend Dilip's marriage was a great adventure. This, in Pran's own words, is what happened...

'Miraculously, the rain stopped and I was able to get to Delhi. But at Delhi airport I couldn't get tickets for the connecting flight to Bombay – and his wedding was to take place that very night!

'Just then two Sardarjis came into the airport. Swaraj Suri, my friend who had come to see me off at the airport, happened to know them.

He found out that one of them was to fly to Bombay on the very flight that I was hoping to board. Suri told them about my plight, saying: "Pran *Saab* is very upset. He simply *has* to reach Bombay for Dilip *Saab's* marriage, but he doesn't have a seat on this flight."

'They immediately said: "We'll get the seat for you." They went to Indian Airlines and asked for a seat on the morning flight, and gave away their seat to me.'

As their luggage was already checked in, so they had to exchange luggage tags too. 'They gave me their boarding card and their luggage tags also. They said that they would bring my luggage. I finally reached Bombay but since I was getting late, I forgot to pick up their luggage from the conveyor belt. I came home, had a shower and hurried to the wedding, having completely forgotten about their luggage!'

Weddings are times when pranks are played on the newly weds, and Dilip's friends were all in the mood to play one on him that night. Pran recalls: 'All of us, Raj Kapoor and the gang, got totally drunk and went boisterously to bang on Dilip Kumar's bedroom door, forcing him to open up and to say "hello" to all of us on his wedding night!' Perhaps that was the last prank they played on their friend, who had graduated from being 'just one of the boys' to being the husband of a young and beautiful wife.

'After the whirlwind courtship and wedding, Dilip and Saira went on their honeymoon to Madras, where Dilip had to shoot for *Ram Aur Shyam*. I too had to report for work. So I was with them on their engagement day, their wedding day and even on their honeymoon!' chuckles Pran.

And what about that poor Sardarji's luggage? The morning after Dilip and Saira's wedding, when Pran finally woke up, his wife told him that she had got a call from some Sardarjis, who were asking for their luggage! 'I suddenly realized that I had forgotten it at the airport! So we called the airport and, to our relief, found that the luggage was still there!' said Pran.

Pran's other films with Dilip Kumar are *Sadhu Aur Shaitan* (1968), in which Dilip made a guest appearance, *Gopi* (1970), directed by A. Bhim Singh, with both Dilip Kumar and Saira Banu in the lead. Then after a long gap, Pran worked with Dilip in Yash Johar's *Duniya* (1984). Saira Banu too was in that film.

Pran, Shukla and Dilip Kumar (2000) – cementing old relationships.

Dilip Kumar's last film with Pran was *Dharam Adhikari* in 1986.

Says Pran about his friend: 'I have done many films with Dilip *Saab* and I have a good friendship with him till today, for more than half a century now. Earlier I used to meet Dilip *Saab* more often, perhaps twice or thrice a week. But even now our friendship is as it was in the beginning. He is an interesting man and has been a good friend.'

5

'Throughout my life, I have had a very close association with Dilip Kumar as well as Raj Kapoor,'[15] says Pran. But, with the third part of The Big Three, Raj Kapoor, Pran's equation was slightly different.

Raj Kapoor was one of the earliest producer-directors to look beyond the obvious. Pran had been struggling to establish himself in films in Bombay during the late 1940s, so if a villain's part was all that was offered, he went ahead and accepted it. Hence, Pran's villain image, which had become established due to the sheer number of 'bad man' roles he did, got even more deeply etched into the public mind. His earlier hero roles were all but forgotten.

---

[15] Raj was the youngest of 'The Big Three', born in 1924.

It is a sign of the times that every era throws up its own genius. It happened over a half century ago (in 1947) when Raj Kapoor, a fledgling actor whom none except himself took very seriously, turned to direction, and made *Aag*. A couple of films later[16] he decided to make *Aah*.

Raj Kapoor now approached Pran with the offer of a 'good man's' role in *Aah* (1953), the fourth film to come out of the newly formed R.K. Films and Studios. In this film, Pran was to play a noble doctor who very nearly ends up marrying the heroine.

However, Pran is very candid about what happened to the film and his brief venture into the realm of playing 'good man'. He said: 'I tried to play a good man way back in Raj Kapoor's *Aah*. But the movie flopped and with it, I also flopped!'

Soon after the debacle of his film *Aah*, I remember the Fabulous Showman (as Raj Kapoor was popularly known) discussing Pran with me (Bunny Reuben): 'There has always been the yen for "good man's" roles lurking in the heart of this wonderful human being who has always excelled in playing "bad man's" roles.' Apparently, the audiences were not ready for a change, for when he saw the film in the theatre along with the first-day-first-show crowd, he quickly realized where he had gone wrong.'

'I had given Pran the role of a doctor, spectacles and all. We had worked out the depiction of his role in our pre-production discussions,' Raj *Saab* continued, 'and we both agreed that, since he was playing a doctor, he should be restrained and dignified.

'But when the film went into release, and I...sat quietly in the darkened auditorium to gauge audience reaction, my heart sank.

'I had gone wrong elsewhere also – I mean, there were things in which I had gone wrong, things other than Pran's role. But in the theatre I could see that the audiences felt Pran's character was too passive. Perhaps if we had interpreted the character differently, made him something of a hearty, jocular extrovert, then that character would have come across with a greater impact.'

---

[16] After *Aag* (1948), Raj Kapoor made *Barsaat* (1949), *Awaara* (1951) and then *Aah* in 1953.

'I don't know, really. Perhaps this was also one of the reasons why my film *Aah* did not do well,' Raj Kapoor concluded.

One point, however, must be made: Even though *Aah* did not fare well at the box office in its initial release, what is commendable is the fact that Raj Kapoor had visualized Pran in a role that was tangential to what he had done until then.

Raj Kapoor, however, continued to work with Pran, not only because of his impeccable histrionic talent, but also because they were good friends. Raj knew that Pran was the kind of painstaking artiste who put a lot of thought and advance preparation into each of his roles, and Raj Kapoor always had a passion for dedicated artistes – there were so few of them around.

Pran also played a small role in Raj Kapoor's multistarrer *Jagte Raho* (1956). The film is a comment about the false values that people have, and the erroneous judgements they make based on the appearance of a person. It also exposed the so-called respectability of city dwellers and encouraged everyone to view things with eyes of innocence (role played by the child artiste Daisy Irani) or piety (the final song sequence featuring Nargis as the one who eventually quenches the villager's thirst). The story of the film was such that it was necessary for every character, other than Raj Kapoor, to make only a brief appearance in the film. In 1957, *Jagte Raho* won the Grand Prix at the International Film Festival at Karlovy Vary in Czechoslovakia.

'From *Aah* (1953) to *Bobby* (1973), I acted in many of Raj Kapoor's films,' declared Pran, 'but the most unforgettable role among them all was the one in *Jis Desh Mein Ganga Behti Hai*…'[17]

'When Raj Kapoor narrated the story of this film to me and asked me to play the role of the dacoit Raaka, I became extremely eager to do the role,' said Pran. 'I put in a lot of thought for the development of that character, his fiery personality, look and get-up.'[18]

Thus, *Jis Desh Mein Ganga Behti Hai* revealed a far more effectively projected dacoit (named Raaka) than the doctor whom Pran had played in *Aah*. And although Pran did not get the *Filmfare* Award for his

---

[17] Released in 1960.
[18] Details about the choice of his get-up are given in Chapter 11.

Pran and Raj Kapoor in a jolly mood (November 1961).

performance that year, Raj Kapoor himself presented him with a shield in appreciation of the brilliant job he had done in the film at a ceremony in Calcutta.

Raj Kapoor's labour of love, *Mera Naam Joker,* released in 1970, had almost wiped him out financially, taking away almost every penny that he had earned with his earlier film *Sangam* (1964).

So, he decided to make one more film – a film with a finger on the pulse of the cinema-going public. He decided to make a teenage love story with his second son *Chintu* (the family's nickname for Rishi Kapoor) and a young new girl, Dimple Kapadia.

The film *Bobby* was Raj *Saab's* attempt to 'show' everyone that he was not wiped out yet. Everything depended on *Bobby* doing well.

The late Satish Bhalla,[19] Pran's long-time friend and *samdhi,*[20] recalled during an interview for this biography that Raj Kapoor wanted Pran to be the hero's father. At that time Pran was on the top of his profession

---

[19] Satish Bhalla passed away in 2003.
[20] Daughter's father-in-law.

and he used to take about two and a half to three lakh rupees for each role. In those days, that was *big* money.

'Pran*jee* was too courteous to talk about money,' Satish Bhalla revealed, 'but it was Raj*jee* himself who said: "I'm afraid, I'll not be able to pay you anything right now."

'Keeping an expressionless face, Pran*jee* asked Raj*jee* in a serious tone: "Do you have a one rupee coin in your pocket?"

'Raj*jee* looked perplexed. But before he could say anything, Pran*jee* said: "Give me a one rupee coin and your deal is signed! That is my fee! I'll shoot the movie whenever you want!"'

Pran played the role of the strict and domineering father (of Rishi Kapoor) in *Bobby*.

Undoubtedly, this reaction from Pran left Raj Kapoor astounded. Pran had asked to neither listen to the story nor know details about his role, and yet he had agreed to sign the deal!

However, Pran was very sure that in a Raj Kapoor film none of the characters would be inconsequential. Each character and each artiste who would play that particular role would be selected with great forethought and insight.

Besides, Pran felt at that point of time that it would be graceless and in bad taste to talk either about money or about the nature of his role. 'So he completed that movie with that one rupee!' Bhalla disclosed with a smile.

Reminiscing about this same event, Ramesh Khosla, a very close friend of Raj Kapoor as well as Pran *Saab* threw some more light on the subject, which is of relevance in view of what happened later. Khosla said in an interview for this book: 'Regarding this noble act of Pran*jee*, Raj *Saab* mentioned to me that Pran*jee* had told him: "Okay, *if your picture is a hit, pay me my price.* If not, then I'll not charge you a single *naya paisa.*"'

Bobby was a superduper hit. It helped Raj Kapoor recoup all the losses he had incurred in *Mera Naam Joker*. It appears that Raj Kapoor had not forgotten Pran's magnanimous gesture and now asked Pran to quote his price, which he did! Taken aback, Raj sent Pran a cheque of one lakh rupees, which was just a fraction of what Pran had quoted.

Pran promptly returned it, saying that it would be an insult to accept a cheque worth three thousand rupees! Pran later explained to Raj*jee* that a cheque of one lakh rupees would ultimately be worth only three thousand because of the heavy taxes one had to pay at that time!

Undoubtedly, any misunderstanding about money must have eventually been cleared and any hurt feelings sorted out, because on the day of Raj Kapoor's funeral,[21] Pran was very much present at R. K. Studios.

Pran recalled an incident during the making of *Bobby*: 'I played Rishi Kapoor's father and Premnath played Dimple's father. In the climax of the film, Rishi and Dimple run away from home and jump into a river. When they begin to drown, Premnath and I jump into the river to save them. Raj Kapoor wanted to do this scene with doubles. But I insisted on doing it myself.

'When I jumped into the water, I found the current was so strong that I lost control and began to drown. I started to thrash about in the raging river. Raj Kapoor and the unit members were standing on the banks of the river and marvelling at my "acting". Eventually, my hand managed to find a rock which I gripped to save myself.

'Later, when I told Raj Kapoor exactly what had happened he said to me: "*Laale*, don't do this sort of thing. We still need you." '

'The day I heard of Raj Kapoor's death, I rushed to R. K. Studios. Seeing Raj Kapoor lying there dead, I suddenly remembered his words. I inwardly said to Raj: "*Laale*, what have *you* done? This is when *cinema* needs *you* the most."

'Raj Kapoor was a director who lived each moment for his film,' emphasized Pran. 'Whatever he did during the making of a film, it was done for his film, and went hand in hand with his creation of it. Film making was his passion and obsession.'

---

[21] Raj Kapoor died on 2 June 1989.

What did Raj Kapoor think of Pran as a person and as an actor? He once said: 'A bit shy in life, Pran on the screen is a beaming, dynamic character. He is all inspiration before the camera, and fully understands what he has to do and does it with a proper emphasis and in an individualistic style.

'He is not at all conventional, nor is he bound to any old traditions of acting. He is mercurial and subtle and, when need be, he is most powerful in his expression. A very fine actor indeed, and a great friend. We have acted in many movies together, and beyond doubt, he has risen to the greatest heights in his performances.'

6

Considering that Pran had watched each of 'The Big Three' enter and then grow in filmdom, what was Pran's personal view of their acting? When asked in the year 1989 by Delhi-based journalist (the late) Bachchan Srivastava as to who was the better actor – Raj Kapoor or Dilip Kumar, Pran, well-known for his plain-speak, replied: 'My vote goes to Dilip

Prem Chopra, Dilip Kumar, Pran and Raj Kapoor,
among others, at a function (late 1960s).

Kumar.' Elaborating further, Pran said: 'Dev Anand has developed a certain style for himself. Raj Kapoor did develop as an actor but once he reached a certain point, he stopped developing and growing as an actor. On the other hand, Dilip Kumar is still growing.'

By some strange coincidence, 'The Big Three' had really proven to be the triumvirate of Hindi cinema, doing an equal number of films with the 'Villain of the Millennium' – nine films each![22]

Although Raj Kapoor is no more and age has caught up with all of them, Pran's decades-long bonds with Dev, Dilip and Raj's family are still intact.

Till today, Raj Kapoor's sons, Randhir (*Dabboo*) and Rishi (*Chintu*) Kapoor have kept up relations with their father's dear friend and colleague. Both of them look up to Pran as a father figure, and make an effort to visit him now and then.

Recently, *Dabboo* mentioned that he and *Chintu* decided in early 2004 to visit Pran. With characteristic frankness, and in complete dissonance from filmdom's general mentality of *'raat gayee, baat gayee'*,[23] *Dabboo* declared: 'I don't believe in ignoring a person when he is alive and then mourn his death by giving some sound-bytes to television channels!'

So when they called him up, Pran told them: 'Don't come for lunch, come in the evening so that I can share a drink with you before dinner.'

'Although he told us he would have just the one drink,' Randhir said warmly, 'he so enjoyed talking about old times and the fun we had on the sets of the umpteen films we've done together, that not only did he have a second drink but he kept offering us some more too... "Have

---

[22] The nine films that Dev Anand and Pran acted in are: *Ziddi* (1948); *Munimji* (1955); *Amardeep* (1958); *Jab Pyar Kisise Hota Hai* (1961); *Johny Mera Naam* (1970); *Yeh Gulistan Hamara* (1972); *Joshila* (1973); *Warrant* (1975); and *Des Pardes* (1978).
Not counting *Sadhu Aur Shaitan* (Dilip Kumar only made a guest appearance in the film), the nine films Dilip Kumar and Pran did together are: *Azaad* (1955); *Devdas* (1956); *Madhumati* (1958); *Dil Diya Dard Liya* (1966); *Ram Aur Shyam* (1967); *Aadmi* (1968); *Gopi* (1970); *Duniya* (1984); and *Dharam Adhikari* (1986).
Raj Kapoor and Pran acted in the following films: *Aah* (1953); *Chori Chori* (1956); *Jagte Raho* (1956); *Chhalia* (1960); *Jis Desh Mein Ganga Behti Hai* (1960); *Dil Hi To Hai* (1963); *Around the World* (1967); *Bobby* (1973); and *Chandi Sona* (1977).

[23] Loosely translated as: 'The night is gone, the matter is forgotten' referring to short memories and shallow relationships.

one more! Have one more!" he urged us, in an attempt to keep us there longer.' *Dabboo's* eyes mist over with warmth and affection for Pran, with whom their father and they have created so much cinematic history.

Certainly, these villain-hero combinations, Pran with Dev Anand, Pran with Dilip Kumar and Pran with Raj Kapoor, have given Hindi cinema many memorable celluloid moments which are forever preserved in the hearts of cinemagoers everywhere.

ELEVEN

The Actor Prepares

1

By the end of the 1940s, when Pran's career had resumed, he had vowed never to let it get ruined again. He had known that he would have to prepare for each role. But it soon became increasingly obvious to him that if he wanted his name to have a long innings on the marquee, then he would have to do much more than just a perfunctory preparation for his roles. He would have to slog it out.

There was good reason for him to feel this way.

Consider the scene in Bombay into which he had stepped as villain. There was already quite a formidable line-up of competitors, in terms of actors who were already doing villainous roles.

The well-established villains of the day had already specialized in their own particular brand of villainy. So, while some 'baddies' such as Jeevan, Hiralal and Kanhaiyalal had mastered the typical *senapati*, *zamindar*, *munimji*, and *sethji*[1] type of roles, other 'baddies' such as Madan Puri and

---

[1] Meaning: chief of the army, landowner, accountant and businessman, respectively.

Anwar Hussain were mostly approached to do either their 'hoodlum', 'gangster' or 'lecher' act.

At the same time, Yakub had paved the way for a more understated brand of villainy, going easy on the patently obvious portrayal of badness and the accompanying hysterics. And ace-villain K.N. Singh had so perfected a highly stylized form of wickedness through facial contortions that for Pran to attempt to carve a niche for himself may have, to a casual observer, seemed to be an uphill task.

All these bad men of cinema were so strongly entrenched in their portrayal of moral turpitude that until *Badi Bahen* (in 1949) their names completely dominated the rollcalls when producers were casting for a negative role in their films. But after *Badi Bahen*, Pran's name too was in the reckoning.

Since Pran could not do anything by halves, his preparation for his roles too was not token – neither unthinking nor mechanical. And in a curious way, the kind of roles which had begun to come his way in the 1950s had ensured that.

From the first decade itself, Pran had been carefully observing whatever happened on the sets from moment to moment. And he had mastered the finer points of his profession with uncanny precision.

He had already observed that there were two broad distinctions in the kind of directors who made commercial Hindi films. The first category, in which there were unfortunately very few, consisted of individuals confident of their own mastery over the medium; they knew exactly what they wanted on screen and they knew how to put it there.

The second kind, of which there were unfortunately far too many, were the *kaam-chalaoo*[2] directors, those who were eager and willing to please their heroes, especially the very 'big' leading men, even at the film's expense. They would happily make script changes to suit these heroes and to arrange to take shots as these heroes dictated.

Of course, the more intelligent of the leading men did not dictate – they suggested. But the *kaam-chalaoo* directors were under no illusions – they knew that their heroes' 'suggestions' were actually laid-down laws. Pran had observed all the goings-on.

---

2   The mediocre 'let's-get-on-with-it' type.

Pran knew that this latter lot of directors would be more than happy to let their actors do all the work in terms of deciding how the character should be interpreted, or how he should look, walk, talk and behave, in addition to actually enacting the scenes.

By the second decade of his career, with the exception of a few roles as parallel hero, Pran was almost exclusively being offered only villain's roles. In a 1952 interview to *Screen,* he declared with conviction: 'I know producers have typed me as a villain. . .but honestly, I do not mind. I very much like to do comedy roles but I certainly do not want to be a goody-goody hero. I love acting very much and I would like to play different types of roles but I fear I will never get them. *I can only aspire to be the greatest villain of the screen.'*

Indeed, Pran was well aware that to aspire to such greatness, he would have to hold his own against the hero, whose character was always given greater weight by the script writer and, of course, by the demands of commerce, whereas his, the villain's character, predictably got his come-uppance at the end of the film.

In the same interview, Pran went on to say: 'To show yourself as a villain you must work very hard. A villain gets only five to ten scenes in a story and within these he must portray his characteristics convincingly.'

Another good reason for him to inject newness into each role was the unfortunate typecasting to which he was subjected and the same sort of dialogue he was made to deliver. To do this, most of his colleagues were getting their 'inspiration' from heroes from the West. Pran, however, was looking at real-life people around him – at ordinary people and their peculiarities.

Pran was firmly of the opinion that there was no point looking to the West and its movies for ideas. As he put it: 'Some film people say that if they see more English movies, they get new ideas. My opinion is totally different. I believe that when you copy somebody else, you learn less. All you become is a copycat. We must remember that after all, those actors also gave it much thought and then acted in a particular way. *So why can't we too think?'*

To *avoid* getting 'inspired' by any film or a character in it, Pran, as far as was possible, eschewed watching films, especially the Hollywood variety: 'I have seen very few English films, and I go to see my films only when I have no other choice.'

2

So, how did Pran learn to prepare the actor within him for each role he was to play? His first and most cardinal principal was *never* to duplicate the 'look' of a character or the accents of that character from one film to another.

Regarding this aspect, Pran's younger son Sunil said: 'Dad always worked hard on his get-ups and his costumes. He says: "If you look the role, most of your battle is won already. You find youngsters with long hair, in a police uniform – no matter what acting you put in, you aren't convincing because you don't look like a policeman. The film is a visual medium – if the look is not there, then you are lost." '

As the varied film assignments came, and with them the preparation, Pran learnt and learnt fast. It was not often that one gets to view the inner secrets of how a good actor prepares, hence listening to Pran speak on this subject is important to any narration of the story of his life and work.

Pran reflected: 'I started concentrating on the *look* of the role and the vocal accents of the role early on in my career. By the time I'd had my first half a dozen films in release, I knew what was important, what was essential, if one had to go to the top of the class.'

'Initially,' Pran went on, 'I didn't have any interest in this business of the "look" of the role. But then gradually, *shauk chad gaya*.[3] It started running in my blood. *I constantly thought of, and incorporated, new mannerisms into every character I was to depict in each of the films I had signed.'*

'I also had to have a new voice, new make-up, new gait. I did not want to repeat my actions. Unlike most other artistes, I always carefully avoided the repetition of a mannerism. If you have observed my work from film to film, you'll find that each character has a unusual way of talking, gesticulating, eating *paan*, smoking a cigarette, or even drinking

---

[3] 'I developed a liking for it.'

tea! My make-up, my wigs, my beard, my overall "look", all have without fail been distinctly dissimilar from film to film,' Pran elaborated with justifiable pride.

There were several styles of cigarette and *bidi* (rolled tobacco leaf) smoking that Pran used in his films. One of them became extremely popular; Pran developed and used this for a film called *Maryada*,[4] where he perfected flipping a lit cigarette with his tongue and placing it back between his lips, without missing a beat or burning his lips. Years later, in 1999, Aamir Khan, no doubt inspired by this 'cool' trick, did a similar routine in *Ghulam* — flipping a lit cigarette in his mouth and extinguishing it with his tongue.

In another film, *Dil Tera Diwana*,[5] Pran used a *bidi* hanging out of his mouth all through the film, and when he was speaking, he would slide the *bidi*, which sat precariously on his lower lip, from one side of his mouth to the other with his tongue.

'The only time that *bidi* left my lips was when I had to drink a glass of water in one of the scenes. That was when I removed the *bidi* from my lips with my left hand,' says Pran, gesticulating to show what he did, 'and used my right hand to drink the glass of water.'

These were just a few examples of the little touches that Pran added to the overall development of the character, but they served to make each of the characters Pran played authentic and believable.

Pran's skills of observation had been honed early in life. Having lived his childhood in a succession of towns and cities in various parts of undivided India meant that Pran had, very early on in life, come in contact with the human diversity of this land — people with their individual cultural backgrounds, physical features, voices, manner of dressing, hairstyles and gestures. Undoubtedly, all these observations had been filed away like data to be retrieved for use later on.

Pran's need to pursue perfection in his interpretation of the character he was chosen to play caused him to constantly scan the montage of people with whom he came in contact, and to (without their knowledge,

---

[4]   Produced and directed by Arabind Sen, this film, co-starring Raaj Kumar, Mala Sinha and Rajesh Khanna, was released in 1971.

[5]   Released in 1962, starring Shammi Kapoor, Mala Sinha and Mehmood.

of course) carefully observe them and imprint in his memory – in his 'library of looks, accents, gaits, and mannerisms' – all that he found particularly distinctive and fascinating.

Pinky Bhalla, Pran's daughter, spoke of her father's penchant for strikingly uncommon and unique get-ups and 'looks' for each of the films in which he starred: 'Very often the get-ups were based on his own ideas. He used to go through magazines and books to see if somebody had an unusual beard, or get-up, or wig. Then he would try and incorporate that into any of his roles.... [He] was a very observant person as well. If, in real life, he had seen somebody with a striking or distinctive mannerism, he would bear it in mind and copy it whenever he could – like he copied my dance teacher's walking style! That helped him to get his teeth into the character.'

Pran agrees with his daughter: 'I used to observe common people and copy their actions or mannerisms. My daughter Pinky had a dance teacher who was physically challenged. Interestingly, he never used crutches; he used just a stick. And even his way of using that stick was very unique — he used to rest his lame leg on the stick while walking. So, when I got a chance to do a lame person's role, of Kaido in *Heer Ranjha*, I copied his style of walking, which I felt was extremely unusual.'

Producer-director Chander Sadanah, who directed Pran in *Chor Ke Ghar Chor*, revealed how Pran had thought up something new for his film: 'Pran *Saab* was always *fascinated* with get-ups and the look of his role. In *Chor Ke Ghar Chor*, we wanted the character of a mad person. He said he had seen a mad fellow in Bandra who used to wear a military uniform, with medals. Using that as the base, he worked on the character in such detail that in seven days, he even gave us a rough sketch of that character!'

Those were Chander Sadanah's recollections. But a good insight into the way Pran imprinted these observations on the pages of his memory can be gained from the fact that when this biography was being written, Pran recalled that this man was actually an eccentric fellow who used to visit various people in the film industry. Dressed in a military outfit, complete with medals, he used to also carry around a cardboard bugle, which he used to sound by pretending to blow it, but would actually make a bugle-like sound with his voice!

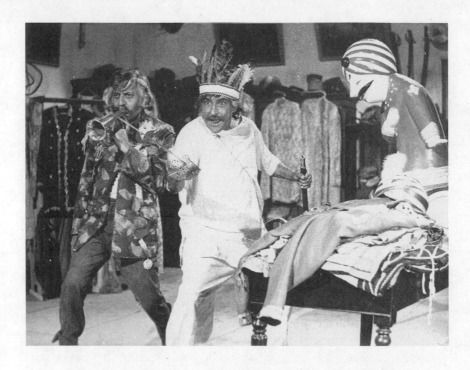

Pran and Ashok Kumar in a comic sequence in *Chor Ke Ghar Chor*.

With regard to the authenticity that emerged from the hard work and details that Pran worked into the overall presentation of his character, Arvind Sikand recounted an amusing incident which took place when he visited the sets of *Gambler*:[6] He said: 'His get-up was really amazing. He had full beard and longish hair and I remember coming to the set one day to pick him up. I walked on to the set and looked around for him. Then I heard my name being called out. Turning around but not seeing my father anywhere, I was puzzled. I scanned the sets again, until he called out to me again. It was then that I suddenly realized that there he was in get-up and *even I* hadn't recognized him!'

Illustrating the point that Pran did achieve what he set out to do – that is, being different in every film he did – is the following incident that took place at a star night in Ahmedabad, Gujarat.

---

6 This version of *Gambler* (1960) starred Premnath, Shakila, Pran, K. N. Singh, Shammi, Madan Puri, Cuckoo, and Agha and is not to be confused with Amarjeet's *Gambler* (1971) starring Dev Anand, Zahida and Zaherra.

A mimic was imitating actors such as Dilip Kumar, Raj Kapoor, Dev Anand, Raaj Kumar and Mehmood. He was doing an excellent job and the audience was enjoying it. Somebody from the audience then asked the mimic to imitate Pran. The mimic fell silent. Then he asked the person who had made the request: 'Which role of Pran's should I mimic?'

3

'Sight' is supplemented by 'sound' in the medium of cinema. So, even while mastering the intricacies of creating a strikingly distinct 'look' for each of the roles he played, Pran began also to think up various ways to making his portrayal truly unforgettable.

This generation of filmgoers knows of present-day film villains who have employed the use of catch phrases and may have enjoyed and even imitated these. But it is interesting to note that as far back as the late 1940s and early 1950s Pran had already started employing catch phrases in his films and very successfully too.

'Some of the dialogues that I have used are also taken from observing people whom I have closely known,' Pran disclosed. 'For instance, there was a really funny incident which involved someone I personally knew in Lahore.... It was the time I was working in a couple of Roop K. Shorey's pictures [*Badnami* and *Khamosh Nigahen*].[7] Roop K. Shorey had a *mama*[8] who was in charge of Shorey's studios. He used to sit in a low studio armchair puffing away at a *bidi* or a cigarette, expounding on some subject or the other.

'*Mamajee* had a very unusual way of holding his cigarette in his crooked right forefinger, the tip of which he tucked into the space between the base of his thumb and forefinger. Every now and then he would draw a puff and say: *"Kyon? Theek hai na, theek?"*[9] with a typically Punjabi accent which places emphasis on the "k" sound in the final *theek*. And finally, perhaps to flick off the ash, he would tap his nose with the same crooked forefinger that held the cigarette – all of these

---

[7]   Both released in 1946.
[8]   Maternal uncle.
[9]   'What say? That's right, isn't it?'

done in one smooth sequence! This gesture and the sentence that punctuated the end of each of his expositions had become his *takia kalaam* or catch phrase.

'*Mamajee* would always be in the studios and he loved drinking. Once he got so badly drunk that he fell down and hurt his nose. The next day, he was holding forth as usual, puffing away at his cigarette. As with most people, he had forgotten what had happened the night before and was holding forth on some topic of the moment. Then, drawing in deeply, he used his catch phrase and he tapped his nose as was his habit. But this time, his *takia kalaam* changed, albeit involuntarily! For added on to the end of "*Kyon? Theek hai na, theek*" was an agonized "*Haiiiieee!*" Apparently, he had only then realized that he had badly hurt his nose!

'I used this in one of my films, *Patthar Ke Sanam*, and it became my *takia kalaam* throughout the film!'

Pran went on to tell us about a couple of other remarkable films and the freshness he injected in them: 'In *Dus Lakh*,[10] I injected the comedy element by translating all my dialogue into wrong English! And in *Heer Ranjha*,[11] I had to speak all my dialogue in blank verse, since the entire film's dialogue was in blank verse!'[12]

As one of the very few persons to have used the maximum amount of get-ups and 'looks' in his career, which also include the way he spoke his dialogues, it would be impossible to chronicle each and every one of them. However, these few instances to which Pran referred show how varied and interesting he tried to make each of the characters he was given to play, and, having played them, how the remembrance of those performances is still capable of bringing that gleam of satisfaction to his eyes.

4

Although Pran never went to any acting school, where he could have undergone voice training, nor did he work in the theatre where he could

---

[10] Released in 1966.

[11] Released in 1970.

[12] Blank verse is verse without rhyme. The dialogues for *Heer Ranjha* were penned by the eminent Urdu poet Kaifi Azmi.

have learnt to use his voice effectively, he instinctively grasped that here was a new medium where his voice and his ability to mimic accents could be used to good advantage.

Pran now began to create *distinctive voices* for the characters he played. The sheer number of his successful films has shown that he gave much thought to this vital aspect of delineating a character. Rather than undergo any sort of voice culture and training to do this, Pran used his powers of observation to make his unusual voice produce what he wanted it to!

Mastering accents was the most important factor. There are as many accents to India's spoken Urdu-Hindustani-Hindi as there are states in our country. So Pran assiduously went about the task of mastering the various accents of Hindi. He paid careful attention to the way people from different parts of the subcontinent would speak it. For instance, how a Nepali-Gurkha would speak the language would be vastly different from how a South Indian would speak it. Or a Maharastrian's Hindi diction would be totally unlike that of a Bihari or a Bhopali. This proved particularly useful when, as per the director's concept, a role being played by him needed comic shades to it.

Regarding Pran's distinctive voice, his daughter, Pinky Bhalla added: 'It is his natural voice. I don't think he underwent any training. He didn't have to. He was very professional. He would use a different accent in every film of his.

'If you remember, in *Kasauti*,[13] he adopted a Nepali accent because the character he was playing was from Nepal. People enjoyed it, especially in that song, *"Hum Bolega Toh Boloye Ke Bolta Hai"*[14] which endeared him to the public and is a hit even to this day.'

The first line of the song itself was Pran's catch phrase all through the film and people still remember it and use it at opportune moments in their own lives!

However, there was no easy method to gaining proficiency at speaking in different accents. Intricacies of tone and cadences, sense stress and

---

[13] Released in 1974.

[14] Sung by Kishore Kumar, penned by Varma Malik and composed by Kalyanji Anandji, this song was picturized on Pran (who lip-synched the words). The movie featured Amitabh Bachchan and Hema Malini as well. It means: 'If I speak up now, you are going to blame me!'

modulation were the finer points of voice control over which Pran gained mastery, and, although he was an instinctive mimic, it was hard work.

'We make films for audience appreciation not for personal satisfaction,' Pran went on to say. 'Merely by changing a costume or wearing a red beard and wig, I wouldn't have been very impressive as a Pathan[15] in *Zanjeer. So I also changed my voice to sound like a real Pathan.* There have been occasions when I've had to do as many as eighteen retakes to get the pronunciation of a word right.'

However, it was in *Kashmir Ki Kali*[16] that Pran decided to add a touch of the comic to his villainy. Playing the character of the suitor of Champa (played by a very young Sharmila Tagore, who was making her debut in Hindi films with this movie), Pran decided to use a *takia kalaam* with a distinctive Himalayan accent. So, all through the film Pran, who is shown as trying to be a patient man where Champa's affections are concerned, says: *"Shataaley, shataaley, Shampa, apna bhi shamay aayegaa!"*[17]

This comic, yet sweet little touch, succeeded in actually making the audiences feel a little sorry for Pran who eventually lost out to the hero with regard to winning Champa's affections at the end of the film!

S. M. Sagar gave Pran the role of Banné Khan, a Bhopali character, for a film to be directed by him titled *Adhikar.*[18] The story and dialogues were by Salim-Javed.[19] Even as Pran recounts the background to his successful portrayal of Banné Khan, his eyes shine with pleasure at a job well done.

'When I was told the story of *Adhikar,* I liked the role because it was interesting,' recounted Pran. 'But I agreed to do the role on one condition. The condition was that Javed *Miyan* should record two Bhopali scenes in his own voice and give it to me, since I had never been to Bhopal

---

[15] Pathans are a people from Afghanistan, many of whom are settled in India.

[16] Producer-director Shakti Samanta's *Kashmir Ki Kali,* starring Shammi Kapoor, Sharmila Tagore and Pran, was released in 1964.

[17] Meaning: 'Carry on with your teasing, Champa, but remember, every dog has his day!'

[18] Released in 1971.

[19] Salim Khan and Javed Akhtar worked as a team on several successful films such as *Zanjeer* (1973), *Deewar* (1975) and *Sholay* (1975) before ending the partnership to pursue their own individual careers.

nor do I know Bhopali. Javed used to speak Bhopali so well that even the Bhopalis would be put to shame!

'Javed agreed and recorded the two scenes in the Bhopali language for me. I used to listen to the tape in the quiet of the night and practised it very well. That role became a hit. The credit actually goes to Javed, his dialogues in it were so well written.

'For example: in one scene some *goondas*[20] are about to kidnap a girl. The girl is screaming to be set free. Banné Khan Bhopali reaches the spot in time and the villain says: *"Jaan, agar hum tumhe chod denge, toh hum kahan jayenge?"*

'Banne Khan says: *"Miya aap kahan jayenge yeh hum bataaye dete hain. Pehle Bibi koh chhod doh."* Girls are called *bibi* in Bhopali.

'The villain says: *"Chalo, hato saamne se."* To which Banné Khan retorts: *"Agar hum saamne seh hut gaye toh aapki batisi apne haath me aa jayegi!"*[21]

'Urdu has its own distinctive style according to the region where it is spoken – whether in Bhopal, Punjab or Hyderabad. Additionally, each region also has its own peculiar style about certain actions – for instance in the eating of *paan*.[22] Most films show the villain chewing on *paan* in one scene or another, so I made it a point to observe the various habits of *paan* chewers in the country.'

Pran added: 'I had observed that in Bhopal, they eat their *paans* with a lot of *choona* and *katthaa*. The interesting thing is that they apply *choona* with one finger and *kattha* with another finger. In UP, they do it in a different way – if you take *choona* with one finger, they make it spread to all four fingers! Each time I used mannerisms like these, the role became a hit beyond words. It gave both me and the public great satisfaction.'

Long before the villains of today rediscovered the use of comedy to enliven the proceedings, Pran had already successfully used this dimension in several of his villainous roles, making them even more memorable.

---

[20] Ruffians.
[21] Loosely translated: Villain: 'My love, if I let you go then where will I go?' Pran: 'Sir, I will tell you where to go, but first, leave the lady alone.' Villain: 'Come come, get out of the way.' Pran: 'If I get out of the way, then I assure you that with me, your entire set of teeth will also get out of the way!'
[22] Betel leaf.

5

Despite the comic touch, Pran also succeeded in striking terror into the hearts of millions of moviegoers.

To be a villain consistently and yet be universally popular is a remarkable feat which has been achieved by comparatively very few 'bad men' of the screen. It has been said that perhaps Pran is the only screen actor who acts with his brain and his facial muscles. He even cocks a sinister eyebrow with finesse and perfect timing.

In this context, Pran explained: 'Certain characteristics are generally associated with bad characters. The thin lips always sneering and always puffing away at a cigarette; the bloodshot eyes, always narrowed to dangerous slits – and of course, the ability to down gallons of booze!'

More than these stock-in-the-trade characteristics of the 'bad man' are little individual characteristics that help create a vivid screen personality – these have helped Pran to avoid monotony and stereotyping in the numerous roles he has enacted.

To be a convincing villain, the individual characteristics should imply vanity, conceit or an overweening cocksureness. As an example, Pran referred to the film *Kab, Kyon Aur Kahan*.[23] 'In that film,' he said, 'I keep flipping a coin and deftly capture it on the back of my hand. It always lands on the back of my hand; it never falls.

'A lot of practice went into mastering this [skill], but it was worth the effort because the audience enjoyed it. You see, that gesture implied both overconfidence as well as extra-cleverness. It suited the character. Many fans did write to me about this particular mannerism. It made me happy that I had a very intelligent section of fans amongst the millions of cinegoers who see my films.'

Moviegoers who have seen any of Pran's films will agree that one of his most striking features are his eyes, which he has used to good effect in all his performances. Ever since that first time, when the magistrate in Lahore had admired Pran's eyes and waived the fine for rash driving, and then, when *Saheb Mama* (Shri Fatehlal of Prabhat) had said '*doley*

---

[23] Released in 1970.

tsangley aahet'[24] about his eyes, Pran knew for sure the effect his eyes had on people.

He would use this knowledge to his advantage. Filmgoers will agree that Pran has been the only villain who, right from his first scene in a film, could instil fear in the audience – usually with consummate use of his eyes. Whether he needed to convey hatred, malice, disdain, lechery or – as he had to do in the final scenes of most of his villainous roles – to convey remorse, regret or sorrow, Pran has been able to do so with a mere look, a glance or even a flick of his eyebrow.

'I believe the eyes and the voice can play an important role in the creation of the right tone of menace,' emphasized Pran. '*I believe in underplaying and using my eyes well.* A mere fraction of movement can convey a great deal. The narrowing of eyes can build up tension. And the voice can do wonders if you use tonal variations. I am never loud. I have never laughed loudly, except in *Dil Diya Dard Liya*, where the role demanded it.'[25]

Over and above all this, Pran also decided not to always leave the very vital part of the preparation for his role to chance – or to the film's costume department! Since he had already played a major part in deciding on his 'look' for each role, he would also take a hand in the designing and procuring of his costumes and wigs and in deciding the kind of make-up he would use for a particular role.

To do that, his preparation would have to continue...

---

[24] Meaning: 'He has beautiful eyes.'
[25] *Dil Diya Dard Liya* (1966) in which Pran co-starred with Dilip Kumar, Waheeda Rehman and Rehman.

TWELVE

The Preparation Continues...

1

Yes, to hold his own against the author-backed role of a hero, right up until the very end of the film, Pran would have to be outstandingly believable as a villain. To achieve this goal would require not just solid effort, but also the help of a few well-chosen people. Why?

From among his three self-imposed requisites — *a new voice, new make-up and a new style of walking* — for the first and last requirements, Pran had drawn heavily on his own depository of knowledge, experience and talent.

However, there was one area in which he would need the help of trained professionals who would work in tandem with him — and that was in connection with being able to meet the requisite of having a new look, a new get-up and make-up for every character he played.

Even a casual glance at the way he transformed himself in the decade of the 1950s and 1960s for films like *Aleef Laila, Halaku, Adalat* and *Jis Desh Mein Ganga Behti Hai* testifies to Pran's own dedication and the talent and

Pran in a sorcerer's get-up in *Aleef Laila*.

proficiency of his make-up man and wig-maker, both working as a team with him, in each of the films in which he acted.

Whenever Pran signed a new role, he, of course, would first spend a lot of time thinking about the character itself. He would call up his make-up artiste, Pandhari Juker, and his wig-maker, S. Kabir, and would explain what he had in mind. Then, in one or several brainstorming sessions, which inevitably threw up the best of ideas and innovations, Pran's talented and trustworthy team would get to work.

Veteran make-up artist, Pandhari Juker started his career in Bombay at around the same time that Pran started his in Lahore. He did Pran's make-up in more films than he can remember! 'No other person has done as many get-ups and experimented with different kinds of make-up as Pran *Saab* has done,' Pandhari *Dada*, as he is popularly known, revealed. 'Pran *Saab* would know the script thoroughly,' Pandhari *Dada* went on. 'In fact, he would be totally immersed in it. He would give much thought to which make-up would suit the role best. He would even ask how he could enhance the get-up. Then according to the get-up, he would go through his "library" and match a moustache or beard.

S. Kabir – wig-maker *par excellence*.

'Initially, he had artists who would make rough sketches. This used to help us get a good idea of what he wanted, and then to execute it. So, we too used to enjoy the work, especially since he, the artiste, was so involved in the creative process.'

'Very few people have a passion for make-up like Pran *Saab* has,' continued Pandhari *Dada*. 'The unique thing about him was that the moment he would put on his make-up, complete with wig, with or without a beard and moustache, he would become, both in "look" and in manner of speech, gait, mannerism – everything – the character he was playing. For instance, if Pran *Saab* had to do the role of a lame villager, he would give the perfect impression of that villager!

'In a way we can say that half the battle of the challenge of portraying another human is won by the make-up itself. An actor cannot act properly if his make-up is not done perfectly,' Pandhari *Dada* emphasized.

Highlighting Pran's dedication to his art and his profession, Pandhari Juker further remarked: 'Pran *Saab* was always punctual. He would give his full time to the make-up artist saying, "I have come for the shooting, and I am under your direction." He would never hurry make-up just for the sake of doing make-up. He would want it to be perfect, so he never gave any problem while getting his make-up done.' Having worked for some foreign films in addition to scores of Indian ones, Pandhari *Dada* compared Pran's methodology and approach to acting with some of the best foreign artistes' methods of working.

With regard to the man for whose visage he has always enjoyed doing make-up. Pandhari *Dada* was exultant: 'Pran *Saab* offers a make-up artiste the scope to rise above the ordinary, to always produce something superlative.'

Pandhari *Dada* highlighted another interesting feature: 'The artistes of today remove their beard after just one shot. But till today Pran *Saab* has never removed his beard or make-up until the whole day's shoot was over, however difficult or uncomfortable the make-up might be. Because he understood that once the make-up is removed and redone, it is not done so perfectly. The first effort is always the best one.'

Pran's habit of being ready well before the work shift and being available on the sets, regardless of whether he was needed immediately or not, enabled him to be immersed in the film as a whole, *in its totality*. Observing what each of his co-artistes was doing enabled Pran to view his role, not in isolation, but to be aware of how that role would have to be played in tandem with his co-actors.

Because of immense effort he put into his preparation, he was able to deliver one superlative performance after another, which still stand out in the memory of the cinema-going public.

2

Right from the early years, Pran had kept close tabs on all the reviews of his films. Undoubtedly, he would have read the *Movie Times* review of Gope Productions' *Malkin* which, while praising 'the consummate artistry of Pran', also made a slightly negative comment about his 'unnatural and odd hairstyle' in the film. Pran would have decided to do something about it so as to ensure that never again would such comments come his way.

Rigorous preparation was required, and Pran did not hold back. Going into some detail about how he would prepare for the actual look of the role, he said: 'If I saw something unusual printed in any newspaper or magazine, I would cut it out and file it. Then if I got that sort of role, I would incorporate it in my acting. I would also use the actual press clipping to show to the costume designer, the make-up man and wig-maker, the sort of idea I had in mind for my get-up, or for my hair, beard and moustache.

'World-famous personalities have always fascinated me. Therefore I have imitated [their] make-up.... In *Khandaan* (1965) my make-up was based on Hitler – his hairstyle and his moustache. I copied Abraham

Lincoln's make-up in *Amar Akbar Anthony*.[1] In *Jugnu*,[2] I was playing a professor and I copied Mujibur Rehman's get-up – the *kurta*,[3] the wig, the glasses, the moustache. Though the viewers felt it looked familiar, they could not pinpoint whom I had copied. That was a revolutionary role. And in *Nigahen*,[4] I used a beard which is exactly like the one the late Rajiv Gandhi's man, Sam Pitroda,[5] sported.'

Pran chuckled as he revealed the name of the person whose beard he had copied for the film *Joshila*:[6] 'I even copied Shashi Kapoor's father-in-law, Geoffrey Kendall's beard![7] I studied his photographs, showed it to my make-up man, and there I was, having this interesting beard and playing the role of a crippled man.'

Raj Mehra and Pran (in the Mujibur Rehman get-up) in *Jugnu*.

---

[1] *Amar Akbar Anthony* – 1977.
[2] *Jugnu* – 1973.
[3] Mujibur Rehman was one of the main leaders responsible for the creation of Bangladesh in early 1971. A *kurta* is a full-sleeved, long and loose Indian shirt that is usually worn either over loose 'parallels' or jodhpur-type *churidaars*.
[4] *Nigahen* – 1989.
[5] Sam Pitroda was Rajiv Gandhi's telecommunications advisor.
[6] *Joshila* –1973.
[7] Geoffrey Kendall, father of (the late) Jennifer and Felicity Kendall, had a touring theatre company called Shakespeareana, which performed the Bard's works for Indian audiences.

The late S.Kabir, wig-maker nonpareil, played an indispensable role in the successful transformation of Pran, the man, into Pran, the character of any particular film. Siraj, Kabir's younger son[8] offered this nugget of information: 'Whenever our father worked for a film of Pran *Saab*'s, he was required to be on the sets every day.'

Pran himself acknowledged the role played by this remarkable wig-maker: 'It was Kabir who executed the wigs that went to make each of my get-ups so memorable. Kabir's wigs were so good that even if you took it out of a box after a few years, the shape and the fall of the wig would be just the way it was when first made.'

Then, Kabir added this insightful comment: 'The moment Pran *Saab* would put on those hairpieces and the full make-up, it was as if he became the very person he was playing. Pran *Saab*'s face suits any kind of role. *He has that kind of god-gifted face which, when made up, can appear to be that of a millionaire or of a beggar – all actors do not have this gift.* As a result, it is difficult to point out which of his get-ups was the most effective. All of them were.'

Interestingly, that view was seconded by popular heroine and later vamp, Shashikala, who referred to an incident that took place during the shooting of Saawan Kumar Tak's *Salma Pe Dil Aa Gaya*,[9] where she saw Pran for the first time on the sets for that film. He had chosen the get-up of a *pir* or holy man and Shashikala recalls the impression he gave as he walked onto the sets: 'It felt as if the whole set was filled with his presence and persona. He was exuding a certain holiness.'

While Pran relied on his team of experts, over the years, he had also developed his own techniques that enhanced the effectiveness of his make-up. Pandhari Juker revealed that Pran had taught him an effective way to camouflage the wig line: 'I learnt from Pran *Saab* how to make the wig look as if it were part of the person's head. After sticking the neck area, Pran *Saab* used to shade the area with a brown pencil, blending the colour of the wig and the skin in such a way that no one would realize that this is a hairpiece and not the real thing!'

---

[8] Kabir's two sons, Farooque and Siraj, apprenticed with their father, before donning the mantle passed on to them by Kabir's untimely demise.
[9] *Salma Pe Dil Aa Gaya* – 1997.

Pran was so passionate about the get-ups and make-up which he had created for the various characters he played, that he commissioned Dharamdas, an artist from Jaipur to paint him in his most memorable get-ups. The artist was provided with a suitable picture of Pran from the films in which he acted and these were executed amazingly well. In all, this artist has painted about sixteen paintings, some of which still hang on the walls of Pran's home.

In the pursuit of authenticity with regard to the costumes he would use for his roles, Pran sought the help of friends. In the film *Kasauti*,[10] where he played a Gurkha character from Nepal, he had to wear a typical Gurkha outfit and also have with him the knife that the Gurkhas always carry. Since he urgently needed both the outfit and the indispensable accessory – the *khukri*, which is a short and extremely sharp knife – Pran enlisted the help of a Nepali.

Pran recounted: 'I had a Nepali friend, called Netra Rana, who lived close by. I borrowed an outfit from him which I got copied for my role as a Nepali and had also got a real *khukri* from him because in some of my scenes I would need it. When on the first day of my scene with the villain, I took the *khukri* with me. I had to place the *khukri* on the villain's throat. The villain took one look at the *khukri* and got really worried! The *khukri* was so sharp that if my hand had moved even slightly, there would surely have been a messy accident. So he requested me to get a fake knife lest something untoward happened!'

3

Pran didn't stop his groundwork at just get-ups, costumes, and accents. There was still one aspect that went to complete his preparation as an actor: Fights.

Screen fighting or '*dishum-dishum*,' as it is popularly called due to the extra-loud sound effects, was an essential part of his job as villain, because inevitably, when any film has major confrontations between hero and villain, that grand finale climactic fight sequence is a *must*. So, Pran's preparation as an actor extended also to those inevitable fight scenes.

---

[10] *Kasauti* – 1974.

Pran found yet another novel and unusual way during the 1970s by which to make each villain he played distinctive and unique. Whenever he travelled to any foreign country, he would try to visit places where he was likely to find the low life of the town, folks who were rough-and-ready with their fists, the kind of people whom we, in our colourful Hindi, term as 'goondas', all so that he could observe how they fought and what sort of tactics they employed.

Being a villain meant that he needed to make each fight sequence authentic. Whenever required, he took lessons to master any fighting technique that was needed for a role. When swashbuckling roles began to come his way, Pran learnt the art of fencing. For two years, he practised daily with the fight master.

In this context, Pran's elder son, Arvind recounted: 'As a very young boy, I remember going to the sets of Sindbad the Sailor,[11] a film in which he co-starred with Ranjan.[12] It was one of those swashbuckler kind of films – a lot of sword-fencing and what not. In order to be able to do it to perfection, my dad joined classes to learn fencing. He would go early in the morning.

'Sometimes, I also used to get up early...and go with him to these fencing lessons. I must have been only about five or six years old then. I'll never forget how he got a special little sword made for me and also gave me a few lessons! It was quite fascinating to participate in this kind of unusual routine and to see the pains my father took and the extent to which he went to bring realism and conviction into his performances.'

Beneath the seriousness with which Pran approached his work, he had an underlying sense of humour that held him in good stead at tense or awkward moments, which could well arise during the course of the shooting of any film.

Successful screen vamp Shashikala highlighted an interesting incident about Pran's quick thinking, his sporting spirit and his ability to know when not to make an issue of things, which took place on the sets of Filmistan's Aab-e-Hayat.[13]

---

[11] Sindbad the Sailor – 1952.
[12] Ranjan was from South India and was mainly known for his swashbuckling roles.
[13] Aab-e-Hayat – 1955.

'[In this film] Premnath played the hero, Pran*jee* was the villain and I was playing the heroine.... Premnath's temper on the sets used to be quite famous, and most of the time we couldn't figure out when he was angry or upset about something. This tested our patience sometimes.

'During one of the sword-fencing scenes, both Premnath and Pran had to wear wigs. I don't know into what sort of mood Premnath had worked himself, but that day he was a little too energetic with his sword and before we knew it, Premnath's sword had deliberately and completely lifted Pran's wig from off his head!! Everybody started laughing at what they thought was a funny joke. I quickly looked at Pran, knowing that he must be very angry. Pran looked shocked for a moment, but then he too began to laugh and thus, defused that tense situation.'

Commonly, actors prefer body doubles or stand-ins to do those stunts or fights, which, though fraught with danger, have to be performed, being part and parcel of the commercial requirement labelled in the credit titles as '*thrills, fights and action*'.

Many junior artistes who started off as stuntmen were eventually able to make it to the big time, due, in no small part, to the largesse that was shown to them by the actor for whom they composed fight sequences.

Pran encouraged and helped some of them become fight directors in their own right. Notable among these were Baggad, who made a debut as fight director with S. K. Kapoor's films, and the famous 'baldie' Shetty, who went from being a 'double' for Pran, to composing fight sequences and acting as villain. Veeru Devgan[14] too 'doubled' for Pran until *Zanjeer*,[15] and then went on to become a fight director by virtue of his own abilities and accomplishments.

For Pran, however, it was only in the most dangerous scenes that he used a 'double'. In most other scenes, he did his fights himself!

In *Upkar*,[16] Pran played the unforgettable role of an amputee named Malang Baba, who hobbled around on one leg. Pran's other leg had been bent at the knee and tied back to his thigh to give the appearance of it being amputated at the knee. In one fighting sequence, Pran

---

[14] Veeru Devgan's son, Ajay Devgan is a popular hero today.

[15] *Zanjeer* – 1973.

[16] *Upkar* – 1967.

performed his own fight scene and did the entire shooting on his one 'good' leg!

Another quite painful incident happened during the shooting of *Tumsa Nahin Dekha*.[17] The hero, Shammi Kapoor, had to shoot certain parts of a fight sequence with Pran and they rehearsed quite well together. The main fighting shots were being picturized on 'doubles' and only a few close-up and mid-shots were to be intercut.

Shammi Kapoor recalls how it all happened: 'We did most of our mid-shots and close-ups ourselves. As usual, we were doing one mid-shot for the climax, in which I was supposed to hit him. There were three shots in which I punch him in the face. His reaction in all three shots should have been to move his face back so as not to get hit by my punch. We had rehearsed the whole thing very well.

'But in the take itself, while the first two punches went okay, unfortunately, during the third punch, instead of going back, he came forward and caught my blow.'

Shammi Kapoor's punch that caught Pran in the nose during the shooting of *Tumsa Nahin Dekha*.

---

17 *Tumsa Nahin Dekha* — 1957.

'Once I had started the punch, I couldn't pull it back. My punch caught him right on the nose and it started bleeding. I felt so sorry after that that I apologized and I followed him all over the place. He turned to me and said: "Come on. Don't be stupid. It was my fault. This sort of thing happens." And without pausing called out to Nasir Hussain saying, "Nasir, what is the next shot?"

'I marvelled at him. Here I was – I had just punched his nose, and he was being so nice about it!'

On occasion though, Pran has broken more than just his nose. In 1975, while shooting for Madan Mohla's *Dus Numbri*,[18] Pran met with an accident doing his own stunts, which landed him in hospital with a broken ankle.

Despite the producer's protests, Pran, who was fifty-five at the time, had insisted on jumping down from a height of some fifteen feet – and promptly broke an ankle!

That was the second time that Pran had got involved in an accident. The first time was when he rolled down a hill near Mysore, refusing the use of a 'double' and was in bed for nearly a month – which was a rather painful way of taking a holiday!

When asked why he chose to do the scene in *Dus Numbri* himself when he could have easily asked for a stand-in, his explanation was simple: 'How do you keep trim and fit if you use a stand-in all the time? Nowadays, most of the time there is action in our films, so these fight scenes offer me a "built-in" recipe for keeping fit.

'But our heroes fail to take advantage of this and put on fat which reduces their competency as heroes. Due to playing the villain, I have always had to keep myself physically fit. When I switched to character acting, I could have taken it easy but old habits die hard.'

How did he manage to keep trim and look so young? Pran became serious and said: '*It is the discipline of total devotion to work. The only worthwhile assets of an actor are his looks.*'

And it was due to being trim and fit that Pran was able to do some of the most excruciating stunts himself. For example, in the climax of

---

[18] *Dus Numbri* – 1976.

Hatyara,[19] the villain was to tie Pran to a horse and drag him for quite a distance over a muddy road. Pran did this scene himself. Pran recalls the agonizing pain, but according to him: 'It was a job well done.'

The thrilling fight at the climax of *Ram Aur Shyam*[20] helps one understand how much hard work goes into the 'choreography' of a fight – for that is what it is – a composition of actions and stunts making up a unified whole. The scope, dimension and chopping and changing which each such fight traverses, and the unusual things which happen all through such fight scenes, combine to make every such a sequence memorable.

Pran's performance as the absolutely hateful despot in *Ram Aur Shyam*, one of his most memorable roles that was typical of the villainous roles he was getting at the time, won him even more fans, although the critics were, as usual, hard to please. However, one reviewer had to acknowledge this: 'Pran's isn't a convincing characterization, *but as usual he does put up a full blooded fight.*'

Every die-hard cinemagoer, raised on a staple diet of mainstream Hindi films during the 1950s through to the 1970s, will acknowledge that in every fight scene where Pran was bashing up the hero, their own edge-of-the-seat nervousness indicated their growing belief that here was a villain who just might make mincemeat of the not-so-agile hero! In fact, many of them did not *want* to see Pran lose out to the hero!

An incident which occurred during the shooting of *Phir Wohi Dil Laya Hoon*[21] illustrates this fact. The Srinagar schedule was in progress and a fight sequence between Pran and the hero, Joy Mukerji, was being canned. It soon became very difficult to work due to the big crowd that had gathered there to see the shooting. Nasir *Saab* told Pran: '*Bhai*,[22] you handle this crowd. Explain to them and make them leave.'

Pran spoke to the crowd: '*Bhaiyon*, I know that all of you are like me. You all want the things that I get to do on screen – chase girls and make money, what else?'

---

[19] *Hatyara*, directed by Surendra Mohan, co-starred Vinod Khanna, Moushumi Chatterji and Rakesh Roshan, and was released in 1977.

[20] *Ram Aur Shyam* – 1967.

[21] *Phir Wohi Dil Laya Hoon* – 1963.

[22] Brother.

The crowd started laughing and said: 'We will do whatever you tell us.' And then they fell silent. Seeing this, Nasir *Saab* got an idea. He said: 'Why not use the presence of the crowd? The hero will give a punch and the crowds will clap.'

So again Pran was sent to speak to the crowd. This time, however, they did not agree! Instead, they retorted, 'Pran *Saab*, we will clap when *you* deliver a punch!'

Filmgoers had become so stirred by his performances that despite the viciousness of the characters Pran played, he still had a major fan following among India's cinema-going public. When the *Filmfare* Awards[23] were still in their infancy, some of Pran's fans had vociferously opined in the press that *Filmfare* should institute an award for Best Villain. They were convinced that Pran would win hands down — something he did do in the years to come.

4

Given the fact that so much thought and preparation went into the development of each of his roles, it is not difficult to understand why Pran would be at the studios on time. Having prepared well at home, all that remained was to literally get under the 'skin' of the character, that is, under the make-up and in the clothing of the person he was to portray.

Then he would go over to the sets and observe others at work, waiting patiently for his turn to be called. In Bollywood, like elsewhere, the film is rarely shot in chronological sequence, and so, observing his co-artistes enact their scenes would provide a sort of continuity in Pran's mind and allow him to give a competent performance.

Going into the latter half of the 1950s, even a cursory survey of the kind of critical acclaim Pran received from leading journals is enough to explain how Pran had not only reached the top by being 'a thinking actor' but how he had also consolidated his premier position and continued

---

[23] The *Filmfare* Awards were initially known as the *Clare* Awards, named a year after their staffer, Clare Mendonca, died.

to remain there. His numerous fans were the real reviewers, giving him the feedback he needed to better himself, performance by performance.

Acting was no longer just a profession — it was his life, and he intended to live it fully, to the widest extent possible.

THIRTEEN

The Sports Lover

1

The amount of effort and the sheer energy that Pran put into preparing for each of his roles may have caused some to conclude that it was 'all work and no play' for the actor. However, despite the hectic schedules and demands on his time, Pran did have quite a few interests that were far removed from the world of films.

One of his main interests outside the world of cinema was sports. Elder son, Arvind, says: 'My father had several different hobbies, but he was very passionate about sports. He also had a great passion for hockey. He became a member of the Bombay Provincial Hockey Association and [was] very active there.'

In addition to giving him some breathing space outside the studios, away from the arc lights, sports helped Pran stay fit. Whenever he had no shooting schedules, or if there was a match coming up, Pran could be found at the football grounds, kicking the ball around with members of the team.

Pran's inclination towards sports also made for some excellent relaxation, good times with fellow actors and sportsmen and, as we shall see, opportunities to collect funds for charitable causes.

Pran's first introduction to sports was in school in Uttar Pradesh, where as a young schoolboy, he played a little hockey. However, he confesses that he was not that good a player!

His interest in sports was renewed after he came to Bombay in 1947. By becoming a member of Bombay's Cricket Club of India,[1] Pran and his friend, producer-director Ram Kamlani[2] were able to watch every major cricket match played at the Brabourne Stadium!

Pran and Ram Kamlani always liked to sit in two particular seats in the pavilion at the CCI. So, to make sure that they got those two seats and none other, Pran used to be the first in the queue at 5 a.m. outside the CCI!

So strong was Pran's love for cricket that during a test match, he used to be present at the CCI on all five days! It was the same with hockey and football. Pran ardently followed all the hockey and football matches until his schedule did not permit him to do so. It goes without saying that on the day there was an important match, there would be no shooting!

Pran's son Arvind reveals a little known, but interesting, tidbit about his father's friends and their love of sports: 'Dad, Ram Kamlani, Satish Bhalla[3] and others formed a group who would always attend all the cricket test matches and stash away their bottles of hip flasks of whisky, which was all very daring because those were the days of Prohibition!

'I think he didn't miss a single test match until the death of Ram Kamlani, who was a very great, close friend of his. After that he refused to go to the matches because he was, in a sense, grieving for him.'

Yes, many of the friends Pran made during those days also shared Pran's love for sports and they remained friends for life.

---

[1] The Cricket Club of India in Bombay is built at the south end of the Brabourne Stadium so that its privileged members can watch the game from its shaded pavilions.

[2] Ram Kamlani was the brother of the famous comedian, Gope, under whose banner of Gope Productions Pran made the films *Malkin* (1953) and *Biradari* (1966).

[3] Satish Bhalla's son Vivek, later married Pran's daughter, Pinky.

2

One such friend was Akhtar Hussain, Nargis's elder brother.

And it was through Akhtar that Pran came onto the football field. Talking about how his passion for football took root, Pran disclosed:

'Akhtar Husain had signed me to work in his film *Pyar Ki Baaten*.[4] However, I was intrigued to find that Akhtar packed up at 4.30 p.m. In fact, that was not the first time! Akhtar would regularly "pack-up" as early as 4 or 4.30 p.m.! We didn't know why – but soon found out! Actually, Akhtar was a great football fan and even had his own club, which he had named The Globe. He used to rush to the Cooperage[5] whenever his team was playing, or whenever any exciting matches were to be played. I, on the other hand, had never yet seen a football game.

'So one day I joined him to see a football match. I liked it so much that I also started going with him regularly. I made friends with a lot of the footballers. And they made me a member of their club.'

Pran continued his reminiscences: 'I began to like football so much that I wanted to make my own team. I talked about it to Raj Kapoorjee. He said: "Okay, we'll do it and the film*wallahs* will contribute."

'Then there was a man who had [a vast] knowledge of football, and he knew practically everybody. So I met him and he suggested some players' names, and together we formed a team in the early 1950s, calling it the Bombay Dynamos Football Club after the famous Moscow team. Our team had six members who represented Maharashtra including one who represented India at the Olympics...

'The team was pretty good too! Most of them were local Bombay boys. But I recruited Sanjiva, from Calcutta, who was the goalkeeper at the 1948 London Olympics. Another Olympian who played for us was inside forward, Parab...

'In those days, matches were being played for the Nadkarni Cup. Our team entered, and we won all the matches we played, including the

---

[4]   *Pyar Ki Baaten* (1951) produced by Nargis Art, directed by Akhtar Hussain, co-starred Nargis, Trilok Kapoor, Anwar Hussain and Cuckoo.

[5]   The football grounds are situated at Cooperage, opposite which is the Oval in south Bombay, where mostly cricket is played.

A star-studded team (late 1950s) for a noble cause. Seen among the celebrities are Pran, Agha, Nirupa Roy, Waheeda Rehman, Shammi Kapoor, Minoo Mumtaz, Ajit, Premnath, Raaj Kumar, Nimmi and Johnny Walker (reclining).

finals. That was in 1952. Then we also won the Western India Football Championship in 1953. When the league matches started, we also won seven to eight of them. And the crowds used to pour in just to see *when* we would lose! And lose we did, one day! And then lost four to five matches continuously. But my love of football did not diminish. I managed that team for over two years. My team earned [both] name and fame.

'The only drawback was that the film people had backed out.... It was very expensive too, since I had to support around fifteen players, paying for their boarding, lodging and other expenses.... So, sadly, I had to close it down.

'Some of those footballers are still alive and they do ring me up once in while. They ask me to come and see how much the football ground has changed.'

Shammi Kapoor recalled a very amusing incident that dates back to the early 1950s, when Pran's passion for football was at its peak: 'I remember we were shooting for *Hum Sab Chor Hain* at Filmistan.[6] Pranjee and I were fond of football and the finals were on.... Since S. Mukerji

---

6   Sashdhar Mukerji's *Hum Sab Chor Hain* (released in 1956) was directed by I. S. Johar and co-starred Shammi Kapoor, Nalini Jaywant, I. S. Johar, Majnu and Ameeta.

is also very fond of football, we went to his house to ask him permission to leave the sets early so that we could go see the match. "Can we go off after lunch? Today is the finals, East Bengal vs. Mohan Bagan." He said: "No way! Nothing doing! Do the shooting!"

'So all of us hatched a plan and stage-managed the whole scene with Nalini Jaywant's help. She was the heroine in the film. Johar set up a shot in which Nalini Jaywant throws a pillow at me and I throw the pillow back at her. Then she chases me all over the drawing-room and I jump over a sofa.

'During the rehearsal everything was fine. But while doing the take, I tripped on the sofa and fell down and rolled over three times and passed out.... Pran*jee* who was in his make-up room, heard the commotion and came over. Ajit, who was in on the whole thing and also wanted to get away from the shooting of his film *Durgesh Nandini*, being filmed on the next stage, also heard about it. Everybody was agitated. They lifted me and put me in the car to take me away to the hospital.

'No sooner were we out of the studio than I was in the driver's seat – Ajit, I. S. Johar and Pran*jee* were with me – driving like mad to reach the Cooperage in time for the finals between East Bengal and Mohan Bagan! There we were, sitting and enjoying the match, when all of a sudden, we turned around and saw S. Mukerji sitting right behind us! He said: *"Badmash! Idhar kya kar rahe ho?"*[7] Putting on my best hang-dog expression, I said: *"Sir, mujhe chot lag gayi thi na, issliye."*[8]

'It was surprising that S. Mukerji also enjoyed our prank. He smilingly acknowledged: "That *was* a good way to get out of the shooting!" '

3

Since the early 1950s Pran had always been in the forefront along with other luminaries such as Raj Kapoor, Dilip Kumar and Dev Anand in organizing cricket matches in which film stars would play for charitable causes. Some of these matches were played in Delhi, Bombay, Calcutta

---

[7] 'You scoundrel! What are you doing here?'
[8] 'Sir, I got hurt, that's why.'

and Madras. He even organized a football match which featured film stars on both teams. Again, the money collected was donated to charity.

The year 1954 dawned on Indian moviedom with excitement at fever pitch. The immediate reason was that a team of Indian film stars was to fly south to Colombo, Ceylon,[9] on a seven-day goodwill visit.

The highlight of the visit was a film star's cricket match featuring over two dozen prominent film personalities, among whom were Raj Kapoor, Nargis, Shammi Kapoor, Begum Para, Jairaj, Nirupa Roy, Shekhar, Smriti Biswas, Sumitra Devi, comedians Om Prakash and Agha, the suave Motilal and comedienne Meena Shorey, singer Talat Mehmood, music director Jaikishan, character actors David, Dewan Sharar, Hari Shivdasani and Jagirdar, vice-president of the Film Federation of India, B. D. Bharucha as well as 'baddies' Sajjan, Anwar Hussain and Pran.

'We were given an enthusiastic reception at the Ratmalana Airport,' Pran remembered. 'The crowds there were huge and star-crazy! They broke the police cordon and rushed on the tarmac to embrace their favourite stars!

'We performed three shows presided over by the then prime minister of Ceylon, Sir John Kotelawala,' Pran reminisced. 'All three of our shows drew full houses but it was the one-day festival cricket match that really took Ceylon's capital by storm.'

The widely publicized film stars' cricket match attracted large crowds and the grounds were packed long before the game commenced. So many stargazers and cricket fans went across to a adjoining property to see if they could find a way to watch the match. The owners charged a flat rate of eight annas.(half a rupee) per person for a grand view — which could be had by being perched on a tree!

As Pran related: 'I remember the two rival teams were skippered by Raj Kapoor and Nargis. Sinhalese film stars Rukmani Devi and Sita Jayawardena also played with us. Raj Kapoor scored the highest with fifty runs and Begum Para lived up to her cricket reputation by scoring thirty-six runs! And we all played great cricket that day. It was a basically a fun match — it didn't really matter which team won. What mattered was

---

9   As Sri Lanka was then known.

that a sizeable amount was collected in aid of various charitable institutions of that country.'

4

India is a cricket-loving nation. Cricket unifies the diverse peoples of the Indian subcontinent like nothing has ever done; normally 'sane' people go completely 'crazy' every time a significant match with high-profile, talented cricketers is being played.

Cricket's pull on the film fraternity was no less powerful. Film folk would either find ways to stay at home, or cancel shooting during an important match, or if that couldn't be done, carry a portable TV to the sets! However, before the days of portable TV, before a wire-free generation got glued to their mobile phones, pocket radios could be found in palms that never left peoples' ears. Even more amusing was to see two or three people trying to 'ear' their way for a 'listen-in' to the running commentary!

This craze is amply illustrated by what happened on the sets of Prakash Kapoor's *Humjoli*.[10] A transistor radio was playing full blast. The commentary revealed that the match was on in full swing and the Indian side was slow on runs and fast on getting out. The Indian side was poised to lose. Spirits were at an all-time low and, although there were a few scenes of Jeetendra's and Pran's to be filmed, no one was in a mood to work. Everyone felt that unless the Indian team scored 'fours' and 'sixes', there was no way that they were going to get back their mood for acting in this fun-filled potboiler.

Pran had to enact a 'sad' scene that day. He said that with the Indian team losing, his acting sad was no acting! It was genuine!

5

Pran's generosity combined with his love for sports resulted in his being very active in all kinds of social and charitable work. He developed a

---

[10] *Humjoli* (1970) was directed by Ramanna.

special knack for staging concerts and various entertainment shows for charitable purposes.

One such occasion in particular proved to be quite eventful. Pran's eldest son Arvind recalls what happened:

'Some friends of mine from London approached me to help them to put on a charity event in Ahmedabad. They wanted to set up a college for people from disadvantaged backgrounds. They wanted to raise funds for this purpose. I thought it was a good cause, so I spoke to my father.'

In a letter from London, Arvind's friend, Gautam Appa,[11] elaborated: 'The Lok Jagruti Kendra in Ahmedabad decided to start a new commerce college which would also be used for other socially relevant educational work.... But the task of finding the initial capital outlay of about ten lakh rupees was daunting.... My friends in Ahmedabad had said a film star's cricket match would be ideal. As Arvind and I were working together at the time in the Indian Workers' Association's London branch, I spoke to him and asked about getting his Dad to help raise some money.

'So I set out on a special journey from London with the sole purpose of persuading Pran to help. In the event it took all of four minutes for him to agree!

'Arvind had arranged for me to stay at the Pran family home. I was told that he would be busy shooting all day and would return late, with an early start the next day. All I could do was wait, and keep out of the way of that ferocious dog they had at the time!

'The next day, there was no sign of Pran Uncle till around 3 p.m. Although he looked very tired, he said hello, asked if I needed anything, and retired straight to his room. I had a ticket booked for Ahmedabad that evening.... So with a lot of fear that I might incur his wrath and spoil my only chance to persuade him, I walked up to the door and knocked.

' "Come in", said the dreaded, all-too-familiar voice that sent shivers down the spine. I entered, full of trepidation. Pran Uncle was having his massage. Having made my apologies for barging in, I spoke about the plan for a college and gave him the information sheets I had been clutching all this time. He asked me a few questions. I was too terrified

---

[11] Gautam Appa is a reader in operational research at the London School of Economics.

to tell anything but the truth. His gaze was on me as I talked. He then asked what I wanted from him. I asked him if he could bring a group of film stars to Ahmedabad to play cricket.

' *"It shall be done,"* he said, and putting the papers under his pillow, closed his eyes. I took the cue and left the room.

'It *was* done. And how! The headlines of the Ahmedabad edition of the *Times of India* had this running right across the front page: CINEMA LOVERS' DREAMS COME TRUE!

'Pran had roped in many famous actors and actresses. But he was not satisfied. Then one day, on one of my many visits that year, he greeted me with a big broad smile and announced that Amitabh Bachchan had agreed to come along; it would be his first appearance after his accident.[12] Pran also made sure that everyone who had agreed to come would definitely come. He drafted a letter of agreement and got them all to sign it!

'But getting the stars across to Ahmedabad wasn't easy.'

Arvind continued with the narrative: 'The match was to be held on 13 February 1983...

'An aircraft was chartered to fly to Ahmedabad. Unfortunately, in those days...Indian Airlines would only offer you an Avro, which is a slow propeller plane. And their fleet of Avros was either based at Hyderabad or Bangalore...

'The match was scheduled to start at 11.30 a.m.... Everybody was to meet at the Santa Cruz Airport [in Bombay] at eight in the morning, and the flight would depart by 8.30 or 8.45 a.m. As it happened, on the morning of that eventful day was the only time I have ever seen fog in Bombay. It was severe fog...

'We all managed to get to the airport by about eight. *I must say that Dad's dedication and pulling power was such that everybody was there* – Rishi Kapoor, Amitabh Bachchan, Amjad Khan, Nutan, Aruna Irani, altogether about forty films stars, all going to this match in Ahmedabad! None of

---

[12] Amitabh Bachchan had been seriously injured on the sets of Manmohan Desai's *Coolie* in the early 1980s in Bangalore, and had nearly lost his life. After many months of being laid low, Amitabh was scheduled to make his first public appearance at the Ahmedabad cricket match.

them really knew what college was being instituted – very few of them probably even understood the cause, *but it was because of my father that they were prepared to make the trip.*

'When we arrived at the airport, we found that the aircraft hadn't arrived yet. It hadn't taken off from Hyderabad because they hadn't allowed it to take off until it would be able to land in Bombay.

'And being a slow plane, it would take three hours to reach Bombay. So my father decided that he would not tell the other stars what had happened, because if they came to know, they may quietly disappear! So my father told them that the flight was on its way and it would arrive in an hour's time. He suggested that they go and have breakfast in a restaurant.'

Gautam Appa continued his report about what was simultaneously happening in Ahmedabad at this sudden turn of events. He wrote: 'The tents were filling up by nine o'clock…and rumours were rife that it was all a hoax…. We approached the chief minister and the home minister of Gujarat to come to the pitch and tell the crowd that it was only the weather that had delayed the plane. They refused.

'But fortune works mysteriously. A rival group, bent on damaging our reputation and that of Pran had organized a "Film Star Nite" the same evening, even getting some of the [stars whom] Pran was bringing to stay over for the evening's event. Some of them had arrived the previous night…

'Eventually a group of us went to see Sunil Dutt[13] who had arrived the previous night. Hangers-on would not let us speak to him in confidence. Finally, he agreed to go into the bathroom with the two of us and locked the door! We told him of our predicament. He agreed to come out with other actors who were there. We got him and others in a jeep that drove round and round the stadium as slowly as I could make the driver go.

'That was enough! The crowd had seen some actors and was prepared to wait.'

Arvind went on to say: 'If it were not for Sunil Dutt, there would have been chaos. Eventually, the match started at about 2 p.m. and

---

[13] Producer-director-actor in Hindi films; he was married to Nargis and Sanjay Dutt is his son. He is also in politics.

everybody had a lot of fun. We returned home that evening after nine, dog-tired but satisfied and happy.'

Gautam finished his report by adding: 'Pran asked me to draft a Thank You letter from him to all the stars who had supported the event. I was to mention that *he was overwhelmed by their support in spite of the hard time they had getting to Ahmedabad* and how on top of that they had sung (with Amitabh starting it) "For He's a Jolly Good Fellow!" on the way back.

'That match raised more than four lakh rupees directly and about the same indirectly due to the reputation that the venture gained. The college is established and is now the leading college of commerce in Ahmedabad.

'Were it not for Pran Uncle's help none of this would have ever been accomplished!'

6

Pran has never been one to tolerate autocratic behaviour. At some point of time during the Emergency,[14] when the television network in India (known as Doordarshan or DD) was controlled by the Central Government, an important sports event was being telecast. Half way through the event, DD, in its supreme wisdom decided to discontinue the telecast. Along with numerous sports aficionados, Pran was also watching the proceedings with keen interest. He was rather upset at this high-handedness on the part of the state authorities. He promptly called up Khalid Ansari (of the well-known magazine *Sportsweek* and newspaper *Mid-Day*) and requested him to persuade the DD officials to resume the telecast!

Kapil Dev, the famous cricketer, also feels indebted to Pran. A long time ago when he was an upcoming player, the Cricket Board wanted to send Kapil to the Cricket Academy in Australia to polish up the finer points of his bowling skills. But it was not able to pay the funds for his training.

When Khalid Ansari announced in his magazine and few newspapers that while he would pay for Kapil's air fare to Australia, a sponsor was

---

[14] June 1975 to February 1977.

being sought who could cover his other expenses. Pran *Saab* offered to pay for the entire trip – air fare and everything else too!

Later Kapil revealed: 'Actually, the board had *refused* to pay for the training and that report got published in the newspapers. This came to the notice of Pran *Saab*, an avid cricket lover.

'Pran *Saab* always felt that I had the potential of becoming a good player. So he wrote a nasty letter to the board and said: "If you don't pay for his training, I'll pay it!" Miraculously, the board decided to finance me and I underwent the required training – all thanks to Pran *Saab*!'

Since Pran was extremely knowledgeable about cricket, he always had an opinion to give. As late as 1990, in an interview given to *Sportsworld*, Pran went on record to make a typically 'Pran' statement: 'Ever since international matches started being held at Wankhede Stadium,[15] I stopped watching the five-day test matches.'

When asked by journalist V. Gangadhar as to why he stopped going to see cricket matches, Pran replied: 'You must have been to Brabourne Stadium. Tell me, is there a better venue for international cricket? It is one of the finest grounds in the world. Wankhede Stadium was created to satisfy the ego of certain people. What a waste of money and material!'

Pran's love for sports and sports people earned him many friends in all parts of the world – especially the cricketing world. One of his close friends was Sir Frank Worrell (a former captain of the West indies), who met Pran every time he came to Bombay. The comedian, Om Prakash, used to be with Pran when he would go to meet Sir Frank.

In this context, Pran observed: '[Sir] Frank was a wonderful man. Om and I would go to the airport to receive him and spend time with him. We used to speak with him on politics, entertainment, racism, etc. He was really well informed on so many issues.'

Another of Pran's dear friends was the cricketer Vinoo Mankad, whom Pran called 'the greatest all-rounder we have ever produced'. And about another legend, Pran said: '[Lala] Amarnath was a shrewd captain, and because of him we defeated Pakistan at Bombay in 1952.'

---

[15] The Wankhede Stadium is near Churchgate railway station.

Om Prakash (*second from left*) and Sir Frank Worrell (*third from left*) seen along with Pran and others during the shooting of *Around the World* (1967).

From among the film stars, though, Pran rated Dilip Kumar as 'a good all-rounder', adding that Raj Kapoor and Nargis used to love cricket and that the comedian Gope 'was a good and useful bowler', although he was rather obese.

Pran's love for cricket goes beyond political boundaries. He enjoys watching both Indian and Pakistani cricketers play. With reference to an incident which brought home the fact that political barriers should not interfere with sports, Pran recollected: 'When the Pakistani team under Asif Iqbal was on the verge of winning the test match in Delhi in 1979, some of their board officials announced that gold medals would be given to the team members. Mind you, this was even before the match was actually won.

'That match was the one when Pakistan's Sikandar Bakht took eight wickets, but India was saved by [Dilip] Vengsarkar's century. I prayed and prayed for a draw. I told our board officials that I would present gold medals to our players if they saved the match. They did and got the medals, but I also gave medals to some Pakistani players, including Sikandar Bakht. *I think cricket is a gentleman's game, not a war between our nations.'*

For voicing these not often popular sentiments Pran deserves all praise.

Where once he took along a portable television to the sets of his films, pleasing both his producer (by not bunking work) and his unit (by letting them watch the match on his TV!), Pran, in the golden years of life, now enjoys watching hockey, football and cricket matches on the screen of a large television set placed in his living room.

And yes, he does not like to be disturbed while he is watching his much-loved sports programmes!

PART THREE

FOURTEEN

The Splendid Sixties:
Riding a Tidal Wave of Success

1

By the end of what came to be known as the fabulous decade of the 1950s, Pran had become even more firmly established in Hindi filmdom and had become one of Hindi cinema's most popular villains.

The 1960s would prove even more exciting and fulfilling than the previous decade and some of the films that would come to Pran would present him with opportunities to explore new avenues.

Producers from both the South and Bombay queued up to sign him up for their films. While there were other popular choices for villainous roles, producers used to prefer working with Pran because they knew that he would give tremendous inputs for every role he played, making each one of them memorable in one way or the other.

Frequently, Pran was the natural choice for many of the roles he was assigned because, from early on in his career, he had developed an excellent counterpoint with some of the popular heroes of the time. The almost mathematical precision which these heroes and villains brought to the depiction of their scenes together – different but harmonious, with a thrust forward here or a drawing back there – contributed to the making of some eminently 'watchable' films in the 1960s.

For instance, Pran did three films with Dilip Kumar during the 1960s, four films with Raj Kapoor, one with Dev Anand, four with Ashok Kumar, and a whopping eleven films out of the twenty films in all that he acted with Shammi Kapoor!

Two of the eleven films that Pran did with Shammi Kapoor during the 1960s are worthy of mention: *An Evening in Paris*, a fun-filled musical with Sharmila Tagore as the heroine, and the breezy *Brahmachari*, with the beautiful Rajshree and oomph-girl Mumtaz in the lead. These were among the films Pran did during this decade that were 'big' as far as name, star cast and box-office success were concerned.

Film buffs will still remember the tremendous amount of energy and excitement these hero–villain combinations generated in films such as *Jis Desh Mein Ganga Behti Hai, Jab Pyar Kisise Hota Hai, Do Badan, An Evening in Paris* and *Ram Aur Shyam*, to name just a few.

From *Chhalia* in 1960 to *Aansoo Ban Gaye Phool* in 1969, Pran acted in as many as about sixty films during this decade.

Most of Pran's films in this period were big hits and had him playing the obligatory villain that every Hindi cinema potboiler required. It is to Pran's credit that in spite of the 'formula' films he was mostly being offered at the time, he endeavoured to rise above the mediocrity by, in effect, taking the role he had been given by the horns, subjecting it to the fire of his scrutiny and rendering it malleable, beating it until it assumed a shape that he could work with and make credible.

Due to his immense dedication to his work, it is no wonder that films were pouring into his lap right then.

Among his more important films in the first half of the decade was Subhash Desai's *Chhalia*, which was directed by his brother Manmohan Desai. This film had Raj Kapoor, Nutan and Rehman playing lead roles. Pran played the role of an Afghan bandit who is ostensibly a 'bad', but essentially good man, caring for the heroine and her child who have been abandoned by her family during Partition.

After *Aah*, this was another attempt by Pran to accept a character role, but one more in keeping with his accepted image. That he succeeded in this endeavour is proven by the fact that thousands of fans today remember his performance as being one of his more noteworthy ones.

The film critics too, although being extremely stingy with their words of praise, managed to say this in one of the reviews: 'Pran infuses life and colour into his role.'[1]

Although the Desai brothers, Subhash and Manmohan, had made *Bedard Zamana Kya Jaane* in 1959, it was *Chhalia* that marked the beginning of a warm and close relationship with them. Over the years, Pran would act in many films, first made jointly by them, and then made by Manmohan alone. Moviegoers still remember the success of their films *Bluff Master, Amar Akbar Anthony, Dharam Veer* and *Naseeb*.

Due to that close and friendly relationship, years later, Pran would place his second son, Sunil *Tunni* Sikand, as an assistant to Manmohan. Pran also acted in Ketan Desai's (Manmohan's son) *Toofan* in 1989. However, that film did not do well. After Manmohan's death (in June 1992), Pran felt he had lost a very dear friend and colleague.

2

Raj Kapoor's politically and socially relevant *Jis Desh Mein Ganga Behti Hai* was also released in 1960. The credits showed Radhu Karmakar as director, but it was well known that its real director was Raj Kapoor, directing himself, Padmini, Pran and the whole supporting cast. The next chapter deals with this film and Pran's contribution to that film in greater detail.

Cine Technicians' *Half Ticket* (1962), directed by Kalidas and starring Madhubala, Kishore Kumar and Pran, was such a hit with the audience that years later, on 20 May 2000 to be precise, a fan wrote:

Respected Pran *Saab,*

Namaskar! May I introduce myself as Sucheta Joshee from Pune. I am a scientist working on medicinal and edible mushrooms...I still

---

[1] *Filmfare*, 21 October 1960.

cannot believe I am actually writing a letter to you...I thought of sharing a secret with you.... A day before my XII Std. Board exams, I saw one of your unforgettable movies *Half Ticket* without telling my mother!

It was not a surprise that I kept remembering the scenes between Kishore Kumar and his *chacha* [paternal uncle]... you! While writing my exam paper I goofed up in maths and though I passed with a first class, I did not get a medical seat. So, I ended being a botanist... Sir, had I not laughed at maths (because of you and Kishore*da* in the film); I would have been forced to become a doctor without my heart involved in it. Today, I cannot imagine myself without field trips to various forest patches, endless working in labs, raising plants and mushrooms. All this, thanks to *Half Ticket* (I have seen it twenty-four times)! My husband Pradeep and my eight-year-old son Salil also know the movie and its songs by heart!

Sincere regards,

'Dr (Mrs) Sucheta Joshee, Pune.

No doubt, it has been fans like Sucheta who have provided the best 'reviews' of Pran's work.

Another riveting film in which Pran acted was the suspense thriller *Gumnaam*, released in 1965. Directed by Raja Nawathe, the film had an impressive line-up of baddies, including Madan Puri, Tarun Bose, Hiralal and Manmohan. In the lead were Manoj Kumar and Nanda to provide the mandatory love interest, with Helen and Mehmood in supporting roles.

The film also had some striking and unusual music by Shankar Jaikishan. The title song, '*Gumnaam Hai Koi*...,' succeeded in heightening the mystery behind the identity of the murderer amongst them. And Mehmood's enactment of the song '*Hum Kaale Hain Toh Kya Hua Dilwaale Hain!*' is still remembered by fans. Although, in its review, *Filmfare* awarded the film only two stars, which proclaimed it 'fair', the film had quite a good run and ultimately, that was what mattered to the actors who starred in it, for in film land you are only as good as your last 'hit film.

Another noteworthy film in which Pran acted during the latter half of the 1960s was *Do Badan*, directed by Raj Khosla and starring Manoj Kumar, Asha Parekh and Simi.

In this film, Pran, who played a negative role, plots and machinates until he gets the girl halfway through the film. The tragedy for the character he portrayed is that although he has managed to marry her, he is unable to win her love. Pran beautifully conveyed the frustration and helpless anger he feels at the girl's response to his love.

As Pran observed: 'I had a very good role of a bad man, who is in love with the heroine (played by Asha Parekh*jee*) and he even marries her. He tells her: "I will sleep in the other room until you say you love me." At the same time, he keeps torturing her for her inability to forget the hero and love him instead.'

Although *Do Badan* was a serious film, off-screen, there were some humorous moments during its shooting. Pran recounted: 'Now, there was a scene where I enter the room in anger and I pick up a "whisky" bottle from the table and pour it in the glass, then I open a soda bottle, pour soda in the glass and gulp it down in one swig. Then, I start the dialogue. We had about eleven retakes of it. And I had to drink eleven glasses of soda! When the shot was over, everybody was having a good laugh. When I asked them what was funny, they told me: "You've saved your money today. When you go home this evening, just have whisky. You won't need to add any soda because there is enough soda in your tummy already!" '

Tangentially remembering what had taken place on the sets of the first film he signed in Bombay after Partition, *Ziddi*, in 1948, he referred to a similar predicament in which the actor Nawab found himself, but with more serious consequences:

'In the story a misunderstanding occurs between the hero and the heroine. When their problem is solved, then actor Nawab, who plays the grandfather, has to express his happiness. 'The director told Nawab, "the heroine will bring a glass of milk, you just have to sip it," ' recalled Pran.

'But Nawab said: "No, I'll drink the whole glass." Then the director said: "Okay, it's your choice. But even a sip is enough for the take." Still Nawab kept insisting on drinking the entire glass! The director said, "fine!" and did retakes of the scene with Nawab. Actually, I wonder whether the additional retakes that the director called for were really needed; but Nawab had to drink *five glasses* of milk that day! Because of all that milk, poor Nawab developed a bad case of diarrhoea and the shooting had to be cancelled for next three days!' chuckled Pran.

3

During the 1960s, not only did Pran have plenty of work in Bombay, but also he continued to get a lot of work in the South for the same reasons that have been highlighted earlier: his dedication to his art, his punctuality and his principles. Thus, observing the entire graph of Pran's career, one aspect stands out immediately; that is, several producers and directors repeatedly cast him for their films.

Pramod Chakraborty was one such person.

Chakki-da, as Pramod Chakraborty is affectionately called, first signed Pran for his film *Love in Tokyo* in 1965,[2] and since then, he has tried to have Pran act in all his films. Over the years, his experiences with Pran, the actor, and Pran, the human being, have served to strengthen his determination to do so.

Chakki-da recalled that one of the shooting schedules for the film *Love in Tokyo* was fixed for the holiday period of December 1965–January 1966. By the beginning of December, some two weeks of shooting had already been completed in Bombay. Shooting was on in full swing and, as was his custom, *Chakki-da* intended to carry on shooting through the final day of the old year and on into the first day of the new one. His belief was that this foreboded well for one's career: 'I told this to Pranjee and he agreed. He only asked me: "If I come a bit late on 1 January, will it be okay?"

'How late?' I asked.

Chakki-da exclaimed: 'And I was really surprised when Pranjee said: "I'll come by nine-thirty in the morning on New Year's Day!" '

Chakki-da continued: 'I agreed promptly, thinking "*maybe he is just saying it, and it may not be possible to celebrate New Year's Eve and then report for*

---

[2]   *Love in Tokyo*, released in 1966, co-starred Joy Mukerji and Asha Parekh.

work at nine-thirty in the morning on New Year's Day!" So I went late but Pran*jee* was *already* there, well before me!'

Another very touching gesture that Pran made towards Pramod Chakraborty was with regard to his payments. What happened was this: Although it had been agreed that Pran would get an allowance of money while shooting abroad, *Chakki-da* was unable at that time to honour his commitment. He says: 'Not only did Pran *Saab* refuse to take his money, [but] he also borrowed from a friend, and until we had finished more than sixty per cent of my picture, *he did not take even a single rupee from me!* Whether he remembers all this or not, I do not know, but I will never forget this!

'While we were shooting in Tokyo, we were staying in the same hotel, and every evening he would ask me: "What time do you need me tomorrow?" Do you know, other than staying in the room we had booked, he used to spend his own money eating out and going places. *But whenever needed, he would always be there on the sets, on the dot!'*

During the latter half of the 1960s, three of Pran's films with Dilip Kumar were released in quick succession. The first of these was *Dil Diya Dard Liya*,[3] the second, B. Nagi Reddi's superduper hit, *Ram Aur Shyam*,[4] in which Pran had a major role pitted opposite Dilip Kumar in his first ever double role. Waheeda Rehman and Mumtaz played the two heroines opposite Dilip Kumar and Nirupa Roy played the much-beleaguered wife of Pran. And the third film, *Aadmi*,[5] too, co-starred Waheeda Rehman, and Manoj Kumar.

Waheeda Rehman who was the common factor with Dilip Kumar and Pran in all three films, recalled some features she noticed about Pran: 'We were shooting in Madras for *Dil Diya Dard Liya*. There was only one hotel there, so sometimes we used to have dinner together and chat. Dilip *Saab* would also be there and they would be reciting *sher-o-shairee*.

'I would remain there only up to midnight. Then I would say: "If I don't go now, I might not be able to get up for the shooting the next

---

[3]   A. R. Kardar's *Dil Diya Dard Liya* (1966) co-starred Dilip Kumar, Waheeda Rehman, Rehman and Pran.
[4]   Released in 1967.
[5]   Released in 1968.

morning." I would thus run away, while Pran *Saab*, Dilip *Saab* and others would linger on sometimes till 2 o'clock in the morning! But the next morning at 9 o'clock sharp, Mr Pran would be there in the studio looking as fresh as ever! I used to wonder what his secret was and so I asked him one day: "Pran *Saab*, tell me your secret: how can you have such late nights continuously and still come to the sets on the dot and look so fresh too? Okay, somebody *must* be waking you up but how can you *look* so fresh?"

'He sincerely replied: "I don't know." Since he has excellent memory for his dialogue and *sher-o-shairee*, he gave me the reason for that, saying: "All I can say is that I eat *badam*[6] in the mornings." I said: "Okay, I too will start eating *badam*. I know people say that it improves one's memory but you *still* haven't told me how you can look so fresh?" He said: "*I really don't have an answer for that one because even I don't know it myself.*" That's something really wonderful about him!' Waheeda exclaimed.

The South's connection with Bollywood was still strong in the 1960s and Pran was still getting major assignments from the producers there. Some of his major 'South' successes were *Pooja Ke Phool, Rajkumar, Khandaan, Milan, Sadhu Aur Shaitan, Nanha Farishta* and *Sachhai*. L.V. Prasad's *Milan*, based on the reincarnation theme, which had Sunil Dutt, Nutan and Jamuna in leading roles, was also a B-I-G musical hit. Its songs, composed by Laxmikant Pyarelal with lyrics by Anand Bakshi, contributed in no small measure to its success and are remembered and sung to this day.

A 'South' co-production with Bollywood was A. Bhim Singh and Mehmood Productions' *Sadhu Aur Shaitan*,[7] released in 1968, was another film in which Pran demonstrated his craft. Reviewing it, *Filmfare* stated: 'Pran is lively, agile and colourful – convincing in his last moments when he refuses to hate the man he has swindled. *Could have done the film a bit of good if they'd kept the "shaitan" alive and shot the "sadhu"!*'[8]

---

[6]   Almonds.

[7]   Essentially a South film, *Sadhu Aur Shaitan* was directed by A. Bhim Singh himself, and co-starred Mehmood, Bharathi, Kishore Kumar, Om Prakash, Nazir Hussain, Tuntun and Keshto Mukherji.

[8]   *Shaitan* means Satan and *sadhu* means a holy man or mendicant.

Pran lurks behind a heavy beard, moustache, dark glasses and turban while playing a comedy sequence with Mehmood in *Sadhu Aur Shaitan* (1968).

4

Films were cascading in during the 1960s. Most producers offered him only the usual villainous roles. But there was clearly a limit to how much he could do to make each 'black' character 'grey'. Pran now wanted to break free from the 'all-black' villainy.

Three films would be offered to him during the 1960s, which would seek to portray the 'villain' in a new light. One of them was a historical subject. The other was based on a slogan[9] propounded by the then prime minister, Lal Bahadur Shastri, and the third was a commercial film – but it was a potboiler with a difference.

Shaheed (1965), was based on the life of Bhagat Singh, martyr to the cause of Indian independence. This film proved to be a turning point of sorts for Pran, who played a character far different to what he had ever played before, making a lot of people sit up and take notice of him as a multidimensional actor.[10]

---

9   The slogan was: '*Jai Jawan, Jai Kisan*'.
10   The film starred Manoj Kumar, Nirupa Roy, Kamini Kaushal, Prem Chopra, Manmohan and Sudhir.

The other important milestone in Pran's career came through the film titled *Upkar*.[11] This was one of the meatiest roles of his life and he did full justice to it.

And the third film that sought to portray Pran in different light was B. Nagi Reddi's film *Nanha Farishta*. Pran, Ajit and Anwar Hussain, as the three kidnappers with hearts of gold, carried the film on their shoulders.

5

Since Pran was one of the first actors from Hindi filmdom to go South, he was able to draw many other artistes to follow suit. While there, he formed many strong professional relationships. One such was with B. Nagi Reddi, the owner of Vijaya International.

Remembering the South Indian film and studio owner magnate who, although superrich, was a cultured and well-mannered man, Pran says fondly: 'B. Nagi Reddi was a very fine gentleman. People used to love and respect him from the heart. He never discriminated [against] anybody.'

Having tasted success with *Ram Aur Shyam*, B. Nagi Reddi decided to make another Hindi film, titled *Nanha Farishta* (1969),[12] this time with Pran in the lead. He assigned its direction to a famous director from Madras itself, T. Prakash Rao, who was going to direct a Hindi film for the first time. This film tackled a touching emotional theme of a little child who has been kidnapped by three hardened criminals and how her innocence and love compel them to change. The three cold-blooded murderers-cum-kidnappers, played by Anwar Hussain, one-time leading man, Ajit, and Pran, gradually undergo a transfomation when they find their emotions stirred by the innocence, the laughter and the tears of the little girl. Padmini, as the child's *ayah*[13] played her role ably. Pran's role was given equal importance to Padmini's role in the film, even though she was a top-level actress then.

---

[11] Produced and directed by Manoj Kumar, *Upkar* (1967) also starred Manoj Kumar, Asha Parekh, Kamini Kaushal, Prem Chopra and Pran.

[12] *Nanha Farishta* had Baby Rani, Pran, Ajit, Padmini, Anwar Hussain, Balraj Sahni and Johnny Walker sharing acting honours. The film was based on an early 1930s' film *We Are No Angels*. It was remade two decades later in 1955, starring Humphrey Bogart, Peter Ustinov, Aldo Ray, Basil Rathbone and other big stars.

[13] An *ayah* is a nanny.

Baby Rani clinging on to Pran in *Nanha Farishta*. The other two 'villains' are Ajit and Anwar Hussain.

In its review of *Nanha Farishta*, *Star & Style* simply said: 'Pran, of course, dominates the scene.'[14] But just after the completion of the film, Pran himself showered lavish praise on what he described as 'the little girl's heart-warming performance'. He said: '*Nanha Farishta* was a very beautiful film.' The beauty of the film lay in the simplicity of its story, the sincerity of its makers as well as the dedication of the performers. The song, '*Bachche Mein Hai Bhagwan,*' lip-synched by Pran, Ajit and Anwar Hussain and picturized on the little girl, her *ayah*, and the three men was one of the highlights of the movie. The feel-good factor with which viewers went home was what made the film a superhit and unforgettable as well.

6

During the 1960s, the trend of presenting the comic-villain had begun. By relieving the all-black picture of badness with the lighter shades of comedy, directors were able to work on a better etched out comedy track, and by using 'pure' comedians like Agha, Mehmood, Asit Sen, Keshto Mukherji, Tuntun, Shammi and Shubha Khote, they could fill any

---

[14] 12 December 1969.

lacunae there was in the 'laughter' department. And laughter was certainly needed to lighten the sombre mood that some 'weepy' subjects produced. Pran himself says that with *Kashmir Ki Kali,* he had started the trend of adding the comic dimension to his acting. This trend soon caught the attention of his producers in the South.

The films that they offered Pran were by and large of the 'family-social' variety and there was a tendency to make these as melodramatic as possible. In an attempt to serve up something for everyone, they usually signed up a fairly large star cast with the mandatory villain and vamp and one or more comedians. This now meant that if each person had to hold his or her own in the film, he or she would have to go along with the flow and *overact* rather than underplay his or her part. The villain, vamp and comedians in the film would also have to significantly turn up their volume if they were to be seen and heard in the three-hour potboiler.

The trend, which had begun to dictate that the villain's role have shades of comedy added to it, got lost in translation, so to speak. The end result was that instead of the portrayal being subtle, the villain's role became loud and caricaturized.

In spite of the obvious lacunae in the script with regard to the development of the characters he had to play, Pran brought his already amply proven mastery of screen histrionics to bear. He used to good effect his ability to bring into his role something different, something new – something that would not only fall in line with the trend, but would also ensure that each of his roles would be significantly different from the ones that went before it. That in itself testifies to Pran's ability as an actor – to be able to do something different in every role, and that too, in spite of the constraints popular Indian cinema laid and continues to lay upon actors.

Take for example, his 1965 starrer *Khandaan.*

For a second time in his career, Pran acted in a superhit film entitled *Khandaan.* Whereas in the earlier Pancholi Pictures' superhit of 1942, directed by Syed Shaukat Hussein Rizvi, Pran had played the hero opposite the now-legendary singer-actress, Noorjehan, in this version directed by hit director A. Bhim Singh, Pran played the villain to hero Sunil Dutt and heroine Nutan. The only difference was that with the first *Khandaan* Pran had newly embarked on his career as an actor, but by the second one, Pran had already scaled the heights as a STAR!

On re-viewing the second *Khandaan* in later years, that film registers as a loud, South-Indian type film. The lead stars were as usual in top form. Interest, however, was on Pran, and it was delightful to see him prove yet again that *here was a thinking actor, a performer who had applied his brains to understand and perfect the niceties and subtleties of a screen characterization, no matter how buffoonish he had to make it for the delight of the multimillions of Hindi cinema's groundlings.*

Critics watching him 'comedify' his villainy with buffoonery in *Khandaan* observed the nervous double twitch, which he used to jerk across one cheek, and how naturally the frequent twitches occurred from scene to scene. One can do no better than to point out that the *Filmfare* reviewer also considered his performance in *Khandaan* important enough to begin the review with this long dissertation:

'The "Gentleman Villain" was never less a gentleman than in *Khandaan*. Come to think of it he was never less a villain. From the Hitler hair-do to badly fitting plus-fours,[15] Pran is a villain on his day off, and apparently enjoying the experience. Had his wardrobe been less outlandish, the role less lopsided, the change would have been welcome: Naurangi Lal (Pran) is supercilious, and there is a certain malicious wit in the way he wrinkles his nose at the world.

'When it comes to villainy, South Indian films have taken over where Bombay left off.... The idea seems to be to make the villain as ludicrous and as artificial as possible, so even the most thick-skulled will not be left in doubt about the nature of the role.'

That was in 1965. In the next five years, Pran was to give much more evidence of his mastery over the histrionic medium. Discerning cinemagoers could observe how well Pran had come to polish two important factors in his process of preparation.

One: knowing that cinema is primarily a visual medium, he knew that 'the look' of the character was of immediate and vital importance to the

---

[15] A suit having long, wide men's knickerbockers, formerly worn while playing games such as golf. They were so called because the overhang at the knee requires an extra four inches of material.

cinemagoer. He had, therefore, devoted a great deal of thought to study everything that would make one particular character stand out distinctly from the rest of the cast.

Two: by adding the 'human' element to all his characterizations, each character that Pran created on screen was not just three-dimensional, but so real that he could as well step out from the screen and into the audience.

Other than Raj Kapoor's *Jis Desh Mein Ganga Behti Hai*, two other films of Pran's – *Shaheed* and *Upkar*, both with Manoj Kumar – contributed greatly to his continuing ride on the highest waves of the high tide of the 1960s. The next few chapters will discuss these three films vis-à-vis Pran and show how they were major factors in the furtherance of his career.

FIFTEEN

Jis Desh Mein Ganga Behti Hai: Understanding Raaka

1

Unlike other film makers who tend to lay the blame for the failure of their films at others' doors, Raj Kapoor squarely took responsibility for the failure of his films. So, after *Aah*, instead of vowing not to cast Pran, or any of the other actors in his cast, in his films ever again, Raj Kapoor cast Pran again, first in a bit role in *Jagte Raho*, and then offered him another role.

A role that was more consonant with his then popular image.

Pran himself declared: 'One of my most challenging and unforgettable roles is the one I got in *Jis Desh Mein Ganga Behti Hai*...'

The unusual storyline had made some people connected with the project think that *Jis Desh Mein Ganga Behti Hai* could essentially be shot either as a documentary or not at all! In fact, when Raj Kapoor sent Arjun Dev Rashk to narrate the story to the music directors Shankar and Jaikishan, Shankar felt it was not fit to be made into a commercial film, and said so! He reportedly grumbled: 'This is a story of ravines and dacoits...where is the scope for music in such a subject?'

How Raj Kapoor invited them over to hear a musical narration of the subject, and how he got Shankar and Jaikishan to give inspiring and emotionally moving music for the film, is another interesting story but doesn't fit in here.

However, this episode made it quite clear to Raj Kapoor that the story he was going to present on celluloid was going to be a real cinematic challenge to narrate. To meet that challenge, he would have to choose his actors carefully.

Hence, for the most dynamic role of the film, next to Raj's own, he chose to approach Pran. Raj Kapoor knew well that professional actors like Pran were impeccable and flawless in what they did because of the careful thought process that governed their meticulous preparation for a role. By offering Pran the unforgettable part of Raaka in his film, Raj Kapoor was giving Pran his vote of confidence even before any portion of the film was shot.[1]

And Pran did not fail him.

2

Raj Kapoor's style of working was unusual, to say the least. Most of Raj's work would start only very late in the afternoon and extend late into the night. Frequently, he worked on his script into the early hours of the following morning, using his close associates as sounding boards for his own creativity. Those brainstorming sessions over whisky and food resulted in some of the most exciting, moving and entertaining moments ever to be seen on the big screen.

Pran remembers that Raj Kapoor also worked very hard with Shankar and Jaikishan in experimenting with a new aspect of film music. The score of one entire musical sequence in the film featured a musical instrument called the *duff*, a sort of tambourine. In the first portion of that sequence, the composition expresses the girl's anger and gradually

---

[1] The film was released in 1960.

moves on to express the pangs of love. Pran felt that Shankar Jaikishan's compositions replaced spoken dialogues in some of the scenes.

It was a known fact that Raj Kapoor stimulated his creative team and artistes to produce some of their most inspired work for his films. So when an actor, who had already established a histrionic pattern of thinking out his roles and working out his own get-ups and the 'look' of his character, worked with Raj Kapoor, one could expect something really phenomenal!

Pran had already done the initial spadework in consultation with Raj Kapoor even before shooting began. Then just before the actual shooting started, Raj Kapoor told him: 'Pran, you are famous because of your mannerisms. So think of something for my film also. You know the story, your dialogue and your role. Think of something effective.'

Every actor worth his salt has his own methods and techniques of preparing a role and preparing *for* a role. And each one of them has learnt through an arduous process of trial and error and by keeping *his inner ear* and his instincts attuned to the voices which speak to all creative persons from within.

Pran ruminated over how this tuning in to one's instincts helped him develop his character in the film: 'When Raj Kapoor narrated the story of this film to me and asked me to play the role of the dacoit Raaka, I became extremely eager to do the role. From that moment on, I thought only of my role – and what my "look", my moustache, wig and costume would be. That's because Raj Kapoor had left the choice of those things to me. After wracking my brains for quite some time, I was still finding it difficult to figure out how I would portray this character.

'Eventually, one day an English "daily" came to my rescue. There was a news item about the capture of a gang of dacoits and they had published a photograph of one of them. If that particular dacoit had not been caught, details about him and his capture would not have been known. It turned out that he was the most cruel dacoit of his gang. When he was killed in the police encounter, his body was found riddled with twenty-one bullets! Looking at his picture, I felt: *"This* is Raaka"!

'I cut out a clipping and showed it to Raj Kapoor who agreed with me. We made the wig and moustache according to the photo. When I appeared before Raj Kapoor in full costume, make-up, wig and moustache, he was very happy and said: "You are looking just like a dacoit, totally dangerous."'

Pran had created a striking, terrifying 'look' for his character. But more would be needed to make the character come to life. He highlights how he achieved this objective:

'I was a dacoit in that film, and I literally slept with that character, dreaming about him, trying to *see* him in the inner being of my mind and heart. I tried to understand the psychology of the man, and tried to probe his secret fears.

'And it came to me one night. I was in deep sleep, and it was a dream that woke me up with a start, and I sat up, rubbing a finger across the throat as though I was suffocating.

'I realized that in the subconscious mind of every dacoit is a deep-rooted fear with which he lives that one day he will be caught and hung for his crimes, or that one day an enemy may slit his throat.

'Right then I knew that I had to use this mannerism for Raj Kapoor's film. And on the very first day of the shooting of *Jis Desh*...when I used it, everyone on the sets were deeply impressed and congratulated me.

'What happened was this: for this particular scene in which I featured, Raj *Saab* was behind the camera [directing the others]. So he couldn't quite see what I was doing. So, after the shot he asked me what I had been doing with my hand.

'I said: "I was constantly running my finger around my neck inside my collar, moving my finger from the top to the bottom of my neck – like this" – and I demonstrated the action to him.

'For some moments Raj *Saab* was quiet. Then it struck him! He said it was superb.

'I felt I should explain how I thought up this mannerism. I told him that how I had been trying to *see* him as a person rather than a character in a film and had tried to think as he would. I also told him how, waking up with a start from a dream one night, I found myself rubbing my fingers across my throat because I felt I was suffocating. I then decided that this gesture would convey what every dacoit must know – that justice or nemesis will eventually catch up with him.

'Raj *Saab* was an intelligent man, he appreciated that I had applied some constructive thinking to my role. I really enjoyed working with him.'

3

Referring to Raj Kapoor, on another occasion, Pran waxed eloquent: 'One of the biggest human beings India ever produced was Raj Kapoor. He was a great director, a big producer. Whenever he used to extract work from people for his films, he used to give them so much love and respect. He knew how to treat his actors well.'

Speaking about his own experience while working with Raj Kapoor in *Jis Desh Mein Ganga Behti Hai*, Pran disclosed:

'The song sequence of *"Hum Bhi Hain, Tum Bhi Ho, Dono Hain Aamne-saamne"* was in progress.

Pran and Chanchal (Madhubala's sister) in a scene from
Jis Desh Mein Ganga Behti Hai.

'Towards the end of the first day of shooting, at around 9 p.m. Raj *Saab* came to me and said: "You drink daily and I know it's time for your drink."

'But I said: "I don't drink with my make-up on."

'He replied: "I was worried that if you drink with make-up on, then I too may have to do the same — which you know I never do. So now, we'll drink together after the shooting."

'After the shooting was over, we freshened up, had drinks, had our food and it was about 3 a.m. by that time. He asked me then: "How are you going home?"

'I said: "I have my vehicle."

'He asked: "Do you have a driver?"

'I said: "No."

'He then said: "Then you won't drive and go. Our company's vehicle will drop you."

'I said: "It's okay that your company's vehicle will drop me, but my vehicle will remain here. Then how will I come to the shooting on time tomorrow?"

'He said: "Don't worry about that. You'll have your vehicle at your door by 9 a.m. tomorrow morning."

'In this way, all the days that we were shooting, his vehicle used to drop me home at night and then his driver would bring my vehicle back to my place in the morning. He was such a great man!'

4

Ironically, the gesture to which Pran had given so much thought and which had actually brought Raaka to life was a result of such perceptive reasoning (which is precisely why it was so natural) that, although some journalists who had been shown the film had *observed* the action, *they had completely failed to understand its significance!*

Pran recalled how those journalists were effusive in their praise for his performance, but clueless about its significance: 'They said: "As the dacoit Raaka in *Jis Desh*… your mannerism of constantly moving a finger from under one ear across your neck right around the throat to the other ear was superb."

'So I asked them: "Did you get the meaning behind that mannerism?" They looked a little bewildered and asked: "It was just a habit, wasn't it?"

'"No," I said. "It wasn't '*just a habit*'. One does not give the mannerisms of royalty to a sweeper – and vice versa!"

'I then went on to tell them the significance of the mannerism and how it was not an unconscious habit but a well-thought out action based on the background of the character I was playing in the film!'

Pran as he appeared in *Rehana* (1946). ▶

◀ Pran exhibiting a
brooding, baleful expression.

◄ Pran played a powerful role
in *Aansoo Ban Gaye Phool* (1969).

The 'hunted' look: ▶
Pran in *Nanha Farishta* (1969).

Thus, the primary way in which Pran approached the preparation of any role was to first analyse the motivations of the character, his *raison d'être* and his manner of thinking. Which is why, Pran was able to make an astute observation about many of his roles, but especially about his role as Raaka:

'In Hindi films, the villain is supposed to be bad, but I don't think all my roles have been "bad", even when I was playing the villain. Take Raaka in *Jis Desh....* He torched villages and shot people, but in the end, he laid down his weapons for the girl he loved and lost. I would term him as one of the most unforgettable lovers in the world, not a villain.'

5

Thus, aided by competent actors and technicians, Raj Kapoor's vision had transformed a 'dry' subject of the laying down of arms by the dacoits of the Chambal (an area spread over parts of Uttar Pradesh and Madhya Pradesh) into an emotional drama with many undercurrents, which even today, leaves audiences not just stimulated but also entertained.

Raj Kapoor took his film, his stars and technicians with him to different centres in India to promote *Jis Desh Mein Ganga Behti Hai*. Since Pran was one of the central characters of the film, he too accompanied Raj on this promotional tour.

Before that, however, a special premiere of this film was held in Calcutta, in January 1961. The chief guest at the premiere was Padmaja Naidu, the governor of West Bengal.

Dr B. C. Roy, the chief minister, also graced the occasion and enjoyed seeing the film in the company of Raj Kapoor, Padmini, Pran, music directors Shankar and Jaikishan and writer Arjun Dev Rashk.

During the interval, Raj Kapoor made his bow to the audience from the stage. Introducing himself, he started: 'Mera naam...'[2] But before he could finish the sentence the whole house in one voice completed it for him, yelling 'Raju!' – the name of the character he portrays in the film.

When Padmini expressed her inability to address the gathering, the fans yelled out to her saying: 'No speech! Just say "Oi—Oi—Oi" ' (the

---

[2]   My name is...

expression with which her song-and-dance number in the film begins).

And Pran still remembers how the entire auditorium cheered when veteran Bengali actor Pahari Sanyal went up to him and said: 'Although I have seen you on the screen, I do not know you personally, but I must congratulate you on your wonderful performance in this film.'

As a matter of fact, the *Filmfare* reviewer echoed Pahari Sanyal's sentiments: 'Pran looks every bit a fierce criminal. *His is an unforgettable performance.*'

It is such moments and such words that remain as treasured memories in an actor's life.

Pran himself considers Raj Kapoor's *Jis Desh...* among his exceptional films. And in terms of the banner, his role and his 'look' in the film, all these factors succeeded in pushing up Pran's market value considerably.

SIXTEEN

Shaheed: A Landmark Film

1

It had struck!

Struck sometime during the 1950s.

It was an inner restlessness, and it had begun to grow. His urge to do something different in every role, and the upper limit he had reached in the 'bad-man' genre, now impelled Pran to look for something that would challenge his creativity. It prompted him to seek a new outlet to express himself.

This yearning took on a definite shape and slowly metamorphosed into a new career path when he signed a few films that would present him in a very different light with reference to what he had done so far.

One of those films was *Shaheed.*[1]

'I used to enjoy his good performances as a villain, but when he did this role of a hard-core criminal, I knew that *this* was a turning point in

---

[1] A martyr.

his career,' Sunil, Pran's younger son, observed about his father's character as Kehar Singh in *Shaheed*.

'His performance in *Shaheed* was excellent! Just five minutes, but what a performance!' exclaimed businessman-producer Ramesh Khosla, a friend of Pran.

The journey to reach this point of unanimous personal and public acclaim had not been easy. For *Shaheed*, it had begun virtually from scratch.

Consider the disincentives to this film being made. For a start, two films about Bhagat Singh[2] made in the then recent past had not done well at the box office. The first, released in 1952, starred Prem Adib in the role of the martyr. Then in 1963 came *Shaheed Bhagat Singh*, which starred Shammi Kapoor in the title role. Moreover, there was a dearth of informative material about Bhagat Singh. Available information actually filled just a few paragraphs in the history books of that time!

So when one-time publicist-turned-producer Kewal P. Kashyap approached Pran to play the role of a condemned prisoner in his film *Shaheed*, he naturally felt quite hesitant. 'In fact,' Pran admitted, 'I initially made a negative response to his offer. Firstly, there were barely six scenes for me in the film and, secondly, the money offered was negligible.'

It must be emphasized here that Pran was then riding the crest of the high tide of success. It must have initially seemed foolish to accept a film in which his role would consist of a mere handful of scenes. Besides, the obvious time to make hay is when the sun shines. Yes, Pran definitely had had second thoughts about his doing this film. Second thoughts, since earlier he had shown interest in this very role.[3]

Kewal Kashyap and Manoj Kumar, childhood friends who were collaborating on this project, had reached a very crucial juncture in their lives. Manoj, who was already tasting success as a popular hero, was now

---

[2]   A young freedom fighter, born in 1907, and executed on 23 March 1931 for his role in India's freedom struggle against British rule.

[3]   Apparently, while on the sets of *Do Badan*, Pran overheard Manoj Kumar narrating portions of the script of *Shaheed* to Raj Khosla and enquired about Kehar Singh's role. When told that the project was not ready, he asked Manoj to send Kewal Kashyap to him when it was ready. Eventually, *Shaheed* was released in 1965, a year before *Do Badan*.

itching to also get involved with script-writing and direction, while his dear friend, Kewal, wanted to move away from the soul-killing profession of film publicity and get more involved with producing films. Together, they had decided to make *Shaheed*. They would need 'big names' for their first project.

Since Pran had already shown interest in this role, what better course of action could they have adopted than to approach him? But when it was obvious that Pran had now become reluctant to do the role, it became a do-or-die situation for them, one where they had to tread carefully.

A few days after the meeting with Kewal Kashyap, Pran met Manoj Kumar on the sets of another film and Manoj asked him why he had refused the role. Pran bluntly told him it was 'bad pay' – the money wasn't good enough. Whereupon Manoj told Pran: 'I have written the story and that character with you in mind. I have worked with you in *Do Badan*[4] and I know what you are capable of. You *have* to do that role. That character has no mother, no father or brother or sister. It is a lone character in jail and who is hanged in the end. If you don't do it I'll write the character out of the script. It won't be a hassle because he is not a part of the story. But if you do it, and I *know* only *you* can play the role, then I can assure you that it will leave a lasting impression.'

At the outset itself, Manoj had made it very clear to Pran that his role was *a small but powerful one*. Pran not only liked his frankness, he was also touched by the faith Manoj had in his abilities. 'I was quite taken aback,' Pran revealed, 'especially when he said that if I refused this role he would eliminate the character altogether from the film!'

Evidently, after this meeting, Pran must have pondered a good deal over what Manoj Kumar had said, for when Kewal Kashyap, at Manoj Kumar's insistence, rather apprehensively approached Pran again, it appears that the actor-villain had already decided in their favour.

'They felt that only I could do justice to that role and so,' Pran went on to say, 'despite my initial reluctance, I agreed – and I'm glad I did! My role in *Shaheed* was that of Kehar Singh *Daku*,[5] who is incarcerated

---

[4] Released in 1966.
[5] A dacoit.

along with the *satyagrahis*[6] and who eventually experiences a change of heart. I also felt that the role was a very effective one. I think that by telling me he would remove Kehar Singh's role from the script if I did not agree to play it was the height of trust and faith which Manoj Kumar placed in me. That is why I agreed to play Kehar Singh's role in *Shaheed*.... So many years have passed since then but even today, when I am asked about my favourite roles, I flashback to the role of Kehar Singh in *Shaheed*. That film will always be special to me.'

Let us go back a little and take the long, wide-angle view of the making of *Shaheed* and how the project had narrowed unerringly to the point of getting Pran into the film and to the actual making of the film.

2

Many years ago, in Delhi, some sixth standard schoolboys staged a play, complete with bed sheets for curtains and camp cots for seats. The play was 'Bhagat Singh' and in the title role was cast a young lad full of vigour and confidence – that is, until the curtain went up!

According to him, after one look at the intimidating audience, the young 'martyr' bolted! But acting was in his blood and the young fellow continued to aspire to an acting career even when his classmates jeered at him for that initial and unforgettable disaster!

However, there was in that group of schoolboys, a youngster who had a flair for journalism. The two young men became firm friends and decided some years later to migrate to Bombay, to seek both fame and fortune in the movie industry.

The boy who loved acting and who dreamt of portraying Bhagat Singh one day, somehow, seemed to be stuck behind the camera as he had become a production assistant. The other one found it easier to become a publicity man for some important film stars.

Even though they didn't know it then, both Manoj Kumar and Kewal Kashyap were laying the foundation for a great project which was later to bring them undreamt-of acclaim and respect. Manoj, who had, by the

---

6   People who adopted the method of 'passive resistance' in opposing the British during the struggle for freedom.

early 1960s, started acting in 'bit' roles, soon graduated to hero level. Yet he and Kewal continued to be close to each other. Inevitably, the time came when they decided that Kewal should produce a film and that Manoj would star in it.

'What subject should I take?' Kewal asked.

'Bhagat Singh, of course,' Manoj promptly replied.

Manoj himself wrote the script. A tremendous amount of research and expense was involved. Manoj and Kewal followed up every lead and drank in every bit of information about Bhagat Singh. If they heard of a man in some remote place with whom Bhagat Singh had stayed even for a few days, they would rush up there to gather more material. Manoj pored endlessly over old newspapers, magazines, books, letters and manuscripts. Every time he got paid for his work in other films, he would invest the money into the making of their film on Bhagat Singh. All this was done while Manoj was working as a hero and Kewal as a publicist.

For his part, Kewal Kashyap withdrew all his assets from the bank, sold his Fiat car and sank all his money into the picture. Several times Manoj and Kewal met and conferred with the martyr's brother and mother (she was an active woman then, even at the age of eighty-one), who supplied them plenty of material with which to work.

The two never-say-die researchers unearthed little-known facts about this great hero of Indian history. For instance, that Bhagat was actually named Bhagya, for the day Bhagat Singh was born, his uncle – also a great freedom fighter – and his brother were released from jail. His grandfather thought that the newborn was *lucky* and so named him Bhagya. Another touching detail was also divulged: the girl who was to have married Bhagat Singh later married another man through circumstances beyond her control. The day Bhagat Singh went to the gallows, on 23 March 1931, her husband suddenly expired. Tearfully, she told the martyr's mother: 'If it was fated that I become a widow, I would rather have been Bhagat Singh's widow.' All that research did not go into the script, but it did help to make *Shaheed* a memorable movie.

After they had made three reels of the film on a shoestring budget, their hopes were raised when a certain distributor asked to see what they had shot – only to be dashed when he gave his verdict. He said: 'You will never be able to complete this film; if you complete it, you won't

be able to sell it; if you manage to sell it, it won't run; and if it runs –
I'll change my name!'

3

Shaheed, which was shot on location in Ludhiana jail, had Pran as its most
violent prisoner wreaking havoc while awaiting his turn to go to the
gallows.

'Madan Puri[7] played the jailor while Anwar Hussain[8] was a fellow-
prisoner in the film. Since it was shot in the Ludhiana jail, several real
prisoners also featured in the film,' revealed Manoj Kumar.

'That's true,' interjected Pran, 'we had not used a *filmi* jail constructed
inside the studio, as is done in most movies. We had shot inside a real
jail. So it was amusing to read one of the critics write that the jail scenes
did not look convincing enough because the sets were not right! The
critic was obviously unaware of what the inside of a real jail looked like!'

Talking about his role, Pran amplified: 'Kehar Singh is a dangerous
man. He has killed, looted, plundered and is waiting to be hanged. He
even beats up the jailor himself. But at heart he is a guileless man. He
does not understand the freedom fighters – that people can kill each
other for their motherland too! Initially, he hates all the *naare-bazee*
(sloganeering) but later undergoes a transformation, wondering how
there can be the same kind of punishment for him, a dacoit, as well as
for the son of Bharatmata[9] – Shaheed Bhagat Singh.'

'The remarkable thing in the film was that throughout the film Kehar
Singh does not get to meet Bhagat Singh. Now when he is about to be
hanged, his last wish is to meet Bhagat Singh, who is also on death row.
With his hands tied up behind his back, he begins the walk towards the
hangman's noose,' recounted Pran, reviewing the scene in his mind's eye.
'As he passes by, Kehar Singh says: *"Bhagat Singh, pehli aur aakhri baar Sat-
Sri-Akaal!"*[10] Bhagat says: "Kehar Singh?" He says: "Yes, it's me. I am a

---

7   Madan Puri began as a villain but later switched over to playing character roles.
8   Nargis' brother, he also suffered being typecast as a 'villain'.
9   Mother India.
10 Loosely translated, *Sat-Sri-Akaal* means 'May Truth Triumph Forever!' Sikhs use this
    term is used as a greeting. The dialogue means: 'Bhagat Singh, for the first and last
    time, greetings!'

bad man. So I should be punished for my acts, but why does the world treat you and me in the same way?" I am going up and I'll ask God: "What is this happening in the world created by you that Bhagat Singh and Kehar Singh are treated as one?"

'"Will you do me one favour? I have never in all my life shaken hands with a *nek aadmi*.[11] Will you shake hands with me?" Both condemned men shake hands back to back, because their hands are tied. Then he says: "Hold it tight." When the time inevitably comes for them to part, Kehar Singh comes out to where the scaffold is and tells the character played by Anwar Hussain to take care of his "children", meaning Bhagat Singh and his companions.'

Cinemagoers will recall that scene which bought a lump to many a throat and made tears roll down many a cheek. The film must have had a tremendous impact on Pran himself, because even after the passing of so many decades since *Shaheed* was made, he is able to recall every shot, every dialogue and every expression in those scenes. Even today, Pran expresses admiration for the dialogue Manoj Kumar penned for the film and for visualizing a character like Kehar Singh.

For his part, Manoj Kumar says: 'I am grateful to him for accepting the role in *Shaheed*, that too for a meagre remuneration. And the *way* he performed in it! He put in his best effort! From that day on, I have been won over by him.'

4

The *Shaheed* team proved all the pessimists wrong. Not only did they complete the film, but they also sold it and released it. And how!

Shaheed hit the screen in 1965 at the same time when the Indo–Pakistan war was being fought. India's first prime minister, Jawaharlal Nehru, had already blessed *Shaheed* when it was still in the project stage. Then, at its New Delhi premiere, the new prime minister of India, Lal Bahadur Shastri, was the chief guest.

Shastri, in his gentle way, asked the film makers if it would not be against the fitness of things for him to inaugurate a film at a crucial time like that.

---

[11] Righteous man.

Manoj Kumar and Kewal Kashyap begged him to come for just fifteen minutes and decide for himself. Not only did the prime minister come, but also he stayed on for the entire three hours and made an inspired speech commending the film!

Reminiscing about this episode, Manoj said: 'War had broken out and patriotic fervour in our country was at its peak. That helped *Shaheed* because the film was about patriotism and it went on to become a big hit.'

Thereafter, in every state where the film was to be shown, the chief minister or some important state minister inaugurated its release.

The young film makers had been confident that this picture would bring them credit, but the outcome went beyond their wildest expectations!

The film went on to do great box-office business wherever it was released. Then, it won three major state awards – the All-India Certificate of Merit for the Best Story, the President's Silver Medal for the Best Hindi Film of 1965 and a cash prize of Rs 20,000 for the Best Film on National Unity and Emotional Integration. Additionally, at all centres, *Shaheed* got an exemption from the heavy entertainment tax that is imposed on Indian films! And as final proof of its worth, it was selected to be screened at film festivals abroad.

Shaheed had come full circle. The acclaim it won when the film was presented the three awards mentioned above by the prime minister in Delhi finally silenced all the prophets of doom. However, the best award of all was the one the film makers got in Ludhiana – when Bhagat Singh's old mother sat through the entire film, crying all the way, remembering the all-too-short life of her son, Bhagya, grateful for this tribute to his memory.

What happened to the distributor who was sure that *Shaheed* would be a dead loss if it ever got completed and released? No one knows if he actually changed his name, but he must certainly have had to eat his words, not to mention how much he must have wept for all the money he would otherwise have made!

5

Already a 'top' star by 1965, Manoj gained a new dimension with this film. Although the direction of this film was credited to S. Ram Sharma, everybody knew that Manoj Kumar had cut his directorial teeth on *Shaheed*. Erstwhile publicist Kewal Kashyap became an important member of the ranks of producers. But both of them knew they could not have done it alone. The entire unit of *Shaheed*, but especially Pran, for whom the film proved to be one of the most memorable of his career, shared the kudos that the film earned.

After talking about the performances given by the rest of the cast, the *Filmfare* reviewer, headlining *Shaheed* as 'A MOMENT REBORN' went on to say: '*...but it is Pran who dominates the latter part of the film from his whirlwind entry as the berserk convict through the tragi-comic transformation and his final scene when he says goodbye to the condemned man — brilliant all the way.*'[12]

Pran acknowledged that he adopted an unconventional approach for this role: 'In Manoj Kumar's *Shaheed*, I played a dacoit Kehar Singh without a beard or a moustache...I even *performed* Kehar Singh's role differently. In an era where shouting was the standard way a fiery character delivered his dialogues, I decided to speak differently. I had seen an unusual character so I decided to imitate him...Kehar Singh became very popular and even today, whenever *Shaheed* has a rerun, my role is talked about.'

Kamini Kaushal, who played the role of Bhagat Singh's mother in the film, had worked in a number of films earlier with Pran. Commenting on Pran's work in *Shaheed*, Kamini Kaushal recently said: 'He created such an impact. His character in the film is that of a rough-and-ready guy who is about to be executed. During the period of his incarceration, Bhagat Singh and his associates are lodged in the same prison. How he transforms into an admirer of Bhagat Singh is a real treat to watch. Such a lovely graph to portray and he did it so well. And Pran gives his own little twists, little nuances to the character.

'I'm sure he must think about how he wants to play a character. It is not like playing a straightforward, linear role with stock emotions. It is playing a definite character. You have to put in a lot of extra effort. Your gestures, your emotions, the character which you want to create for your image, all that is important. And then, to hold on to that image right through the film, *that* is very important. And this is exactly what Pran achieved in his role.'

---

[12] 10 June 1966.

Prem Chopra (then a rising actor and later villain), who played the role of Sukhdev, one of Bhagat Singh's associates, also spoke about *Shaheed* and Pran's work in it: 'Pran *Saab* had a very small but dramatic role in it. Manoj Kumar, the actor who played Rajguru's role and I were the heroes of the film. But Pran *Saab*? He was its *jaan*![13] Although his character was an imaginary one, entirely created by Manoj Kumar, that role gave Pran *Saab* striking identification and fame as a character actor.'

'Of course, he had such a strong image of a villain that producers in those days would be scared to change the image of any actor who is typecast. But with this film he *forced* the people to see the change. He made them realize what he was capable of,' Prem Chopra marvelled.

However, the greatest compliment probably came from the veteran actor, the late Ashok Kumar: *'If anybody could do the role of Kehar Singh, it was only Pran!'*

6

At the time when Pran finally chose to play Kehar Singh's role in *Shaheed*, he was ruling as the 'king of villainy' in Hindi cinema. He had a virtual monopoly on the best roles available and he made sure that his place and position in the film industry remained unchallenged.

Explaining why he decided to begin the switchover from pure villainy to character roles of varying shades, Pran said: 'I guess I was bored of the same routine, again and again. The problem was that villainous roles kept pouring in and I went on doing them. I had done a positive role in Raj Kapoor *Saab's Aah* in 1953, but when that film didn't run well, nobody dared to give me a positive role and try to change my image after that! It was only much later that I got this unusual role [in *Shaheed*] and *that* was only because of Manoj Kumar.'

Pran's performance as the convict in *Shaheed* was a superb blend of laughter and sorrow, a deliberate underplaying which served as a thin veil for the unstated, all of which was based on a subtle conception and understanding of the role.

---

[13] *Jaan* means 'life' or 'soul'.

Only a thinking actor whose heart would have been touched by what he was going to play could achieve what Pran did with this role. Reminiscing about it, Pran said: 'I think my first *real* tryst with character acting came with Manoj Kumar's *Shaheed*. I was a "baddie" gradually improving and eventually turning good in the end – and people liked me! That was a rare new feeling – being liked even when the character was not all-white.'

Pran was Hindi cinema's arch villain and intended to stay at the top position for a long time yet. Being astute, he realized that in order to do so, he would have to transit to another stage of his career and expand the scope of what he was doing right then.

When he decided to make a switchover to a new kind of role – that of a bad man who was inherently good, Pran had actually done himself a big favour. Agreeing, albeit reluctantly, to act in the small but significant role in Kewal Kashyap's *Shaheed*, he had allowed audiences to have a small taste of big things to come.

And by letting the audiences see what he was capable of delivering, he himself had also been able to test the waters regarding their reaction to his image change. *Shaheed*'s success 'told' him what his next step should be – a full-fledged character actor good man's role.

The intelligently thought-out transition period was a part of that gradual metamorphosis and had begun at just the right time. Younger villains had begun to enter the scene just then and their youth and newness could have served to catalyse the fall of the older actor-villain from the position of numero uno. This switchover not only prevented that from happening, but it also gave him a new lease of screen life and the further opportunity to prove himself to be one of the screen's most versatile and durable stars.

The news about his urge to do something different, a 'good man's' role, i.e., a character role, had begun to spread. This prompted film land's voices to excitedly whisper and conjecture about whether or not an actor of his calibre, already a maestro at 'bad man's' roles, could possibly acquit himself playing 'good man's' roles.

The answer would only be given two years later, in 1967, with his performance in Manoj Kumar's *Upkar*.

SEVENTEEN

The Turning Point: *Upkar*

1

'In Hollywood,' began Manoj Kumar, in an interview exclusively done for this biography, 'it is said that if you do not find an appropriate person for the role that is written, then take Anthony Quinn.' He continued: 'I would say that if you do not find an actor in Bollywood who can do the role that is written, then take Pran *Saab* — he is so versatile and dedicated.'

Yet consider this: Despite the fact that in some of his early films he had done sympathetic roles also, film makers unerringly continued to cast Pran in bad man's roles. Manoj Kumar was one of the few exceptions who could discern in Pran the talent to do something more than what had been demanded of him, or even exploited, up to that point of time.[1]

---

[1] Pran played hero in *Khandaan* (1942); second hero in *Grahasti* (1948); 'bad-good' roles in *Chhalia* (1960), *Shaheed* (1965), *Nanha Farishta* (1969), *Victoria No: 203* and *Majboor* (1974); positive roles in *Apradhi* (1949) and *Aah* (1953), *Zanjeer* (1973) and *Kasauti* (1974); and played 'good man' character roles in *Upkar* (1967), *Aansoo Ban Gaye Phool* (1969) and *Parichay* (1972). These are a few of his roles that were off the well-worn path of villainy.

Between *Halaku* (1956) and *Upkar* (1967), Pran's films gave ample proof of his wide histrionic range. They show an actor who desired to break free of the mould in which film makers and the audience had cast him: an actor, who not only *desired* to do so, but was capable of doing so.

By the late 1950s or early 1960s, it had become apparent that Pran was getting restless and wanted to do something different – *Shaheed* was proof of that. But the question was: After years of playing 'bad man' and even 'good bad man', could he express the kind of emotions and feelings required in a character role? And more importantly, would audiences *now* accept Pran in a full-fledged 'good man's' role?

The time had come for Pran to present the people with an answer.

2

Manoj Kumar's *Upkar* was certainly the turning point in Pran's career. But what was it that made Pran start thinking about doing 'good men's' roles?

'Before this film I had been cast as the "bad man" in film after film,' says Pran. 'I remember that whenever I was spotted in public, or on the roads, I would be greeted with taunts like *"Arrey badmash"*, *"Hey lafanga,"* [or] *"O goonde harami"* [all highly derogatory expletives]. But I would shrug off these jeers nonchalantly! They also left my wife Shukla unperturbed, because she always knew that I was only doing a job and doing it well.

'But one day my daughter Pinky, asked me quietly: "Daddy, why don't you do some decent roles for a change?"[2]

'I realized immediately that her school friends had been talking to her about her Daddy.

'Those days, whenever I came on screen, kids would hide their faces in their mothers' laps and keep enquiring: "Mummy, *gaya kya woh*?[3] Can we open our eyes now?" '

'There was one particular film, *Kab, Kyon Aur Kahan,*[4] in which I play a man who returns from the dead, his pupils dilating horribly. I gave the little ones (and some of their parents too) the jitters,' Pran recalls.

---

[2] Born on 8 November 1952, Pinky would have been a young teenager when she asked her father this question.

[3] 'Mummy, has he gone?'

[4] Released in 1970.

But despite the shivers he sent down many spines, Pran loved playing the villain. How then could he convince his daughter Pinky?

After much thought he called her to his side and asked: 'Tell me... at the end of eighteen reels when bad men like me have been killed and the hero and the heroine are about to walk away into the sunset, what do you do?'

Pat came Pinky's answer: 'Return home! The movie is over!'

'So you see, you're only interested in the film till I'm around. Once I make my exit – you make yours too!' he reminded her, and that, on a lighter note, ended the argument of his playing the hero!

3

How did Pran come to be part of the cast of *Upkar*?

Elaborating on how he came close to Pran, Manoj Kumar recounted: 'My friendship with him started with *Do Badan* and *Shaheed*.[5]

'Until then, I hadn't had much of a chance to work with Pran *Saab*. I had started as a junior artiste. I used to do two or four scenes in a film and very gradually went on to become a hero. Side by side, I developed another skill. Raj Khosla *Saab* was the director of *Woh Kaun Thi*.[6] He had made me write a lot of the scenes for that film.... Then Raj Khosla *Saab* was chosen to direct a film called *Do Badan*. He must have liked what I did before, because he made me write scenes for this film too.'

'I used to notice Pran *Saab* looking at me with a peculiar expression. He may have been thinking: *"Is kal ke chhokre koh toh dekho!*[7] He has hardly started acting and now he is presuming to write!"* But after working together for three-four days, it appeared that he liked the scenes I had written. Soon he and I became more friendly with each other, revealed Manoj.

Another factor contributed to the closeness that was developing between the older man and his younger contemporary: 'Pran *Saab* was

---

5   Although *Shaheed* (1965) was released before *Do Badan* (1966), it went on the floors only after the latter had started being made.
6   Released in 1964. The heroine was Sadhana.
7   Loosely translated: 'Just look at this greenhorn!'

an expert in Urdu and English but at the time he wasn't very accustomed to Hindi,' divulged Manoj. 'In one scene, there was a dialogue which had the words *puschatap*[8] and *prayaschit*.[9] Being more comfortable with the Urdu language, he naturally found these words quite hard to pronounce. So he requested me: "Would you please change these words to Urdu, *Panditjee*?" '[10]

Interestingly, since then, Pran has always called Manoj, '*Panditjee*'!

'Anyway,' Manoj continued, 'I said to him, "Pran *Sahab*, the language is such that the Urdu words for these words would be very difficult." Pran said, "But I am not able to pronounce these." So I said, "You just do the lip movement for these words and we'll handle it in the dubbing." Then Pran *Saab* remarked, "Nowadays, the wind of Hindi is blowing too hard and there are certain words I find really tough." Since I could also write Urdu, he requested me to write out those words for him in Urdu. And from that time on we have shared a rapport.'

Speaking further, Manoj declared: 'There is no producer who has not repeated Pran *Saab* in his productions,' Manoj declared. 'I have spent some forty-five to forty-seven years in this film industry, and Pran *Saab* has been there to share the joys and sorrows of everybody. He has always thought of this industry as a family. There is no producer who can say that he could not shoot because Pran *Saab* gave some trouble, or that Pran *Saab* cancelled the dates of the old films because got a new film.'

In his justifiably lengthy[11] interview, Manoj narrated an incident that highlights Pran's total dedication to his work:

'Once we were shooting a fight sequence for *Upkar*…which he did on crutches. After two or three days, I noticed that something was different about Pran *Saab*. Since the sequence was so strenuous, I thought he was probably tired. He would do a shot and then sit in the corner or have a cigarette. Upon asking him whether anything was wrong, he would say, "no".

---

[8] '*Puschatap karna*' means 'to repent' or 'to feel remorse'.

[9] '*Prayaschit karna*' means 'to atone'.

[10] *Panditjee* means a 'scholar' or a 'learned person'.

[11] For the record, Pran worked with Manoj Kumar in thirteen films. They are: *Gumnaam* (1965), *Shaheed* (1965), *Do Badan* (1966), *Sawan Ki Ghata* (1966), *Patthar Ke Sanam* (1967), *Upkar* (1967), *Aadmi* (1968), *Purab Aur Paschim* (1970), *Yaadgaar* (1970), *Be-imaan* (1972), *Sanyasi* (1975), *Dus Numbri* (1976) and *Jai Hind* (1999).

'We shared the same make-up room. That night after pack-up at 10.30 or so, I found that he was a bit silent, not the usual jolly person. I put my hand on his shoulder and asked him if he was tired? I could feel his body trembling and he made a sound as if he had hiccupped, then he said: "Yesterday, at eleven in the night, I went home after pack-up. After a bath, as I was about to eat, I got a trunk call from Calcutta informing me that my sister had died." It was but natural that he could not have slept after he got that call. But what was amazing is that the next morning at seven sharp, he was on my sets!

'And he never told me a thing about his bereavement that entire day! I said to him: "If you had told me this earlier, I could have cancelled the shooting and you could have gone to Calcutta." He said: "I thought, I know you can cancel the shooting, but today is my outdoor shooting and there are a lot of combinations with other artistes also in this shooting, and if I had mentioned this news to you, then not only you, but seven other producers too would have had to suffer. *Sab ka beda gark ho jata. Sister toh meri mari hai, main un producers ki maa ko kyun maarta?*" '[12]

Manoj paused in his narration, deeply impressed not just by Pran, the actor, but by Pran, the human being as well, and then said: '*This is Pran Saab.*'

'People say that *I* gave him that role in *Upkar,* but I did not do anything extraordinary. *I always used to think, "if a good man can do the acting of a villain, why can't he do the acting of a good man?*" '

Why ever not, indeed?

4

Chhalia (1960) and *Shaheed* (1965) had already provided part of the answer to the questions about whether or not Pran would be able to acquit himself in 'character' roles with shades of both good and bad. These films had given Pran's career an added dimension, which he could now explore. In spite of the run-of-the-mill Hindi films that were being

---

[12] Loosely translated as: 'Everyone's project would have come to a standstill. It was my sister who died, why then should I put the producers to such a great inconvenience?'

churned out by the studios and independent producers, some individuals were attempting films with unusual subjects and unusual characters — those which had more than one facet to them.

With *Shaheed*, Manoj Kumar had already demonstrated what quality he was capable of producing. Having hit the bull's eye with its success, Manoj was hooked to not only acting in, but also making, films — films that would awaken and arouse the collective conscience of the Indian people; films that would stay in the public memory for a long time.

So how was *Upkar* born?

The seeds of the idea were sown during two meetings which Manoj Kumar had in New Delhi.

One meeting was with his school friend from way back in the late 1940s. This young man was the son of a rich *zamindar* (landowner) with many fields and farms. But yet, he had turned his back on agriculture and had come to the city to make a living — as a clerk! This situation, where farmers had to leave their traditional occupation and move to the cities for meagerly paid jobs, had worried Manoj.

The other meeting was with the then prime minister of India, Lal Bahadur Shastri, whom Manoj had invited to the premiere of his starring vehicle *Shaheed*. The soft-spoken prime minister had asked Manoj: 'Couldn't a film be made on the theme of "Jai Jawan, Jai Kisan"?'

'Jai Jawan, Jai Kisan' was Lal Bahadur Shastri's slogan to encourage India's self-sufficiency with regard to military preparedness as well as food for the nation. Manoj Kumar was inspired by this clarion call and decided that the theme of *Upkar* would focus on India's Green Revolution. It would depict a modern India which had not been able to smoothly synthesize the village and the city. It would depict a country in a state of flux and upheaval, trying to grow despite the uncertainties.

The challenge of *Upkar* was to make a film that would rouse Indians in the far-flung corners of the country to value the land of their birth and to contribute to the Green Revolution. To accomplish all this without the film ending up looking like a documentary was the challenge to creativity. In order to achieve all that he had set out to do, Manoj Kumar not only made sure that his story and script were crisp and tight, but he also sought out actors who would be very, very convincing and would share his passion, dedication and zeal for good and wholesome cinema.

Pran as the unforgettable Malang Chacha in *Upkar* (1967).

Manoj recalled: 'Even while I was working on the script, as the scenes of [the character] Malang Chacha developed, I began constantly to *see* in my mind's eye Pran *Saab* doing that role.

'As my script progressed, the character sort of escaped from my hands — it simply grew and grew!'

5

In *Upkar*, Manoj Kumar decided to do something that few others would have dared attempt at that stage. Manoj had no doubt that Pran would be able to deliver the goods with regard to what he had in mind for him.

The fact is, Manoj had been so impressed with Pran's on-the-sets histrionics that he decided to picturize one of the film's best songs on him. That famous song was *'Kasme Vaade, Pyar Wafaa Sab, Baatein Hain...Baaton Ka Kya...'*[13]

Music directors Kalyanji Anandji were distraught when they heard that one of their most sensitive songs, written by lyricist Indivar, was

---

[13] This means: 'Promises, vows, love, loyalty, all mere words...of what value are words?'

going to be sung on screen by Pran. They virtually wailed: 'Are you mad? He'll ruin our song! Please take somebody else! Raj Kapoor flopped in *Aah* by giving a positive role to Pran *Saab*.'

Manoj found it hard to explain to them that it was not Raj Kapoor who had failed, but it was actually the film that had failed. It was clear that even Kalyanji*bhai* and Anandji*bhai* were influenced by Pran's hitherto strongly entrenched 'villain' image. But they soon realized that despite their protestations, and despite Kalyanji's daily phone calls to Delhi imploring Manoj to let the song play in the background, the latter was not going to give in.

However, a bigger shock awaited Manoj when Kishore Kumar was approached to sing the song. He absolutely refused to do so, and not even a personal request from Pran himself could get him to change his mind!

Whereupon Manoj went ahead and told Kalyanji and Anandji that they should take another singer for this beautiful song which he could 'see' being sung only by Pran.

Finally the song was sung by Manna Dey, and what a rendition! Even today it stands out not only among Kalyanji Anandji's best compositions, but also as one of Manna*da's* most soulfully rendered songs. That Pran had lip-synched the entire song so naturally only served to add to its beauty.

Manoj Kumar recalled how he got Pran to prepare for the picturization of this song: 'When it was time to film the song, we asked Pran to sit in one place and placed the camera [in position]. He kept singing and we kept shooting for some one and half hours. And then at pack up he said: "*Panditjee*, I didn't enjoy the shot much today. You kept the camera in one place and took many close-ups of me." I said: "Pran *Saab*, actually, we didn't switch on the camera at all!" He asked [for] the reason. I said: "Where your dialogues are concerned, I have no doubt about your acting. But I have never seen you singing and I wanted to make sure that my hunch about your abilities was not wrong. In the song sequence, as an actor, I will be in the background and not be behind the camera to see you. So I just wanted to know whether I was right about you." '

'He asked: "Was there any problem with my acting [while picturizing the song]?" I said: "No, except there was a slight break when singing the words 'Kasme Vaade'. That was the only thing. The rest was fine." To help him with something he did not feel comfortable doing, I used to keep the speakers very close to his ears and, at Pran Saab's request, I myself would sing along,' elaborated Manoj Kumar.

No one had anticipated that the song would become such a big hit! The first congratulations came from none other than Kalyanji. Manoj Kumar reported that the music director told Pran: 'I have to admit that we [Kalyanji and Anandji] were the ones who were the most vehemently opposed to you being spotlighted in the song but now, after seeing the first print, we have to admit that most stars sing our songs only with their lips. *Many have sung our songs, but nobody has sung it the way you did! You are the only one who has sung it from the heart, with all the feeling you could put into your voice, so much so that all the veins in your neck were visible.*'[14]

Referring to his preparation for the song sequence in *Upkar*, Pran divulged: 'I used to bring the cassette home and hear the songs many times.... Since so much hard work was involved in the picturization of the song, I requested Manoj to turn on the tape full blast and mouth the words along with me, loudly singing the song!

'I personally liked the song done on me in *Upkar*. The song was good, the wordings were nice, and the picturization was also excellent. It was only me who was nervous! So I worked very hard for that song.'

6

No matter what the role, the hallmark of a good actor is when he or she goes prepared to play it in a way that the character depicted no longer remains just that – he or she becomes a real-life person, with whom people can identify and empathize and feel a oneness at some level.

Speaking about Pran's preparation for his film *Upkar*, Manoj Kumar said: 'After he took the first scene of *Upkar* from me, he came to my

---

[14] Although there is a section of film stars who, rather than produce any sound with their voices, only mouth the words of the song being filmed, there have been a number of stars who actually *sang* the song that was being picturized on them.

house, and said: "Kidar Sharma's[15] assistant talks like this, and I want to use that style of speaking." '

It is a well-documented fact that Pran worked assiduously not only on his 'look' and 'get-up' but also on his mannerisms, accents and voice. In this context, Manoj pointed out an interesting fact about that ability: 'Pran used to work in ten to twenty films simultaneously, but never in his entire career did any of the directors or their assistants need to remind [him] that his tone or mannerism had to be such and such. Pran could remember what he had to do, and in which film!'

'I have directed actors ranging from Ashok Kumar to Dilip Kumar but Pran Saab was such a person who used to ask for the dialogues one day in advance. He prepares! He was not in the habit of thinking: "Go to the set, take the dialogue and do what you can,"' asserted Manoj Kumar.

While emphasizing Pran's insistence on *not* mediocre and substandard work, but on quality work, Manoj disclosed: 'If he did not like a scene, he'd get behind me until I had sat down, worked on it and improved it! Until he was fully satisfied with a scene, he would compel me to rewrite the scene – again and again. Mercifully, such occasions were few! But his greatness is that he always gave credit for other people's good work as well.

'And if a scene didn't come off well, Pranjee would ask for retakes, but not just for himself. If he noticed that another artiste's work wasn't good in that particular scene, he would quietly come and say to the director: "That artiste's work was weak, so please explain to him what to do, and then have a retake." Pranjee was never selfish. He would never ask for a retake just for himself. He was always interested in the film as a whole.

'He would always abandon himself totally to the director. If, however, at times he felt certain talents [were] lacking in the director, then without saying anything, he would do the work and also develop his role himself, without offending the director.

---

[15] The late Kidar Sharma was an eminent producer-director-writer-poet-lyricist and star maker, who gave Hindi cinema great stars, such as Raj Kapoor, Madhubala and Geeta Bali, and music directors such as Roshan. His most famous works include *Devdas, Vidyapati, Chitralekha* (both versions), *Neel Kamal, Neki Aur Badi, Bawre Nain* and *Hamari Yaad Aayegi*. Songs written by him, and mostly sung by K.L. Saigal, include the famous 'Mai Kya Jaanoo Kya Jaadoo Hai' and the lullaby 'So Ja, Rajkumari, So Ja'.

'I salute Pran *Saab* for his patience. If his shooting was scheduled for ten o'clock, then he would always reach by seven – because to put on his make-up or his beard (if he needed one for that shooting) would take four hours. I can understand that for one film you may need to give many hours to have your make-up done, like Nargis*jee* needed for the old-age portion in *Mother India* [a 1957 film]. But Pran *Saab* has done this for *all* his films and for *all* his get-ups!'

That Pran himself had enjoyed working in *Upkar* and was equally impressed with Manoj Kumar's film is evident from what happened when he was interviewed for this book. In the process of repeating a dialogue in precisely the same style as he spoke it in the film, he paused first and then said in his characteristic gravelly voice, '*Raashan par bhaashan bahut hai! Bhaashan par koi raashan nahin! Sirf yeh: jab bhi bolta hun, zyaada hi bolta hun, samjhe!*'[16]

After more than thirty-six years, to be able to meet an actor who could remember not just his lines, but also its pitch, pace, power and tonal inflections, is a rare and priceless treat.

Pran remembered yet another memorable scene from *Upkar* and his dialogue in it: 'In the film, Manoj Kumar's name is Bharat. The scene is that the brothers have had a fight. So I say...'

Here, Pran paused to recall the dialogue and to get into the mood of the moment. Then he continued: '*Bharat, tu duniya ki chhod! Pehle apni soch! Ram ne har yug mein janam liya hai, lekin Lakshman jaisa bhai dobara paida nahin hua!*'[17] When he finished repeating this dialogue, one could see the quiet satisfaction in his face, the satisfaction that comes from knowing that both the film and his job in it were well done.

7

The audience reaction to Pran's delineation of the Malang Chacha role started right at the premiere show of *Upkar* itself, which was held in New

---

[16] 'There are lots of speeches on rationing, but no rationing on speeches! Just this: whenever I speak, I speak a little too much, got it?'

[17] 'Bharat, forget about the world! Think about yourself! In every era, a Ram [the hero of the epic *Ramayana*, a paragon of virtue] has been born, but a brother like Lakshman [Ram's devoted younger brother] has yet to be born again!'

Delhi. The then president of India, Dr Zakir Hussain,[18] had been invited as the chief guest.

After the screening of the film, Manoj Kumar presented the members of the cast to the president, starting off with Asha Parekh, who played his sweetheart in the film, Kamini Kaushal who played his mother, Prem Chopra, who played his brother, and so on till most of his stars had been introduced. The president was politely moving along, responding to everyone's greetings with his hands joint together in a *namaste*.

Finally, stopping in front of Pran, Manoj Kumar said: 'This is Pran, who has played the role of Malang Chacha in the film.' On hearing this, the president stood-stock still, and he kept looking at Pran as if he was unable to believe what he had just heard! Then with a great deal of enthusiasm he stepped forward towards Pran and, after congratulating him on his excellent performance, shook his hand and patted him on the back!

Dr Zakir Hussain's surprise when he was introduced to Pran reveals how, even in the mind of the president of India, Pran's villain image had

Pran with President Dr Zakir Hussain at the premiere of *Upkar*.

---

[18] Dr Zakir Hussain passed away on 3 May 1969.

been so firmly fixed. The president was astonished to find out that it was the famous villain who had played Malang Chacha's role with such finesse!

Whether from the movie-going public, film-industry professionals or even the president of India himself, the reaction to Pran's performance in *Upkar* was one of resounding approval. Pran, who had been anxious about the response to his 'good man's' role, had now succeeded beyond his wildest expectations!

The industry was abuzz with talk about *Upkar* and Pran's role in it. Asha Parekh, who was the heroine of the film, commented: 'I had seen Pranjee over the years constantly doing villain's roles. In *Upkar*, however, Manoj was daring enough to visualize him in a very different and striking role, one which was tremendously sympathetic.'

'It must have been very difficult for him,' Asha continued, 'especially because the character is supposed to be lame and walks on crutches. But Pran *Saab* did a fabulous job of it! He carried the role very well and it is one of the most memorable roles he has ever done.'

In similar vein, Kamini Kaushal, who was cast as Manoj Kumar's mother in *Upkar*, spoke about Pran's image change: 'He [Pran] did it so well. To overcome the strongly-established negative image and to fit into an image that is most lovable is a very big feat. He did it superbly. Casting a thorough, full-blooded villain into a most dynamic kind of characterization was fantastic to see and the credit goes as much to Manoj Kumar who "saw" him in that role, as it goes to Pran who "lived" up to his director's expectations.'

Crediting Manoj Kumar for giving Pran some of the strongest roles of his career, Kamini went on to say: 'Actually, Manoj has been a very big help in creating these striking characters for Pran, the kind of characters which made his talent come across strongly. Otherwise if the role is not there, how can any artiste do anything?'

The dedication that Manoj Kumar had expected, and got, from his team ensured that the sense of conviction and commitment was palpable in every frame of *Upkar*.

Upkar, having achieved what its inspired creator hoped it would, surged with dynamic power, and nobody even faintly interested in films could be apathetic to it. The audience, which could scarcely be expected to understand the intricacies of 'taking', 'composition' or 'inter-cutting', strongly felt the startling impact of the directorial cohesion of all these elements, among many others, on the screen.

Between 1940 and 1967, Pran had, of course, done quite a few 'good man's' roles in films, some of which had scored significantly, box office-wise as well as in terms of critical appreciation. But it took a Manoj Kumar to create and give a memorable 'good man's' role, the role of Malang Chacha in *Upkar*, not to any of the well-known character actors who had specialized in doing 'good man's' roles, but to Pran.

Star & Style (15 October 1967) carried a review of *Upkar*. Here is a relevant excerpt: 'Pran has got yet another off-beat role (as the cripple) after *Shaheed*. A little loud perhaps, *but loud about issues in which we should be involved.*'

Another critic of that period remarked: 'The best performance [in the film] comes from Pran. Released from his eternal villain roles, he brings to life the character of Malang Chacha, the sharp-tongued village philosopher.'

Upkar won for Pran his first amply deserved *Filmfare* Award for Best Supporting Actor.

8

Manoj Kumar has added reason to be eternally grateful to Pran. In his interview he spoke of the time when Pran helped him out of a financial mess. Manoj's producer-partner of *Upkar*, Harkishen R. Mirchandani (who was also world rights controller of *Do Badan*) had taken huge loans from some persons. Those devolved to *Upkar*. Even Manoj Kumar's mother was drawn into the case. 'Eventually,' Manoj remembers gratefully, 'Pran *Saab* was the only man to solve [the problem]! We surrendered *Upkar* for nine years to Mirchandani. That means I didn't get money for acting, writing or directing it. But Pran *Saab* was the one who took us out of that tension!'

Typically, when asked for his version, Pran did not remember all the details of how he helped Manoj, but acknowledged that Manoj did have 'some problem' which he helped solve!

Most people in the film industry are well aware of the fact that Manoj Kumar never travelled by air; he always travelled by train. Referring to this aspect, Manoj Kumar continued:

'When *Upkar* was released, I tried to obtain a "tax-free" certificate for the film. Being a "train man" myself, I could not quickly get to different places to pursue the tax exemption matters. So Pran *Saab* did this for me. He went by air to Punjab, to Guwahati and other places, and in most places he got the tax exemption done himself. So naturally he had to sit through the screenings of *Upkar* each time a screening for tax exemption purposes was held!

'I'll never forget a sweet compliment which Pran paid me one day soon after that. He said to me: "Till today, I always thought of Manoj as a big writer and director. Now that I have seen *Upkar* so many times, I realized that as an actor also, he had done such excellent work, such striking mannerisms." Noticing one particular mannerism of mine, Pran *Saab* said, "I am going to copy this particular mannerism in one of my forthcoming films!" It was such a touching compliment!'

9

The ultimate verdict about whether or not he had acquitted himself well enough for his 'villain' tag to be obliterated came some time after *Upkar* was released. This verdict would tell Pran whether or not audiences had accepted him in a 'good-man's' role, after *Aah*.

Pran remembers all his public appearances before the release of *Upkar* quite well. Wherever he went, he would invariably be greeted by hoots and all kinds of taunting epithets!

So when Pran had to attend the wedding of Om Prakash's daughter in Delhi and was asked to park his car a good distance away and to walk the rest of the way to the *mandap* (the venue), Pran was terrified – especially about what the star-crazy fans would want to do to him because of not realizing that there was a world of a difference between his on-screen image and his real self. Other film stars who had been going in before him had already been mobbed by fans, almost as soon as they had left the safe haven of their cars.

When he alighted from his car, a little apprehensive about what was going to happen, he couldn't believe the reception he got – there was an awed silence! Then someone stage-whispered, '*Malang Chacha aa rahen hain!*[19] Make way for him!'

As the crowds moved back and made way for him to walk through, gazing at him with a new respect in their eyes, Pran continued, amazed at the change in the public's reaction to him. 'I still marvel at that almost overnight change in people's perception of me,' Pran beamed reminiscently.

After *Upkar* Pran began to be *flooded* with appreciative fan mail.

One of them was from a young man who told him that since the day he saw *Upkar*, he had been thinking only of Pran. As he put it:

'I think that just like the prime minister was addressed as "*Chacha Nehru*", you should also be addressed as "*Chacha* Pran".'

The 'bad man' had come a long way...finally to be transformed in the public mind into a 'good' and kindly uncle.

---

[19] 'Here comes Malang *Chacha!*'

EIGHTEEN

The Family and Friends in the 1960s

1

By the dawn of the 1960s, Pran and his family were well and truly settled in their bungalow at Union Park.

Despite being in the largely abnormal world of films, where most people's lives take on a surreal quality and every occurrence may appear to be an episode from a film viewed on the silver screen, the Sikands, like any other normal Indian family, had their own aspirations, hopes and goals in life.

To that end, Pran and Shukla's eldest son, Arvind, was being educated at one of India's premier educational institutions, at Sanawar,[1] where he excelled.

Arvind would be home every summer and winter and recalled how other star kids and the Sikand children would assemble for some fun:

---

[1] Near Simla, in Himachal Pradesh.

'We kids…would get together for birthdays. *Dabboo*,[2] Jalal Agha,[3] all of us, would get together.'

'In those days, Republic Days were a big thing and would make for a great evening out. All the film stars would have their own trucks decorated with their own *dholaks*[4] and bands. And we kids would fight for the best seat, which would be on the top of the driver's cab, the vantage point. People like *Dabboo*, Jalal and myself, we'd all be there. It used to be great fun,' said Arvind nostalgically.

The festival of Holi[5] too was a big event at Pran's home. Like Raj Kapoor's R. K. Studios in Chembur, Pran's home in Bandra used to be the hub of the traditional Holi celebrations with all its colour and hilarity.

The tradition of celebrating Holi at Pran's residence had been started in 1959. The 2 April 1959 issue of *Cine Advance* reported that although

Holi celebrations galore. Seen among other are Raj Kapoor (with a cigarette dangling between his lips) and Pran.

---

2   Randhir Kapoor.
3   Jalal Agha was the actor-son of the late Agha, who started out as a hero and later became a comedian.
4   An elongated kind of drum.
5   Holi is the festival of colour, which celebrates spring as well as the triumph of good over evil. Much of the hilarity during Holi is due to the consumption of *bhaang*, which is a drink made from freshly ground hemp.

Pran had been inviting his friends for three years, they had only that year accepted his invitation. And how!

After kicking off the merrymaking at R. K. Studios, with all the drinking and dunking that are the hallmarks of the festival, many of the stars had then gone in a long convoy to Pran's residence in Bandra. Elaborate arrangements had been made to host hundreds of stars, friends and relatives. As was the custom, everyone was dunked in a huge pool of coloured water. Those who did not willingly jump in, were thrown in! The festivities were climaxed by a sumptuous lunch.

Brother-in-law, Ajit Walia[6] added vibrant detail to the description: 'They would celebrate Holi with the kind of pomp and ceremony seen normally only at very wealthy weddings! Tents were put up, there was drinking and eating and dancing with utter abandon. And Raj Kapoor would outdance all of them!'

Once the tradition of celebrating Holi at Pran's was established, it was customary to find filmdom's Holi revellers at either R. K. Studios or at Pran's bungalow in Bandra.

But during 1961, when both Pran and Raj Kapoor were busy in Madras shooting for their films there, the popular film journal *Filmfare* reported that the Holi celebrations that year lacked the gaiety and verve that were normally to be seen when both the large-hearted and larger-than-life stars were around!

2

In the early half of the 1960s, Arvind completed his education at Lawrence School, Sanawar.

Pran is immensely proud of Arvind's academic achievements, which is manifest when he speaks: 'It is amazing that being in the environment such as ours, the film world, Arvind was still so good in studies! He always came *first class first*. In those days, there was a master, an Englishman, who had devoted his entire life to education and to the school. The gentleman had bought a small tract of land there and given instructions that upon his death, he should be buried there itself.'

---

[6] Pran's wife, Shukla, has a sister, Pushpa Walia. Ajit is her husband.

Shukla carried forward the narrative: 'So when Arvind passed the Senior Cambridge exam with a first class, this teacher recommended him for a scholarship in England. So it was because of him that Arvind got a scholarship, and at the age of seventeen itself, went to London for higher studies, first to Gresham's, a school in Norfolk, and then to Birmingham University.'

Shortly before Arvind left for England, Pran arranged to give him a grand farewell party. Underscoring the relationship the father and the firstborn shared, Pran reminisced: 'That night, I went to him with a glass of whisky in my hand and said: "*Bubboo*,

Pran affectionately bidding goodbye to Arvind (in 1963), who was to leave for England..

have a sip." He said: "Dad, you know that I don't drink." I said: "Yes, but when you go to London, you'll go to parties, and what if somebody offers you a beer or some champagne? Why don't you start from now. Your Daddy is a good drunkard." He said: "Yes, Daddy, I'll have a sip." That's when he took his very first sip!'

3

Pran made no bones about that fact that he worked hard and played hard. But he never allowed his relaxation to interfere with his work. Arvind recalled some of those carefree days in Union Park: 'Mr Satish Bhalla, my father, Dilip *Saab* and Mr Balraj Kohli[7] were all living within a half mile of each other. Mr Balraj Kohli used to live in a house opposite us. He was a very affectionate man and was fond of us children. This gang

---

[7] Balraj Kohli, known to everybody simply as Balli, was the son of a goldsmith. He came from Rawalpindi to Bombay and made it home. He was very close to Pran, Dilip Kumar, Raj Kapoor and several other film personalities.

of four was a great one for partying and wild times. At least three or four times a week, they would be at one or the other's house drinking till two or three in the morning.'

Sunil also spoke of how their parents enjoyed the good things of life together. Of their regular parties at home, Sunil said: 'The regulars were Raj *Saab*, Shammi *Saab*,[8] Mr Balraj Kohli, Mr Satish Bhalla, and, of course, Dilip *Saab*.[9] It was a regular thing; they'd be over once or twice a week. They were all healthy drinkers. Quarter bottle...half bottle was easy.

'The conversation used to be liberally sprinkled with ribald humour, *sher-o-shairee* and anecdotes about various films and colleagues. Every time someone felt the pangs of hunger, they'd say '*khaana garam karo*', and while it was getting heated, another round of drinking and conversation would start and carry on for one more hour. And the food would go cold again. This would happen at least three-four times during the party.'

Recalling one memorable incident, Sunil revealed: 'I remember waking up one morning and finding evidence of quite a party...I was then told that the "gang"...had been partying all night. My mother does have one or maximum two pegs to give company, so she along with Mrs Kohli and Mrs Bhalla had all joined in. I don't think Dilip *Saab* was married at that time.

'Apparently, after having partied all night, they had decided to go for a swim early in the morning at Juhu Beach! So they all landed up on the beach at about 5 a.m., dressed in their *lungis* and whatever! Mr Balraj Kohli tipsily claimed that he was the best-dressed person because he was in a *lungi* and a tie! This was the kind of fun my parents and their gang of friends had. They all lived their lives fully.'

'But,' Arvind adds, 'one thing about my father, and this is something that will be borne out by all of his directors and producers, is that *no matter how late he was up the night before, he would be on the sets by 9.30 a.m., in time for work.* That *is something that he has inculcated in all of us children, to give a full day's work.*'

During this period, one particularly amusing anecdote highlighted the easy camaraderie between Pran and Dilip Kumar, with whom Pran did

---

8   Raj Kapoor and his brother, Shammi Kapoor.
9   Dilip Kumar.

some of his most memorable films. On the flight back to Bombay after a film stars' cricket match in Hyderabad, which Pran had helped to organize, Dilip Kumar, Premnath and Vyjayanthimala were carrying on an animated conversation in the aisle. Wanting to make his way to the pilot's cabin, Pran tried, in vain, to squeeze his way through between Dilip Kumar and Vyjayanthimala. At which, Dilip Kumar pulled Pran back, saying: 'Must a villain always be a villain? You should at least be considerate to a lady!'

Pran's repartee was instantaneous: 'A villain's place is always between the hero and the heroine!'

4

During the early part of his career, Pran had made several good friends from among his colleagues. One hero with whom Pran had a tremendous 'tuning' was Shammi Kapoor — with whom he acted in twenty films — not just on the sets, but beyond them too.

Arvind says: 'When they performed together, there was a lot of non-verbal communication between them; their instinctive interaction with each other made for some very good scenes together.'

Arvind remembers going to Switzerland with his father and Shammi Kapoor for the shooting of *An Evening in Paris*.[10] Arvind was studying in England then, so his father had taken him over during the summer. Arvind recalled that time: 'I met them when they were shooting at the Rhein Fälle — the large waterfalls on the River Rhine in Switzerland and I remember having a fun time with Shammi*jee*. One day, when there was no shooting, we spent the entire day playing on the pinball machines and drinking wine and eating chicken and chips which was a standard fare in Switzerland with lots of Tabasco® all over it!

'One evening after that, when the two of them returned from their shift, they got dressed and took me along with them on a pub crawl. That was a fun exercise except that it was impossible to keep up with these two hardened drinkers.

'I remember after the third bar that we visited. I was only about twenty years' old and recently introduced to drink. I was definitely

---

[10] Released in 1967.

feeling a little bit tipsy, having had wine all day and now these whiskies in the evening! At the fourth pub we visited, whilst neither of them was looking, I tipped half the contents of my glass into Shammi Uncle's glass and the remainder into Dad's glass! But I don't think it bothered them at all. They just carried on drinking!' smiled Arvind at the memory of that unforgettable day in Switzerland.

Shammi Kapoor himself remembered the latter half of the 1960s, when his hero days were almost coming to an end. He reminisced about how the relationship between producers, directors and co-artistes was not limited to the sets: 'We had a kind of ritual. We used to pack up at 6.30 p.m. at Natraj Studios, which was Modern Studios before that. We would remove our make-up and get going by 7 p.m. Within twenty minutes we would be at that bridge near the studios. Since the Andheri bridge was just being built, we could park our cars there. Three or four of us, Pranjee, Ramesh Sippy, Bhappi Sonie and myself, would stop here. We'd take out our own little deck chairs, which we used to keep in the boot, and sit on the pavement. In later days, Rajesh Khanna also used to join us. And a bar used to open up right there on the roadside. Soda water, ice, whisky – everything was ready. We used to have two drinks. Not one, not three but two drinks. We'd enquire how each other's day went and say, "Fine! Bye-bye, cheers! and good night!" and then go home. We were not boozers that we couldn't do without a drink. We were drinking people; we knew how to hold our drink. But this gave us an opportunity to chill out with the boys!

'Those were the days! We did this for about two years. But times have changed. Today there is no contact, no communication whatsoever. You are called on the sets when the shot is on. You give it, and that is that. Then you go back to your airconditioned bus outside.

'In our case, we are all working in different films, but we made it a point to meet at one place, have a couple of drinks, share notes, and then it was "bye-bye". Sometimes we would meet again at a party the same night. But this was how we stayed in touch,' recollected Shammi Kapoor.

Speaking about Shammi, with whom he enjoyed working, Pran said: 'With him, it was a different delight altogether. He was lovable even with all his *wild* ways and is still lovable with all his *mild* ways.'

5

By 1962, Sunil had finished with Lawrence School and was back in Bombay and studying at the Cathedral and John Connon High School. 'I think I had more opportunities to twirl my mother around my little finger than Arvind or Pinky,' says Sunil matter-of-factly. 'Did she ever talk about my escapades to Dad? I don't know what they talked between each other. But I think she hid a lot of my escapades. Otherwise I would have been in trouble more often.'

Meanwhile, Pinky had continued to be with her parents in Bombay, leaving for Sanawar only after her brothers had finished studying there: 'I was in St. Joseph's Convent, Bandra, till the fourth or fifth standard, but I was not really bothered about my studies. So my parents decided to pack me off to boarding school. I don't think it was planned that I would be sent to Sanawar, otherwise I would have been sent when my brothers were there.'

Life in Union Park had fallen into a pattern. Normal family activities went on as usual. Pran would return home from the studios every evening and would be welcomed by his dogs. Pinky remembers: 'Once he came home, the dogs used to be after him. He used to feed them biscuits, have tea, sit in the garden. There was no mention of which studio he had come from or who had acted with him. It was a complete "switch-off" where his work was concerned. He never actually asked me about my studies. He used to come home in the evening from the shootings, he was there every evening, unless he had a double shift. Say from 6 p.m. onwards he would be there at home. He would have his bath and drinks and then relax.'

Shukla knew that her husband was in a highly demanding profession. She made it her business to ensure that his home life was free from the stresses he surely experienced in the studios. Like Pran, she had not forgotten their hard times and she knew that this was the time for them to establish themselves. She knew what went on in the world of films and knew what she had to do to make certain that the family remained on even keel, which would have been impossible without her quiet support.

So, Shukla went about her home-making tasks quietly and with dignity, making sure that things moved in a well-oiled manner, things that only a caring woman would think of. Sunil says: 'My mother is a wonderful woman who's always been there for us.'

However, to occupy the long hours during which she had to sacrifice her husband to the arc lights and cameras, she spent time pursuing her vastly diverse interests – one, a deep love for spiritual things and the other, going daily to the Cricket Club of India to play rummy.

Pran and Shukla share a common love for dogs. So, when Pran decided to get his house refurbished, he also decided that he would have special kennels built for his seven dogs. But by the time the house was readied, some of his beloved dogs had died. Pran summed up his feeling of loss by saying: 'I lost four of my dogs. I remember the joyous barking of those dogs who would give me a grand welcome whenever I came home from late-night shootings, and I remember to this day how sorely I used to miss the rich barking of those dogs. Although three dogs were still around, everything used to sound quite subdued.'

However, on the professional front, things were far from subdued. Pran was riding the crest of the tide of success and the rate at which he was going, this particular tide would not wane for a long, long time to come.

NINETEEN

The Splendid Sixties
Draw to a Close

1

The 1960s had definitely ushered in a change with regard to the kind of roles Pran began to be offered. Films like *Chhalia, Shaheed, Upkar, Nanha Farishta* and *Aansoo Ban Gaye Phool* had confirmed that Pran could successfully transit from doing villainous roles to doing character-actor roles and 'good men's' roles.

With his role in *Shaheed*, Pran got people to sit up and take notice. Buoyed by its successful acceptance in the public mind, Pran went on to do the out-and-out 'good-man's' role in *Upkar*.

Pran's daughter, Pinky Bhalla, spoke about the switch Pran made in his choice of roles: 'When he switched to doing "good" roles, *I felt that at least now his full potential would be used* .... It was the film *Upkar*, which proved to be the real defining moment of his career. That movie put him in a position where he would now not really have to look back and go to doing the "bad man" roles.'

Until that happened, however, the follow-the-leader mentality adopted by some film makers had meant that Pran continued to be offered only those roles where he would have to play an out-and-out, blacker-than-black villain. Playing villain in film after film for well over twenty years had such an impact on the public psyche that, despite the shift towards character roles, the 'bad man' image continued to hold strong sway.

Pran's decision to rise above the mediocrity had been a wise one. The scant attention being paid to the etching out of even the main characters in the story, and the casual handling of a run-of-the mill script in general, meant that the villain's character often did not get the kind of treatment that one sees happen in cinema that is governed by art, rather than by just a ringing of cash registers.

He had perfected the art of preparation by paying attention to detail. This had made him an actor strongly in demand. Roles were now being written *for him*, or roles were *worked into* the scripts of important film makers who were pleased that here was an actor who worked with dedication on creating memorable characterizations for their films.

By the end of the 1960s Pran, already an outstanding actor, had now become a *star* in his own right. In the minds of both the producers and the public, Pran was synonymous with 'BAD'! When producers discussed their upcoming projects with their regular distributor-financiers, the demand was invariably stated: 'If the villain's role in your film is strong – take Pran!' This was because distributors, having their fingers constantly on the pulse of the box office, knew that audiences looked forward to seeing the next distinctive and colourful character Pran would play.

What this meant in terms of lucre was that when Pran's name was added to the star cast of a newly announced film, producers upped their sale prices – and distributors willingly paid because, in terms of film selling, Pran's name had acquired star dimensions.

2

The manner in which a film is conceived, the joys, problems and difficulties in its making, the blood, sweat, toil and tears of each and every person on and behind the screen, all of which contribute to the final product, and then the wide gap between the year or two of its making and the final release date, are all insignificant compared to the expressed opinions of the 'first day, first show' viewers and the film critics. It is only these opinions which have prime importance for the film maker.

There were more reviews during this decade, most of which contained just a one-line acknowledgment of fact – that Pran had done his job well. The sameness of the reviews became tedious – 'Pran is the usual polished villain', 'Pran as the villain is convincing', 'Pran makes an interesting villain', and so on and so forth.

Interestingly, even when the reviewer felt that Pran was acting a role which was repetitiously seen in film after film, he pointed out that there was a difference in the way Pran had etched each role. For example, about a 1965 film, *Filmfare* wrote:[1] 'This must be the umpteenth time Pran does the kind of role he has in *Do Dil, yet the sameness does not pall.* Thanks to the script which does not make him rant and rave, *he lets the character come through with an expressive face and an ironic inflection of voice*' [italics added].

With the exception of this review, the rest of the reviews made it obvious to the reader that reviewers sometimes fail to paint an accurate picture of the performance of the individual artiste who has put in a phenomenal amount of hard work into his or her performance. While most would have been discouraged due the lack of column space devoted to him and his work in the most popular film journals of the day, not so Pran.

Pran's dictum was to work hard on each film – before and during its making. But after its release, he left it up to the *public* to make judgements and decide its fate. And the public did not once let him down.

Pran would merely move on to his next film characterization and intensely concentrate on the task at hand. This ensured that Pran's level of performance was not affected by the box-office success or failure of his preceding film.

About his ability to bring something new into each role, Pran said: 'I had always striven to present something new...[ideas for which] come only in my sleep or when I am alone.'

---

[1] *Filmfare*, 10 December 1965.

Revealing another habit that helped him not to be repetitive, Pran said: 'I go to see my films only when I have no other choice. *Main majboori mein hee jaataa hoon.*' Pran would consciously try not to see the film in which he had finished working. As a result, although by this time Pran had acted in over 150 films, he had seen just a handful of them!

Although he received little critical acclaim in the film journals of the period, he harvested a rich crop of awards.[2] Among the many awards won, some were for his supporting portrayal in Anoop Kumar Productions' *Aansoo Ban Gaye Phool.*[3]

Pran remembers his role in *Aansoo Ban Gaye Phool*, a film based on a successful Marathi drama by Vasant Kanetkar titled *Ashroonchi Zaali Phule.*[4] When Pran was chosen for his role as the *dada,*[5] someone suggested that they all go see the drama. While the other actors dutifully went to see

Pran trying to impress Helen in *Aansoo Ban Gaye Phool.*

---

[2]   See Appendix 2, which gives details of some of the awards won by Pran.
[3]   Released in 1969, *Aansoo Ban Gaye Phool*, directed by Satyen Bose, co-starred Ashok Kumar, Deb Mukerji, Alka, Nirupa Roy, Anoop Kumar and Helen.
[4]   Loosely translated as 'The Tears Have Changed to Flowers'.
[5]   Street-smart don.

it, Pran didn't go. He believed that if he had gone, he might have been influenced by the other actor's style and might not be able to act freely for the film, delineating the role in his own way.

For the first time, Pran was going to play a Maharashtrian character, and as usual, in his dedication to perfection, Pran took the trouble in advance to perfect the accent which Maharashtrians have when speaking Hindi. Pran recalls how he was able to do that: 'Not knowing any Marathi, I picked up a few Marathi words from the electrician and used it in my dialogue. Since it was a Hindi film, the use of occasional Marathi words was not incongruous.'

So although he did not see the play, his acting in *Aansoo Ban Gaye Phool* was so good that it appeared as if he was the life and soul of the film!

Aansoo Ban Gaye Phool did very good business at the box office. It further added to Pran's superstardom by also winning for him his *second Filmfare* Award (for Best Supporting Actor) during this decade. Recognition for his hard work from within the film industry had come in late, but it had begun to come – and it was coming in fast.[6] And recognition from one's colleagues is what is important for anybody, but especially so for an actor.

This kind of success kept Pran where he was at that point of time – right at the very top!

3

By the conclusion of the 1960s, Pran's thirty-year-old career was at its peak. Pran's own restlessness and that catalysing question asked by his young daughter, Pinky, had led to his career exploring new avenues; the result was that from successfully playing the stereotypical arch villain, Pran also achieved success as an impressive character actor.

---

6 The first, much-delayed *Filmfare* Award was for Manoj Kumar's *Upkar*, just two years prior, in 1967. Before its present form marked by glitz, glamour, hype and corporate sponsorships, the *Filmfare* Awards constituted recognition from within the film industry, with only the top-notchers of the film world invited to its awards' functions which were usually held at the Shanmukhananda Hall, at Sion–King's Circle, Bombay.

With about sixty films to his credit, the 1960s had indeed been splendid, a memorable decade for Pran's career. Riding the crest of incredible success, Pran faced the emerging 1970s with a silent prayer on his lips.

For things were going to change dramatically in the 1970s, changes of which even the film industry was unaware. These changes would reflect the uncertainties to which mankind was being subjected, over which none had control. Art had been mirroring life, but that trend would soon change...to life mirroring art.

The decade to come, the angry, turmoil-filled decade of the 1970s, would soon put to test Pran's staying power in filmdom. As per the law of the jungle where newer, younger males challenge the authority of the king lion, newer, younger villains with promising abilities began to appear on the scene and they would present a challenge to the position which Pran traditionally occupied.

Additionally, the emergence of a new type hero, the 'angry, young man' as hero – as against the hitherto goody-goody hero of Indian cinema – would redefine not only films and the traditional set of characters in them, but also social mores and the established ways of life.

Pran's career was now poised on a springboard for his leap into the 1970s.

PART FOUR

TWENTY

The 1970s:
Scaling New Heights

1

If the 1960s sent Pran's star status zooming to significant heights, the decade of the 1970s saw Pran achieve superstar status.

At the beginning of the decade of the 1970s, Hindi film makers sought to make something different. Even as society went about its way with its ages-old traditions and ways of life, which is what cinema had mirrored until then, subtle changes were taking place beneath the surface. During the 1970s, these changes would reflect themselves in the subjects that would be chosen as celluloid entertainment in not just the new-wave genre of film making, but also in the commercial format of Hindi cinema.

Films would aim to more accurately mirror the new mood that was afflicting humankind – the mood of frustration and of anger at the inequalities of this system – but they would do so within the framework of '*the formula*'.

2

Between 1970 and 1979, about seventy-five of Pran starrers went into release, most of which were box-office hits.

Some of the most important among them were the Madras-produced *Gopi*[1] and Chetan Anand's *Heer Ranjha*.[2] This film was unusual in that the entire film's dialogue was in blank verse.

Both Gulshan Rai's *Johny Mera Naam*[3] and Manoj Kumar's *Purab Aur Paschim*[4] had a huge and impressive star cast in keeping with the multistarrer genre that was slowly beginning to take shape.

S. M. Sagar's *Adhikar*, Gemini's *Lakhon Mein Ek*, Rajendra Bhatia's *Jangal Mein Mangal*, Raj Kapoor's *Bobby*, Ravi Tandon's *Majboor*, Madan Mohla's *Dus Numbri* and Sanjay Khan's *Chandi Sona* were among Pran's prestigious film assignments.

'Pran *Saab* always gave us more than our money's worth,' director-producer Arabind Sen had told me (Bunny Reuben) long ago. 'He is an added brain for the director right from the script stage to the final editing of the film.' Despite being involved in each project, Pran never presumed to overstep his contribution to it.

Producer-director Pramod Chakraborty remarked, rather gratefully, in an interview for this book: 'One more beautiful thing about Pran*jee* was that he would not tamper with the script; at least he did not do it with me. He never said, "my role is less, increase it"! He may change the delivery of the dialogues – which is common, any artiste would do it – but he doesn't change the topic of the film.' With a certificate like that, is it any wonder that Pran was a favourite with many producers and directors?

In fact, after working once with Pran, many of them would repeat him in their future projects. Crosschecking with the list of films done during this decade, we see that many film makers had chosen to repeat him within the same decade! For instance, Arabind Sen gave him

---

[1] *Gopi* was released in 1970.
[2] *Heer Ranjha* was released in 1970.
[3] *Johny Mera Naam* was released in 1970.
[4] *Purab Aur Paschim,* was released in 1970.

Pran as a 'professor' in ▶
Jangal Mein Mangal (1972).

fr

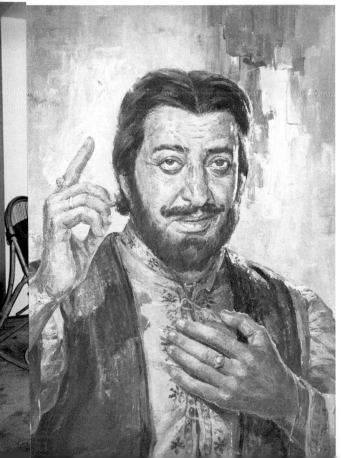

◀ Pran as the inimitable
Sher Khan in *Zanjeer* (1973).

Pran in the company of old friends Nimmi and her husband Ali Raza (February 2000).

Pran with some of his trophies on display (February 2000).

memorable cameos in *Maryada* and *Kasauti*, while Pramod Chakraborty featured him in important roles in *Naya Zamana* and *Jugnu*.

It appeared as if Sohanlal Kanwar had made Pran a permanent figure in his films, for he featured him prominently in four films during the decade – *Be-imaan, Do Jhoot, Sanyasi* and *Atmaram!* Brij Sadanah's *Victoria No: 203* was a masterpiece of landmark proportions, due to which he went on to make *Chori Mera Kaam*, and his brother, Chander Sadanah, made *Chor Ke Ghar Chor*, all of which featured Pran.

Good friend, S.K. Kapoor's *Dharma, Shankar Dada* and *Apna Khoon*, Prakash Mehra's *Ek Kunwari Ek Kunwara* and *Zanjeer* and Manmohan Desai's *Amar Akbar Anthony* and *Dharam Veer*, all demonstrated that talent, hard work *and* good relations *do* pay.

Pran's steady upward graph in the 1970s confirmed what Arabind Sen and Pramod Chakraborty said more firmly than ever before. And it was in the decade of the 1970s that Pran, already noted for his substantial contribution – along with that of the writer and the director – to making each and every role in his starring vehicles, striking and individualistic, enacted some of his most outstanding roles in some of his most memorable films. In further chapters in this section, these roles are dealt with in detail.

3

One of the more commercially successful films of the 1970s was *Johny Mera Naam*, which Vijay Anand (Dev Anand's younger brother) directed for Gulshan Rai and in which Pran played the role of a villain who finally turns good when he discovers that the hero (played by Dev Anand) is his long-lost brother.

Gulshan Rai was already a big-time exhibitor-distributor when he decided to make a film titled *Johny Mera Naam* based on a script by K.A. Narayan. *Johny Mera Naam* and Raj Kapoor's *Mera Naam Joker* both went into release within weeks of one another at the tail end of 1970 – perhaps a deliberate move by Gulshan Rai, who for reasons best known to him, had decided to use *Mera Naam* in the title of his own film. Since the film was readied for release at the same time as *Mera Naam Joker*,

Pran disguised as a *sadhu* in *Johny Mera Naam*.

Gulshan Rai had made sure that it would stand up to a Raj Kapoor film. Much bad blood was generated as a result of this episode.[5]

Remembering the year of release, Pran said: '1970 for me was a memorable year because some of my important films became superhits. Among them was *Johny Mera Naam*.'

But Pran almost did not do *Johny Mera Naam*

What happened was this: After Gulshan Rai decided to make his first film, he made up his mind to rope in Dev Anand and Pran for the two most important roles of the film.

Director Vijay Anand amplified:[6] 'Gulshanjee wanted both Dev *Saab* as well as Pran*jee*, because when he became a producer, he was already a well-established distributor — and he knew that big names sell.'

He then decided to cast Hema Malini as the leading lady because he was quite fascinated by the immense publicity and promotion that had already gone into launching her in Hindi films as the *'dream girl'*.

5 See Chapter titled 'Gulshan Rai – vs – Raj Kapoor: The "Mera Naam" Controversy' in Bunny Reuben's *Follywood Flashback...A Collection of Movie Memories* (Indus, an imprint of HarperCollins Publishers India, New Delhi, 1993).

6 Vijay Anand passed away on 23 February 2004, some months after giving a lengthy interview for this book.

After the initial spadework was done, it appears that a few of the industry*wallahs* known to Gulshan Rai warned him in no uncertain terms about turning producer – especially due to the high risk involved.

'But Gulshan*jee* got irritated, being told off like that!' observed Vijay Anand. 'So he told me to make sure that this film would be a commercial hit. *That is the only time that I went into the making of a film keeping in mind primarily box-office appeal, that the film should be a hit from A to Z.* Naturally therefore, I agreed to take whoever Gulshan*jee* wanted for his film. However, when K. A. Narayan and Gulshan*jee* went to meet Pran*jee*, he told them: "I don't have the time".'

Gulshan Rai was naturally terribly dejected and asked Goldie[7] to go over and try and persuade Pran to sign up for the film.

But when Goldie went over, Pran honestly showed him his fully booked diary and the back-to-back shooting schedules in it, and so regretfully declined to work in Gulshan Rai's film. On so hearing, Goldie decided not to push matters further.

However, Goldie's quiet acceptance that Pran was busy and his view that Pran should not be pushed into doing the role had evidently impressed the star. Recalling those events Vijay Anand said: 'Gulshan Rai, however, informed me that Pran*jee* had told him that he had been impressed by my demeanour and had said: "Such a strange young man! When I showed him my diary, he just got up and left! He never tried to argue or discuss. Therefore, I must do something." '

Once it was decided that everyone would do his or her best to accommodate Pran's schedule and make adjustments as required, he agreed to sign on the dotted line. And that is how Pran came into the star cast of *Johny Mera Naam*.

'In *Johny Mera Naam* I knew exactly what I wanted out of Pran,' revealed Vijay Anand when interviewed for this book. 'For me as a director, I found him perfect as an actor within his own specific range. And within that range, I got what I wanted from Pran *Saab*.

'I wanted him to be stylized most of the time, except when it is revealed that he too is a victim of circumstances. Then his inner emotional conflict comes out, and he emerges in a very sympathetic light.

---

[7] Goldie was Vijay Anand's nickname.

'*That is the only time when I needed much more from Pran Saab than what he had customarily been doing in most of his other films.*

'I explained to him the twist of the story. The twist is that to save her real son (Dev Anand) by diverting the attention of the villains away from him, the mother points out to Pran telling the bad characters, "you can kill *him*, he is my real son" — not knowing that he too is her real son. That day Pran *Saab* was very, very committed and was intensely preparing himself well before waiting for that scene to begin shooting.

'He did it very well. He has to break down and hug his mother, a role played by Sulochana. The key moment of the scene comes when it is revealed that Pran is also her son and that they had been parted long ago. When that moment of revelation comes, they embrace each other and weep.

'I think, that day my brother Dev *Saab* paid the highest compliment to Pranjee. He said to Narayan: '*Yaar, yeh Goldie ko samjhao.*[8] Is he making the film on me or on Pran? What a scene he has given Pran! He will take all the credit for the film!'

Pran told us that apart from his striking role in *Johny Mera Naam*, there were several things noteworthy about the film. '*Johny Mera Naam* was fast paced and because of that, it swept the audiences along with it. It did not give them any time to think.' This achievement was in no small part due to some slick editing by director Vijay Anand.

4

Although the decade of the 1970s saw a great many releases in which a number of top heroes had acted, there were also many films in which character actors were featured more prominently. This was something unprecedented in the film industry.

It was only after being an actor for more than thirty years that, in the early 1970s, Pran opted for his first double role — as that of the misogynistic bachelor-professor and his hippie nephew, the effeminate student, in Rajendra Bhatia's *Jangal Mein Mangal.*[9]

---

[8] 'My friend, why don't you make Goldie understand something?'
[9] Released in 1972.

The story of the film revolves around the misogynistic professor who takes a group of his male students on a botanical excursion. There he meets a man-hating woman-professor who has brought her own batch of lady students, also for botanical studies. In making frantic efforts to keep the two batches of students separate, the old man and the old lady fall in love!

Jangal Mein Mangal was derived from a Malayalam-language comedy written by Kuttan Pillai Kottaarakkara, from whom producer-director Rajendra Bhatia had obtained the Hindi film rights. The major role in the earlier film version of this subject, titled *Rest House*,[10] had been portrayed by P.K. Bahadur, a famous comedian of Malayalam cinema, and was in fact a double role.

Producer Rajendra Bhatia was in a quandary as to whom to cast in this role. He was not in favour of getting one of the known comedians to depict the character. In a flash of inspiration, he thought of Pran.

Would Pran accept the assignment? Rajendra Bhatia knew, of course, that he held the trump card: he was aware that Pran was no longer interested in playing the villain and was looking for either sympathetic roles or 'different' roles, roles which would give him the opportunity to widen the scope of his histrionics.

How would he react to a direct offer to play straight slapstick?

Instead of straightaway offering the role to Pran, Bhatia arranged for a video-screening of the Malayalam film at his own residence where he, very casually, invited Pran to dinner.

After Pran saw the film, his first impression was that Bhatia was trying to interest him in the villain's role, and so he said, 'no, thanks', to Bhatia. It was only then that Bhatia let the cat out of the bag.

'Pranjee,' he said, 'I am sure you are a great comedian. What about doing the main comedy role in the film?'

Pran was intrigued as well as interested.

'Which role are you thinking of?' he asked Rajendra Bhatia.

'Both!' Rajendra Bhatia exclaimed. 'This will be Pran's first double role!'

That did it! The same night Pran consented to do the film!

---

[10] *Rest House*, directed by Sasikumar, was released in 1969.

By the time the shooting of *Jangal Mein Mangal* ended, Pran had appeared in no less than four different characterizations – as a sedate professor, a 'high' hippie, a 'woman' and an aboriginal warrior!

Besides wearing the clothes and facial make-up of a woman, it was Pran's first attempt at playing a woman's character. To cash in on this publicity angle, the film's producer also added, in bold letters, in the advertisements of the film along with the cast names, also 'and co-starring Pran, Pran – and Prani!'

Pran in one of his many distinctive facial get-ups (as the hippie) in *Jangal Mein Mangal.*

Referring to his attempt at doing a role in drag, Pran remembers that it was the immortal Charlie Chaplin who was the first actor in cinema history to play the role of a woman in one of his silent films.

Commenting on the many comic characterizations that Pran did in this film, a leading daily observed:

'*Jangal Mein Mangal* may well turn out to be Pran's most important film to date, and may yet make a confirmed comedian out of this very accomplished thespian.'

Among his 1970s' films, Pran makes special note of *Jangal Mein Mangal*, not only because of his vivid triple role – actually a double role, the third being a role within a role – but also because he was so happy with these films that he opened his own distribution office in Delhi and added film distribution to his cinematic activities.

5

Pran counts Manoj Kumar's *Purab Aur Paschim*, director S.S. Balan's *Lakhon Mein Ek*, S.M. Sagar's *Adhikar* and S.K. Kapoor's *Dharma* among the important films he did in the early-to-mid 1970s.

Coming as it did after the memorable *Upkar*,[11] the eyes of the movie industry as well as the entire country were on *Purab Aur Paschim* and the expectations from this film were tremendous. Manoj's film *Upkar* had resounded with the cry of 'this land is my land, let us be proud of it, cherish it, protect it'. *Purab Aur Paschim* further elaborated on and consolidated this nationalistic theme.

When Manoj Kumar had first given Pran the 'good man's' role in *Upkar*, the results, both on-screen as well as in terms of audience reaction, had been sensational. 'By giving me a strikingly outstanding role of the "good man" in his *Upkar*,' Pran commented, 'Manoj Kumar did something very significant in terms of my career – he broke my conventional image of the "bad man".'

'*Purab Aur Paschim* followed *Upkar*', Pran pointed out, 'and Manoj Kumar gave me yet another off-beat role. Here I started off as a villain, a traitor. Actually, I betray a nationalist to the British and they shoot the patriot. This [incident] took place during the Freedom Movement. In the story, I take my son, then a little boy, and run away to England for good. Years later, circumstances compel me to return to India, to come face to face with the great betrayal – not of the man who died – but of myself as an Indian and as a man.

'When I first heard the story from Manoj,' Pran continued, 'my first reaction was professional: how will he manage to balance so many different characters in a coherent whole? Each one had an important contribution to make towards furthering the theme. Yet they all had to fit in well. He's done it brilliantly, of course. You can see that when you see the finished project.'

If *Upkar* was a poem glorifying India's Green Revolution, *Purab Aur Paschim* tackled another vital national problem: the brain drain. Here again, as in the case of *Upkar*, it is the writer in Manoj Kumar who first sets afire the director in him. It is the theme first – then the telling of it.

Pran said: 'I remember the subject of *Purab Aur Paschim* grew out of a short story which Mrs Manoj Kumar had written. It was based on a single character, some distant uncle of his wife's, who had gone and

---

[11] Released in 1967.

settled in London, and never returned to India. It set Manoj thinking: "Why do India's best brains, her writers and scientists, her painters, technicians, poets, architects, her brilliant students of philosophy and mathematics, why do they leave the motherland never to return?"

'Money, of course. There is that. But the problem goes essentially deeper than money. It has become a challenge of "cultural values". Like in *Upkar*, the canvas in *Purab Aur Paschim* too was vast. The characters too, were larger than life. And in the depiction of his theme, Manoj Kumar chose to paint in vivid, heavy brush strokes, as it were.

'As in *Upkar*, there were in *Purab Aur Paschim* memorable shots, a vivid panorama of striking visuals. In both films, Manoj Kumar, the writer, never allowed Manoj Kumar, the director, the slightest latitude. In consequence, *Purab Aur Paschim* emerged as a flamboyant successor to *Upkar*: a writer's and a director's film, a film for both the mind and the heart, a film which made you feel overwhelmingly proud to be an Indian.'

Concluding his reminiscences about the film, Pran noted: 'I consider *Purab Aur Paschim* to be one of the more memorable films of my career.'

Yet, although he did such a superb job in *Shaheed, Upkar* and *Purab Aur Paschim*, Pran did not act in a Manoj Kumar-directed film for nearly thirty years. Why this happened will be discussed a few chapters later.

6

To switch from drama to comedy is a transition which most actors cannot easily make. This is generally known to most people who are knowledgeable about Indian cinema because in Indian films there are distinct 'character slots'.

This means that one is typecast as an artiste who specializes in senior roles, or in villain's roles, or in comedy roles, and so on.

In Pran's case, however, his histrionic range made it particularly challenging to accept roles which took him from one extreme of characterization to another.

Consider director S. S. Balan's *Lakhon Mein Ek*, for instance.[12] This film is remembered till today because of Pran's extraordinary performance

---

[12] Released in 1971.

as a truck driver in it. Writing about this film one newspaper remarked:

'Pran's performance in *Lakhon Mein Ek* has proved that he is a brilliant comedian too; and when he comes to dance "Bhangra" very few can stand in front of him. With his tremendous range of acting, he is undoubtedly *"lakhon mein ek"* or "one in a lakh".'

The actor had matured over the years; the rough edges had long since been smoothened. He had also attained such a high level of performance that no matter however nit-picking a critic could be, that critic would find it difficult to condemn Pran as 'bad' in any of his performances.

Let us focus on *Adhikar* then.[13] Produced by S. Noor and directed by S. M. Sagar, this film had Ashok Kumar heading the cast. The Hindi-language journal *Madhuri* praised the goodness of the 'bad man' Pran in the film, and went on to make a comment on Pran's role and performance, which, in essence, said:

'Although Pran has a good role in this film, it appears to be a specially created role for Pran. Additionally, his deportment and manner of speech also seem unnatural. His style fits the *film* very well but his way of speaking seems a bit out of place. He has been given good dialogues because of which he got claps for his performance.'

Evidently, the writer of this piece may have been unacquainted with the way in which certain people from Bhopal speak! But the fans loved Pran's depiction of Banné Khan Bhopali.

The critic of a leading English daily (*Hindustan Times*) of New Delhi went out of his way to use the most impressive phrase in Hindi to praise Pran. He said: *'Pran, tera jawab nahin!'*[14]

For any daily to give so much importance to any star or character actor in their critic's column was a totally new feature. But everybody who had seen the movie felt that Pran really deserved such praise.

Now that Pran had stripped off the 'bad man's' image, he had become a very successful character actor displaying the widest range of histrionics.

---

[13] Released in 1971.
[14] It means: 'Pran, you have no equal!'

This is how three important dailies headlined Pran's performance in *Adhikar* in their reviews:

Times of India: 'Three cheers for the bad man.'

Indian Express: 'A new image for Pran.'

Statesman (Calcutta): 'Pran again proves to be one of our most intelligent actors.'

.7

The fact remained, however, that Pran seemed to have, within himself, arrived at a plateau, that difficult stage which every good actor must reach, and then transcend, with regard to the manner in which he delineates each of his different characterizations.

Then came *Dharma*,[15] with its *qawwali*: '*Raaz Ki Baat Keh Doon Toh, Jaane Mehfil Mein Phir Kya Ho, Ishaaron Ko Agar Samjho, Raaz Ko Raaz Rehne Doh.*' Pran's performance to the music and his lip-synching made audiences go crazy![16]

Pran's played the title role in *Dharma*, who was a *nawab*-cum-*daku*[17], a good-bad man, and the film's most popular song was picturized on him and Bindu. Mohammed Rafi and Asha Bhonsle sang the *qawwali*, which was a composition by Sonik Omi, and it restarted the trend of having *qawwalis* in films.

In 1974, journalist Uma Rao commented about what she saw happen while watching this film, when this *qawwali* came on. She wrote: 'I particularly remember the way the crowd in the theatre reacted to Pran's rendering of the *qawwali*...I had witnessed such a spontaneous, excited and stimulated response to an actor on screen only once before in my life – when Rajesh Khanna had sung [another *qawwali*] "*Vaada Tera Vaada*" in *Dushman*.[18] The crowd had gone hysterical then. It was the same in Pran's case, and I admit I was a little taken aback. After all, it's easy for

---

[15] Released in 1973.

[16] This episode is the one referred to in the Prologue of this book.

[17] A dacoit.

[18] Premji's *Dushman* (1971) directed by Dulal Guha, co-starred Rajesh Khanna, Meena Kumari, Mumtaz and Bindu.

a young, good-looking hero with that "certain" smile to get mass adulation. It's different — and difficult — for a character actor to arouse that kind of mass appreciation. Pran has done it. That's why I call him a superstar.' [19]

From actor to villain to character actor and now superstar — Pran had certainly achieved a lot in the more than thirty years of his career.

His next lot of successful films proved that Pran was nowhere near hanging up his boots. There was yet much to be done.

---

[19] 'Pran — A Superstar at 54!', *Stardust*, February 1974.

TWENTY-ONE

Raja and Rana Ride in *Victoria No: 203*

1

Studying the movie industry in depth one finds, among its many facets, this interesting tidbit: most trendsetting films emerge quite unexpectedly from financial compulsions.

From the flopping of one film to the starting of another, any film maker can, and frequently does, grasp at straws. And sometimes, as it turned out in the case of Brij Sadanah,[1] he can be lucky.

The characters played by Ashok Kumar and Pran in *Victoria No: 203* were based on the film *We're No Angels* (1955), in which Humphrey Bogart, Peter Ustinov and Aldo Ray play three crooks who escape from prison on Devil's Island, find shelter with a French family and help extricate them from various problems.[2]

---

[1] The late Brij was the director of *Victoria No: 203*.
[2] *We're No Angels* was remade (using the same title) in 1989. Instead of three escapees (as shown in the original), the remake featured only two escaped convicts, played by Robert De Niro and Sean Penn.

Released in 1972, *Victoria No: 203* is remembered to this day as one of the prime examples of the palpable results which actors can achieve on screen when their mutual tuning is excellent. *These two thespians presented, in this film, an ideal example of coordinated acting.* They were at their naughtiest best in *Victoria No: 203* and were almost entirely responsible for the box-office success of the film.[3]

Ashok Kumar and Pran, who had, both individually as well as in films in which they co-starred,[4] regaled audiences for decades, went on to make their first-time comic teaming a delightful experience in Brij's *Victoria No: 203* which today stands as one of the landmark films, not just in Pran's career, but also in the careers of Ashok Kumar and director Brij.

Pran had met Ashok Kumar for the first time in Bombay Talkies,[5] where he was signed up for a role in *Ziddi*,[6] the film that ended the phase of unemployment. Once struck, this friendship lasted through the decades. No doubt, one of the things that endeared Ashok Kumar to Pran was that he never used to speak against anybody. 'If however, somebody happened to get on his nerves and annoy him to the point where he could not bear it anymore,' said Pran, 'and if he really wanted to say something bad about such a person, then all he would say was this: "Pran, just be careful of this man here. Keep your distance." In Ashok Kumar's language, it was as if he had cursed him to the limit!'

Pran continued: 'During the shooting of *Afsana* [see also Chapter 7], in spite of the fact that I had met Ashokjee earlier, I was very nervous since this was the first picture in which both of us would be acting together. So I went and told Choprajee: "Ashokjee is not only a very big star, he is also a BA graduate. I feel nervous. What should I do?"

'Choprajee reassured me saying: "Don't worry! Just go along and meet him. Everything will be fine. Come, I'll take you with me." Choprajee then took me to Ashok Kumar and introduced us.

---

[3]   *Victoria No: 203* co-starred Saira Banu and Navin Nischol.
[4]   Before *Victoria No: 203*, Ashok Kumar and Pran were usually on opposite sides of the fence, Ashok (Dadamoni) Kumar used to be the hero and Pran the villain. By the time *Victoria No: 203* began to be made, Ashok Kumar and Pran had worked together in sixteen films.
[5]   Ashok Kumar was also employed by Bombay Talkies, but did not have a role in *Ziddi*.
[6]   Released in 1948.

'I'm sure Ashok Kumar must have sensed my nervousness because he took my hands and held them for a long time. I felt as though he was infusing energy into me by holding my hands. I also felt more relaxed by the informality with which he talked to me, like we were old friends. From that day till his death on 10 December 2001, we had always enjoyed a very close relationship.'

So close were Pran and Ashok Kumar that Pran recalled Dadamoni saying that if he (Ashok Kumar) was in the bathroom and Pran's movie was being shown on TV, he would immediately recognize the voice and say: 'That's Pran speaking, isn't it?'

That friendship was certainly one of the most enduring ones in filmdom.

After *Afsana*, in which they were on 'opposite sides of the fence,' as it were – Ashok Kumar was the hero (in a double role), and Pran the villain of the piece. Among their many memorable films until then, were *Inspector*, directed by Shakti Samanta, *Mr X*, H.S. Rawail's *Mere Mehboob*, AVM's *Pooja Ke Phool*, Anoop Kumar Productions' *Aansoo Ban Gaye Phool*, A. Bhim Singh's *Bhai Bahen*, apart from *Purab Aur Paschim*, *Adhikar* and *Sazaa*.[7]

Then, in 1971, they were approached by Brij and Chander Sadanah to do *Victoria No: 203*, a film with a storyline but no script. Why? Because there was simply no time to sit down and write one!

Remembering the pre-production history of *Victoria No: 203*, Chander Sadanah who had worked as an assistant with his brother Brij, said: 'My brother and I had earlier made *Kathputli*[8] which had flopped very badly – hence the financial crisis.

'We needed to start a film immediately, but that's no easy matter, because one does not get star's dates as fast as one would like (due to their innumerable simultaneous assignments). But, as I said, we needed to launch a new film in a month's time – and no script can be written in just one month!'

At the time when Brij Sadanah decided to make a film on this subject, Ashok Kumar and Pran were both very big stars, and both took up this

---

[7]   For further details, please see Filmography.
[8]   *Kathputli* (1971), co-starred Jeetendra and Mumtaz.

assignment as a challenge because it widened the scope of their creative talents far beyond acting alone.

Pran especially, in keeping with his avowed principle of helping new directors-producers to establish themselves, was not concerned whether it was a big banner or a new one – he only wanted the role to be interesting so that he could take it forward from interesting to memorable.

2

K. A. Narayan's story of *Victoria No: 203* initially revolved only around an innocent hack-victoria driver who had been falsely implicated in a murder. Narayan's story also featured the man's daughter, who disguised as a boy, drives the horse carriage to eke out a living.

But that would have made the story run-of-the-mill. So, they decided to 'borrow' the characters of the two crooks from *We're No Angels*, and assimilate them into the storyline. The result was an utterly delightful film – *Victoria No: 203!*

In the film, the two thieves, Raja and Rana, come out of jail, resolving never to do anything that would send them back there. But no sooner are they out of the prison than they read in the newspapers that some diamonds have been stolen from a museum.

Next, when they find a key inside the wig of a dead man they wonder about the lock that the key would fit. This situation prepared the way for one of cinema's most humorous song situations to be filmed. The lyrics contributed to the humour and, of course, Ashok Kumar and Pran, as Raja and Rana, were terrific in it! Film fans will still recall the song, written by Varma Malik, sung by Kishore Kumar and Mahendra Kapoor and composed by Kalyanji Anandji, which went:

Do bechare, bina sahare,
Dekho poochch-poochch kar haare;
Bin taale ki chaabi lekar,
Phirte maare-maare;
Main hoon Raja, yeh hai Rana,
Yeh diwana, main mastana,

Dono milke gaaye gaana;
Oh, haseena...:zaraa ruk jaaana![9]

Raja and Rana's pride in their professionalism challenged, they get on to the trail of these diamonds and learn in due course that the treasure is hidden in a hack-victoria (*ghoda-gadi*) – hence the title.

In their search for the diamonds, they get involved in many adventures and come across the heroine, Saira Banu, the innocent victoria driver's daughter who, in her father's absence, has to fend for herself by disguising her identity and driving the horse carriage.

The story was the usual crime-and-action type of potboiler, but Brij added to it rib-tickling comedy by putting in two comic characters, the spectacular combination of Ashok Kumar and Pran. This surprise comedy duo carried the film on their shoulders. Together, Ashok Kumar as Raja, and Pran as Rana, elevated this film from ordinary to extraordinary!

Reminiscing about the making of *Victoria No: 203*, Chander Sadanah revealed: 'Once the storyline of *Victoria*...took on new shape with the characters of the two crooks being added, Narayan had decided to add an emotional dimension to the character [Rana] by making him the long-lost father of the hero, Navin Nischol.

'Brij and myself already had a vague idea about who should do which role, but we worried that both actors may want the same role, the one with the "extra" dimension to it. So, we went to Pran *Saab* and narrated him the story. And he said, "I'll do *this* role" – meaning the role that we'd had in mind for him! We heard his choice and didn't commit anything because we had yet to meet Dadamoni.

'Then we went to Dadamoni and narrated *him* the full story. And he said, "I'll do *this* role!" – meaning thereby the role we had originally thought for *him*! Amazingly, whatever we had wanted them to accept is what they themselves selected!'

---

[9]   Loosely translated: We're two poor chaps, without any support;
                Have asked everyone, but received naught;
                Got a key, but not the lock;
                We've searched for it all about,
                I am Raja, he is Rana,
                And we're singing you this song...
                O pretty one, why don't you stop?!

3

With this very smooth beginning, the actual shooting of the film began. Recalling those days, Chander Sadanah said: 'I remember that the making of *Victoria No: 203* was great fun all the way through. There was a lot of friendly competition between Pran and Dadamoni.'[10]

'Dadamoni and I would sit on the sets and write our dialogues,' said Pran. 'His habits were child-like, he would…play lots of mischief and tease everybody, but nobody minded.'

'The film was full of punches and little touches, many of which were not in the original script but which we made up as we went along,' recalled Pran.

Chander Sadanah carried forward the narrative, saying: 'For example, there was this one sequence where the two of them are in a boat. Both of them are tied up and the boat is sinking. Anwar Hussain, the villain, has made a hole in it since he wants them to drown.

'Now in the film, Ashok Kumar is shown to be in the habit of drinking. So Pran asks him: "Where is your bottle?" On being told that the bottle is in his rear pocket, Pran takes it out with his mouth, breaks the bottle and cuts the rope with its jagged edge. This is a normal thrill sequence. But the "punch" that was added by both of them was this: Ashok Kumar's hands are free. Despite that, he takes the bottle from Pran and puts it in his mouth to cut the rope! So these types of "punches" were added to each scene by them!'

Brij, always an expert in creating thrills, had made sure that this film was full of them, but the extra zing which the two thespians brought into their scenes, made the film an absolute delight to watch.

Establishing rapport with these two formidable artistes was easy for Brij. Pran revealed his director's methodology:

'Brij gave us plenty of scope to improvise and innovate. He would work out the general pattern of the scene, bring it to the studio, and then ask both of us to sit with him on it.

'After that, he'd literally hand over charge of the scene to both Dadamoni and myself! We always worked out the scene in fairly great

---

[10] The total number of films in which they have acted together is twenty-nine.

detail and would go before the cameras ad-libbing as we went along, and bubbling over with the fun of the whole thing!

'There was a great deal of slapstick in the way in which we worked out our roles, and we really hit the bull's eye with this one, because when the film was released, the public was in fits of laughter all through.' Corroborating what Pran had said, a reporter, while visiting the Sun 'n' Sand Hotel in Bombay (where the shooting of *Victoria No: 203* was in progress), wrote that he saw Pran discussing a particular shot with the director Brij in one of the make-up rooms. It appeared to him that Ashok Kumar was not in agreement with something which Brij had suggested, contending that it was not realistic enough.

Although Brij tried to explain the significance of the shot to him, Dadamoni was not satisfied. When Brij gave Pran a helpless look, Pran stepped in and told Ashok Kumar: 'Dadamoni, this is an important shot.'

'Okay then,' Dadamoni replied, 'we'll do it.'

Apparently after this, there were no more arguments, no doubts and no hesitation. Ashok Kumar then asked his make-up man to get him ready for the shot.

The same reporter went on to describe what else happened on the sets. Before they got started, Dadamoni and Pran discussed the shot, and then had one rehearsal. However, after the first rehearsal they felt the scene was rather flat, lacking punch. So they studied the scene and then improvised on it, took another trial, and improved the camera set-up and the pattern of lighting as well.

Ashok Kumar would try to get to the marrow of the character he was portraying; the physical get-ups did not fascinate him as much as they did Pran. In most of his films, Ashok Kumar looked like his usual, everyday self. Pran, on the other hand, would always study other people on a day-to-day basis, make mental notes of faces and get-ups which interested him and re-create some of their distinctive physical characteristics for the roles he played in various films.

The role Pran played in this film was different; it was something new. 'I was the father of the hero,' Pran reminisced, 'while Dadamoni, my friend from my jail days, was a hobo with a penchant for wine and women!'

In most films, Pran would be the one to run after girls and somebody would have to stop him but in this film it was Ashok Kumar who was

doing what Pran normally did in his films! Ashok Kumar had to chase
the girls and Pran had to try and stop him!

4

A few months before his death on 10 December 2001, Ashok Kumar,
in a special interview, discussed *Victoria No: 203* as well as his friend and
co-star Pran.

'It was a pleasure working with Pran. Now, as you well know, all
actors have big egos. Pran was different. He was proud of his talent as
an actor but his was a positive and constructive ego. It contributed to
the betterment of every film in which he worked – and it never belittled
anybody, from the biggest to the smallest.

'When I first heard the subject, its script was in its first draft. Brij,
however, was in a hurry to start and I encouraged him. "You go ahead,"
I told Brij. "Leave the rest to Pran and me."

'When production actually started I realized that *Victoria No: 203* was
a new kind of challenge. It wasn't a challenge in the negative sense of
"let's see who does better – Ashok Kumar or Pran!" No, more than a
challenge, it was an opportunity to work in tandem with a very talented
actor.'

Discussing his teaming with Ashok Kumar, Pran said: 'It's always a
delight working with Dadamoni. I learned so much from him!

'We both had very memorable roles in *Adhikar* and *Aansoo Ban Gaye
Phool* – but in producer-director Brij's *Victoria No: 203*, our combination
was unbeatable!

'In our earlier years we used to appear as hero and villain. Subsequently,
we became accustomed to playing distinctive "characters", but in *Victoria
No: 203*, for the first time we were together from start to finish. There
are scarcely a few bits in the entire film when we are separated!'

5

Both Ashok Kumar and Pran won much critical acclaim for their
performances in *Victoria No: 203*, but each one was quick to give the other
credit for their brilliantly coordinated performances in the film.

In a TV interview around its post-jubilee period, Pran emphatically declared: 'The credit for our performances, which both press and public have praised, goes to Dadamoni, who has even written the dialogues for our scenes.'

In response, Dadamoni, at the silver jubilee celebrations of Pramod Chakraborty's *Naya Zamana*, insisted that he had done nothing and that Pran was unnecessarily giving him credit for the things he (Dadamoni) had not done!

'Who says that I was writing the dialogue of our scenes as we went along?' Dadamoni exclaimed. 'Nonsense! I was sleeping all the time, while it was Pran who wrote all our dialogues!

'I only spoke the dialogue he wrote and now, just because he goes on TV, he tells the world that I did it all, doesn't mean that I did it! In fact, all the credit goes to Pran as well as to director Brij,' pointed out the thespian.

However, heroine Saira Banu had the last word on the subject: 'If we knew why *Victoria No: 203* clicked in such a big way or if we studied the formulae for making successful movies, we would all be jackpot winners with each film. *But as far as* Victoria No: 203 *goes, its success was due to Brijjee's deft handling and the brilliant cameos from Dadamoni and Pran* Saab.'

The pairing of Pran with Ashok Kumar in *Victoria No: 203* is a prime example of how two accomplished actors can lift the totality of a film to memorable heights when they merge their talents with each other's, in the larger interest of the end result. Their punch lines in *Victoria No: 203* are unmatched. As Pran observes: 'We shared an almost telepathic rapport. Whenever any director would go to Dadamoni with the dialogue sheet he'd wave it away saying: "Whatever Pran does I'll do." Most of the lines of *Victoria No: 203* were improvised on the sets. Dadamoni would start a sentence and I'd complete it or vice versa.'

'That was an exchange you'd never seen on screen before and it worked wonderfully,' Pran beams.

That totality showed at the box offices everywhere. *Victoria No: 203* was a runaway hit and completed its well-deserved golden jubilee. It is remembered to this day not only as one of Pran's landmark films, but also as an entertainer which, because it was successfully 'different', really entertained!

TWENTY-TWO

The *Be-imaan* Controversy:
A Matter of Principle

1

Film awards are always big news. Today there are dozens of them, given by film industry organizations, film magazines, newspaper conglomerates and television channels. But from the early 1950s through the 1980s, the *Filmfare* Awards started by the fortnightly magazine *Filmfare*, a *Times of India* group publication, were the most prestigious, the only *major* film award eagerly looked forward to, to be won by film industry personalities, both big and small.

If winning a *Filmfare* Award every year was considered big news by the winners, refusing one would be almost unthinkable! Therefore, when an incident occurred in 1973, of a *Filmfare* Award being turned down, it hit the headlines everywhere and became the most talked about subject all around.

The case in point was Pran's refusal to accept, in 1973, the *Filmfare* Award for his performance as a policeman in *Be-imaan*.[1]

---

[1] Producer-director's Sohanlal Kanwar's *Be-imaan* (1972).

This was, however, not the first time that the *Filmfare* Award had been refused.

Both Vyjayanthimala and K. Asif had refused it earlier. But they did so on personal grounds. Vyjayanthimala had refused the Best Supporting Actress Award because she felt that she was the heroine and not the supporting actress in Bimal Roy's *Devdas*.[2]

Pran as he appeared in *Be-imaan*.

In the case of K. Asif, he had received the *Filmfare* Best Picture Award for *Mughal-e-Azam*,[3] but not the Best Director Award. He felt that the Best Picture Award must certainly go hand in hand with the Best Director Award, if not some other awards as well, in order to really merit the award of the best picture.

Pran's case was different. Pran refused the award not on personal grounds – he refused it as a matter of principle, a matter that had nothing to do with him, but rather, concerned someone else.

That immediately made it the hottest of controversial discussions in film industry circles. There were a few who felt that Pran had done it for the sake of getting more publicity. There were others who pointed out that if it was publicity he was seeking, then he could have got much more of it as well as applause, just by going to the awards function and then refusing the award in front of the audience!

Whatever may have been the reason for Pran not accepting that award, he had certainly – and strongly – made a point and had also expressed the opinion of the majority of film people about the *Filmfare* Awards that year.

By refusing his own award, Pran had certainly emphasized the need for greater awareness amongst those authorities who give the awards,

---

2 Released in 1956.
3 Released in 1960.

and it was generally felt that they would be more careful in future before taking such weighty decisions.

Doing the 'almost unthinkable', Pran was refusing a *Filmfare* Award on behalf of two people, no more in the world, but whose enormous genius and talent had contributed in no small measure to Indian cinema. Those two people were Ghulam Mohammed, the music director of Kamal Amrohi's much-awaited film, *Pakeezah*, and Meena Kumari, its heroine.

2

'Why bother?' would be the kind of reaction one would expect today. Back then, undoubtedly, many thought the same way. But then, Pran was not 'many'.

A man of principles and a lover of good music, who believed in fair play, Pran could not let himself sit back and do nothing – so what if the two deserving people were dead?! Pran strongly felt that a statement must be made – and so he chose to refuse the award – which, of course, set the cat among the pigeons!

The controversy that resulted is highlighted by an exchange of letters between Pran and B. K. Karanjia, the then editor of *Filmfare*, through the pages of the *Journal of the Film Industry*, which used to be published in newspaper-size by the Indian Motion Picture Producers' Association (IMPPA).

Commenting on the whole issue, the editor of the *Journal of the Film Industry*, S. Kumar, among other things, wrote:

'The biggest news this week in the industry was Pran's decision not to accept the Best Supporting Actor's Award given to him by *Filmfare*. He felt that the award for the Best Music Direction should have gone to *Pakeezah* only. It appears that the whole industry has liked this gesture of Pran; and by not accepting the Supporting Actor's Award he has become the hero of the day.

'I have discussed the issue with Mr Pran as well as Mr Karanjia (of *Filmfare*). I am giving below both the versions. Both of them have their reasons.'

S. Kumar continued by saying that he had just met Pran earlier at the *Shama-Sushma* Awards in Delhi and the latter had told him that he was not happy with what had been announced by *Filmfare* that year.

'He [Pran] had said: "Shankar is a good music director [4] but this year the Best Music Award *should* have gone to the late Ghulam Mohammed for his music of *Pakeezah*.'

'"But why blame Mr Karanjia, when he has to abide by the decision of the judges?" I asked Mr Pran.

' "Who knows the judges? We recognize only Mr Karanjia. *He is praised when the awards are liked; and he is blamed when the awards are not liked,"* ' said Mr Pran.

Pran's comments showed that he bore no personal grudge against Karanjia, but that his objection was purely based on principle. If Pran's letters were being addressed to Karanjia, it was because Karanjia was the man at the helm of affairs in *Filmfare* at the time, and he would naturally be the one in the line of fire if something had not been dealt with satisfactorily.

S. Kumar went on to report that when Pran and he had met in Delhi, the latter had only told him of his disapproval of this year's choices, but had not informed him about his decision *not* to accept the *Filmfare* Award which *he* had won that year for his role in *Be-imaan*. 'Perhaps,' suggested S. Kumar, 'he did not know it himself then.'

Unbeknownst to S. Kumar, Pran had written a personal letter to Karanjia on 19 April 1973, just two days before the *Filmfare* Awards Nite were to be held.

In that letter, Pran had explained his stand at length:

Dear Sir,

I would be failing in my duty towards the film industry – which has made me whatever I am today – by accepting one of the awards which are not fair this time.

I strongly feel that the Filmfare Awards Committee has been unfair in not giving the Award of the Best Music Director to the late Mr Ghulam Mohammed for his music direction of Pakeezah.

---

[4] That year (1972) music director Shankar (of the Shankar Jaikishan duo) was awarded the Best Music Director Award for the film *Be-imaan* as Jaikishan had passed away in September 1971.

Since the days these awards were announced, my conscience has been biting me, and I cannot bear it any more.

I would appreciate it if you please relieve me from the burden of receiving the Best Supporting Actor's trophy.

By not accepting this award I do not mean any personal disrespect to you or to my numerous fans who have voted for me. On the contrary I am thankful to them.

I regret the inconvenience caused to you, but I could not reconcile with the idea of a Filmfare Award trophy (for Be-imaan) staring at me when I am alone at home and reminding me that I have been a party to something unfair. Please forgive me.

Pran.

3

All was quiet until the morning after the *Filmfare* Awards Nite, which was held on 21 April 1973.

Then S. Kumar telephoned Pran on the morning of 22 April and informed him that there had been a rumour going around about his having refused the award and that no mention of it was made at the function, when Pran's name had been announced.

'Why did you not come to the function and *refuse* the award there?' S. Kumar asked him.

Pran answered: 'They have been unfair in not referring during the function to my letter. *Even then, I would not have liked the idea of going to the function and insulting the host by reading out the letter and then refusing the award. I know that the whole house would have applauded my decision but it would have been unfair on my part. Here too, I did not want to be a party to something unfair.*'

When asked what his next course of action would be, Pran asked S. Kumar to print the same letter that he had first sent Karanjia, and which he was now also going to release to the general press. 'This letter must be brought to the notice of the public,' Pran emphasized.

S. Kumar, along with the letter (reproduced earlier), also published this 'question and-answer' discussion between the editor of the *Journal of the Film Industry* and Pran. This is what emerged:

Q: *Could you not write this letter earlier, say when the awards were announced?*

A: *In life we tolerate a lot of things which we do not like. But there comes a time when we cannot tolerate them any more. Just because we have been tolerating something unfair for some time does not mean that we must always tolerate it. We can always take decisions for the better, can't we?*

Q: *We can, but you could have taken it earlier.*

A: *In fact, I am happy that I did not take the decision earlier. After I wrote the letter, some of my good friends persuaded me to withdraw that letter and in spite of my very friendly relations with them I had to say "no". Had I written this letter to Filmfare earlier, more of my friends would have been sent to persuade me to change my decision and reconcile with something against my conscience. I would have had to hurt their feelings too. Now it is all over in two days and there is no room for discussions.'*

S. Kumar's report in the *Journal of the Film Industry* continued as follows:

Before reporting this matter, I talked to Mr Karanjia. He explained that the purpose of the awards was not only to honour the "bests" but also to encourage the newcomers. "That's why the judges preferred to give the award to Hema Malini [for Seeta Aur Geeta] instead of giving it to the late Meena Kumari. When the issue of Best Music was being discussed the judges felt that though the Pakeezah music was very good the award could not be given to the late Ghulam Mohammed as it was not given to the late Meena Kumari," said Mr Karanjia.

It appeared from Mr Karanjia's explanation that the Awards Committee was not in favour of giving awards to the dead!

"Why then did you give the Award to the late Mr K.R. Reddy?" I asked him.

"He died after the awards were announced," said Mr Karanjia.

"And to Jaikishan, last year?"

"Jaikishan's case is different because it was a combined award for Shankar Jaikishan."

"But I don't think this point was ever clarified, that the award would not be given to dead people," I remarked.

"No, it wasn't," he agreed.

"It was not mentioned, even while publishing some letters from readers of Filmfare suggesting that the Best Music Award should have gone to Ghulam Mohammed," I pointed out.

"No, it was not mentioned there. But the matter was discussed while the judges were finalizing the awards. In the case of Best Colour Photography, two names were recommended by the Association of Cinematographers. Those were of the late Joseph Wirsching and of K. Vaikunth. The matter was referred to the judges and they felt that since the award was not given to the late Meena Kumari and the late Ghulam Mohammed, it should also not be given to the late Joseph Wirsching for his photography of Pakeezah," said Mr Karanjia.

It was also obvious that Karanjia had not liked being told about Pran's decision barely two days before the Awards Function on 21 April.

'He could have done it earlier when Mr Pran received the invitation to accept the Filmfare Award that year, and his secretary sent a telegram thanking us for it,' B. K. Karanjia pointed out to S. Kumar. He added: 'He even asked for some extra seats when he accepted the invitation for the function. And then suddenly he changed his mind and wrote that letter. I wish he could have done this earlier.'

When asked by S. Kumar whether or not Pran's letter should have been read out at the awards ceremony, Karanjia answered in the affirmative.

'I would have,' said B. K., 'but when I talked to him on the phone after receiving his letter and expressed the desire to meet him for further discussion, Mr Pran told me that he had made up his mind and there was no use of further discussion as he was not going to change it.

'Obviously, I did not like it, otherwise I would have requested Mr David Abraham [the compere] to read out that letter at the function and also explain our reasons for not giving the award to the late Ghulam Mohammed, in spite of the fact that the music of Pakeezah was excellent.'

4

The interesting fact about the entire episode was that Pran was refusing a Filmfare Award for Best Suppporting Actor for his role in Be-imaan on the grounds that the Best Music Director Award was unfairly won by Shankar for the same film! Where others may have gone along with everything and been happy for the fact that the film in which they had starred was the recipient of so many awards, it was not so for Pran. He was going to see this controversy through to its logical end.

The next instalment of the controversy came in the form of a letter that S. Kumar received from Pran on 30 April 1973, and which he chose to reproduce in his journal:

Dear Mr Kumar,

Thank you for printing in your column in the Journal of the Film Industry *my letter to* Filmfare *and other discussions I had with you.*

I have also read Mr Karanjia's statement. In his heart of hearts he appears to be convinced that the music of Pakeezah *was the Best Music and yet he is only trying to justify an unfair decision by saying that the Filmfare Award is not given to dead people.*

In his anxiety to justify a wrong decision he has made a wrong statement also. He says that Mr K. R. Reddy (who gets the Best Telugu Director Award) died after the Filmfare Awards were announced. No Sir. Mr Reddy died on 16 September 1972. The Award could not [have been] announced before 31 December 1972.

If a Filmfare Award could be given to Mr K. R. Reddy after his death, it could also be given to Mr Ghulam Mohammed after his death.

In our culture, the dead are no less respected than the living. It is strange that Filmfare *seems to be having more consideration for the living than for the dead. Moreover, by making such statements (that the award is not given to dead people), he has humiliated both the dead as well as the living.*

No award winner would like the idea of getting an award just because the better one had died unfortunately (or fortunately, for the award winner!) before the awards were announced. From Mr Karanjia's version published by you it is obvious that the awards would have gone to Ghulam Mohammed Saab and Meena Kumarijee had they been alive.

One more point. Mr Karanjia, has often blamed the film stars for their lack of sportsmanship. At least he could himself have shown some by reading my letter at the Awards Function.

Yours sincerely,

Pran.

Commenting on the entire affair, S. Kumar went on to say:

'Pran's action should be an eye-opener to Filmfare. *It has taken about two decades for the* Filmfare *Awards to reach the position of "the most-coveted one in the industry," as described by Ashok Kumar, who was the chief guest at the function. It has to make some drastic changes and assure an infallible system of judgement to maintain that prestigious position.*

'Any change in the award rules should be announced before the polling so that there may not be any misunderstanding. For example, if the purpose of the award is to encourage new talent rather than to honour the best ones (as is presumed), it has to be clearly stated much in advance. Otherwise, the judges' intentions are likely to be misinterpreted by the common people.'

S. Kumar went on to conclude his report as follows:

'I have mentioned here both the sides. But as I wrote the above, we do not live by reasoning alone. These explanations may not convince most of the people who have already formed their opinions about the decision of the judges of the Filmfare *Awards Committee as well as about the decision of Mr Pran.*

'Personally, I feel that Mr Pran has gained more popularity and prestige by making his non-acceptance of the award a tribute to the music director of Pakeezah, *while* Filmfare *has suffered a setback. It has to be more careful in future. What is built in decades can be sometimes destroyed in a year. Let it not happen to the* Filmfare *Awards.'*

The editor then said that he 'would like to close this controversy between Mr Pran and Mr Karanjia, unless of course Mr Karanjia happens to write a letter in reply to Mr Pran's.'

Obviously upset, Mr Karanjia took recourse to silence.

However, Pran was too much of a gentleman to let an award come in the way of a relationship built over the years with the reputed and respected magazine, which had given him two earlier awards – for *Upkar* (1967) and *Aansoo Ban Gaye Phool* (1969) – both of which he had graciously accepted.

So, at *Filmfare's* Silver Jubilee Year Party held in March 1977, Pran sent his best wishes and a bouquet to the magazine, which was reported as follows:

'Another bouquet was from Pran – a specially touching gesture. Pran had once declined a *Filmfare* Award but the gentleman-villain obviously wanted to show that he had nothing against the paper itself and anyway he wasn't going to take a quarrel – if it was that – too far.'

It was obvious that *Filmfare* too was in a mood to let bygones be bygones.

5

Both the English-language press and the regional-languages press had carried the news of Pran's refusal of the *Filmfare* Award. When approached by the Hindi-language weekly *Palki*, Pran issued a clarification, and went on record to say: '*I refused to accept the award on the grounds of principle. Though* everybody knows that I have nothing to do with *Pakeezah* or with Ghulam Mohammed, *I was objecting to the award being given wrongly. And I expressed it by not accepting my award. That's all.*'

When asked about the *Be-imaan* controversy during an interview for this book, *it was obvious that Pran still stood strongly for what he had felt at that time.* After repeating much of what was printed by the media earlier, he added:

'I had heard people say that the awards were being bought and not being given to deserving ones. That year's best music was of Master Ghulam Mohammed in *Pakeezah* [1971]. They didn't give him the award and gave it to *Be-imaan* instead, so in protest, I refused to take my award. The picture's name was *Be-imaan*[5] and I found that I could not stand with the dishonest ones to take the award.

'This created a lot of *hungama*[6] and they came to me. I said "you change your system". They said "we'll change it from next year". Then I said "then I'll take the award from next year only".'

Pran somehow did not win another *Filmfare* Award for the next twenty-five years! It was only in 1997 that *Filmfare* awarded Pran with a Special Veterans' Award for his lifetime contribution to cinema.

Although Pran did not accept his *Filmfare* Award for *Be-imaan*, he did accept the *Shama-Sushma* Award for the same film as Best Supporting Actor, because he did not see any injustice done to any deserving persons in those awards.

---

[5] Meaning, 'dishonest'.
[6] Meaning, 'hullabaloo'.

Though both of them were not alive then, *Shama-Sushma* had given Meena Kumari the Best Actress Award for *Pakeezah* and music director Ghulam Mohammed the Best Music Award for the same film. The first *Shama-Sushma* Film Awards Function was held at Hotel Ashoka, New Delhi, on 11 March 1973. It was one of the best − if not the best − star shows held in the capital. The convention hall of the hotel was overflowing. The trophies were presented by I. K. Gujral, who was then the minister for information and broadcasting. Except for the famous Urdu poet Kaifi Azmi (who was not well) and Zeenat Aman (who had returned to Bombay from Hong Kong only a day earlier), all the award winners were present − except, of course, Meena Kumari and Ghulam Mohammed.

Another important film journal covering the event reported: 'The loudest and [the] longest applause was reserved for Pran. It was an experience to see him walking towards the dais to receive his trophy while the whole house was thundering with claps. It appeared that before I. K. Gujral could give him the *Shama* trophy, the audience had already given Pran a much greater trophy by way of its tremendous applause.'

6

Controversies of a wide variety have always dogged Pran's footsteps. Yet another interesting case took place involving the same film, *Be-imaan*. Pran played the role of a police constable in it, who happened to be Manoj Kumar's father, and during its shooting, one scene required Pran to hit the idol of a deity with his baton. While doing this, the head of the deity fell off.

When the film was released to the public, this scene apparently hurt the religious sentiments of one great devotee, a *panwaari*[7] in Rajkot. He filed a case in the Magistrate's Court against both Pran as well as the director, Sohanlal Kanwar.

Pran created a very positive impression in court, just like he had done many decades ago in Lahore. One of the arguments he gave in his defence was that throughout his screen career he had 'murdered' over

---

[7] A *panwaari* is a man who sells betel nut and mouth-freshening spice mixes wrapped in betel leaf.

two hundred people and committed more than forty 'rapes', but he had never been hauled up before a court of law. 'Surely this "criminal record" of mine is far more serious than the breaking of a plaster of Paris statue!' Pran remarked.

7

All things considered, *Be-imaan* was unremarkable as a film. In its review, *Star & Style* (1 September 1972) described it as 'a messy formula film', the theme of which 'is simple and age-old. There are lots of *"bada chors"* in high society, so why blame the *"chota chors"* in low society, who are only earning a living?'

With regard to Pran, the review noted: 'But we wish they had not made Pran's character play to the gallery to a point where it makes you uncomfortable.'

Pran's refusal to accept the *Filmfare* Award brought *Be-imaan* into the limelight and garnered much media exposure for it. Even so, although the film did not get good reviews and it was not such a big hit, it won for Pran at least four other awards that year, including the one given by *Shama-Sushma.*

Despite the fact that Pran emerged victorious after this episode, it did not go to his head. A gentleman to the fingertips, and possessor of a racy tongue, Pran has always been a man of principles, even when he had nothing to gain from them.

And the *Be-imaan* controversy proved it.

TWENTY-THREE

Zanjeer: Setting a New Trend

1

The 1970s had not only ushered in newer actors who were testing their wings in negative roles, but also this decade was about to bring to the fore a new phenomenon. That was the phenomenon of the new hero, an antithesis of all that heroes had stood for, until then – the anti hero.

This new type of hero was deeply angry and rebelled against the Establishment, after finding that all the hitherto accepted rules of society applied, not to the *rulers*, but only to the *ruled*. The Rebel would take the law into his hands and rid society (read: the hero's immediate locality) of all the evil that had been amassed sky-high – a sort of social messiah.

This new hero would now not only redefine the subject matter of the films being made, but would also have a direct and somewhat worrying impact as a role model for the youth of the land.

In this scenario, consider what happened to actor-villain Pran. In the late 1960s, Pran had taken a successful step towards positive character-actor roles, thereby changing the only image he had cultivated until then.

That, as it turns out, was a very fortunate step because the demarcating lines between the villain's sphere of activity and the hero's would soon be blurred. In some films, any villain would now be only slightly 'darker' than the hero.

At the start of 1970s, Pran not only wanted to continue proving his versatility by playing a variety of characters of varying shades (which he had done in his most memorable roles of the late 1960s–early 1970s), but also he needed a break from the routine activity that playing 'villain' had become.

It was at such a time that producer-director Prakash Mehra approached Pran to play the role of Sher Khan, a tough Pathan[1] with a heart of gold.

2

'Had it not been for Pran *Saab*, *Zanjeer* would never have been made; it would have remained a dream.'

That was the very first statement which producer-director Prakash Mehra made when asked to reminisce about the making of his superhit film, *Zanjeer*.[2]

Prakash Mehra's association with Pran was relatively new: Pran had worked with him in only two films until then: *Aan Baan*[3] and *Ek Kunwari Ek Kunwara*.[4] Watching him work in *Aan Baan*,[5] Prakash Mehra had already been impressed by his dedication to work.

Aan Baan had a twist wherein Pran, who plays Rajendra Kumar's brother, does not know that the girl he is to marry is actually his brother's sweetheart. The entire scene of the elaborate marriage sequence was to be shot with Pran on horseback. During the picturization of that sequence, he had to even give the 'long shots'[6] without the use of a

---

[1]   According to *The New Oxford Dictionary of English*, a Pathan is a member of a Pushto-speaking people inhabiting north-west Pakistan and south-east Afghanistan.

[2]   Released in 1973.

[3]   *Aan Baan* (1972).

[4]   *Ek Kunwari Ek Kunwara* (1973).

[5]   A film titled *Aan Baan* in which Pran had acted was made earlier in 1956, and then again with the same title in 1972, again with Pran in the cast. Interestingly, Pran acted in quite a few pairs of films which had the same title but were made years apart.

[6]   A long shot is where the camera is placed at a good distance from the subject.

'double'.[7] It was a long shot involving a whole lot of junior artistes crowding in the verandas of the houses on both sides of the huge street set. The hero, Rajendra Kumar had to sing the song 'Lo Aaye Hum Dulhe Bhaiya Ke Baraati Banke'[8] as the baraatis proceeded down the street.

Talking about it to a film journalist years ago, (the late) Rajendra Kumar said: 'Pran Saab is so dedicated to his work that never did he ask to dismount. He sat the whole day on the horse in that heat – and he never once lost his cool!'

Pran had proved that he was one hassle-free artiste who would give his directors consistently good work. So for his own film, Prakash Mehra decided that he would like to have Pran in a key role. As Prakash Mehra elucidated:

'Though both Pran Saab and I had been in the movie industry from long before Zanjeer, it had been just a "hi-hello" kind of interaction. Although we had worked in Aan Baan and Ek Kunwara Ek Kunwari before, I was just the assigned director in those films. What better common ground than working closely together on my own film in order to grow close to one another?

'Pran Saab – as I was to learn when the time came to plan Zanjeer – has always been a man of strict principles.

'Let me explain.... About the same time that we started the groundwork for the film Zanjeer, Manoj Kumar was also working on his film, Shor. I had heard the script of Zanjeer narrated by Salim [and] Javed[9] and while listening to the character of the Pathan in it, the image of Pran came to my mind because I had seen his work in Chhalia in 1960. I therefore immediately approached Pran Saab for that role – and he accepted.'

'After Pran Saab had said "yes" to the Pathan's role in my Zanjeer, I heard that Manoj Kumar approached him a few days later to do a similar

---

7 'Doubles' or 'duplicates' are people who are chosen on the basis of their general appearance matching that of the star for whom they have to stand-in. 'Doubles' are often used for fight sequences, difficult or dangerous stunts and long shots.

8 Baraatis are those invited guests who walk in procession with the bridegroom as he makes his way to the bride's house.

9 Salim Khan and Javed Akhtar were a writer-duo who would skyrocket to fame with this film, and with Trimurti Films' Deewaar, directed by Yash Chopra, and Ramesh Sippy's Sholay (both released in 1975).

role...in *Shor*. It must have taken a lot of courage to say "no" to Manoj Kumar, who had, not very much earlier, given Pran that memorable role of a good man in *Upkar*,' Prakash Mehra observed.

Pran reportedly told Manoj Kumar that he would work in *Shor* should Prakash Mehra decide not to make *Zanjeer*. But both knew that the likelihood of that happening was virtually nil, since Prakash Mehra's recent films like *Haseena Maan Jayegi*,[10] *Mela*[11] and *Samadhi*[12] had all become jubilee hits!

Recalling what happened in an interview to *Cine Blitz* (December 1989) Pran said: 'I enjoyed working with Manoj Kumar.... Unfortunately, I didn't work with him after *Upkar* and *Purab Aur Paschim*. When he was planning *Shor*, he did come to me and asked me to play a Pathan in the film. But I had to refuse the offer because I had already agreed to play one in Prakash Mehra's *Zanjeer*. And I didn't want to be unfair. He felt bad because after all he had given me *Upkar*. I think till today he's annoyed. But if he sits down and thinks, he'll realize how right I was.'[13]

However, it is interesting to hear what Manoj himself had to say about Pran's commitment, which, in the case of Manoj Kumar's *Shor*, happened to come up against the actor-film maker's own sense of commitment: 'Since I was so close to Pran, I asked him to hear the story of *Shor*.'

When asked about the story, Pran reportedly told Manoj: 'It's difficult to make.' Continuing his narrative, Manoj said: 'So I asked him, "Pran Saab, what's the point in making an easy film? There's no fun in it." Later on, he telephoned me and said: "*Panditjee*, don't mind. Can you please change that character of the Pathan to somebody else?"

---

[10] *Haseena Maan Jayegi* (1968) had Shashi Kapoor in a double role with Babita as the heroine.

[11] *Mela* (1971) featured the brothers Feroz Khan and Sanjay Khan with Mumtaz as the heroine.

[12] *Samadhi* (1972) starred Dharmendra (in a father-son double role) with Asha Parekh and Jaya Bhaduri as the leading ladies. The much 'remixed' song *'Kaanta lagaa...'* (written by Majrooh Sultanpuri, tuned by R.D. Burman and sung by Lata Mangeshkar) was originally in *Samadhi*.

[13] This interview was obviously given before Manoj Kumar signed Pran to work in his film *Jai Hind* (released in 1999).

'I asked: "Why?" "I have already agreed to do a film of Prakash Mehra and I am doing the role of a Pathan in it. I am committed," he told me. To which I replied: "Pran *Saab*, I appreciate your commitment. You are committed to Prakash Mehra and I am committed to my script. I cannot change it. So, no ill feelings."

'We took Premnath*jee* instead. This makes people think that something has gone wrong between Pran and Manoj Kumar. But it's not like that. The very third day, he was sitting at my house and hearing the story of *Dus Numbri*.[14] I appreciated him for saying that he was already doing a Pathan role. But I *needed* a Pathan for my film. *Pran* Saab *is a man of principles!* I had my own commitments which he too appreciated.'

Not only was this refusal a matter of principle that Prakash Mehra had approached him first, but also the other reason why Pran had turned down Manoj Kumar needs to be mentioned here.

The unique factor about Pran's career always was that he tried never to repeat a 'get-up' or character. If he had to accept Manoj's offer, it would mean doing two Pathan roles in quick succession, since both films were being made almost simultaneously.[15] Although the stories of both films were substantially different, Pran reasoned that the Pathan character would be similar and, after all, how many different ways *are* there in which to play a Pathan? Inevitably, with the simultaneous filming and the similar characters, it would not be inconceivable that certain repetitions in delineation of the two characterizations would creep in. Therefore, Pran explained his stand to Manoj and rejected his offer.

The moment Pran accepted *Zanjeer*, he went much beyond himself, far beyond merely visualizing and preparing for his own role.

He went out of his way to help Prakash Mehra in some other important ways as well.

---

[14] Released in 1976, this film co-starred Manoj Kumar, Hema Malini, Premnath and Pran.

[15] Prakash Mehra stated very definitely in his taped interview that he was motivated to cast Pran as a Pathan in *Zanjeer* since he had been stirred by his performance *as a Pathan* in Subhash Pictures' *Chhalia*, directed by Manmohan Desai. However, that get-up was used nearly thirteen years previously, in 1960.

3

'Pran *Saab* helped me in many ways in *Zanjeer*,' Prakash Mehra recounted. 'For one thing, we were not able to finalize a hero, so Pran arranged a meeting for me with Dev Anand *Saab*, whose *Kala Pani*[16] I had seen.

'When I had seen *Kala Pani*, I had strongly felt that the role he played in that film would transform Dev's entire image – from the song-singing, goody-goody hero doing light, romantic roles to something far more impactive.'

When Prakash Mehra mentioned that he was considering Dev Anand for the hero's role in *Zanjeer*, both Salim and Javed felt that it would be a case of total miscasting.

Prakash Mehra continued: 'I had already paid three visits to Dev *Saab* and had narrated the script to him; then Dev Anand mentioned that he should be given two or three songs to sing in the film. I said: "No Dev *Saab*, this character will not be singing. This is not that kind of character."

'Dev *Saab* immediately said: "Alright Prakash, you do one thing. This is a beautiful subject. You give it to me. I'll make it in Nav Ketan and you direct it – and I'll give you whatever money you want."

'I laughed and said: "Dev *Saab*, I have come to give *you* work – and now you are offering to give *me* work!" We both laughed and parted as friends.'

There was, of course, another reason why Prakash Mehra refused to hand over the subject to Dev Anand. It had to do with an earlier arrangement Prakash Mehra had had with Dharmendra!

Prakash Mehra, by virtue of a verbal commitment made earlier, was bound by an understanding with Dharmendra. 'He and I were partners,' Prakash Mehra revealed. 'The story had been bought by Dharmendra, who was to be the leading man of the film.' However, Dharmendra had other commitments and so, although their partnership was dissolved, he let Prakash Mehra use that story.

The story of *Zanjeer* was then narrated to Raaj Kumar, who in his classic style said: '*Jaani*, this is my kind of subject. I was once an inspector

---

[16] *Kala Pani* (1958) was directed by Raj Khosla and co-starred Dev Anand, Madhubala and Nalini Jaywant.

in Mahim.[17] But for this film, you do the shooting in Madras!' When Prakash Mehra explained that the story's setting was in Bombay and that it would be impossible to shoot a film like that in Madras, Raaj Kumar also declined to do the film.

This business of finding a leading man for *Zanjeer* was going from perplexing to annoying. Prakash Mehra had by now considered *three* heroes and he was getting increasingly frustrated about not yet being able to zero in on the right candidate. Besides, rumours had already spread about his not being able to *decide* on a hero for *Zanjeer.*

Pran's younger son Sunil (*Tunni*) was working in Madras and staying with his friend Ajitabh Bachchan, whose elder brother was already in films. When he heard from his father that Prakash Mehra was looking for a hero for his new film, he told him: 'Dad, I have a friend who is in films. Though his recent films have flopped, this guy is real good.'

That hero was Amitabh Bachchan, who had started his career with K. A. Abbas' *Saat Hindustani,* released in 1969, and had done an excellent cameo in Sunil Dutt's *Reshma Aur Shera,* released in 1971. Though Hrishikesh Mukherjee's *Anand* was the third film he had signed, it was released earlier in 1970, and became a hit.[18]

Getting in touch with Prakash Mehra, Pran told him: 'You go and see *Bombay to Goa.*[19] It's recently been released. I haven't seen it myself but you check out the hero in it.[20] My son *Tunni* is praising him a lot.'

---

[17] An area in western-central Bombay .

[18] Amitabh Bachchan's other early films such as *Parwana* (1971), *Pyar Ki Kahani* (1971), *Sanjog* (1971), *Bansi Birju* (1972), *Ek Nazar* (1972) and *Bandhe Haath* (1973) were not huge commercial successes. *Anand* (1970), *Bombay to Goa* (1972) and *Abhimaan* (released in the same year as *Zanjeer,* 1973) clicked in a big way at the box office. *Zanjeer* is officially called the beginning of Amitabh's 'angry young man' persona. However, film fans will recall that his role in *Anand* was that of a brooding, serious and introvert doctor, and had won for him rave reviews and predictions of greatness. His performance had stood in sharp contrast to Rajesh Khanna's extrovert performance in the title role of the same film.

[19] N.C. Sippy's *Bombay to Goa* (1972), directed by S. Ramanathan, was a small budget multistarrer which co-starred Amitabh Bachchan, Aruna Irani, Shatrughan Sinha, Mehmood and many other well-known stars.

[20] As far as possible, Pran *Saab* does not like to go to the movies.

So Javed Akhtar and Prakash Mehra went to see *Bombay to Goa*. There is a particular scene in that film which was a fight sequence.

'Even as the film was unfolding,' said Prakash Mehra, 'we came to that fight scene of Amitabh's with Shatrughan in a restaurant. *That scene was enough for us to decide and select the hero.* I screamed: *"Mil gaya!"* The entire hall turned to stare at us! Why, they wondered, was I yelling *"mil gaya!"* for no apparent reason? Without seeing the rest of the film, we came out of the theatre and I said to Javed: "We have found our hero!" '

4

Although they had finally found their leading man, other obstacles emerged, and it would still be a while before Salim and Javed could approach Amitabh.

Mumtaz, originally slated to be the female interest in the film, got married to Mayur Madhvani and decided to leave films. So, she returned the signing amount Prakash Mehra had given her for *Zanjeer*. Then Dharmendra withdrew and the financier backed out as well. Everything was in a shambles.

After eventually sorting out his problems, Prakash Mehra went to Amitabh Bachchan who agreed to do the film.

In an exclusive interview for this biography, Amitabh Bachchan spoke about how *Zanjeer* happened to come to him:[21]

'*Zanjeer* actually came about because of Salim Javed. I was working in *Anand* and Rajesh Khanna was the hero. Salim and Javed were very close to him and used to come and visit him on the sets. I met them once or twice. *Then they saw one of my films called* Bombay to Goa, *and I don't know what they liked, but they came to me and that's how the role came to me.*

'I also believe that apart from Salim Javed, Ajit *Saab* and Pran *Saab* both had recommended my name, perhaps in a very guarded tone because I had not worked with that many actors, to Salim *Saab* and Javed *Saab*. That's how I got the *Zanjeer* role. Why Prakash Mehra chose me,

---

[21] It appears that Amitabh Bachchan could have been unaware of what had transpired before Salim and Javed approached him for the role in *Zanjeer*.

why Salim Javed chose me, why Pran *Saab* endorsed me, why Ajit *Saab* endorsed me remains a mystery to me but I am happy that they did because *Zanjeer* gave me a lovely platform.'

By a happy combination of circumstances and fortuity, not only did Prakash Mehra and *Zanjeer* get a hero, Hindi cinema got itself a new superstar, a super-as-never-before-hero, an icon and a legend, a phenomenon that few have been able to describe or analyse, but at whom all have marvelled.

However, Prakash Mehra recalled that at one point during the making of *Zanjeer*, his hero became quite dejected due to another of his films not having done well at the box office: 'O. P. Ralhan's *Bandhe Haath* had flopped, and our hero got a bit jittery. So I reassured him, saying: "You wait and see, *Zanjeer* will change everything for you." Then I announced my second production, *Hera Pheri*, a comedy with Amitabh Bachchan and Vinod Khanna. This was my way of getting my hero out of his depression.

'Jaya, who was working in the other film I was directing, *Samadhi*, was not keen on another small role [in *Zanjeer*] where [it] would be called a "special appearance". But Amitabh and Jaya were courting and so we once more asked Jaya to do *Zanjeer*, which she did...'

'...and that is the entire behind-the-scenes story of how *Zanjeer* got started,' Prakash Mehra concluded.

5

Zanjeer (meaning: a chain) is the story of Vijay (played by Amitabh Bachchan), who, as a child, has witnessed the murder of his parents by a faceless killer wearing around his wrist a chain, from which dangles a small white horse. Tormented by the image of the chain, Vijay, who becomes a cop in Bombay, determines not only to root out crime from the city, but also to hunt down his parents' murderer. He befriends Sher Khan, a Pathan gambler and local don (Pran), who becomes his ally. Although he is romantically drawn to Mala (Jaya Bhaduri), the serious young man does not sing or dance or romance, but is single minded in his quest to identify the faceless murderer: Teja (Ajit). When he does so, he takes the law into his own hands and avenges the murder of his parents.

Pran and Amitabh Bachchan enact a poignant scene in *Zanjeer*.

Prakash Mehra also revealed details about how Pran not only prepared for his role but also worked hard at it: 'For *Zanjeer* Pran *Saab* used the same get-up as the one he had used for *Chhalia*, since in that film too he was playing a Pathan. He didn't change things too much, but he used a reddish-haired wig and beard for this film. You know that Pran *Saab* has always been very fond of get-ups. If I may be permitted a digression here...it has been my great desire that a public exhibition should be held of Pran *Saab*'s various get-ups from all his films. Film lovers will be fascinated by such an exhibition!'

Highlighting the importance of voice modulation in addition to the choice of costume, make-up and wig and beard, in order to become the character one is portraying, Pran explained: 'Changing one's voice and accent is very important. Merely by changing my costume, or wearing a red beard and wig, I wouldn't have been very impressive as the Pathan in *Zanjeer*. So, I changed my voice, too, to sound like a real Pathan. There have been occasions when I have had to do as many as *eighteen* retakes to get the pronunciation of a word just right.'

6

The shooting of this film started with the picturization of that now-immortal song: 'Yaari Hai Imaan, Mera Yaar Meri Zindagi'.[22] When Prakash Mehra informed Pran that his first shot for the film would be a song sequence which they were picturizing the very next day, the actor told him that he was opting out!

Of course, part of the reason why Pran was upset was because the song and the words were not given to him in advance. Besides, he never liked to 'sing' songs in movies! By his own admission in one of his early interviews: 'I cannot run around trees and sing!'

But now, after Upkar, he came to the conclusion that if the song they wanted him to sing was not there simply for the sake of having a song, but that it would actually enhance the story, he would definitely sing it. He decided that he could do such songs, but he would need the song along with the words in advance so as to be able to prepare for it.

'You haven't sent me my lines, or a cassette of the song – and you expect me to be ready!' Pran virtually shouted at Prakash Mehra. 'You can forget about starting your film tomorrow!'

'I was in a terrible fix,' Prakash Mehra admitted. "If I didn't have the muhurat[23] of Zanjeer the next day, my distributors were going to ditch me.'

On hearing that Pran was going to opt out of the film Prakash Mehra dashed over to his house. Prakash Mehra needed Pran, especially since his new hero was not at that time a bankable proposition. Trying to convince Pran not to let him down, Prakash said: 'We'll do the song tomorrow, then I'll edit it and show you the rush print. If you don't like it – we'll scrap it.' Since that sounded reasonable, Pran agreed to start shooting the very next day.

'Some days after the muhurat,' Pran said, 'I started getting calls from some friends and colleagues who had managed to get a sneak peek at the rushes. "It's brilliant! You're brilliant!" they all raved.'

---

[22] This song, sung by Manna Dey, tuned by Kalyanji Anandji and written by actor-lyricist Gulshan Bawra, who appeared briefly in the film in another song sequence, means: 'Friendship Is My Faith, and My Friend Is My Life.'

[23] The day, date and time fixed by astrologers for the auspicious beginning of a project.

Then, a couple of days later, Prakash Mehra phoned Pran and invited him to come and see the edited rush print of the song.

'I've seen it already,' Pran told Prakash.

Prakash Mehra was astonished: 'When? Where?'

'Through the eyes of those who have seen the rush print!' Pran retorted. 'If so many people have liked it there's no need for me to see it now. Retain it. It'll be a hit.'

And he was right!

Asked to talk about the conception and execution of that song-dance sequence, Prakash Mehra amplified:

'Pran *Saab* was apprehensive about dancing, but, never a man to shirk work, he still danced. I told Pran *Saab* that Pathans dance with a large handkerchief in their hands and this must be done. I explained to Pran *Saab* that this song-dance [sequence] was important for another reason – it was not just as an item.

'The other reason was that though this song-dance item comes in the thirteenth or fourteenth reel, nearer the climax, it is the first time that the hero smiles a little and you will be putting special efforts in that song-dance [sequence] for some eleven solid minutes to make this man smile!

'And that is exactly what Pran *Saab* did!'

Going into more details about that famous number from *Zanjeer*, Prakash Mehra continued: "Satyanarayan*jee* choreographed that item. Pran told Satyanarayan*jee* that he had severe pain in his hip.

'Satyanarayan*jee* said: "Sir, it is a full[-blooded] song with the vigorous dance of a Pathan. And Prakash Mehra is insisting on all the movements with the 'kerchief," and showed him the dance. Pran got panicky because of the pain in his hip and mentioned it.

'So Satyanarayan*jee* told Pran: "Except for the finale of the song when there are major body movements, the rest of the song has only minor movements; and since you are the main character in the dance, I will surround your dance with the dancing of the junior artistes. This will make things easier for you." So they both collaborated, and the song was picturized. That song was the highlight of the film.'

Prakash Mehra went on to say: 'When the song was reaching its peak, Pran *Saab* got so involved in the mood and rhythm of the song that he forgot all about his hip! After that, however, he took to bed for some four or five days. Then when he started reporting for shooting, he would apply medicine, would wear a belt brace for his hip and take painkillers. But never once did he ever miss his shooting, nor would he ever be late for the shooting.'

When asked to comment on Pran's performance in the 'Yaari Hai Imaan...' number, Amitabh Bachchan recalled what happened after the actress Nargis (who was the one to get Amitabh his first film, Saat Hindustani) saw Zanjeer:

'Pran Saab put so much zest and gusto in that Pathan song in Zanjeer; he was very endearing in that song! I still remember Nargisjee was still alive at that time. She saw the trial of that film and actually called him up and said: "You know, you look younger than the hero you are working with." Remarkable!'

That immortal song is still telecast from time to time, and the mass cinegoers remember to this day the enthusiasm with which Pran danced in that item!

Another interesting phenomenon is that whenever participants of the various antakshri[24] music programmess made for television decide to sing 'Yaari Hai Imaan, Mera Yaar Meri Zindagi', the participants get on to the stage and dance to the song exactly like Pran did in Zanjeer!

7

Talking about Prakash Mehra's film in his reminiscences for this book, Pran said: 'Zanjeer proved to be an unforgettable film. When Prakash Mehra narrated the character of Sher Khan Pathan to me, I felt that this character had a lot of scope for interpretation. When the question of costume and get-up arose, Prakash told me that I would have to wear a Pathani pagdi,[25] but I had visualized the Pathan character without a pagdi. Eventually I put on a wig, took a centre parting and dressed up as the Pathan and showed it to Prakash. He was very satisfied since the wig enhanced the effectiveness of the get-up and, hence, the character.

---

[24] Musical chains – songs sung in a chain, a new song beginning with the last letter of the previous song.
[25] A turban tied in the style of the Pathans.

'We started the shooting of the film and I appeared in it without the Pathani *pagdi*. But one day, Prakash came to me during the shooting and placing the *pagdi* in front of me said: "Today you will have to wear the *pagdi* because the scene demands it. Your inspector friend is in jail and you need the money to bail him out, so you have to pawn your *pagdi* at the Marwari's shop;[26] you obviously will not be able to do it if you are not wearing one." So saying, Prakash moved to one side to observe what I would do.

'I was in quite a fix because I didn't like the idea of pawning the *pagdi* since according to my knowledge, a Pathan's *pagdi* was a symbol of his dignity and respect in the community. And a Pathan would never pawn his dignity! I gave it a lot of thought and eventually found a way out.

'Prakash was obviously worried. He kept asking what I had decided, what would I pawn in place of the *pagdi*, whether or not I would do the scene, how would I do it, and so on. To that I told him: "Don't worry. The scene will be done without the *pagdi* and it will be done well. That's it. Roll the cameras and see what I do!"

'Poor Prakash Mehra started the cameras and started shooting the scene. The scene demanded that I approach the Marwari and ask him for a loan. In answer he says: "Do you have anything to keep as collateral?"

'At this, I immediately pulled out a hair from my moustache and said: "Take this *Laala! Mere mooch ka baal!*[27] What could be more valuable for a Pathan than a hair from his moustache?! Keep this hair as collateral."

'Hearing the Pathan say this, the Marwari immediately agrees to give him the loan. Prakash Mehra was immensely pleased when this shot was over and said: "*Wah!* You were wonderful! This idea of pawning a hair from the moustache is brilliant!"'

'Prakash Mehra's greatness lies in the fact that he respectfully listens to his artistes and where appropriate, incorporates their suggestions. My role in *Zanjeer* gave my career yet another milestone,' noted Pran.

Revealing how that idea of using a hair from his moustache came to him, Pran smilingly said: 'I had heard the story many years ago: A certain

---

[26] Marwaris (originally from Marwar, Rajasthan) are normally depicted as moneylenders or shopkeepers.
[27] Meaning: A hair from my moustache!

nawab sahib[28] had ordered that no one working within his premises could have a moustache with its ends twirled up. This was to be the *nawab*'s privilege alone. Anyone who disobeyed his orders would have to pay a fine of one hundred rupees. No one had the guts to disobey except for a Pathan who would walk in every morning, the ends of his moustache twirled up, pay the hundred rupees fine – and then get down to work!

'The *nawab* was aware of what was happening but there was nothing he could do about it since the man was paying the fine. Then one day the Pathan walked in looking unusually despondent, the ends of his moustache drooping down. That worried the *nawab*. What had happened? Was the Pathan in financial trouble? Being a benevolent employer he called the Pathan and asked him what the matter was.

'*Kal ghar mein ladki paida huyee* (yesterday a girl-child was born to us). Now my moustache will always be drooping,' said the despondent *Pathan*.

'I remembered having heard this story,' Pran reminisced 'and I put it to good use in *Zanjeer*.'

Another incident highlighted how Pran helped Amitabh Bachchan, the comparative newcomer, to forget any background knowledge that could stilt his performance and concentrate on the scene at hand.

Pran's younger son, *Tunni*, was a friend of Amitabh. This fact, and Amitabh's own Allahabadi *tehzeeb*[29] and his Sherwood College[30] upbringing, were making it difficult for the well-behaved, soft-spoken young man to convey the right amount of anger required for the scene.

Pran recalled that scene from *Zanjeer*: 'He was the new inspector who had been shifted to my territory and as was the custom, I (as the villain) was summoned to the police station. I go to him and as I am about to sit on the chair, Amitabh has to kick the chair away and say: "*Yeh police station hai, tumhare baap ka ghar nahin.*" ('This is the police station, not your father's house.')

'I reply: "*Tum vardi pehne hue ho, so aisa keh rahe ho. Itne saalon se kisine mujhse aisa nahin kaha.*" ('You can speak like this because you are wearing the uniform. It's been a long time since someone has dared speak to me like

---

[28] A Muslim nobleman or person of high status.
[29] The polished culture of upper-crust Allahabad.
[30] A public school in Nainital, Uttaranchal.

this!') The scene demanded that he must kick the chair away from me with much force.

"But when it actually came to Amitabh's doing the scene, he simply could not bring himself to kick the chair away from me with enough force! I knew what was happening inside him, so I told him: "Don't think of me as your uncle! Think of me as the villain here. Forget the uncle and kick the chair!" Only then could he do the scene well enough. He was so respectful. He is a very fine man,' said Pran of Amitabh.

8

Jaya Bachchan (*née* Bhaduri) recalls that in *Zanjeer* her role was quite small: 'I had very little work; I happened to be there because they needed a girl in the film! I remember one incident: We were shooting at the R. K. Studios and I had to shoot with Pran Uncle that day. Pran Uncle is a very punctual and disciplined person. He is an actor who is very well prepared. I think he was delayed that day for some reason and as soon as he came, everybody started whispering: "Pran *Saab* is late today. It is unbelievable!"

'As soon as he reached the studio, he came straight to my room and said: "*Look, I am very sorry, I am late.*" I was so embarrassed. I mean, he really didn't have to say "sorry"; I was so used to working with people like Sanjeev Kumar who came late every day!

'Pran Uncle was really very, very sweet. *It showed how much respect he had for co-artistes, whether younger to him or older. He treated us like co-artistes and not like someone very junior to him age-wise or professionally. It speaks volumes about someone who has that kind of regard and respect for the profession. Otherwise, it is hard for someone to last so many years in that profession.*'

This comment by Jaya Bachchan put in a nutshell what almost all the people interviewed for this biography had to say about Pran.

And what did that epitome of punctuality, Amitabh Bachchan, have say about the other epitome, Pran, who (with the exception of that one documented instance where he was late) has always been punctual?

Amitabh said: '*It was difficult keeping pace with his punctuality. He was* always *the first on the sets, and ready with make-up.* You know that in most of his films, he did very intricate make-up, his wig or his dress; that in itself would take two hours. So, if there was a seven o'clock shift, and he is already on the sets at seven, then we can imagine that he must have started doing his make-up at five, and for that he must have got up at four in the morning! That was the kind of commitment he always had. *We used to be very embarrassed because he used to beat us outright!*'

Prakash Mehra also spoke about Pran, the person: 'He is very cordial, very sweet, I mean – he is THE man! He was THE man who gave me such a boost and there was never any talk of money. If the matter came up, he would say: "Don't worry, I'll take only what is committed and that too at your convenience. If you have a problem, pay me later."

'I remember, in this matter of money, Pran *Saab* had a minor tiff with Raj Kapoor over the contractual amount but since Raj *Saab* had a financial crunch during the making of *Bobby*, Pran *Saab* had settled the issue by agreeing to take only one rupee from Raj *Saab*. So, Pran *Saab* said that since he had also committed to work in *Zanjeer*, he would take the same amount from me too. Pran *Saab* has always been a man of principles.

'And he has a very sweet nature and great understanding. He would read the script once and grasp it. He would then tell me: "Will it be okay if I do this in this way?" And I would say: "Pranjee, if you feel comfortable, do it. I am not losing anything, in fact I am gaining from your experience." He had so much dedication for the work.'

9

The date: 11 May 1973. The time of reckoning had arrived. *Zanjeer* was being released.

The first-day-first-show's audience reaction would tell Prakash Mehra and the *Zanjeer* team whether or not all the hard work, sweat and toil had been judged worthy, and whether or not the film would run...

Three hours later, the verdict was out. The resounding applause said it all. *Zanjeer* was a hit, and with it, its star performers were a hit too!

Prakash Mehra remembers what happened in Calcutta. He and Amitabh Bachchan along with the unit of *Zanjeer* had arrived in that city for the premiere, but were not accompanied by Pran. The audience was visibly annoyed. "Where's our hero?" they demanded of Prakash Mehra.

However, after seeing the film never again did the audiences ask:"Where is our hero?"

A few weeks later, at the charity premiere of *Zanjeer* in New Delhi, the whole hall of Vigyan Bhavan reverberated with the sound of applause the moment Pran set foot on stage. Standing quietly till the ovation died down, Pran then addressed the audience:

'Thank you very much for your claps; your love has now bound me with a *zanjeer* (a chain). But this is such a loving *zanjeer* that I wish to be bound by it forever. Today with the *zanjeer* of your love, we are going to present you another *Zanjeer* – that of Prakash Mehra.

'This *Zanjeer* that has bound me to you people ... has also bound two people forever — they are Amitjee and Jayajee. I could not attend their marriage and here I am meeting them for the first time since their marriage. Maybe you all are also seeing them for the first time after their marriage. So I am congratulating them on behalf of you all and from my side, I am blessing them.'

Yes, with the success of *Zanjeer*, Amitabh and Jaya who had been seeing each other for some time, decided that marriage could no longer be put on hold, and had tied the knot in a private ceremony on 3 June 1973.

In spite of a 'poor' review in *Filmfare*, *Zanjeer* was so successful that it went on to complete not just a silver jubilee, but a golden jubilee too!

Amitabh Bachchan, the 'angry young man' had arrived, and how! That Pran had played an important part in Amitabh's success is something that the latter always acknowledges.

Screen had the practice of featuring a single photo of a hero or a heroine, each Friday when a new film would be released, on the front page. Proof that Pran's name had added weight to the film is gathered from the fact that during the week *Zanjeer* was to be released, *Screen* broke its unwritten rule for the first time and featured not one actor, but two actors, in their front page photo – Amitabh Bachchan and Pran!

Zanjeer is an example of a film made *primarily* on the strength of the character actor's name, along with factors such as the choice of heroine, the story, the tight script and an audience readied by the then-prevailing times to accept a new tough and angry hero with a purpose. All these inputs contributed to *Zanjeer's* stupendous success.

So successful was the film that it was heartily appreciated even by international audiences! Pran, as part of a cultural delegation visiting the erstwhile Soviet Union to participate in the thirthieth anniversary celebrations of Indian independence, was mobbed in one of Moscow's largest theatres where *Zanjeer* was screened as the opening attraction of a week-long festival of Indian films.

After *Zanjeer*, Pran and Amitabh made a successful team and worked in as many as fourteen *more* films together.[31] When Amitabh was asked which film he did with Pran did he consider the most memorable and why, he replied:

'I would say that there are so many, [it's] very difficult to pick any one. Quite obviously *Zanjeer* is one because it was my first experience with him, I found him quite phenomenal in the film. Pran *Saab* was the biggest star of that film at that point of time. Jaya was very big, I was a nobody, Prakash Mehra was big…. But Pran *Saab* was really the true thespian, the true veteran. He played that role immaculately. So I would rate *Zanjeer* as my most memorable film with him.'

Today, *Zanjeer* is remembered as much for its 'angry young man' as for its famous *qawwali*: '*Yaari Hai Imaan Mera, Yaar Meri Zindagi.*'

---

[31] The fifteen films that Pran and Amitabh Bachchan have done together are: *Zanjeer* (1973), *Kasauti* (1974), *Majboor* (1974), *Amar Akbar Anthony* (1977), *Don* (1978), *Ganga Ki Saugandh* (1978), *Dostana* (1980), *Kaalia* (1981), *Naseeb* (1981), *Andha Kanoon* (1983), *Nastik* (1983), *Sharabi* (1984), *Shahenshah* (1988), *Jadugar* (1989) and *Toofan* (1989).

TWENTY-FOUR

The Wheel of Life Turns...

1

Much of the reason why Pran could immerse himself single-mindedly in his roles, and cooperate to the utmost with his directors and producers was due to the fact that his home life was happy and content. And that was primarily due to family traditions and values.

Casting her memory backwards, Pran's wife Shukla, when asked how she managed to adjust between 'the good man' in real life and 'the bad man' on the screen, replied: 'I always knew perfectly well that it was actually only make-believe, only a role he was playing. I have been so close to him over the decades and he never carried his role or his work home, nor did he allow it to permeate his inner self, his real self, or that of his family.'

'That's right!' Pinky reiterated. 'Whenever he came home, he would have a bath, freshen up and only then sit down to have his drink. Even if he came from work and saw that there were people already waiting for him, and that the drinks had already started, he wouldn't immediately join them. He would say: "First let me have a bath."'

Pinky added: 'My mother is such that whoever comes to visit at home, be it a close relative or distant acquaintances, she would definitely invite them in and offer them lunch or dinner.... Dad would never say that "I am tired and you have called so many people". We never, ever heard that from him. Whoever came to the house, he was always there to socialize with them. Mother has always been very fond of calling relatives and friends, everybody, home and this practice continues till today.'

So, it was only natural that when Shukla and Pran's silver wedding anniversary approached in 1970, both of them as well as their children were unanimous about celebrating it.

On the evening of 18 April 1970, film personalities, relatives and close friends turned up at Pran and Shukla's bungalow in enthusiastic numbers for an evening of merrymaking.

Although Pran does not remember all the details, he does recall some of the events: 'At our silver anniversary, I remember that I gave her cash. Since we had finished twenty-five years, I gave her a thousand rupees for each year, that is 25,000. I gave her an additional 25,000 rupees for being a good wife.'

That evening, as their guests began showing up, the family members ushered them on to the spacious lawns to begin the celebrations.

Pran and Shukla garlanded each other on this important milestone in their lives. Recollects Pran: 'The *haar*[1] had come from Madras; the real thick ones.' Without a doubt, those thick, intertwined garlands would have symbolized the strong relationship between them and the fragrance of the sweet smelling flowers, the harmony and equilibrium they had achieved in their years together.

Remembering the celebrations, a close friend said: 'I was there at that party. It was memorable. Lots of film people, co-stars and friends had turned up. Pranjee himself was the life and soul of those celebrations which were enlivened by the attendance of Ashok Kumar, Raj Kapoor, Dilip Kumar, Manoj Kumar, Dharmendra and many others.

'Pranjee was only fifty, active and enthusiastic. At that time the entire world was unfolding before him because he had mastered the secrets of

---

[1] Garlands.

A gathering of celebrities during Pran and Shukla's silver wedding anniversary.
Seen (among others) are Dharmendra, Manoj Kumar, Pran,
Raj Kapoor and Ram Kamlani.

success in his profession. I remember how some of us were amused by
the very different image Pranjee presented that night — so much in
contrast to his colorful screen get-ups! He was clad in a simple white
dhoti and *kurta*, and looked more like a middle-class family man than a
film star.'

The alcohol flowed like water and by two in the morning, both Raj
Kapoor and Dilip Kumar were singing duets! As both their families hailed
from Peshawar, one may rightly presume that they may have been singing
North Indian folk songs, but no! They were singing popular Bengali
songs!

While their impromptu song session was in progress, Shukla looked
after Saira Banu (who was now Mrs Dilip Kumar) as well as Mrs Krishna
Raj Kapoor who, unlike their husbands, preferred not to sing duets together!

2

Meanwhile, the time had come for Pran and Shukla's children, all of
whom were now grown up, to begin making decisions — important
decisions which would affect the future course of their lives.

Arvind, their eldest child, was now a young man and had been in England since 1963. After having postgraduated and, after completing his Ph.D. in chemical engineering, he obtained a research position at the Imperial College, London. In this context, Pran said: 'After Arvind finished his chemical engineering, he didn't come back – he decided to settle down in England itself. He got a job and then went into business.'

Pran loved his son dearly. He must have felt a pang at knowing that Arvind would stay on in England, but he knew he would not interfere in that decision of his. In fact, Pran's love for his son was so great that sometimes it overrode even some of his personal preferences...like for instance, his choice of clothing!

After indulging in the fanciest of clothes possible, Pran had gradually developed a taste for wearing only white clothes. So much so that at the height of his career his standard clothing was a white shirt and a pair of white trousers. They were almost like a trademark.

Rishi Kapoor spoke about this habit: 'In his personal life, Pran *Saab* has always had a very standard way of dressing – white T-shirt, white trousers and white *chappals*.[2] *When I was younger, I used to think he never used to change his clothes at all, but was wearing the same shirt everyday! But he actually had several of those identical T-shirts and trousers!*' But soon Pran began sporting some flamboyant T-shirts. When questioned about this, Pran once said in an interview: 'My son spoilt me. He sent me some colourful T-shirts from London and from that day onwards I no longer wear strictly white clothes.'[3]

Pran and Shukla's love for their son also meant that they would have to start looking for a suitable wife for him, since by the beginning of the 1970s, Arvind had already reached his mid-twenties. Of course, offers of marriage had begun to pour it for this 'prize catch', who was not only tall and handsome, but was also extremely well educated and well settled. 'But,' shrugged Pran, 'as they say, marriages are made in heaven.'

However, much before Arvind could even *think* of tying the knot, Pran and Shukla's second son, Sunil, had jumped the queue.

---

[2] Slippers.
[3] Rafique Baghdadi and Rajiv Rao, 'Pran: Arch Villain Turned Character Actor', *Screen*, 17 June 1983.

After finishing his schooling, Sunil joined the St Xavier's College in Bombay, but dropped out in 1968. Understandably, his parents were none too happy about it. They were even more apprehensive when he fell in love with an air hostess from New Delhi, Jyoti Das (the daughter of a retired general), who used to frequently fly in and out of Bombay.

But their son was in love, and Pran and Shukla thought it best to let him settle down. As is customary, the auspicious dates for this important occasion were sought. Three dates were suggested – 12, 25 and 28 February 1972. 'When I offered him his choice from these dates,' Pran reminisced, 'Sunil said: "Keep my wedding on 12 February since that is your birthday. That way, one year *I* will throw the party and the next year *you* will throw the party!"'

Sunil recalls that since his was the first wedding in the Pran Sikand family, they did not have much of an idea about the intricacies of the various rituals during Punjabi weddings. That is when Raj Kapoor and his wife Krishna came to their rescue. Raj told them that before the *baraat* could depart for the marriage venue, they would have to perform the ritual of *'ghodi ko channe khilana'*.[4] Only then could the *baraat* start! And after that, Raj Kapoor directed the whole *baraat* till the *baaraatis* reached the venue.

The wedding reception was held at Bombay's Taj Mahal Hotel, where Pran and his wife had started off in Bombay in that long-ago year of 1947. Maharashtra's governor at the time, Nawab Ali Yawar Jung and his wife, and Maharashtra's minister for power and irrigation, Vasantrao Patil, with his wife were among the guests from officialdom.

From the film industry viewpoint, it was a star-studded affair. Most notable amongst whom were Raj Kapoor with wife Krishna and son Rishi, Nargis Sunil Dutt, Nimmi and her husband Ali Raza, Mr and Mrs Dilip Kumar and the veteran Jairaj.[5]

A couple of years later, on 6 January 1974, Sunil and Jyoti presented Pran and his wife with their first grandchild, a boy whom they named Siddharth.

---

[4]   The ritual involves feeding cooked horse gram to the mare on which the bridegroom is to be seated.

[5]   Now deceased.

At Sunil Sikand's wedding. *Right to left*: Elder brother Prem, Shukla, Pran, younger brother Kirpal, sister Pramila, *bhabbi* Kuldeep, Pinky and Raj Kapoor.

Having lived in England since 1963, it was but natural for Arvind to have formed his own circle of friends. Through them he met Chitra, who is the daughter of a brigadier in the army. Shukla recalls: 'When Arvind told us that he wanted to marry her, we gave him the green signal. Our son's happiness came first. And since Chitra's father was posted in Delhi at the time, we decided to have the wedding in Delhi itself.'

Arvind and Chitra were married on 21 September 1974, and just short of two years later, on 7 August 1976, became proud parents of a daughter, whom they named Sunaina. Some six years later, on 5 March 1980, their second child, a son was born, whom they named Arjun.

Arvind Sikand and Pran on the former's wedding day.

Grandmother Shukla looked after this child in Bombay until he was a year-and-a-half old. She explained: 'When the younger son was four-five months old, I brought him over to Bombay. Since both Arvind and Chitra were working, they were finding it difficult to manage, and putting him in a nursery was not good. Besides, he used to cry a lot. So I took him under my wing for some time, after which he was sent back to his parents. When Sunaina and Arjun were young, I used go to London every year and stay for some months. I wanted the children to know that there are other relatives too, who are their own.'

As a result, despite the fact that Arvind and his family are settled in London, a close bond has been maintained with his parents. Also, a close bond has developed between the grandchildren and the grandparents.

3

Unlike her brothers, daughter Pinky was sent to boarding school only much later. It was but natural that Pran grew closer to her. She was also instrumental in the changes he effected in his career – from villain to character actor and back again to villain!

'Daddy treated me like a princess,' Pinky declared. 'My mother used to call me *Gudiya Rani*.[6] And for their friends too, it was like I was something special. Dilip Uncle used to call me Princess Margaret.'

Well, the 'princess' had to grow up and, inevitably, also found her 'prince charming' – no, not from a distant land but from up the road on Pali Hill, in the family of Pran's closest friends, Satish and Shalu Bhalla – Vivek Bhalla.

Satish Bhalla[7] was the son of wealthy landowners and had initially been a fan, then become a friend, and finally was made a *samdhi*[8], of Pran. He used to have a factory manufacturing bone china crockery for export. His reminiscences of Pran, given in a detailed interview a few months

---

[6] Doll princess.
[7] Sadly, Satish Bhalla passed away during the writing of this biography.
[8] The word *samdhi* is used when referring to the father of the son-in-law or father of the daughter-in-law. Likewise, the word *samdhan* is used to refer to the female parent of either son-in-law or daughter-in-law.

before his death, allow us insight into the soft heart of a supposedly harsh man. Yes, Pran is a *badnaam farishta*[9] to those who know him intimately!

Satish Bhalla remembered him from the time in Lahore when he himself was in his tender years: 'I was about thirteen years old.... Pran*jee* was our hero.... But we never got to know him at that time.

'Initially when we were in Lahore, he was not a "villain". It came only later. And when Partition occurred, we lost contact. After Partition, he came to Bombay and started working here. I then met him for the first time at around 1955, through some common friends. That is the time when we became friends.'

Satish Bhalla was connected to the film industry in an indirect sort of way. His father had a film finance and distribution office in Bombay and it was through those business interests that he came in contact with Pran.

'By the end of 1957, I shifted to Bombay, and we [then] were living in Malabar Hill in Darshan Apartments,' Satish Bhalla elaborated. 'It was during our stay there that Pran*jee* started coming to our house and we became very close.'

Among the many incidents Satish Bhalla recalled for this biography, this one stands out as an example of the closeness that Pran and he shared. He remembered the time during the 1950s when Pran used to get paid a mere Rs 60 to 70 thousand for a role. One day, however, it all changed.

'One night, Pran came to my house at Pali Hill. It must have been about one o'clock in the morning. He knocked on my window. My wife and myself were fast asleep,' recounted Satish Bhalla. 'He woke us up and he said: "I want a drink because I want to tell you some good news." He came into the bedroom, we poured a drink, and he gave my wife a present, a saree. I asked him: "What is this in aid of at this time of the night?" His words were: "Today I have broken the...barrier. I have signed a movie for a lakh of rupees." He told us that it was the first movie he had signed for such a big amount (which it was in those days) and so, he had wanted to share the happiness with us.'

---

[9] A maligned angel.

Satish Bhalla continued: 'I have known Pranjee for over fifty years now. There are a few things which are quite exceptional in this man. One is his total generosity. I have never known or heard from any person in the industry or outside who complained that Pranjee had tried to harm anybody or spoken ill of anybody.

'And it is a privilege beyond words that he is my *samdhi*. For this I am totally grateful to my son and daughter-in-law. *I think they decided the issue more than either I or Pranjee decided!* To be very honest, we had no clue that something like this was going on. The families were so close, we were in and out of each other's homes. We had no idea that something like this would turn up. But it did. And I am so happy it did. I am very proud of the fact that Pranjee and *Bhabhi*jee are my *samdhis* and that Pinky is my daughter-in-law!'

Pinky recalled her easy relationship with her in-laws: 'Since I was very fond of children and used to collect them together and have fun at home, Daddy [Satish Bhalla] used to call me Pinku Aunty and still did till his death some months ago.'

For his part Pran observed: 'Satish Bhalla, who [was] my *samdhi* had been my good friend over the decades. He was a very lively person; he had a very unique personality. Because he was very handsome, everybody used to ask him why he didn't become a hero. He would always reply saying: *"Unkey peth peh laath nahi maarna chahta;* I have so many friends who are heroes that I don't want to rob them of their livelihood by becoming a hero myself!"* '[10]

'Since both my brothers were married, my parents had wanted me to settle down too. They had been getting a lot of proposals for me while I was still in the final year of college [1974],' Pinky revealed.

Pinky had known Vivek from childhood. The families had grown up together and used to frequent each other's homes and it was not long before Pinky and Vivek fell in love with each other. So while they were quite young they decided to make their future together and then told their parents about it. But like all other parents, Pran and Shukla were worried about the fact that Vivek had still to finish his education.

---

[10] Many more incidents and anecdotes involving Pran and Satish Bhalla are strewn throughout this biography.

On Pinky and Vivek's wedding day. *Left to right*: Arvind, Chitra, Pran, Vivek, Pinky, Shukla, Jyoti and Sunil.

'That is why initially, my parents were not very happy with the idea,' confesses Pinky. 'They knew that Vivek would be away in America, in San Diego, for four years doing his business administration. But eventually they came around when they saw that we were genuinely in love. So I didn't go for any further studies but waited till Vivek came back and we could marry.'

And so, four years later, on 19 January 1978, Pinky married Vivek Bhalla. The children further cemented the friendship between the two families, which had already stood the test of time.

While reporting on Pinky's wedding celebrations held at the Turf Club in Bombay's Mahalaxmi Racecourse, *Star & Style* (10–23 February 1978) noted that practically everybody who was anybody had turned up. The magazine added: 'The most touching part of the evening is seeing ex-villain Pran in tears, bidding farewell to his very pretty daughter Pinky.' Apparently the newlyweds were to settle in Canada. Although Pran would not have dreamt of interfering in their plans, he must have breathed a big sigh of relief when they changed their decision to go abroad and decided to settle in Bombay itself.

Pinky and Vivek Bhalla had their first child on 30 December 1979, whom they named Swati and who is a replica of her mother. The princess now had her own little princess. And some four years later, on 17 October 1983, a little boy was born to Pinky and Vivek – who is appropriately named Yuvraj![11]

Commenting on his children's choice of life partners, Pran stated: 'In olden days, love marriages were rare, maybe one in ten thousand. Today, in our family, all my children have opted for a love marriage.' Then Pran added, a trifle sheepishly: 'Even *my* marriage is partially a love marriage!'

The wheel of life had turned. Within this ten-year period itself, Pran and Shukla had not only completed twenty-five years of togetherness, but also their children had, in quick succession, made them graduate from being parents to becoming in-laws and then to becoming grandparents!

Contemplating on how the circle was completed and a new one begun, Pran said: 'My daughter married, and just when I was thinking I had finished my responsibility, I realized it had doubled. I now have five grandchildren!'[12]

---

[11] Meaning 'prince'.
[12] Taken from an article by Santosh Sud, 'Unforgettable Pran', *Cine Blitz*, December 1989.

TWENTY-FIVE

The Successful Seventies Continue

1

After the fantastic success of *Zanjeer* in 1973 the Pran and Amitabh *jodi* (teaming) was repeated with equal success in *Kasauti*,[1] *Majboor*,[2] *Amar Akbar Anthony*,[3] *Don*[4] and *Ganga Ki Saugandh*.[5]

In *Kasauti*, Pran did that absolutely delightful role of a Nepali Gurkha who makes friends with the hero, Amitabh Bachchan. It wasn't just a colourful and an important role; no, Arabind Sen, with whom Pran had already worked in many films, had worked into the scenario what turned out to be a terrific song sequence to be picturized on Pran.

No doubt, Pran's song item in *Zanjeer* was a key factor in getting him to sing a song in *Kasauti* also. The song, penned by Varma Malik and playbacked by the one-time-reluctant-to-sing-for-Pran Kishore Kumar,

---

[1] *Kasauti* (released in 1974).
[2] *Majboor* (released in 1974).
[3] *Amar Akbar Anthony* (released in 1977).
[4] *Don* (released in 1978).
[5] *Ganga Ki Saugandh* (released in 1978).

is the very catchy '*Hum Bolegaa Toh Bologey Ke Boltaa Hai*', sung in an endearing Nepali accent. This style of singing not only delighted audiences everywhere, but also the song became the top hit of the time and also contributed to the film turning out to become a superhit.

However, Pran, noted for his earlier allergy to singing songs, later said in an interview to *Star & Style*: 'I keep telling these people not to overdo a good thing. But they won't listen.... Contrary to rumours, I don't insist on singing songs either. In fact, I fold my hands and request them: "Please, don't make me sing!" But the songs in *Zanjeer*, *Kasauti* and *Majboor* were all hits! *In Kasauti, for instance, there was no need for me to sing. But that song became a highlight of the film!*'

In director Ravi Tandon's *Majboor*, Pran played a key character called Michael D'Souza, a good bad man. Pran animatedly recalls his role: 'My character in *Majboor* was a small but striking one. I saw the movie for the first time on Delhi TV when I went there to discuss the government's new excise levy.[6] I think I made an entrance only in the twelfth or thirteenth reel, but what an entrance!'

The post-interval entry by a key character was not only an unusual ploy, but also the entire introduction itself was superbly done. Film buffs will recall the scene where a camera is shown to be focusing on a person,

Pran in a memorable role as Michael D'Souza in *Majboor*.

---

[6]   It may be recalled that Pran does not like to see his films once they are released.

apparently through a pair of binoculars. But the point is that the circular view is not through binoculars at all, it is through an *imaginary* pair of binoculars formed by the thumb and four fingers of two hands – Pran's hands.

Pran's character, who is always looking at things and people through the formed-by-his-fingers binoculars, proved to be an attraction in the film. Eventually, it is this *durbeen* (the binoculars) that leads him to identify the real villain of the film. Tandon's action thriller, with Amitabh Bachchan in the lead and Pran as his improbable ally, turned out to be a smash hit.

The idea of forming mock binoculars by using his fingers came from Pran himself, who had been closely observing Ravi Tandon during the shooting of the very first scene that Pran shot for the film, which happened to be the death scene of the character he played.

Even as he was 'drawing his last breaths', Pran noticed Ravi Tandon visualizing the camera angle through the circle of his thumb and four fingers. Pran asked him why he did not do that with both his hands. Thus the idea of viewing things through the circles formed by his fingers was born! It was not only used in the opening shot for the introduction of Michael, but Pran decided to use it as a mannerism throughout the film!

Some of the inputs Pran gave to each of his scenes, and the little touches he added to his performance, succeeded in raising them from the mediocre to the superlative.

Director Ravi Tandon was specially impressed with the interest Pran showed with regard to his work by coming up with various innovations. In his character's death scene, Pran has been wounded by a bullet, but has managed to corner the villain and hold him at gunpoint. Growing weaker by the minute, he is supposed to try and hold out till Amitabh gets to the scene with a doctor in tow. To build up the suspense, the scene was a protracted one. Ravi Tandon acknowledged Pran's contribution to making this scene a memorable one: 'Pran suggested that he change his make-up several times during his death scene. He said that the long-drawn-out climax would require that subtle changes be shown in the dying man's condition. I must say that Pran's idea to change his make-up for every edited minute of the sequence made a tremendous difference to that long and important scene. Pran was so involved and interested that he did his make-up himself, and the careful use of varying shades and colours came across most effectively on the screen.'

This brief but shining performance by Pran was made all the more special by his song and dance sequence: '*Daaru ki botal mein, kaahe paani bharta hai? Phir na kehna Michael daaru peeke danga karta hai! Hey! Haanv Goincho Saheba, lal-la-la, lal-la-la, la, hey!*'[7]

Pran's performance in *Majboor* was instrumental in furthering his new character-actor image, letting him, as it were, to bring to his producers' and his audiences' notice that he was capable of *much more* than what was being asked of him.

Another surprise that Pran sprung on audiences was in his role as an outwardly stern, but soft-hearted, grandfather in Tirupati Pictures' *Parichay* directed and co-scripted by Gulzar. Deprived of the love of his only son (played by Sanjeev Kumar), who after marrying for love and leaving home due to unexpected opposition from the father, eventually dies in penury, the old man finally finds fulfilment in his orphaned grandchildren, who by now consider him the villain of the piece and have become defiant of his authority. To cope with their rebelliousness, he hires a tutor (played by Jeetendra) to help 'civilize' them. The tutor finally succeeds in changing their attitude towards their grandfather.

In the role of the oldest of the children is Jaya Bhaduri, who essayed her character superbly as a young girl, forced to grow up after her mother's death, take charge of her dying father and younger siblings, and, upon the death of their father, return to their grandfather who is a stickler for discipline.

Portions of the film were inspired by the 1965 film, *The Sound of Music*.[8] However, in this version, the governess is replaced by a male tutor, played by Jeetendra. The music of *Parichay* was by R. D. Burman, whose songs delight us even today.

---

[7] This Hindi-mixed-with-Konkani song means: 'Why are you cheating by filling the liquor bottles with water? Then don't you grumble that Michael creates a ruckus after he's drunk. I am the gentleman from Goa!'

[8] Produced and directed by Robert Wise, *The Sound of Music*, co-starring Christopher Plummer and Julie Andrews, was adapted from a Broadway musical that was based on a true-life story of the Von Trapp family who fled their homeland in 1938 to escape from Nazi rule. The lyrics of the all-time hit songs were by Oscar Hammerstein and the music was composed by Richard Rodgers.

For Pran this role was a difficult one since he did not have the luxury of either having lengthy dialogue or descriptive actions to convey the feelings of the character. In the final scene with Jaya Bhaduri, Pran superbly conveyed the throwing-off of the final vestiges of the character's sternness and self-discipline.

In that scene, Pran asks Jaya if Jeetendra has met her. Out of shyness, Jaya lowers her eyes. Pran then tells Jaya to come near him, looks at her while polishing his spectacles, then wears them and closely examines Jaya's expression – and then slowly smiles in approval. The entire scene was done with a minimum of words, allowing Pran to show the cultivated hardness of expression being dissolved by the power of love. Conceptualized by writer-director Gulzar, the scene was splendidly enacted by Pran. As Pran himself acknowledges: 'The most difficult roles I had were in *Bobby* and *Parichay*. I was walking on the sword's edge with them. If, in either film, I had made the character a little more sympathetic or a little more villainous, then it would have completely lost its desired impact.'

2

At the beginning of the 1970s, in view of the newer and younger villains coming up in the firmament and the fact that the villainous characters were getting increasingly repetitious, Pran had switched to character actor roles and tried to find ways in which to expand his repertoire.

For starters, Pran went back to doing some regional-language films. It may be recalled that Pran's earlier films were mostly in Punjabi. In 1970, Pran acted in producer-director Dara Singh's *Nanak Dukhiya Sab Sansar*, which starred Dara Singh himself along with Prithviraj Kapoor, Balraj Sahni and Achala Sachdev and was rather a big hit in the Punjabi circuit.

Pran has also acted in some Bengali films. Newspaper reports indicate that around the time Pran was shooting for Manoj Kumar's *Purab Aur Paschim* (1970), he signed his first Bengali film, titled *Sonai Dighe*, directed by Ashim Banerjee. *Sonai Dighe* was based on a famous 'hit' drama of the same name and featured Joy Mukerji as hero, for whom this film was also the first one in Bengali. Pran's role was also an important one, but one in which he would only have to speak broken Bengali, which was fine by him! However, no mention was made about the film's release date.

Another film, titled *Jeevan Rahasya* (1973), directed by Salil Ray, starring Tarun Kumar and Madhabi (Chakraborty) Mukherjee in the lead, did get made during 1973–74.

A brief write-up in *Filmfare* (9 March 1973) about the film during its making shows that Pran faced similar problems in Tollygunge[9] as he did in Bombay with regard to the punctuality of his co-artistes! *Filmfare*'s correspondent reported that 'the heroine was very late in coming to the studio on the day of his [Pran's] leaving for Bombay and the irked Pran remarked: "I am from a place which is thousands of miles away and I am on the set correct to the minute – but the heroine who is in Calcutta is late!" ' Another report from a New Delhi journalist revealed that Pran had made every effort to speak his Bengali dialogues himself, showing that no matter what the film, or the language, Pran did not adopt a lackadaisical approach to his role.

After this write-up, and after another photographic mention of *Jeevan Rahasya* in *Star & Style* (1 February 1974), no more was heard of the film.

However, Pran was open to the idea of working in regional-language cinema and did do so in later decades.

3

In the history of this film industry, whenever an actor has achieved fame and position, a pattern has emerged regarding how he has handled them. Usually, the actor allows success to go to his head and becomes a trifle difficult to deal with. Did this happen to Pran?

During Pran's peak period as villain and then as character actor, allegations were made in the media that he had begun to view himself as superior to the heroes with whom he acted.

Was that really true? Consider what happened some decades ago when a fiery hero turned flamboyant film maker picked up a fight with Pran after downing quite a few drinks at a private party. Nadira (a heroine

---

9   Tollygunge is used to refer to Bengali cinema, especially those films which are shot in the studios of Calcutta.

of yesteryears who later did character roles), who witnessed the entire tiff recalled the episode, and said bemusedly: 'This young hot-blooded hero said to Pran: "You are a bloody so-and-so, you one-eyed actor!" Whereupon Pran smoothly replied: "Whatever I could do with one eye, you can't even do with both of them!" So that was the beginning and the end of the fight!'

Pran's repartee had actually prevented the whole episode from turning ugly and was sorely needed to bring the 'high' actor down more than a few notches!

Similarly, there were occasions (as reported in the press) when Pran seemed to have got into a controversy by the simple expedient of speaking his mind. The root cause of the matter may have been some negligible thing, and yet, at the time, it did create ruffled feathers and did hurt feelings. Fortunately, both sides – heroes and villains – were able to overcome their differences and there were no hard feelings.

Known for being a forthright man, Pran had said in an interview in the mid-1970s:[10]

'I don't like quite a few people in the industry. But I never let it affect my work. I avoid doing a film with them. But if there's any film already signed with a person I don't quite like, I finish the film quickly. I don't let these things affect my profession.

'Rajesh Khanna.... Ah! He claimed in one article that his films never have a Mehmood or a Pran in them because he doesn't need them to boost his films. Did he realize then that he was actually paying us a compliment by admitting that we do boost a film?' countered Pran.

Needless to say, Pran must have been more than a little hurt by Rajesh Khanna's assertions, because Pran revealed that during the shooting of *Aurat* (1967)[11] in Madras, he had helped Rajesh get medical help for a serious hand injury. By refusing to shoot and requesting S.S. Vasan (the film's co-director-producer) to take a few more dates from him, if necessary, Pran had ensured that Rajesh received medical treatment and rest.

---

[10] *Star & Style*, 18 June 1976.

[11] *Aurat* was one of Rajesh Khanna's earliest films, and was directed jointly by S.S. Vasan and S.S. Balan. The title role was played by Padmini; Feroz Khan was also in the cast.

Similarly, with regard to the controversy with Shashi Kapoor, which purportedly started due to Pran quipping in response to former's dialogue in a scene from the film *Shankar Dada* (1976). *Star & Style* wrote: 'The story goes that Shashi Kapoor had been signed to play the title role in *Shankar Dada*. While shooting one day, he suddenly found himself saying: *"Mera naam Shankar hai"* to which Pran replied suavely: *"Tumhara naam Shankar hai to mera naam Shankar Dada hai!"* '

While the quip was probably meant to be just that, a quip, it appears that Shashi Kapoor was rather miffed. In that same interview to *Star & Style*, Pran clarified: 'It has been a big misunderstanding. Someone has given him the wrong impression that I wanted to snatch the title role from him. He is the Shankar Dada of the film. I'm not aspiring for title roles.'

Pran frankly admitted in that interview that he *does* get into trouble for his plain speaking: 'I'm always getting into hot water for my frankness.'

Neverthless, it appears that Pran and Shashi were able to reconcile differences and they co-starred in eight *more* films.[12]

Reminiscing for this biography about working with Pran, Shashi Kapoor affirmed: 'He was almost British-like in his punctuality and [in] his sense of dedication to his work...I attribute that to his belonging to the old school, to people who lived by the motto that "work is worship".'

4

Pran had always striven to work with the new blood in the industry. Perhaps that was one way he could ensure that he brought an element of newness to each character he played. One of the newer directors with whom he worked during the 1970s was Subhash Ghai, who recalled how he got Pran to work for his second film *Vishwanath* (1978).

Subhash Ghai had originally aspired to be an actor. However, he soon realized that his true métier was directing films, not acting in them. His first film as director was *Kalicharan* (1975) starring Shatrughan Sinha,

---

[12] In all, Shashi Kapoor and Pran worked together in twelve films. These were *Sanskar* (1952); *Biradari* (1966); *Chori Mera Kaam* (1975); *Shankar Dada* (1976); *Chakkar Pe Chakkar* (1977); *Apna Khoon* (1978); *Do Musafir* (1978); *Phaansi* (1978); *Rahu Ketu* (1978); *Maan Gaye Ustad* (1981); *Krodhi* (1981); and *Maa Beti* (1987).

Reena Roy and Premnath, which was a big hit. Emboldened by his success, he decided to start his next film again in association with Shatrughan Sinha.

Although Pran was at the peak of his success, on the recommendation of his secretary who had seen what Ghai had done with *Kalicharan*, the old-timer decided to hear the newcomer out. Understandably, Subhash Ghai was nervous. Having seen Pran in films from childhood, he knew that he would be dealing with a veteran.

Referring to that period, Subhash Ghai said: 'I don't think any other actor has done the number of characters that Pran *Saab* has enacted, and that too, with such realism. I knew that Pran Saab gives much attention and time to listen carefully to the story and then finds better ways in which to depict the character. Besides, Pran is an actor who knows the language, style and definition of acting.

'...Pran Sahab's price was also equal to that of the hero! But more important for us was that he knew the style of acting, which meant that I, as a writer-director, would have to work doubly hard.

'So before I went to him with the story, I spent three nights working on his character in detail. It was as though I was going to give an examination and that I had to pass! Pran *Saab* called me over and heard the story. When he heard my story and the character, he was much impressed. He talked to me very lovingly and chased away any fears I may have had. He said: "It has been ages since I have seen a director work in so much detail. You are a new director but I can tell you that you will become successful because you know how to put effort in your work."

'That was my first meeting with him. I knew that his price was quite high, but I was taking responsibility to ensure that the decision to take Pran in the film was worth it. I convinced my producer that the character in this film is very important and we needed a good artiste. That is how Pran came to work in *Vishwanath*.'

Talking about the film and Pran's role in it, Subhash Ghai elaborated: 'In the film *Vishwanath*, I had written the character of Golu Gavah, who is a small-time lawyer. He stands outside the court and gives a false witness for money. He is a professional *gavah*.[13] Give him money and he

---

[13] Witness.

will give any false testimony in court. He would sell himself like the black marketeers outside cinema halls.

'It is a very beautiful character. As the story unfolds, Golu Gavah sees an honest lawyer getting punished, which makes him feel quite sad. So the film is about how Golu Gavah supports the lawyer Vishwanath (played by Shatrughan Sinha) and says in the end that: "All the testimony that I have given till today has been false, but today the testimony that I am about to give is true. This man (Pran had to say pointing to the Shatrughan Sinha) his name is Vishwanath...." And the film takes an emotional turn.'

Subhash Ghai remembers the homework stage of Pran's preparation for the role: 'Pran called me for the get-up and I sketched it and explained [the finer points]. He liked the sketches, and was very much impressed. Then we called the make-up man and explained that this character is a Punjabi, so he should be made-up accordingly. Pran was also going to use a Punjabi accent for the film.'

Speaking about the experience of working with such a senior star, Subhash Ghai recollected: 'The first day of shooting required a shot of Golu Gavah. I remember that right in the first scene itself, Pran *Saab* and I got into a bit of a dispute. When I said, "do it like this," he disagreed by saying, "why not like this?" So I said: "This character has to walk in from there like this and stand here and talk." I could see that he didn't like what I said at the time. I thought to myself that it is important for me to handle this carefully, giving him due respect.

'So I had the lights switched off, and asked him if I could talk to him privately. Then, I explained the meaning of that scene in great detail to him. He listened very carefully. I admire that man! He said: *"Bete,*[14] I am very sorry, I misunderstood the scene. You are right. From here onwards, I will not speak, you will direct."

'It was a great reward for me to get that comment from such a great actor! Once we got over that hiccup, it was smooth sailing with Pran *Saab!*'

---

[14] Son.

5

Pran's many and varied successful characterizations during the 1970s, the fourth decade of his career in films, proved not only that he was a good actor, but also that he had been able to maintain a steady graph in spite of the onslaught of youth and the changing trends in cinema.

His abilities as an actor, his dedication to his work and skilful navigation through the minefield of stardom had helped him to stay on top.

However, what would the next two decades bring for an actor who loved his work and who had sought ways in which to expand his acting prowess? The *successful seventies* were drawing to a close and the 1980s and 1990s were at already at hand...

PART FIVE

TWENTY-SIX

Pran in the 1980s:
Five Decades in Showbiz

1

The 1980s began with popular cinema retrogressing with regard to the depiction of certain features. Vendetta, vigilante violence and overt sex were the main ingredients being used in films made during this decade.

Also, the trend which had started in the 1970s — that of making multistarrers — continued in the 1980s. But big budgets, big stars and ambitious projects did not always ensure success.

In such a scenario, as Pran entered the fifth decade of his career, he found himself frequently being offered roles in multistarrers. When once asked about his increasing appearances in smaller roles, Pran shot back: 'What was wrong with small roles? To do small roles and make them stand out is a challenge. It's not how much or how little footage they give you. What counts is what you *do* in that footage. You don't lose your dignity by appearing in just a couple of scenes in a film!'

Another change Pran experienced during the 1980s was in terms of the degeneration with respect to the attitude of the dominant stars to their work.

His attitude to work is revealed in what he said when comparing the work ethic during his heyday as against that of the present day: 'To my batch of artistes, work was their religion, the next batch was dedicated, and present day artistes say they're professional – though God knows what kind of professionalism it is. Three shifts a day, dozens of films on hand, shuttling from one set to another, in one film you're Ram, in another Gopal, how on earth can you give *any* kind of performance?' wondered Pran.

Pran also believed that one's attitude to work was manifest in one's consciousness of time, especially other people's time. However, times had changed and an incident which occurred on the sets of *Souten*,[1] highlighted this aspect.

Veteran character actress Shashikala recalled an incident which occurred during the shooting of *Souten*: 'I was playing Pran's wife in the film. We had gone to Mauritius for the outdoor schedule. Sawan*jee* used to say: "Come at 9 a.m. sharp!" Among the artistes, we three seniors, Pran, Prem Chopra and myself, were always there on time having on our full make-up. We were always conscious of every minute of the producer. At no time did the producer, the director or any assistant have to be sent to us with the call: "Shot *taiyyar hai*, please *aaiye*."[2] But *Kaka*[3] and Sawan*jee* used to always come in the afternoon – at 2 p.m.'

'Well, Pran observed this situation for three days. On the third day, when he saw both these men coming, he stood up and said: "Pack up!" When Sawan*jee* asked him what was happening, Pran censured him and said that for three days the three of us had been getting ready for work at 9 a.m. and here are the director and hero strolling in at 2 p.m.! But when we found that it made no difference to the attitudes of both *Kaka* and Sawan*jee*, we too started appearing for shooting only at 2 p.m.!' said Shashikala.

---

1   Saawan Kumar Tak's *Souten* was released in 1983 and co-starred Rajesh Khanna, Tina Munim and Padmini Kolhapure.
2   'The camera and light settings are ready, please come.'
3   Rajesh Khanna's nickname.

Veterans of the Hindi cinema industry are usually asked to speak about the changes that have occurred within the industry over the years, and most of them will rue the change in attitude towards senior stars. Once Pran was asked if he was still treated with the same respect as in his heyday. Completely ignoring all negative incidents, Pran replied in the affirmative, adding that if some of his contemporaries did not feel that way then it was because 'they haven't learnt to adjust to changed circumstances; we can't expect the kind of adulation that we had when we were at the top'.

Yes, the tide had changed but Pran had learnt to swim with it, and had survived so many decades in Hindi filmdom.

2

Pran acted in at least seventy-six films during the 1980s. Though many of the films made in during that period were duds at the box office, fizzling out within the first couple of weeks, others did moderate to good business.

Some of the top-grossing films in which Pran acted during this decade were Yash Johar's *Dostana* in 1980, which had 'hit' songs that still play on radio and TV today. Based on the film, *The Reincarnation of Peter Proud*,[4] Subhash Ghai's *Karz*, also released in 1980, had some excellent music by Laxmikant Pyarelal. Then came Tinnu Anand's *Kaalia*, Manmohan Desai's *Naseeb*, Satyendra Pal's *Sharabi* and, in 1985, Gulshan Rai's *Yudh*, a multistarrer directed by his talented son Rajiv Rai.[5]

The big-banner films of the decade in which Pran had roles were Yash Johar's *Duniya* and *Muqaddar Ka Faisla*; Tinnu Anand's *Shahenshah*; Prakash Mehra's *Jadugar*; and Manmohan Desai's *Toofan*. Unfortunately, these films did not do well commercially.

Interestingly, during this decade, two of Pran's incomplete films, which had been started years ago, but due to factors beyond everyone's control had been in deep freeze, were finally released.

---

[4] Based on Max Ehrlich's book, *The Reincarnation of Peter Proud*, (1975) directed by J. Lee Thompson, starred Michael Sarrazin, Jennifer O'Neill and Margot Kidder.
[5] For details of these films, please check the Filmography.

One of these was K. Asif's *Love and God*, which was left incomplete when Asif died in the 1970s. Akhtar Asif (who was Dilip Kumar's sister and Asif's wife) had managed to get this film completed and released in 1986. The other was Kalpanalok's *Chingari*, directed by Ram Maheshwari, written by Gulshan Nanda, and starring Sanjay Khan and Leena Chandavarkar, which was released in 1989.

Unfortunately, due to unforeseen factors such as long delays, death of certain artistes and the change in appearance of those left behind, these films failed to get any response from the public.

3

In 1983, a film by Shahab Ahmed was made, entitled *Film Hi Film*. The film's unusual feature was that Pran was its only real star. The rest of the cast were rank newcomers, who fitted the subject being made. Shahab Ahmed, who had earlier made a film titled *Cinema Cinema*, stumbled upon the idea for this film during one of his visits to the Bombay Film Laboratories.

Having stopped at a pile of what looked like junk, Shahab Ahmed was amazed to find out that these were the abandoned rolls of those films which could not be completed due to a stoppage of finance, ego hang-ups, accidents, deaths or legal wrangles. Some of those films had just a day's worth of shooting, some had much more. He found films made by K. Asif, Kishore Sahu, Manibhai Vyas, Nandlal Jaswantlal, Kamal Amrohi, Ramesh Saigal and Raj Khosla, among others, which starred greats like Dilip Kumar, Madhubala, Raj Kapoor, Dev Anand, Bina Rai, Vyjayanthimala, Nutan, Raaj Kumar, Mala Sinha, Amitabh Bachchan and Jaya Bhaduri. There was a treasure trove of over two thousand films!

Shahab Ahmed came up with the novel idea of building a story around these abandoned films, since moviegoers are unaware of the hurt and pain that go into the making of a film.

The story of *Film Hi Film* revolved around a veteran producer and father figure of the movie industry, Seth Gyanchand, who is at the top of his profession, but due to various reasons, finds himself stripped of all that he possesses, including his honour and prestige. After a lot of hard work and a few lucky coincidences, his dream of making a film again is realized.

Pran played the role of Seth Gyanchand, a character loosely modelled on Chandulal Shah, the owner of Ranjit Studios, whose own production company Ranjit Movietone had hit hard times.[6] He even went so far as to re-create Chandulal Shah's 'look' and 'get-up' for his role. *Screen* recorded about *Film Hi Film*: 'The way Pran looks and behaves in the film is what is eye catching. There is a striking resemblance to the late Chandulal Shah, one of the dream merchants who lived like a king and died a heart-broken man.'

And *Trade Guide* commented on *Film Hi Film* thus: 'The idea is different. The excerpts from unreleased films are so woven with the story that they are a part of *Film Hi Film*.'

Film Hi Film may not have done major box-office business, but it was certainly a novel and bold experiment. What Shahab Ahmed had done was to take on a team of veterans in their own field of expertise – people like Hiren Nag as director, Kamleshwar as writer and Mukhtar Ahmed as editor – who would help make his dream come true.

While Ramesh Deo and Seema Deo were the only other stars in the cast, it was Pran who was the real backbone of the film. Certainly, as a character actor, this was one film in which Pran must surely have found fulfilment! His portrayal of a heart-broken film maker is one that touches the viewer's heart.

Over the previous two decades, Pran had worked with great directors like Manoj Kumar and Prakash Mehra, both of whom used to pay a lot of attention to the story and the music. That is why most of their films have a strong storyline and good music.

However, Prakash Mehra's repeated use of 'the formula' and misjudgements in his storylines caused even *Jadugar* to fail at the box office. '*Jadugar* was my last movie with Prakash Mehra but he was not able to work his magic like before,' rued Pran. And, unfortunately, the opportunity to work with Manoj Kumar did not come again (after the offer to do *Shor* had been turned down by Pran) until the late 1990s for a film titled *Jai Hind* (1999), which failed to light up the box office.[7]

---

6   Chandulal Shah was an acclaimed film producer of the 1930s through the 1950s. Now a mere shadow of its former glory, Ranjit Studios (or sadly, whatever remains of it in the face of encroachments and tenants) still exists on Dada Saheb Phalke Marg in Dadar, central Bombay.

7   For details of these films, please see the Filmography.

Says Pran regarding these gifted film makers whose early work he has always admired: 'If I ever get to work with such talented directors again, I shall consider myself fortunate.'

4

Among the new crop of film makers, apart from Subhash Ghai, Tinnu Anand was another director with whom Pran got the opportunity to work.

Subhash Ghai recalled with reference to *Karz*: 'Pran played the role of Kabira. He plays the role of a person who does not know whether he is Hindu or Muslim. But since the person who raises him is Muslim, he considers himself Muslim. Later on, Kabira raises a little girl.

'The character is shown not to have married. He is portrayed as always narrating *dohas*, sometimes of Kabir and sometimes of Amir Khusro. Whatever he says, he takes from everyday life. The character was meant to be saintly, but Pran breathed life into it and made it believable.'

Subhash Ghai continued: 'In *Krodhi* (1981), Pran's get-up was like Moses and his character was to be like that of a *maharshi*.[8] The story is of a don who gradually becomes saint-like by living in the company of *rishis*.[9] Eventually, people start thinking that he too is a saint.

'Dharmendra played the don who comes under the *maharshi*, Pran Saab's wing. Pran Saab accepts him but does not reveal that he recognizes Dharmendra's true identity. Before his death, he begins the process of handing over his responsibilities to Dharmendra. Dharmendra is now forced to live the life of a saint till the end.

'Pran Saab's *ruthba*[10] in that film is of a spiritual man, a guru. There is one main scene in *Krodhi* where Pran Saab and Dharmendra are there. Pran points to a *shila*,[11] which has some dung drying on it. The scene shows Dharmendra objecting to Pran's views about God, saying that God is a myth.

---

[8]   A spiritually enlightened person.
[9]   *Rishis* are men who have undergone intense study of the Hindu scriptures and allied texts.
[10]   Position or status.
[11]   A large stone with inscriptions, like a stela.

'Then Pran *Saab* is supposed to remove the dung with a stick and point to the now-visible inscriptions on the stela. The village folk are unaware of the true value of those inscriptions and they look at it as a good place on which to dry cow pats. The scene shows *Pran Saab telling Dharmendra that even your mind is fogged; however, if the fog is cleared away, you too can become very wise.*'

'Pran *Saab* did that scene very well!' exulted Ghai. 'I think that is one of the best performances an actor could do. During shooting, *Pran* Saab *would become one with the role – that's what makes him a great actor.* He lives the character. He would take his role seriously. He has been a great example as an actor.'

Ghai went on to add: 'When I went to Pran *Saab's* house to sign him for *Krodhi*, he showed me all the paintings that have been done of him in his various get-ups. And since he had already done so many and such varied characters, it was difficult for me to create a character which would be new. He was very fond of his work and that fondness makes one put forth all effort.

'*It is unfortunate that because of his health and age we cannot work with him any more. But Pran* Saab's *name will always be written in the golden history of actors of Indian cinema.*'

Pran acted in two films made by director Tinnu Anand, son of the well-known writer Inder Raj Anand. Speaking with admiration about the veteran actor, Tinnu Anand elaborated about his experiences:

'I may not have made many films with Pran *Saab*, but my father…wrote lots of films with Pran *Saab*. Pran *Saab* acted in a lot of films where, more than action, he had to speak lengthy dialogue. So there was a relationship with him right from my father's days.

'For *Kaalia*, I came up with the story of a jailer and his convict. There were two very strong personalities in it. Because of Amitabh's established image, we had chosen him to play the strong hero but we wanted an equally strong personality to play the jailer. The story really starts when the hero runs away from jail, and the jailer is on his trail trying to get him back into prison.

'So we knew it had to be someone very, very important, someone who had an image, someone who people could believe that yes, this character could stand up to a fight sequence with Amitabh Bachchan. *Plus, he had to be a senior actor. Because he was playing a much more senior role.*

'I don't think anyone knows this, but I had approached Sanjeev Kumar for the role which I ultimately gave to Pran *Saab*. I had a very long session narrating my story to Sanjeev and discussing his get-up and everything for the role. Then at 4.30 in the morning, he got up and he said he was doing my film....

'When I went to Sanjeev's place at about 1 o'clock in the afternoon of the following day, which was about the time when Sanjeev used to wake up, I was told by Jamnadas, his secretary, that Sanjeev Kumar would not be doing my film! This was only because that very morning a full-page advertisement had appeared in *Screen*, which announced that Amitabh had green-lighted *Kalia*. So he felt very hurt, slighted that we had not waited for his announcement before putting in the ad.

'But the ad had ensured that everyone came to know that it was Amitabh who was playing the title role of Kaalia. Sadly, I didn't get a chance to work with Sanjeev Kumar again. That very day I decided that I would give the role which Sanjeev had left vacant to Pran *Saab*. This was because my father and I felt very strongly that if there was anyone, apart from Sanjeev Kumar, who could play this role, it was Pran *Saab*.

'When I narrated the story to Pran *Saab* he was very happy he was going to play a role in a film to be written by my father, since he was always a great admirer of my father's dialogue writing.

'Pran *Saab* would come prepared for his scenes. Pran always asked for his dialogues ahead of time – in fact, he needed to. This was because most dialogue writers write only in Hindi, and Pran *Saab* has difficulty reading Hindi. He used to tell everybody that he could read only Urdu. He would request the director to send an assistant who could write out the dialogue for him in Urdu and, if such a person was not available, he would offer to take down the dialogue in Urdu script himself!

'Fortunately, I did not need such an assistant because my advantage was that my father wrote only in Urdu. So there was this great combination between Pran *Saab* and my father, not only because of the Urdu but because my dad also hails from [what is now] Pakistan.

'*Kalia* was a great hit.[12] It made a lot of money. It still is making a lot of money with distributors. In *Kaalia*, Pran *Saab* is the father of

---

[12] *Kaalia* was released in 1981.

Parveen Babi. She is the girl who falls in love with his convict Amitabh Bachchan. And they have this total hate relationship because, as warden of the jail, Pran *Saab* hates indiscipline, whereas Amitabh, as Kaalia, breaks all the prison rules! So that was the triangle in the film.

'My father used to say, referring to both Pran *Saab* and Amitabh: *"Tumhare paas* actor *jo hain, woh lafzon ke rakhshas hain* — they are insatiable when it comes to powerful dialogue." That is exactly what my father wrote for them in the film — very powerful and impactive dialogues.'

'That is why I got the idea of interspersing dialogue with the music track and it became a hit! So much so that in Delhi, music cassette vendors, who had erected little stalls outside the theatres showing *Kaalia*, were playing the dialogue track of the film rather than the song tracks!' pointed out Tinnu Anand, and added, *'Pran* Saab *had a major share of the best dialogues spoken in Kalia.'*

Tinnu Anand went on: 'Whenever people talk about *Kaalia*, they remember only two names — one is Mr Bachchan's, the other is Pran *Saab*'s. And that is because *Kaalia* was a film that was famous more for the dialogues between Amitabh and Pran *Saab* than for its music!

'I have always admired Pran *Saab*. Why I keep mentioning *Kaalia* is because [it] *had two very disciplined actors — Amitabh and Pran* Saab.... If you called them at seven in the morning, they would be there! Pran *Saab* was a remarkable example of punctuality. He would be on the sets at 7 o'clock...ready with his make-up!

'Working with Pran Saab *has always been a matter of love.* He never questioned you about anything. He has never said that he would not speak a certain line or dialogue. He's always been cooperative, genuinely from the heart. I have never had any problems with Pran *Saab*; in fact, I have always enjoyed working with him.'

'Sometimes though,' conceded Tinnu Anand, 'Pran *Saab* being a stickler for discipline would be a source of slight irritation, since he is so punctual and such a perfectionist actor! As a result, sometimes we too would feel pressured since he would always come on time and once he was there, we felt that we just bloody well had to take a shot. We didn't feel good about making him wait! However, it's a great advantage for a director or producer to work with disciplined actors, especially in the present scenario. *And Pran* Saab *is one of the very few disciplined actors left in the industry...'*

Tinnu paused and then continued: 'I must narrate to you an incident which took place on the sets of *Kaalia* which revealed Pran *Saab*'s way of conducting himself of the sets.

'One day Amitabh and myself had a disagreement about a particular piece of dialogue which Amitabh did not want to speak. Pran *Saab* was present on the sets but he did not interfere either way.

'The matter took a serious turn and it was touch and go whether Amitabh would continue to work in the film if I continued as director. Amitabh even indicated that he would be willing to drop out of the project so as not to affect my career. I said that the producer would prefer to keep Amitabh rather than a Tinnu.

'There was a bit of a standoff so Amitabh called me back on the sets and asked me why I was being so stubborn. I told him that my father and I had sat up till three in the morning working on the *dhamakedaar*[13] dialogue which was the very one he was refusing to speak! Since it was a key scene between Amitabh and Pran, I wanted that when Pran *Saab* finished speaking his dialogue, Amitabh should end the scene with the kind of repartee that would elicit claps from the audience.

'Amitabh said: "How many films have you worked in?"

'I said: "None."

'"How many films have I worked in?" said Amitabh

'I said: "More than forty."

'He said: "Every director that I worked with says that the audience will clap at this scene or that, but when I go to the cinema, I hear no claps!"

'Then I replied: "If I don't get claps for this particular dialogue, then I will leave this profession! I swear this by my mother and father and my profession."

'There was a stunned silence. Everyone was shocked that a director who was totally new could speak to a superstar like this on the sets! Pran *Saab* who was sitting right opposite me did not say a word.

'Amitabh then got up quietly, looked up and told the lightman: "*Kya dekh rahe ho bhai, bahut dheett hai!* [14] I will have to say the dialogue. You better put on the lights."'

---

[13] Literally, 'explosive'.

[14] Loosely translated as: 'What are you looking at, my friend, he's very stubborn.'

'That evening, after the shooting, I got a bouquet of flowers. It was from Pran *Saab*. He had been a silent observer, not wanting to take sides but he also wanted to see whether I would succumb or not. The flowers showed that he was happy that I did not.

'That was a good thing because twenty days later, Amitabh sent producers Tito and Tony to me. They were announcing two films and they had signed Rakesh Kumar for one film and they wanted Amitabh to suggest the name of another director. Amitabh said: "Go and sign Tinnu Anand."

'I think I got the film only because I stood by what I believed in. I also admire Amitabh's qualities because, in front of everybody, he gave in to a director and spoke the dialogue that the director wanted him to. That shows his greatness as an actor!'

Did Tinnu Anand get any claps for the scene between Pran and Amitabh on which he had gambled his entire career?

'Of course, I got claps. *Meri puri jaan usme atki hui thi!*[15] I was praying for it too.

'In this industry everything turns out well in the end. If people would only sit down and sort out problems instead of letting it be hidden behind a façade, like whatever happened between Sanjeev and me…but ultimately everybody said that fate had played a very good hand with me. *Maybe I could not have done with Sanjeev what I was able to do with Pran Sahab,*' confessed Tinnu.

Tinnu went on: 'I must tell you about another film that I have done with Pran *Saab*. The name of the film is *Ek Hindustani*…. Although I have just got one scene of Pran *Saab*, I am certain that this scene will get him the maximum claps from the audience!

'Danny [Denzongpa] plays the villain in the film and Pran *Saab* is playing the freedom fighter, who is the father of the hero. There is a confrontation scene with Danny and there are powerful dialogues between the two of them. In fact, when people heard this scene on the sets they thought that since Pran *Saab* was backed by such powerful dialogue in the scene, Danny would most probably refuse to do this scene! Which, of course, did not happen since Danny too is such a disciplined actor.'

---

[15] 'My entire life was caught up in that one scene!'

'And what is more, when Danny heard the scene, he was clapping at every dialogue. He said: "If I am clapping at every dialogue of Pran *Saab*, the audience is going to go crazy!" It is a tremendous scene and it was performed very well by Pran *Saab*,' beamed Tinnu Anand.

Tinnu further recounted: 'Despite the huge time gap between *Kaalia* and *Ek Hindustani* and the fact that Pran *Saab* has aged, he came to the sets with his dialogue totally prepared! He questioned me privately saying: "Is Danny going to do this scene?" I could sense that Pran was excited at the prospect of doing this challenging scene with Danny.

'It is very strange that when I switched over from direction to acting, there was one more aspect about Pran *Saab* that made me realize just how completely disciplined he is! I had to wear the same kind of wigs and beards that Pran *Saab* used to wear for his roles and I found that I would feel irritated at having to wear a beard, because of the discomfort caused by the spirit gum. *But Pran Saab has never ever complained about anything! You give him any kind of get-up, he is most happy to wear that comfortably all day long.* One can see why he has enjoyed such a long stint as a villain and character actor, but he'll always be remembered as a villain.

'I wish he had never grown old. *At least in my mind, he has never grown old!*' Tinnu Anand concluded, echoing the sentiments of many of Pran's fans the world over.

5

For a man who, over the years, has been as close to Pran as Yash Johar[16] has, it is surprising that they did only three films together.

'I know him for a very long time, right from the time I entered the film industry...', Yash Johar said reminiscently referring to those many years before he graduated from production manager to controller of production, to eventually becoming a well-established producer in his own right.

Before becoming a producer however, Yash Johar had worked with Pran in Nasir Hussain Films' *Jab Pyar Kisise Hota Hai* (1961), a Dev Anand–Asha Parekh starrer.

---

[16] Yash Johar passed away on 26 June 2004. He gave this interview before he fell sick in 2003.

Yash Johar recalled: 'His family members and ours were personal friends, mainly because of our common friend, Satish Bhalla. I respected him a lot and we went on to work in some good pictures.

'He worked with me in *Dostana* [released in 1980]. Subsequently, when I made *Duniya* [released in 1984], I requested him to do the villian's role and he readily agreed.'

After a long stint doing character-actor roles, Pran switched to villainy in *Andha Kanoon* (1983), and then, winning the race against newer villains, played chief villain in *Duniya*. It was also after a long time that he worked with Dilip Kumar, with whom he had developed excellent counterpoint in some of the films of the 1960s.

Why did Pran switch back to doing villainous roles after such a successful changeover to character acting?

Pran clarified why he suddenly changed tracks: 'Many years ago, the monotony of having to play villain in film after film hit me. At the same time my young daughter had asked: "Why don't you try something different?" It was the right question at the right time.'

'Then suddenly in the 1980s, I began to feel vaguely restless,' Pran admitted, 'and again it was my daughter who touched the right chord when she said to me: "Papa, now we are fed up with your character roles." That's why I decided to do a few negative roles again.'

Pran, therefore, readily accepted Yash Johar's *Duniya*. Pran clarified: 'I did his second picture only because of Yash, a very dear and good friend of mine. He is one of the finest men I have ever met.'

In his interview for this biography, Rishi Kapoor recalled the time spent with Pran working in Yash Johar's film: 'I did one film which it was a great honour to be associated with. That was Yash Johar's *Duniya* and I had the privilege of working with such great artistes as Ashok Kumar, Dilip Kumar and Pran. Unfortunately, *Pranjee* was playing a negative role in this film and I just couldn't bring myself to accept him as a villain, because in most of my other films, he had played my father. This was the only film in which he played a villain's role with me.

'Dilip *Saab* had a lot of action scenes with Pran *Sahab*…. And how Dadamoni (Ashok Kumar), Dilip *Saab* and Pran *Saab* would talk! Those were great moments for me! I was able to imbibe so much from them as actors and put it to good use in my own work! It was a wonderful experience!' exclaimed Rishi Kapoor.

The third film Pran did with Yash Johar was *Muqaddar Ka Faisla* (released in 1987). Speaking for this biography, Yash Johar remembered an incident which made him make this comment about Pran Sikand. He said: 'I have always liked him as a human being. You can't find another such human being.'

What was it about Pran that caused Yash Johar to make such a glowing remark about Pran, the same as the many others had who were interviewed for this biography? Yash Johar remembers the incident well, dating it to the time when Pran had agreed to work in his *Muqaddar Ka Faisla*.

This time round too, Pran told Yash Johar that he would accept whatever price Yash would give him as signing amount. Yash gave him Rs 11,000 and told him that he would pay him once the work got started. However, as production progressed and Pran saw the expenses mounting, he refused to accept any payment from Yash Johar, saying that he would take his payment later. 'No, first pay others, then pay me,' was what he would say.

This pattern went on all through the making of the film until the entire picture was completed. 'He did not take a single penny from us after that Rs 11,000 which I gave him right in the beginning. And when it was released, my picture bombed really very badly,' said Yash Johar.

Yash continued: 'The result was that I went into a terrible loss and depression. But Pranjee stood by me. And by not a single phone call did he remind me of the money! I was very indebted to him and I would feel awkward about meeting him. But whatever the occasion at his house, a party or anything, I was the first on the guest list; I had to be there.

'One day, he told me: "You don't worry about the money. I will ask for it whenever I come to know that you have got sufficient money. I will not accept it otherwise." '

Yash Johar digressed at this point to tell us how, in spite of not being paid for *Muqaddar Ka Faisla*, Pran still retained a generosity of spirit, which soon became evident when Yash Johar started his next project *Agneepath*. As Yash Johar explained:

'When I signed Mukul Anand[17] for *Agneepath* (1990) I made it clear that come what may, we must ask Pran *Saab* to be a part of the film.

---

[17] Now deceased.

Anyway, Mukul wrote the subject, but the role we thought we would give Pran*jee* was too small.

'I told Mukul: "Never mind, we will credit him with a *guest appearance*." But Mukul said: "A *guest appearance* would not be fitting for an actor of his stature." But I said: "I must offer him *something*! Let us leave it to him to decide. We'll give him a *special appearance*."

'So both Mukul and I went to Pran*jee*. Mukul straightaway told him: "Yash*jee* is insisting on giving you this role, but I am telling you one thing: Is it not true that this role is not important enough for an artiste of your stature? Still, we will leave it to you."

'Pran*jee* said: "I'll never go against the decision of the director, and you are right. Our relationship is not going to end if there is no role for me in your picture."

'That is the kind of man Pran is and the kind of relationship we share!' asserted Yash Johar.

Coming back to the incident involving *Muqaddar Ka Faisla*, Yash Johar continued: 'Despite not being paid for my earlier film, he continued to help me with investments from his family and friends also. Money from sons, daughter and everybody in the family were also invested with me. So I told him: "Please tell me whenever you want the money – whatever you want, I am ready to give it." But still he would not accept the money I owed him.

'When *Kuch Kuch Hota Hai*[18] [released in 1998] became a very big hit, I was able to pay off everybody's dues. So I also went to him with the money. Even then he said: "Keep it for any…." That's when I interrupted him saying, "After *Kuch Kuch Hota Hai*, there *won't* be any more 'anys'!"'

With the passing away of Yash Johar, Pran not only lost a good producer, but he also lost a good neighbour. Yash had chosen to move closer to his office in Khar, and when they took one look at a flat in Pran's building, they decided that they could have no better location for their new home.

In spite of his years, Pran attended the *chautha* rituals held in memory of Yash, sad, yet stoic, at the loss of a very dear friend.

---

[18] Directed by Yash's son, Karan Johar.

6

In the early 1980s, Pran's second son, Sunil Sikand, made his formal entry into the world of films – no, not as a hero or a villain, but as a director.

Growing up in filmdom, watching a lot of films and associating with his father's friends at the numerous parties Pran threw for them, it was but natural that Sunil should nurture the desire to join the film industry. However, Pran had never pushed his children towards the film line.

Pran had made a conscious decision to be different from other star parents, keeping his wife and children away from the limelight. He added that he wanted to give them a variety of career options to choose from. Moreover, he did not want to force them or pressurize them into joining any field or profession.

In an interview with *Star & Style*,[19] Sunil said: 'We were never kept away from films as such. Though Dad never carted us along on outdoor locales or to studio shootings he used to throw a lot of parties where we came into contact with Dad's friends. I have always been a movie buff, I used to watch a lot of films and that's how I developed an interest in films. I was at the crossroads of my life where I had to decide on a career when I realized that I was keen on turning a director. I approached Dad and told him of my desire. My Dad then gave me the choice of deciding to apprentice under either Manmohan Desai or Manoj Kumar. I decided on Manmohan Desai.'

Pran chuckled and added: 'I told my son that apart from direction he was sure to learn how to abuse. "Man" cannot speak without "*gaalis*"!'[20]

Sunil joined Manmohan Desai's unit as his fifth assistant and worked his way up.

But why hadn't Pran ushered his children into the film industry earlier?

Pran replied: 'I kept my children away from my profession because, quite frankly, I didn't want them to follow in my footsteps. At no stage did I impose my will on them, I just gave them a wide choice to choose from.'

---

[19] *Star & Style*, 13–26 April 1984, pp. 12–13.
[20] Abuses.

'I didn't want my sons to become actors. Most of the boys who have joined the industry haven't been exposed to any other field but this. You may point out that I shouldn't be complaining considering I still command respect as a senior artiste. But tell me, how many people here are so lucky? The industry has treated some others very harshly the moment their luck ran out on them. I would never recommend my children to take up acting. Sunil was interested in being a technician and that's why I gave him my total encouragement. It's too late for me now, but given a chance, I too would have preferred to be a technician. A technician's job is definitely more committed and creatively satisfying than an artiste's,' added Pran.

It was clear that Pran had not just seen and experienced the highs of the film industry and the starry glitter and glamour that are associated with it, but also he had experienced firsthand the bitterness of failure and the realities of the people behind the masks. Yes, Pran had seen the underbelly of the film world and, like any responsible father, had wanted to shield his children from what could become a very harsh limelight. He knew that the movie business was intoxicating, and anyone who has had a sip of it, will keep thirsting for his or her next drop.

Under Manmohan Desai's tutelage, it wasn't long before Sunil gained the confidence to handle a project of his own. The Nadiadwalas gave him a break as a director for their film *Karishma*, which was to star Amitabh Bachchan, Parveen Babi and Pran. It may be remembered that Pran had earlier acted in the Nadiadwalas' films *Inspector* and *Ek Raaz*, both of which were directed by Shakti Samanta. However, for reasons best known to the Nadiadwalas, this film was put on hold.

Pran then encouraged Sunil to make his own film quickly, using his own story. *Farishta* (released in 1984) was produced and directed by Sunil Sikand, with Ashok Kumar, Bharat Bhushan, Kanwaljit and Smita Patil. In a special appearance were Master Raju, Ambika Shourie, Master Rajiv Bhatia, Danny and Pran. Unfortunately, the film did not do as well as expected.

However, the question is: Why was *Pran* not tempted to turn to film production or direction earlier on in his career — perhaps as the next stage in the course of progression from being actor to being a producer or taking to direction?

Pran and his son Sunil on the sets of *Farishta*.

While being interviewed for this biography, Pran spoke about this subject in more detail: 'No, I never felt tempted to become a producer. Many did suggest the idea to me but I didn't follow it up. My one-time secretary, Lalit Kumar Doshi, was always after me to produce a film, but I would keep putting him off. I had already tried my hand at film distribution in partnership with Satish Bhalla, but it had proved to be a loss-making venture for me.

'Lalit thought that if all my actor-friends were to be brought round to his way of thinking and if *they* were to start encouraging me to turn a producer, I would not be able to refuse them. So they started convincing me to turn producer. When that did not work, Lalit convinced my wife that I should become a producer and then *she* too told me to start a film, make more money, and whatever else Lalit was telling her. She said this once or twice, and since she was never the type to speak this way, I realized that it was actually Lalit who was behind all this.

'So, becoming fed up of this sort of indirect nagging by Lalit, I asked him to accompany me in my car, and we drove straight to Dilip Kumar's house. There were some eight to ten producers sitting outside Dilip's house. I didn't bother to wait with them, but went straight to the Dilip's private sitting room door, opened the door and barged in. I told Dilip that there were quite a few producers waiting outside to meet him and that he should go finish with them. I talked to Dilip for about five minutes and returned with Lalit.

'Later I asked him: "Do you want me to sit and wait around like those producers or am I better off being able to enter Dilip's room uninvited?" He never brought up the subject of my turning film producer again!' chuckled Pran softly.

7

For a long time, Pran and other leading members of the film fraternity had been aware of the lacunae in social security for artistes and technicians, who had worked silently in the background of the glamorous world of films, and who, due to the working conditions then prevalent (and in some cases, still prevailing) in the film industry, did not have the benefit of a pension plan! To that end, the Cine Artistes' Association had been formed, but that helped only the circle of actors and character actors. There were vast numbers working in the film line who had no financial 'safety nets' at all.

In 1986 something unusual happened, which served as a catalyst to ensure that even the smallest member of the film world would not be left penniless when they could work no more.

For the first time in its history, the *entire* film industry went on strike to protest the levy of the unreasonably high amount of entertainment tax imposed by the government. Earlier, sections of the film industry had struck work, demanding better wages or improved work conditions. However, this time, all of them were united against a common 'enemy' — unjust taxation!

The heavyweights of the film industry decided to organize a silent *morcha*[21] in Bombay that would start at the Chowpatty Beach and end at the Racecourse in Mahalaxmi. There would be no sloganeering: just white clothes with black armbands. And all of them would *walk*, not drive in their cars, to the destination.

On the given day, all the heavyweights and lightweights of the film industry walked, regardless of the heat and humidity. They walked to express their solidarity with each other and to register a strong protest at the unjust way in which the film industry, as compared to other industries, was being treated. Everyone who walked, walked because, by then, enough was enough. (It was walking during this same protest march that caused a heavily-pregnant Smita Patil to become so ill that she passed away a few days later.)

A few days after that historic protest march, a public gathering was held one evening on the sands of the Chowpatty Beach and those assembled were addressed by stalwarts like Dilip Kumar, Pran and Raj Babbar, as well as by actors and film makers from Marathi cinema, including the inimitable Dada Kondke,[22] all of whom elaborated on the taxation and implications it had on every level of film making.

The film industry strike had been so prolonged that it affected just about everyone who was actively or even remotely connected with it. Along with a few others, Pran took the initiative to try and end the strike. Vijay Anand and Yash Chopra, too, realized the need to also help those who were financially affected by it.[23]

They also wisely foresaw that, as time went by, difficulties would increase and even more complex situations would arise. Hence, they felt that this was added reason to maintain a registered fund for the film industry which would render financial aid to any needy person associated with it.

Out of this need arose HOPE '86.

In an unprecedented manner, the film industry united to put on a musical variety show, the proceeds of which would go to build the corpus of the Film Industry Welfare Trust.

---

[21] A *morcha* is a protest march.
[22] Dada Kondke passed away in the 1990s.
[23] Vijay Anand passed away on 23 February 2004, some months after giving a lengthy interview for this book.

The then-reigning kings of music, Kalyanji Anandji, Laxmikant Pyarelal, R. D. Burman and Bappi Lahiri, all dropped their invisible barriers and got together to put on the most fantastic musical show for the public. There was absolutely no sign of any egos whatsoever, as everyone got together to perform and collect money for those affected by the film industry strike.

That night, in addition to the stars in the firmament, a veritable galaxy of stars shone brightly at the Brabourne Stadium[24] – Lata Mangeshkar, Asha Bhonsle, Amitabh Bachchan and Dharmendra; in fact, everybody who was anybody was present and on call, lending weight to the occasion by their performances and mere presence. The sold-out show ended at three in the morning!

The funds generated by HOPE '86 were used to create the Film Industry Welfare Trust, and since then, it has disbursed money to anyone working with the film industry and who has become needy – whether technician, light man, spot boy, junior artiste, character artiste, photographer or screen writer, all have been helped.

Vijay Anand, an associate of Pran's on the HOPE '86 show, had this to say:

'Pran *Saab* was one of the trustees of the Film Industry Welfare Trust for a number of years. He was the one who took the most active interest in it. Our job was to decide who was worthy of this charity and who was not.

'Sometimes I would go to *Pranjee's* house, sometimes he would come to the trust office, and we used to sift through all the applications before deciding the deserving ones. I found in Pran *Saab* a great human spirit and a sense of justice. His memory was sharp and he would say: "He/she is a very old artiste and is now going through hard times, we must help." He would always keep the veterans in mind, those who had fallen on hard times.

'I have learnt some important things from Pran *Saab*. I also came to see that he has a very soft heart. Sometimes out of pity for those in need, he had this tendency to go overboard. But if I felt the case was not deserving I would stop him. We had a very good rapport and worked well as a team.

---

[24] Nestled between Churchgate and Marine Drive, in south Bombay.

'We used to consider those cases who had asked for educational aid...Pran *Saab* made some good suggestions, which we accepted. He said: "A child who gets good or outstanding results in the exams, should be given a hundred rupees extra and his parents should not touch that money. Or, a child who gets outstanding results as well as comes first in his class should get an extra hundred rupees." Sometimes we used to send two to three hundred rupees to the child on his say-so. We still follow this practice started by Pran *Saab*.'

'If some needy person's appeal has touched his heart,' Vijay Anand continued, 'then somehow or the other, Pran *Saab* would find a way to help him out. If the trust could not help, then Pran *Saab* helped that person from his own pocket!'

8

By the final years of the 1980s, Pran again began to feel that perhaps there was something more he could do in his profession as an actor. If ever an artiste has been fortunate enough to have as long a career as Pran has had, surely very few could lay claim to acting in such diverse genres and assortment of roles.

The next few chapters unveil many hitherto unknown aspects of Pran the co-star and the man – through the eyes of his fellow-actors and family – and help us gain added insights into the nature of this superlative human being.

TWENTY-SEVEN

Pran: The Gentleman Villain

1

When an actor has spent over sixty years in the film industry, one can safely assume that he must have interacted professionally and personally with almost the entire spectrum of stars, actors and creative talents that graced the silver screen during those decades. In addition to getting an insight on Pran and on what must be the *longest* career in filmdom, this chapter aims to find out how he got on with his colleagues and fellow-villains.

When Pran entered cinema primarily as a 'bad man', there were already several actors who had graduated from playing hero to side hero to villain. How artistes treated each other in those days of a now long-gone era would provide an interesting sidelight. One incident, which occurred in the 1950s, highlights this aspect clearly. It was the period when Pran's career had taken off and he was being signed for a stream of films, especially for those films being made by producers from South India.

However, it was in Bombay, while shooting concurrently for the many films for which he had been signed, that Pran ran unexpectedly into a professional dilemma – to accept an assignment or to reject it. This was an acute dilemma, since, at that time, Pran was seeking to re-establish not just his career but also his finances, which had taken a beating after Partition. In spite of the need for more work, Pran did not greedily grab all assignments.

His good breeding, culture and chivalry were clearly evidenced when he got an offer for a good role in a D. D. Kashyap film titled *Aan Baan*,[1] which was earlier offered to an actor senior to him.

'Sajjan had been signed up for that particular role,' recalled Pran. 'However, he suddenly decided to bow out of the film, apparently because he had been offered something more tempting in a film being

Pran as seen in *Aan Baan*.

---

[1] Released in 1956.

made in Madras. It was a last-moment thing, and Kashyap, on the eve of his first major shooting schedule, didn't know what to do. He came to me urging me "to save him".'

It was completely in character that Pran did the right thing. 'Ethically speaking,' Pran pointed out, 'what an actor who faces such a situation should do is to confirm with the actor into whose shoes he is being asked to step…whether he is leaving that film of his own accord and whether it's okay to step into his shoes or not?'

'*One should not barge hungrily into such an assignment as if one's evening meal depended on it!*' Pran emphatically declared, but with a smile. 'So putting Kashyap on hold, I went to meet Sajjan and asked him whether it was alright with him if I took up his assignment or not. It was only after Sajjan said okay that I phoned Kashyap and accepted *Aan Baan*.'

Perhaps as a reward for the completely ethical manner in which Pran handled this situation, *Aan Baan* earned for Pran extremely favourable critical appreciation.

Filmfare, for example, headlined its review : 'AAN BAAN IS A WELL-ACTED COSTUME DRAMA WITH GRIPPING STORY' and published a favourable review, going so far as to give Pran special critical acclaim: 'Pran is excellent as the turbulent and contumacious younger son resolved to displace his elder brother.'[2]

Certainly, in the matter of ethics, Pran had conducted himself in a manner which classified him 'a hero', behaving in a far better way than certain other 'reel-life heroes' of his day!

2

Another incident, which occurred in the 1970s, gave proof that his adherence to principles and a strong sense of fair play had not changed despite the passage of years.

Pran found himself in the unenviable position of having to turn down a director who had given him two of his best roles – in *Shaheed* and in *Upkar* – in addition to a really good role in *Purab Aur Paschim*.

---

[2] *Filmfare*, 1 February 1957, p. 28.

When Pran rejected Manoj Kumar's next film,[3] he knew full well that his friend would feel bad. However, with his heightened sense of fairness, he also knew that since another producer[4] had come to him *first*, with the offer to play a role *very similar* to what Manoj was now offering, it would be morally wrong for him to agree to act in both the movies that would be filmed almost simultaneously. It took courage and firm conviction to stand for what is right and say 'no' to a friend, but Pran did it. And commendably, Manoj has remained a dear friend.

Pran's principles would also not allow him to take up endorsement advertising, an activity of which many of today's film heroes and heroines and even sports stars think nothing, except as a superfast means to earn megabucks! Even in the past, corporate houses used to spend large sums of money for endorsements. But Pran remained unswayed in the face of monetary temptation. In his entire career, Pran did just one commercial endorsement – that of a brand of whisky. Why? In an interview given to Bachchan Srivastava for the *Hindustan Times* he said that it would be morally wrong to endorse a product that one does not personally use!

3

The views of Pran's co-villains also need to be documented in this book.

Prem Chopra, one of the earliest villains to enter the line after Pran, had many reminiscences to share when he was interviewed for this biography. He said: 'In the film industry, whether it is a senior or a junior artiste, nobody calls him Pran, they call him Pran *Saab*. This is something that he has automatically created – he commands respect. People would call Om Prakash as Om Prakash*jee*, or other senior actors by their names, but Pran was always called Pran *Saab*.

'Pran *Saab* had created a tremendous image of a bad guy on the screen because of which people in general tended to identify him as a bad guy in real life also. But once they came to know him closely, they knew how wonderful, noble and gentle a person he is.

---

[3] Manoj Kumar's *Shor*, released in 1972, starred Manoj Kumar, Jaya Bhaduri, Premnath and Nanda.

[4] The other producer was Prakash Mehra. For further details, see Chapter 23.

'I used to watch him while he portrayed his character very intensely, *because he was an icon amongst actors.* He had a tremendous range – he could do comedy, dangerous roles, emotional roles and dramatic roles.'

'We have been together and we've had fun too. We used to improvise a lot on the sets; we would give suggestions to each other. We used to work collectively. We would add or subtract according to our mutual discussions,' Prem Chopra noted.

'We played father and son in many pictures like *Anjaana*[5] and *Purab Aur Paschim.*[6] The only difference between father and son roles was that initially he used to snatch away wealth as well as the girl. Now *he* would snatch away the wealth and make *me* pursue the girl! We used to work together so that wealth as well as the girl would come home!' chuckled Prem Chopra.

He added: 'Our team became so popular with the distributors that I remember people saying that Pran and Prem Chopra were the excitement and the "draw" in any film in which they act!'

Prem Chopra went on to talk about the fine example Pran set when it came to taking his guests along for an outdoor shooting schedule. He said: 'Pran *Saab* was an example for us to follow. Even if he took his guest on an outdoor shooting, he would see to it that he stayed in a separate room and he would pay for everything, even for all the phone calls which the guest would make from the room. Additionally, he was never demanding! Generally, his food would come from home.' This was totally opposite to the many who 'had to have only a certain type of (usually expensive) food', and that too at the producer's cost.

'No actor can stay as long as Pran *Saab* has stayed in this disorganized industry. The more talented you are, the harder you have to work. An actor has to be totally involved during the making of a Hindi film. *These stalwarts have had staying power because they were devoted to their work.*

'Off the sets, after the shooting, Pran *Saab* would meet everybody but he would never behave cheaply with anybody. He was a very dignified person. I never saw him fighting. He would retire from any unpleasant situation. When there is a certain dispute between the actors or others

---

5   Released in 1969.
6   Released in 1970.

and if they seek his help, he would help to amicably settle the matter, which he has done many times.'

'He did not carry his reel role into his real life. He was very nice and acceptable company, but he is basically a very private person,' concluded Prem Chopra.

When the veteran actor, the late Madan Puri, was asked in an interview[7] as to which actor, to his knowledge, went deepest into his work, he answered:

'Two – Dilip Kumar and Pran.' When asked the reason why he chose to cite Pran as an example of professionalism, Madan Puri explained:

'Pran is most fantastically professional. When he takes up any assignment you know that for a full two months before shooting starts, the script writer, the assistant directors, the director, the make-up man, the wig-maker, everybody needed for his work – they'll all be drinking whisky at Pran's cost, at his house!

'He goes in very great detail into every aspect of his role, and for this reason I have been a great admirer of Pran for many years.'

'Do you know that Pran and I have been acquainted since 1937? We were on stage as amateur players in Simla in that year! Yes! I was the hero and Pran the heroine, in a drama staged at the Gaiety Theatre.... Pran, though junior to me in age by about four or five years, is senior to me in the acting profession, because he joined films earlier than I did,' said Madan Puri, whom Pran affectionately used to call Maddi.

Another fellow-villain, the late Anwar Hussain (Nargis' brother), commented in his interview to *Star & Style* about how most folk in the film industry had very short memories. Speaking about Pran, he said: 'One man who hasn't changed over all these years is Pran. He is just the way he was decades back in Lahore. A very well-mannered man, Pran welcomes whoever goes to meet him at his bungalow with open arms.'

In 1977, Anwar Hussain suffered a stroke which effectively brought his decades-long film career to an end. Speaking about the film industry's *'raat gayi, baat gayi'* attitude,[8] Anwar Hussain said: 'No film man comes

---

7 'A *Star & Style* discussion with Madan Puri', *Star & Style*, 30 March 1973, p. 17.
8 Loosely translated as: 'recognized today, forgotten tomorrow', referring to short memories and shallow relationships.

to enquire about my health, except for Pran.' '[He] has stood by me as a friend, and he even sends money sometimes,' added Anwar Hussein gratefully.

Lambasting a relatively new villain who had made a very grandiloquent statement that what Pran had done in twenty years, he could do in two, Anwar Hussain said: 'I asked him, "what about the remaining eighteen years?!" ' A simple but effective argument, indeed!

The late Manmohan was another villain who was an avowed Pran fan. He was so crazy about Pran that he too decided to play villain in films. He once said: 'Pran *Sahab* was my idol for a long time. Any movie of his I would never miss at all. Not only that, I would see the same movie several times without getting disgusted at all.'

Indeed, while most villains in Hindi cinema could only come up with a crude portrayal of the baser, animalist qualities of man, Pran managed to render those same qualities in a way that could only be described as 'polished'.

Actor-director Tinnu Anand spoke about the ease with which Pran performed all the 'badness' that the script demanded of him: 'None today measure up to Pran *Saab*'s dedication. Whether it was raping women or fighting or making the hero's nose bloody. He was *comfortable* with anything.'

Pran's younger son, Sunil Sikand too spoke about the films in which his father played villain: 'A lot of films in which my father acted were stylish films, like Nasir Hussain *Saab*'s earlier films and the ones with Shammi Kapoor. When you saw the film you felt that here was a villain with whom the girl also could run off. There is none of that sadistic looking make-up and posturing and screaming all kinds of funny dialogue.'

Commenting on the fact that in earlier times there weren't as many rape scenes, Sunil said that it was because the villain had the honourable intention of marrying the heroine! 'Even though the villain takes the girl to the *shaadi mandap* and the hero comes and rescues her, the fact is that the villain was willing to marry her! And another point to be noted is that the heroine did go to the *shaadi mandap* with the villain!'

'To ensure that the heroines were taken in by the villain, the villain was shown to be very polished. His personality was not at all abrasive. His style of wooing was practised, easy and suave; his words smooth and persuasive. Even where his clothes were concerned, if the hero was shown wearing ordinary trousers and an ordinary shirt, then the villain was probably wearing socks and shoes and a suit and hat and looking as smart, if not smarter, than the hero! It is no wonder then that so many girls would manage to get "seduced" by the villain almost in the beginning of the film itself!' exclaimed Sunil.

4

In response to what contributed to the successful creation of his villain persona, Pran made a pertinent observation: 'My voice has a big hand in my success. There are very few artistes who can change their voice according to the need of the role. I could do so with ease.'

Besides his voice, Pran used those unusual eyes of his to convey all possible emotions − lechery, contempt, red-hot anger, ice-cold rage, ruthlessness and repentance − in some unforgettable roles.

Pran's brand of 'villainy' was so well executed and honed to perfection that almost everyone in the film industry agreed that his name had become synonymous with that word!

It would be appropriate here to cite a really amazing example of the way in which Pran's villain image had become deeply embedded in the psyche of the mass cinegoers of our country. In referring to this synonymy, Pran said: 'As I started receiving more and more villain roles and became famous doing them, people started getting more and more frightened not only of me but also of my name! They stopped naming their children "Pran!" '

Arvind Sikand spoke about this phenomenon: 'I recollect my father relating this to me. It came about because some fans of his had come down from Allahabad to visit him and they rang him up and said: "We've come from Allahabad, we are students and we want to see you." Predictably, Dad asked them to come over and have tea.'

Arvind continued: 'They then told my father: "We have a fan club and one of the things we have discovered is that nobody in our fan club is named 'Pran'. Since we were a little bit surprised by this, we went to our college register and found out that there wasn't any student in our college named 'Pran'. So we checked out other colleges in Allahabad and discovered that none of them had a student named 'Pran'. Casting our search net wider, we went through the entire register of students in Uttar Pradesh and couldn't find a single one by the name of 'Pran'!" In fact, looking back through their rolls, they found that since about 1956 or 1957, there was never any student enrolled in the university or college by the name of "Pran"!'[9]

Pran's reaction? Arvind reports his father as having said: 'This is the biggest compliment anybody could give me. After Raavan,[10] Pran is the only name that a mother hasn't used for her child.'

Throughout the long era during which Pran reigned supreme as India's number one villain, people named their children after many gods and deities from the Hindu pantheon – but interestingly, none risked naming their sons 'Pran' which they obviously viewed as the embodiment of evil!

Interestingly, a letter arrived in March 2000, which revealed an exception. The writer from Mumbai got straight to the point: *'Believe it or not, my name is Pran and I am twenty-four years old and no one could be more aware of the aura of your name than me, for every time someone hears my name I get a look. It is an expression which just cannot be described.'*[11]

Any curiosity as to whether people *still* view the name Pran to be synonymous with villainy was dispelled by the comments made by Pran's ophthalmologist, Dr Nisheeta Agarwala,[12] who recently operated on Pran to remove his cataract.

'Some time back an elderly man and his son walked into my clinic. Since my work was to examine his eyes, I did not pay much attention to either his face or his name. I had my assistant put some drops into

---

9   'The Good Bad Man', *ZEE* magazine (April 2000, pp. 110–15). This article says that Pran's acting was so realistic and his on-screen villainy so convincing that when a survey was done in all the colleges of Maharashtra, UP and Punjab in the 1970s, it was found that not a single school or college student had been named Pran in about three decades!

10 Raavan is the demon-king in the epic Ramayana, who has epitomized evil in all its forms.

11 This letter, dated 14 March, 2000, came via email, the writer giving just his name – 'Pran'.

12 Of Hinduja Hospital, Mumbai.

them, preparatory to doing some more tests and asked them to wait in the waiting area.

'As soon as they left the room, my assistant excitedly asked me: "Did you realize who that was? It was Pran, the actor, whom you just examined!"

'I was astounded. So I went into the waiting room just to take another look at him. And there he was! Sitting there with his eyes closed letting the drops do their work. He had no idea that I had come to check him out!'

'I had imagined him somewhat differently, but when I met him, he was so utterly different to what I had pictured. I realize that on screen actors are portrayed differently and they have a certain image, but in spite of all that, this man here was different. He was so changed and so mild and simple in his ways,' exclaimed Dr Agarwala.

Over the course of the following months, Dr Agarwala was so taken with Pran that when an old friend of Pran, Ramesh Khosla, consulted her, she emphatically told him: *'If ever I have another son, I shall name him Pran!'*

Life had indeed come a long way for the *gentleman villain*, who is now more gentle than villain. Where once one might have been tempted to stick Pran's picture next to the words 'villain' in an encyclopedia and where once parents shied away from naming their offspring 'Pran', Dr Nisheeta Agarwala's words prove that people's perception of Pran has changed – changed dramatically and forever!

TWENTY-EIGHT

The Opposite Sex
...and Pran

1

Any book on a person who has played hero, villain and character actor through a career spanning six decades would be incomplete without talking about his interaction with the fairer sex.

Right from his first film, in which he played villain, Pran was cast opposite some of the most beautiful women in the subcontinent.

Noorjehan was the first of them.

Noorjehan, which means *light of the world*, went on to become the singing sensation of the subcontinent. About her, the famous author Saadat Hasan Manto wrote: 'To me, there was just one thing about her that was phenomenal — her voice! [It] was pure like crystal. Even a suggestion of a note was discernible when she sang, being perfectly in command whether the notes she employed were in the lowest range, the middle one or the highest.... Noorjehan only had to strike a note to make you sit up.'[1] *Mallika-e-Tarranum*

---

[1] From Saadat Hasan Manto's *Stars from Another Sky — The Bombay Film World of the 1940s* (Penguin, New Delhi, 1998).

(the queen of melody) Noorjehan was certainly a well-deserved title.

However, when Pran met her on the sets of *Yamla Jat*, she was just a young teenager being systematically introduced to the realities of the world. Still, in keeping with the artifice of her background, she was given the prefix 'Baby'.

By the time *Khandaan* began to be made, the 'Baby' from her name had been dropped. She had graduated to playing heroine. But Noorjehan was still quite short then and Pran remembers that, in their scenes together, they had to make her stand on some bricks in order to make her look taller!

Although during the making of *Khandaan* she fell in love and eloped with her young director, Shaukat, eventually marrying him, Noorjehan apparently also shared a good rapport with her co-star of three films, Pran. It appears that a common love for Urdu *shairee* and music was at the foundation of their friendship.

That there *may* have been some undercurrents of a romantic nature on Noorjehan's part is revealed in her gesture of running to Pran's house on the day his *baraat*[2] was leaving for Delhi.

Jotting down her memories of Pran especially for this book, Pran's eldest *bhabhi*,[3] Kuldeep Prem Krishen Sikand, recalled the moment: 'Pran was looking so handsome, wearing the *sherwani*[4] specially stitched for the occasion. Sitting there on the mare, with the *sehra*[5] on his head, he really looked regal.

'Suddenly, Noorjehan came running and asked, "Pran *ghodi chad gaya*?"[6] And the people around said: "Yes." '

Apparently, whatever needed to be said would now remain unsaid.

Pran's firstborn, Arvind, who has lived for many years in London, recalled receiving a telephone call in the early 1970s from the legendary

---

[2] Marriage procession.
[3] Brother's wife.
[4] Long, usually brocade, coat buttoned up to the neck; mostly worn at weddings and other formal occasions.
[5] *Sehra* is a veil of flowers tied to the bridegroom's head.
[6] Literally, 'has Pran mounted the mare?' But it could be taken to mean: 'Has Pran said "yes" to marriage?'

singer: 'Out of the blue I got a call from a lady who said: "I am Noorjehan and I am here visiting from Pakistan and I would like to see you."

'I was quite surprised. I mean, I knew that she'd acted in some films with my father. I remember *Khandaan* was her first role as leading lady and it was also my father's first role as leading man. But this was rather unusual – she was my father's first heroine in Lahore, and in the many years that had elapsed since then, we hadn't had much contact with her.

'She came across to our home one evening. She was very affectionate, and as we were having dinner that night she suddenly said to me: "You know, when I look at you, you could have been my child."

'I think it must refer to some, perhaps romance, that they may have had at that time. It was very sweet of her, I must say. I didn't take it at all in any bad way.'

Although Pran and Noorjehan had not kept in touch, for Pran never returned to Pakistan, not even to visit, apparently there was at least one occasion on which they had spoken to each other.

Pran's friend and *samdhi*,[7] Satish Bhalla spoke[8] about that occasion which took place some years ago: 'Pran*jee* had given an interview to the BBC. During the interview he mentioned that, when in Lahore, he had been the hero in a picture opposite Noorjehan. He mentioned that she had been a very famous heroine and a great singer of her time. Then he casually remarked to the interviewer, a trifle regretfully: "She must now be very old."

'This interview must have been telecast a few weeks later and Noorjehan must have seen it. I remember that day very well because I was sitting with Pran*jee* in his house. While we were chatting, an overseas call came through.

'It was Noorjehan – and wherever she was, she was p-r-e-t-t-y annoyed! Because she came right to the point and said: "This is Noorjehan speaking. So? I'm getting old, eh? And what about you? You're not getting any younger!" '

Decades later, during the early half of 1982, thirty-five years after she left for Pakistan, Noorjehan and her daughter, Heena, were coaxed

---

[7] Daughter's father-in-law.
[8] A few months before his death in 2003.

Nooorjehan and Pran − a joyous
reunion.

to make a visit to India, to be special guests at a music programme in celebration of the golden jubilee of the Indian talkie, which would bring together several living legends of the world of music and which, happily for Pran, fell on his birthday, 12 February. There, she sang her famous song, 'Awaaz De Kahaan Hai...' from the 1946 film Anmol Ghadi.

Pran recalled that joyous and affectionate reunion: 'Noorjehan was so nervous about the trip, she called me at least eight−ten times before she boarded the plane, just to be reassured that I'd be waiting for her at the airport with a special bus. It was an evening to remember and she was so thrilled that she'd let herself be persuaded to make that visit to Bombay. I also threw a party in her honour where she could meet many more of her old colleagues and friends.'

That Pran is a fan of Noorjehan's voice, just as the rest of the world of her listeners are, is clear from this very telling incident that took place many years ago on board an aircraft, high up in the skies.[9]

During the flight, there was some sort of heated discussion going on in the neighbouring seats between some Pakistanis and Indians, and the topic was focused on Kashmir which then was, and still is, a flashpoint. One of the passengers asked Pran about his opinion in the matter.

Pran's reply? 'You want Kashmir?' he asked. 'Well, you take Kashmir!' he said. 'But in its place, you will have to give us Noorjehan!'[10]

---

[9]   Pran himself narrated this incident to Satish Bhalla, who, in turn, talked about it in his interview for this biography.

[10] Sadly, Noorjehan passed away on 23 December 2000.

2

Many of Pran's female co-stars used to find it difficult to cut through the several layers of the tissue of Pran's image, to recognize the man within. Later they would embarrassingly confess their reservations about working with him and how their fears and qualms had proved utterly groundless.

One such was the heroine of yesteryears – then young, naïve, innocent and unsophisticated – in the wonderland of cinema: Nimmi.

Nimmi, while discussing how she first met Pran, disclosed: 'I worked with Pran *Bhaiyya*[11] for the first time in K. Amarnath's *Aleef Laila* in the early 1950s. Before that meeting, I had seen Pran *Bhaiyya* only when I used to see movies and in them he used to play mainly villains' roles. In *Aleef Laila*, he had chosen the get-up of a very dangerous looking magician with long nails, wispy beard and moustache, the kind who gazes into a crystal ball to predict the future and all! Seeing him in that get-up on the sets scared me all the more! [See Chapter 12.] At first, we scarcely addressed one another. When he was sitting on the sets, I would involuntarily sit at some distance from him!'

One day, journalist-publicist Rebecca Samson visited the sets of *Aleef Laila* to interview Nimmi. Seeing Pran seated not far from them, Rebecca greeted him in a friendly manner. She was puzzled to see a distant look on Nimmi's face and quietly asked her about it.

'Reluctantly I came out with my fears!' Nimmi said, with a laugh. 'I told Rebecca how I was afraid of this man who always played villain.'

'"But in real life he is really a very good man, the very opposite of the kind of roles he depicts on screen," Rebecca told me and said: "Come, let me introduce you to him properly!" '

Nimmi, although hesitant to actually go up and meet Pran, said: 'Wait! First please go to my car and in it you'll find a box of sweetmeats[12] and a very good *raakhee*.[13] Please fetch them here.'

---

[11] Brother.

[12] Indian confectionery.

[13] A *raakhee* is a piece of decorative string which is customarily tied by a sister on to the wrist of her brother as a symbol of her sisterly devotion, in exchange for which the brother promises her his protection. This ritual cuts across caste and creed and is also used by ladies who wish to proclaim sisterly feelings for a gentleman who is not their real brother (as a blood realation).

As soon as this was done, Rebecca sent a message to Pran, who came across and, moments later, became Nimmi's *raakhee* brother!

'He was very happy when I tied the *raakhee* to him,' Nimmi reminisced. 'He embraced me and from that time onwards, my love and respect for him grew – not only as a brother but as a human being too.'

Nimmi maintains this custom to this day and she and her husband, Ali Raza, are counted among Pran's closest family friends and have been present at all the important milestones celebrated by the Sikand family.

In the early 1950s, with Pran's career in films becoming more established, and his interaction with co-stars having increased, many more who came close to him found out that he was nowhere like the villain he had portrayed in countless films.

The lovely and graceful heroine Waheeda Rehman[14] recalled an anecdote that took place during the late 1960s, around the time of *Aadmi*:[15] 'There was a party in Madras and a few of the invitees were from the Air Force. I hate to say this, but these invitees became a little tipsy and had begun to misbehave. Then they began to insist that I say *"Hai Allah!"* just the way I had said it in *Chaudhvin Ka Chand*.'[16] I said: 'Look, this is not a film set where I am shooting. It's a party. How can one recite dialogue off-hand like that?' Waheeda still felt exasperated at the memory of that situation.

She then made a pertinent observation, saying: 'I have noticed in the industry that when "outsiders" do something, then the film people become very protective. Pran *Saab* who noticed that an Air Force chap was following me around, got up and said: "Waheeda*jee*, now I think it's time up for you to go home and sleep. Come on, now go." The hostess

---

[14] Waheeda Rehman was a top heroine who started her career in Hindi films with Guru Dutt Films' *C. I. D.* (1956) directed by Raj Khosla, co-starring Dev Anand and Shakila. Her role as Rosie in Navketan International's *Guide* (released in Hindi in 1965) directed by Vijay Anand, won her the Best Actress Award for the English version (directed by Ted Danielsky), which was released earlier, in the Chicago Film Festival. She became the first Indian actress to win an international award. This was reported in *Variety*, a famous international film magazine.

[15] Released in 1968.

[16] Released in 1960, Guru Dutt Films' *Chaudhvin Ka Chand*, directed by M. Sadiq, was a Muslim 'social', which also co-starred Guru Dutt, Rehman and Johnny Walker.

began protesting, saying: "No, Pran *Saab*, the evening has just begun. What's this? She's not a little child!"

'But he said: "No, I know that, but she has to look beautiful and fresh and nice in the morning, so she has to go." He got up and ordered for the car and saw to it that he came with me up to the car, sat my assistant and me in the car, and checked who was going to escort us. Then he gave them instructions, saying: "Go right up to her room. See that she is in the room at the hotel. Now you are responsible for her." These are the kind and thoughtful things he did which show that he is a very caring person. I think that is the time people started calling him "the gentleman villain",' declared Waheeda Rehman.

And so, the soubriquet 'the gentleman villain' stuck.

But newer entrants seemed to have been as influenced by Pran's villain image as the on-screen *Guddi* was![17] Veteran actress Aruna Irani recalled in her memoirs[18] the first time she had to work with Pran in a film called *Johar Mehmood in Hong Kong*.[19] As the title suggests, most of the film was filmed in Hong Kong and after a long stint of shooting there, the young Aruna was eager to get back to familiar ground – India.

Finishing her work earlier than the others, Aruna had to fly back from Hong Kong to Calcutta and then to Bombay. Since she was quite young then, Pran was asked to escort her back to Bombay. Their flight from Hong Kong was delayed, so they could not make it in time to catch the connecting flight to Bombay. As a result, they had to spend the night in Calcutta.

In Aruna Irani's imagination, Pran's screen reputation immediately reared its ugly head. Petrified at the prospect of having to spend a night in the same hotel as Pran, she described her feelings in her reminiscences: 'I was terrified. I was sure Pran*jee* would rape me! Once we reached the hotel, he dropped me to my room and said: "Lock your door from inside. I am in the next room. If anybody knocks on the door, don't open it.... Inform me on the phone." I was so touched! He had turned out to be

---

[17] See Chapter 29.

[18] Published in an article by Shubha–Misbah in *Stardust*. Unfortunately, the collector of this clipping neglected to record the date of the issue.

[19] Released in 1971, the comedy, *Johar Mehmood in Hong Kong* co-starred Mehmood with Aruna Irani and I.S. Johar with Sonia Sahni.

such a gentleman. Now that I know him, I just adore that man. You can put him at the top of the list in the whole industry. He is a gem of a person.'

Pran was well aware of the effect of his image on people, but he often used humour to remove the sting from peoples' words and actions.

On the sets of producer-director I. S. Johar's *Bewaqoof*[20] erected in the grounds of Central Studios at Tardeo in Bombay, a very interesting conversation took place between Johar and Pran. Inevitably, the topic turned to girls and as was Johar's wont, he began to find ways in which to tease his colleague.

Johar told Pran that a girl had once told him: 'You know, the other day, I saw Pran – and I ran!'

Not without a piquant sense of humour himself, Pran promptly replied: 'You should have asked her – "in which direction?" Away from me or towards me?'

That was the end of that discussion!

Reflecting on this aspect Pran said: 'Girls, especially schoolgoing girls, wouldn't dare come near me during those days when I used to play the villain.... It amuses me now, but some girls would even bring their parents along when they came to take my autograph!'

Since this was the reaction to his presence, over the years, Pran has invariably been asked this question: 'How do leading ladies feel in your presence?' Pran's reply in the 1960s to this question is valid for all time:

'At first the heroines are ill-at-ease. But after a few days, when they come to know me better, they understand that my screen villainy is not a reflection of my personal self. This dispels their doubts; it sets their minds at ease, and makes it possible for everyone to be normal with one another.'

A few months before her death in 2004, singing star Suraiya, who had played the title role in *Badi Bahen*,[21] made it evident that, over the years, Pran, the real person, had not changed: 'He was absolutely the opposite of the bad-man image...Pran *Bhaiyya*...was always courteous and respectful...to all women.... "Very bad on screen – but very good in real life", that's how I'd like to sum up my feelings about Pran *Saab*.'

---

[20] Released in 1960.
[21] *Badi Bahen* was released in 1949.

Which makes one wonder whether Pran managed to frighten any of his heroines at all. When asked by journalist Roshmilla Bhattacharya, she says that Pran had replied rather sheepishly that he had managed to terrorize none! [22] In her article, she reports Pran as having said: 'In fact, heroines like Mumtaz, who was a real firebrand, would laugh and say about me: "How will he frighten me when he can't even grab me properly?" '

Imagine! For all the hard work he had put into convincingly portraying 'bad man' in film after film, his heroines seemed to have had no problem saying: *Bad man he may be on-screen but off it, everyone knows he is a good man.*

However, in one of his early interviews given to *Screen* (18 January 1952), Pran said: 'I like being "rough" with the females on screen so much so that my friends wonder if I am really the rascal that I portray. I admit I am. I love to give the impression of being a bad man and, sometimes, when I psychoanalyse myself, I feel I enjoy the role of a screen villain because I have not the guts to be one in reality.'

Some time later, in early 1954, it so happened that Pran had to enact a typical rape scene with Bina Rai for *Meenar*.[23] During the filming of the scene, which obviously showed the villain having a go at the heroine and the heroine putting up a hard fight to stave off his advances, it appeared that Pran had put a little too much energy into the 'attack'.

Filmfare (16 April 1954) reported as follows: 'Pran's "attack" on Bina Rai resulted in her having black and blue marks on her arms and legs as a result of a furious struggle with screen villain Pran. She bravely suffered the full onslaught of Pran's savage fury. She had to be carried to her make-up room in a state of collapse, but [nevertheless] reported for work the next day.'

This was the *only* report in his entire career of his having 'manhandled' a heroine. Undoubtedly, after this incident, Pran must have realized how delicate the fairer sex is and would have been extremely careful in his enactment of rape scenes, for every one of the heroines who had at some

---

[22] Roshmilla Bhattacharya's interview with Pran appeared in two magazines (under different titles): 'Destined to Be in the Movies – Nostalgia', *Screen*, April 1998, and 'The Good Bad Man', *Zee Premiere*, April 2000, pp. 110–15.

[23] *Meenar* was released in 1954.

time in their films been 'manhandled', 'raped' or 'attacked' by Pran, said in their interviews for this book, that although he acted 'rough' for dramatic effect on the screen, Pran had actually handled them very carefully.

In many of the films, as per the constraints of the commercial genre, the writer would inevitably write in at least one scene where Pran would grab the heroine by her arm or her wrist and lead her to wherever he wanted her to go.

Remembering those scenes as a whole, Asha Parekh[24] commented thus: 'He was one person that when there was a fight scene, and he is supposed to be catching the heroine and running – he knew how to catch, he knew how to push. *I never felt that I would be bruised by the end of the fight. He knew how to handle the heroine.* That is very creditable; and even at this age, he is so agile. *To be in this industry for some sixty years or more is a very great thing.*'

3

In every Hindi film with a typical 'all-black' villain, there usually was his female counterpart – the vamp. Together, the villain and the vamp would do their worst to stir things up for the hero and heroine before reaching a bad end themselves. Or, if the script writer was feeling generous, the villain was made to reform after being beaten within an inch of his life and the vamp was allowed to turn a new leaf in time for the 'happily-ever-after' ending.

Pran had memorable villain–vamp partnerships with actresses such as Kuldip Kaur,[25] Shashikala, Nadira and Helen. Although all of them also played heroines' roles, Helen was *the* cabaret star of all time! By the late 1970s, Shashikala and Nadira graduated to doing character-actress roles, with Helen joining their ranks in the 1990s, with her comeback role in

---

[24] For the record, Asha Parekh has acted in nine films with Pran. They are *Asha* (1957); *Jab Pyar Kisise Hota Hai* (1961); *Phir Wohi Dil Laya Hoon* (1963); *Mere Sanam* (1965); *Do Badan* (1966); *Love in Tokyo* (1966); *Upkar* (1967); *Bhai Bhai* (1970); and *Jawan Mohabbat* (1971).

[25] Kuldeep Kaur died young.

Sanjay Leela Bhansali's *Khamoshi – The Musical*. Interestingly, these veteran actresses have got some of the best roles late in their careers after the usual run-of-the-mill ones in the earlier part of it.

While Kuldip Kaur and Pran had worked together from the Lahore days and had continued with their careers in Bombay, Shashikala, Nadira and Helen all teamed up professionally with Pran only in Bombay.

A co-artiste with whom Pran has done a lot of work is Helen. She has enjoyed decades-long fame as probably the Indian screen's finest dancing star. The song-and-dance numbers by Helen invariably turned out to be highlight items which enhanced the market value of their films.

Pran and Helen have worked together in twenty-four films, in most of which he was the villain and she was the side heroine, the vamp or the cabaret artiste.

Born in Rangoon, Burma, Helen Richardson came to Bombay along with her parents in the 1940s, during the Second World War years. Life had certainly not been easy for her. Therefore, she values the kindness and friendship that Pran showed her. In this context, she noted:

'We were in the star cast of over twenty films, but the best of the lot in which we did many good scenes together, were *Pyar Ki Rahen*, *Jaalsaaz* and *Dus Lakh*.'[26]

'In *Dus Lakh*,' Helen went on, 'I remember Pran played the comedian-cum-villain. And we had lots of scenes with Manorama and Om Prakash. I was the side heroine in that film. Pran is easily one of the finest persons I have ever known in the industry.'

When the veteran producer P. N. Arora and Helen could not work together any longer, a lot of unpaid financial dues had already accumulated and Helen suddenly found herself in a precarious situation. It was Pran who helped her tide over the crisis. As Helen recalled:

'Though Pran *Saab* and I knew one another as co-artistes, we had never been that close for me to expect any help from him – but when he heard of what had happened to me, he came forward to help me. That can be expected from someone close to you, but Pran *Saab* had always been just a co-artiste. Yet, when he heard of my troubles, he was kind enough to volunteer even monetary help.

---

[26] Released in 1959, 1959 and 1966, respectively.

'I remember to this day that very human gesture of Pran *Saab's*. The only other person who helped me at that time was Nanda.[27]

'Many years have passed since we met but I'll never forget how he helped, when I needed help most. That's better than even the help one expects from close friends, isn't it? When we talk of good people, I always have Pran Saab's *name first on my lips.'*

If during the 1950s through to 1970s Pran was *the* villain, and Helen was *the* cabaret dancer, then Shashikala will be remembered as *the* vamp.

Shashikala first met Pran when she was signed as the heroine of Filmistan's *Aab-e-Hayaat*, in which Premnath was signed to play the film's hero and Pran the villain.[28]

She recalled the time when due to failed business ventures, she and her husband could no longer afford a car, she would either take the taxi home or the folks from Filmistan used to send her home in a studio car:

'Pran *Saab* used to have a car and sometimes he would give me a lift in it. But look at the man's *decency*! In those days, we had a lot of night shootings, but he was so decent that he never touched me. He is a thorough gentleman.'

'He was so wonderful that any woman or girl could fall madly in love with him. During the shootings, however, whenever he had to touch me, I noticed that his skin was a soft and smooth as butter. I know that people may think that I am saying this because I must have had a fling with him! But he never took advantage of his obvious charms.' As Shashikala said this, one could hear the respect in her voice.

'When Pran was at the peak of his career, we did quite a few films together. *Our rapport was so good, that people used to think that something was going on between us and many rumours were afloat because of our working together so often and working so naturally together.* But because we lived in the same area, our families were close and Pran was very fond of my two daughters. He is very fond of children,' remembered Shashikala.

---

[27] Yesteryear's top actress Nanda is the daughter of Master Vinayak, famed Marathi actor-film maker of the 1940s. Some of her famous roles were in V. Shantaram's *Toofan Aur Diya* (1956), *Chhoti Bahen* (1959), *Hum Dono* (1961), *Jab Jab Phool Khile* (1965), *Ittefaq* (1969) and Raj Kapoor's *Prem Rog* (1982).

[28] Released in 1955.

4

Gossip about link-ups with various beautiful women and co-stars is all part of the territory of acting, whether as hero or as villain in films. What did Pran himself have to say about the allegations of 'affairs' with his co-stars made by certain sections of the media?

When journalist Pamela Sethi asked him about his alleged 'relationship' with Helen, his co-star in over twenty films, Pran was very cut and dry with his answer, saying that all he had done was to come to her aid. He said: 'Her flat had been taken over by her friend P. N. Arora and she came to me for help. I helped her to recover her property with the aid of a brilliant lawyer. That's all there was to it – so why must film magazines and gossipmongers start shouting about it? Why? Why? Who are they to write such things?'[29]

On another occasion, freelance journalist Alka Kherdekar interviewed Pran for an article she was doing for *Sunday Mid-Day*.[30] During the course of the interview she asked him how he felt about certain rumours of his alleged 'marriage' to some starlet that were making the rounds of filmdom at the time.

Upset that no one had bothered to cross-check the facts before publishing such irresponsible reports, Pran reacted angrily: 'Have I gone *crazy* to marry again, that too at this age? I am fully content with my life.'

Never one to hide behind any sort of artifice in his real life, Pran candidly said in that same interview: 'I have never claimed to be a saint. But they should not write such things without ascertaining the facts.'

What effect did this sort of gossip have on his wife, Shukla? Pran had once said this about his wife in an interview to *Screen* (18 January 1952): 'I have never argued or quarrelled with my wife all these years. Perhaps, this is due to her good nature. She is a sport and takes me as I am.'

This statement is borne out by what Shukla said when asked how she felt about his job as an actor. She apparently took such reports in

---

[29] Pamela Sethi, 'Small Roles Are a Challenge – Pran', *Filmfare*, 2–15 September 1977, pp. 25–27.

[30] *Sunday Mid-Day*, 28 June 1987.

her stride, knowing that all of this went hand-in-hand with the job of being an actor. However, she did acknowledge that while she preferred him doing 'good man's' roles, she realized that portraying a villain was also part of his work. 'Work is work,' Shukla*jee* said when interviewed for this biography. 'When it came to rape scenes, I have maintained this nonchalant attitude. I think of it as his work. And that his work demanded such scenes. So I didn't feel anything. Even the thought that he may run away with one of the heroines never crossed my mind.'

Since Pran had three growing children, what effect did this sort of scandalmongering have on them? Daughter Pinky spoke about how the matter of gossip was dealt with: 'Film gossip or any other gossip was not allowed at home. He never did it, so we didn't have the guts to do it in front of him. Nobody else's life was discussed at home. What's being written in the magazines, about whom was it written, all this was never talked about at home. We never really did ask him why is so-and-so doing this or that.... It was in the flow of things. We didn't even sort of question him·as to why he was doing this or that. At least I could not. I was quite shy of him. And sometimes, when somebody brought it up, he would say: "What have you got to do with it? How is it going to affect you? So let's leave it at that." There was simply no unnecessary talk of all these kinds of things.'

5

Despite the villainous image which Pran had established and despite the many ladies who were supposedly frightened of him, a lot of people are surprised to learn that Pran has a large number of female fans – including Pran himself!

Once, while in Calcutta for the shooting of Salil Ray's Bengali film *Jeevan Rahasya* (in 1973), Pran had become quite wound up because of having to wait a long time for the heroine to appear for the shooting. But when he realized that a large number of the fans waiting to see him and take his autograph were female, not only was his mood altered, but also he felt quite chuffed. Looking at the number of female fans assembled there, he is reported to have exclaimed: 'Goodness, I never knew I had so many!'

Some of his female co-stars, when interviewed for this book, spoke admiringly of Pran's good looks. 'I have never ever seen such a handsome villain!' exclaimed Shashikala. 'The way he walked, the style with which he talked and the way he used to dress up, and what culture! I have never ever heard Pran referring to any lady in abusive terms.'

The candid and outspoken actress Nadira said that even though Pran enjoyed his drink, it never affected his good looks. When interviewed for this book she said: 'The more he used to drink, the more handsome he used to look. He is a very, very pleasant man to drink with, to talk to and that makes him a wonderful person. I love Pran*jee* as he is an open book. He is a very good human being. Some time back, I had written something about him, and he sent me a bouquet of flowers. These small little gestures go a long way. He is a very sweet, very polite man.'

Pran and Nadira share a tender moment
(in the 1960s).

Shubha Khote (a comedienne turned character actress) added: 'Pran was a very down-to-earth person. I never felt I was working with a great actor and a big star whom I had seen in school and college days in films like *Munimji*.[31] I used to think, "he is such a handsome man, why does he do villain's roles, why doesn't he become the hero?" And come to think of it, the villain *has* to be very handsome if he has to compete with the hero, hasn't he?'

6

Given the fact that in addition to the admirers of Pran's good looks, there were many more women, both within and outside the film industry, who

---

[31] Released in 1955.

were besotted with Pran, it is interesting to find out Pran's views on beauty and women as also his views on his co-stars.

During the early 1950s, in an article titled 'The Bad and the Beautiful' for *Movie Times*, Pran was asked for his opinions on women. He acknowledged that after having worked for so many years in the film industry, it would be fair to say that he had gained some knowledge of the fairer sex through experience.

Although sometimes the experiences had been sad, he said that one had to expect such setbacks in the film world in which so many sensitive, complex and artistic temperaments abounded. In his view: 'Show business has taught me a great many things, and the fair sex can always be an interesting experience – take that as you will! I have worked with most of the ladies on our screen. This has afforded me a "perspective", shall I say. I have at least learnt to see things as they are instead of how I'd like them to be. Time has knocked off the rose-coloured aura. Where once I was taken in by appearances I can now look below the surface and know when a look or a remark is not just "casual". That is why, perhaps, my idea of "beautiful" may not be what someone else's might be.'

That is the kind of profound remark which one may expect from an intellectual, and, over the decades, Pran has modestly concealed that intellectual side of his nature.

In the same interview, Pran went on to speak about several leading ladies opposite whom he had worked. His words held up a mirror not just to them but also to how Pran himself viewed the opposite sex. What emerged was a very telling picture of not just the people about whom he spoke, but of Pran himself – the man, the person within:

'Sometimes we meet very beautiful women who leave us unmoved. Why? Because in my opinion beauty is not skin-deep. It involves a lot more: that is why it is so rare.'

Elaborating on his views of who was truly beautiful, Pran said: 'I think I can explain this giving a few examples of interest. I have had a chance to study most of the screen heroines. All of them have the advantage of good looks, grand wardrobes and expensive jewellery, but it is not from these but from chance remarks, from behaviour with subordinates and colleagues, from conversation and conduct, from little exhibitions of temper that I have discerned a great deal of the reality.' Obviously,

Pran was not taken in by just by mere good looks or by embellishments.

Pran's 'list' of 'truly beautiful women' is revelatory: He spoke of Durga*bai* Khote[32] as 'the embodiment of all that is truly feminine'. He added that it was not her charming smile or her dimples that made him feel that way but it was because she was sincere and gracious. Her attitude towards both the rich and the poor was the same and she never patronized her junior colleagues.

Pran recalled having seen Durga Khote for the first time dressed in rags and without any make-up, ready for a shot in which she was supposed to look old and weary. After the scene was filmed, she talked to a lady about how to nurse a sick person at home and it was during this conversation that Pran looked at Durga*bai* and thought she was the loveliest person he had ever seen – the soul of patience and sympathy, qualities which shone radiantly on her face. Pran remarked that years could never diminish her beauty, which exuded from within.

One other co-star Pran admired was Nargis. He said the main reason was because Nargis never made anyone feel that he or she was working with a great and famous artiste. Pran's first picture with Nargis was her own *Pyar Ki Baaten*,[33] which was directed by her brother, Akhtar Hussain.

Pran, who was eager to work with Nargis, quite frankly felt when he first saw her that 'her beauty did not match her art'. However, over a period of time during which he acted in *Aah*[34] and *Angaray*,[35] he came to realize that although Nargis was not the classic beauty, she was really very 'beautiful' because she had that 'inner radiance' which time could never dull. This innate quality as well as a wonderful sense of humour, along with intelligence and a balanced attitude, made her a wonderful, beautiful person.

Speaking about Nimmi, with whom he first acted in *Sabz Baagh*[36] and then *Aleef Laila*,[37] Pran affirmed that she was every bit as beautiful off-screen as she was on it, with histrionic talents to match.

---

[32] With whom he worked in *Malkin* (1953) and *Lakeeren* (1954).
[33] Released in 1951.
[34] Released in 1953.
[35] Released in 1954.
[36] Released in 1951
[37] Released in 1953.

Recounting an incident which took place when he had organized a charity show in Calcutta to collect funds for his Bombay Dynamos Football Club, Pran said that Nimmi had agreed to come in spite of her heavy shooting schedule. Even though there had been two air crashes just before their departure to Calcutta, Nimmi kept her promise to participate in the show, although several other stars dropped out because they feared that their plane would crash too! Pran recalled how her infectious smile never once left her face and that she was a source of encouragement to all as she went through all her items for the evening.

Although everyone else's nerves were on edge, and tempers frayed, Nimmi never once lost her cool. Pran described the moment, saying: 'With the auditorium in darkness and the spotlight on Nimmi, dressed in pearl-grey, she recited Urdu *"nazms"*.[38] She looked like a beautiful statue come to life. I have forgotten what she recited but I can never forget how she looked that night.... Do you think she would have looked that way if she had lost her temper, sulked and gone into a tantrum? I realized then that she looked beautiful because she was not only a beautiful woman and a good trouper but because inside of her she has all those qualities which go to make a great star and a still greater lady. Her beauty can be taken for granted − not the attributes which make her so.'

Pran also spoke warmly of the excellent rapport he had developed with Nutan and Madhubala, both very talented heroines.

Yes, Pran's concept is that beauty lies in the eyes of the beholder, beyond the obvious outward show of it. That newspaper article, to which Pran had contributed, concluded with these words: 'Therefore, let those women who think they are plain take heart. We men have discrimination. Don't underestimate us. We are never taken in by beauty alone. Other things must go with it − contribute towards keeping it. Someone long ago rightly said:

> The plainest face has beauty,
> If the owner's kind and true.

---

[38] A form of Urdu poetry similar to blank verse.

7

From 18 April 1945 to the present, Pran has had the privilege of walking through life with a truly beautiful and gracious woman at his side – his wife Shukla.

Pran's relationship with Shukla has been based on friendship and mutual trust, to the extent that Shukla could 'tell off' Pran for being unconcerned when she was involved in the car accident which completely damaged their Hillman in the early 1950s!

Pran always spoke of his wife as a friend, and in one early interview he had said: 'I even try to make my wife Shukla see that I am really a rascal. But like all women, she thinks she has made a good "catch" and feels I am improving.'[39]

When interviewed for this biography, Shukla said of Pran: 'I never discussed his career with him. He used to get only such sort of [villainous] roles, so we were happy in whatever we got. I felt, "if he likes doing villainous roles, then it was okay with me". And I found satisfaction when he was happy with his work. His happiness counted first with me. I am happy when he is happy.'

Spoken like a true friend and companion!

---

[39] *Screen*, 18 January 1952.

TWENTY-NINE

The Real Man versus the Reel Image

1

Pran had certainly come a long way since the days when he earned fifty rupees a month in Lahore, at Dalsukh Art Productions, when for a mere seven annas[1] one could buy a Scotch and soda *and* a plateful of crisps!

The journey of Pran the actor is more well known. However, it was in tracing the journey of Pran the real man that many hitherto unknown but interesting aspects emerged.

Almost immediately, it became obvious that there was a vast difference between Pran, the actor, and Pran, the man. The reel image of villain was very far removed from his real self, and many feared him because they could not differentiate between the strongly entrenched image and the real person.

---

[1] Before the monetary system went from Imperial to Metric, 16 *annas* made a rupee (100 *paise*). Hence, one *anna* would be equal to 6.25 *paise*.

Interestingly, one person who attempted to project Pran *as he was in real life – a really kind-hearted human being* – was Hrishikesh Mukherjee, who cast Pran in his film titled *Guddi*. All that was required for Pran to do in this role was play himself!

Guddi[2] dealt with the illusion that is created by the make-believe world of films and the effect it has on young minds. How a young girl is helped to distinguish between that illusion and reality was the theme of the film. In the brief 'footage' in which Pran appeared, director Hrishikesh Mukherjee showed him spontaneously handing over his watch and some money to a needy studio worker. Due to the villain image that has been so firmly established in her mind, the schoolgirl,[3] who is on the sets to watch the shooting of a film, immediately suspects Pran of having some dastardly motive. However, it is pointed out to her that in real life, Pran is totally different from what is projected by his screen persona.

Guddi was a film made not just to entertain, but also to educate and set straight the sort of skewered thinking that is a natural consequence of depicting the fantastic and illusory world of films. By requesting Pran to play himself in *Guddi*, Hrishikesh Mukherji achieved two objectives: one, he enlarged on the basic premise of his film and, two, he did a great service to Pran – by using the medium of cinema to help the audience see the real Pran: he is not at all like what the movies had generally portrayed him.

In an interview given to *Filmfare* in the early 1950s,[4] Pran spoke about how often people mistook the 'reel-life' image for 'real':

'Some time ago in Delhi, I accepted a friend's invitation to dinner. While we chatted of old times, his eight-year-old sister was introduced to me. Later she told her brother that he should not have brought a "bad man" to the house. I was that "bad man".'

Pran contended that his screen persona made an impact not only in India but also abroad. After the release of *Ram Aur Shyam*,[5] Pran played

---

2   Released in 1971.
3   Played by Jaya Bhaduri (now Jaya Bachchan).
4   'No Hope for a Villain!', *Filmfare*, 22 August 1952, pp. 14–15.
5   Released in 1967.

host to some guests from East Africa. Their children were curious to know where Pran kept the whip with which he had flogged Dilip Kumar, the hero. They had mistaken Pran to be the despicable character he played in that film!

Pran was well aware that his villainous image was the cause of these reactions, but there was little he could do about it then. He had family responsibilities and he had to earn enough money to fulfil them.

2

Many little known aspects about Pran were unearthed during the writing of this book. Although all the people interviewed for this biography were unanimous in their praise of him, some of his co-stars, colleagues and relatives revealed specific details of Pran, the man, which were largely not known to the public.

Asha Parekh who, having acted in nine films with Pran, made this very discerning observation: 'Basically, I feel that Pran *Saab* is *an introvert*. He would take a chair and sit in the corner. But then when I started working more with him, he opened up. What I found quite interesting was that, after he gets over his shyness and talks to you, he has got this *great sense of humour*, and comes up with rare anecdotes and jokes.'

Comedian Deven Verma narrated a comical episode, when Pran and he played a practical joke on tourists: 'This interesting incident happened during the shooting of *Aaja Meri Jaan*[6] in Goa. I was the surprise villain in this mystery drama. We were shooting the climax scene outdoors, far away from our five-star hotel. When we packed up I had lots of "blood" splattered on the front of my shirt and coat. I was tired and wanted to have a shower. So I rushed back to the hotel in the same dress and in the same condition.

'In the hotel's lounge, I saw Pran *Saab* and immediately acted as if I was shot. Pran *Saab* immediately caught on, and shouted: "He's been shot! He's been shot!" Some elderly foreign ladies sitting there screamed and ran helter-skelter! The situation was so funny that we both sat down and had a good laugh!'

---

[6]   *Aaja Meri Jaan* was released in 1993.

And Shammi Kapoor revealed yet another facet: 'Pran *Saab* is *basically a very gentle person.*'

Reminiscing about his loyal friend and the precious friendship they have shared for a long, long time, Shammi Kapoor said: 'Pran*jee* and Geeta had worked earlier on, even before Geeta and I got married.[7] I remember him particularly when Geeta's parents died and then when Geeta herself died,[8] Pran*jee* was with us. Pran*jee* used to come forward and willingly help…he knew how to manage things in the world. He's always been a very helpful and resourceful man.'

Manoj Kumar remembers how Pran was there all the time with him as a bulwark when he lost, first his father and then, his mother. He said: '*Pran Saab* was there all the time with me as a support. He was like *an expert friend*, who would divert my attention from thinking about my sorrows, by telling me jokes or something else to cheer me up. *He has shared other people's sorrows but he has never revealed his own sorrows.*'

3

Another noteworthy quality is his strong sense of right and wrong, which sometimes brought him at odds with the political powers of the land. Pran has always stood strongly for human rights and the upholding of human dignity. In early 1977, during the height of the Emergency, Pran had written, outspokenly, against it and the excesses that were being committed in its name.[9] This was an extremely brave act, since there had been a clampdown on free speech by the then information and broadcasting minister, Vidya Charan Shukla, and Pran could easily have been arrested.

---

[7] The brilliant actress Geeta Bali was Shammi Kapoor's first wife. Geeta Bali and Pran had first worked together in *Badi Bahen* (1949).

[8] Geeta Bali contracted a fever, which resulted in her death. She passed away on 21 January 1965, at the age of 35.

[9] Emergency was imposed on 25 June 1975, by Indira Gandhi, when citizens' rights were suspended and censorship was made mandatory. Pran evidently wrote an article for *Screen*, in which he gave vent to his anger and frustration at the government's malpractices.

On reading the article, the trade union leader George Fernandes,[10] who had been lodged in Tihar Jail, New Delhi, surreptitiously wrote a letter appreciating Pran's stand on the matter of free speech. Pran wrote back encouraging him to keep up his courage and good work.

His not tolerating bad governance moved him to remark: 'During the Emergency, I felt excesses were committed, so I...openly supported the Janata Government.' But when he found that regardless of which party rules, the people at the helm are all the same, within six months of the Janata Party coming to power (in late 1977), he wrote against Prime Minister Morarji Desai and the Janata Government's policies.[11]

In an article in Star & Style,[12] Pran spoke out bitterly: 'I campaigned for the Janata Party last year to bring to an end the unbearably oppressive regime of the previous government. We wanted our freedom back. You ask me what the Janata Party has done for the film industry. My answer is, nothing...nothing...

'Where we [the film industry] are concerned, neither the Congress nor the Janata has ever bothered about us. They don't consider [us] an industry. Let alone helping...everybody has only taxed us as heavily as possible. The government gets so much revenue from us. But not a penny is ever ploughed back into the film industry.'

When Mrs Indira Gandhi came back to power in January 1980, Pran's reaction was not surprising: 'I was very happy because the Janata government was turning so bad that the only person who can control everything at this juncture is Mrs Gandhi. I admire her choice of ministers. She had earlier promised not to encourage any defectors and so far she has not brought in the defectors. The rest we cannot comment on until the government starts functioning, it's too early now.'[13]

He later said: 'These days I feel all politicians are just there for themselves, not for the country. What we really need is benevolent dictatorship.'[14]

[10] George Fernandes subsequently became a Union minister.
[11] Rafique Baghdadi and Rajiv Rao, 'Pran: Arch Villain Turned Character Actor', Screen, 17 June 1983.
[12] Pran 's views were published in the article 'Politicians in Filmland', Star & Style, 10–23 March 1978.
[13] Pran 's statement appeared in a column called 'Reactions', published in Star & Style, 8–21 February 1980.
[14] From an article by Sanjay Sayani, published in the Telegraph Magazine.

All those who had even the smallest interaction with Pran knew that although on-screen he was 'bad man', he was a good one off it. Apparently, even the very politicians, about whom Pran did not have a very high opinion, knew about the real Pran. Once a politician, who happens to have the same initials and surname as another famous villain, was asked whether he resented being referred to in a way where he could be equated with a villain, responded imperturbably: 'Why should I be upset? What's in a name? Pran may be the most feared villain in reel life but in real life everyone knows he's a gentlemen, very *shareef*.' [15]

Typically, Pran remembered a *sher*, which reflects his disillusionment with the system: '*Hum hain sab be-imaan, phir bhi kehte hain "hamara desh mahaan"*!'[16]

4

'Kindness passed on will soon embrace the entire human race' is evidently a dictum by which Pran has *silently* chosen to live his life – both personally and professionally. Pran has chosen to 'cast his bread upon many waters'. However, the grateful recipients of his kindness could not keep quiet. His good deeds had to come out some day.

It is impossible to document all the good deeds Pran has done all through his life. The people he helped silently, without motive, are too numerous to be included here, even just by name! From producers and directors to stunt men and fight masters, and from spot boys, light men and extras to old-timers and aged character actors, Pran has never consciously turned anyone away. Instead, he has gone out of his way to help them.

The instances of Pran's strong support to deserving charitable and individual causes are strewn generously throughout the many decades of his career. Wherever possible, Pran expressed his generosity through an organized, registered body – such as the Cine Artistes' Association.

---

[15] This report of Kanwar Natwar Singh's remark on the popular television show, *Aap Ki Adalat*, and the *sher* that Pran remembered, both were published in *Screen* in April 1998, in an article by Roshmila Bhattacharya.

[16] 'All of us are crooks, yet we proclaim "our country is noble"!'

Character actress-comedienne Shammi provided a few details about this association and its functions: 'The Film [Cine] Artistes' Association was actually the Character Artistes' Association. All the character artistes had come together and formed it because invariably it was the character artistes who never used to get their money...Pran was, I think, one of the founder members along with Manmohan Krishna[17] and K. N. Singh.[18] It remained as the Character Artistes' Association for a long time. We used to put our foot down about our remuneration and used to get what we wanted.

'When some heroes and heroines agreed to abide by the rules of the Character Artistes' Association and joined [it], they asked that it be renamed the Cine Artistes' Association.... Pran was a very active member of the association. He really did a lot of work. Because everybody respected him and was fond of him, he could get them to help in our various fund-raising charity programmes.'

Chandrashekhar,[19] the president of the Cine Artistes Association, disclosed how monetary help was being given to some very old and impoverished artistes since there is no social security in film land. The older generation of stars and character actors were not commercial minded; neither did they invest their monies in the kind of businesses that artistes had begun to do in the 1960s. For instance, Rajendra Kumar[20] was the first star to invest his film earnings wisely. Since then, many stars and others have followed his example.

But the stars of the 'silent' and the early 'talkie' era neither had the business sense nor the opportunities to invest in the businesses of today. As a result, their plight during their non-earning years was quite pitiable and many suffered during their old age. For instance, E. Billimoria, a hero

---

[17] Manmohan Krishna, a renowned character actor, gave memorable performances in *Basant Bahar* (1956), *Dhool Ka Phool* (1959), *Waqt* (1965) and *Do Badan* (1966).

[18] K. N. Singh usually played villain 's roles. His role in *Awaara* (1951) as Jagga was outstanding.

[19] Chandrashekhar was a hero turned character actor. His memorable films include *Bara Dari* (1955), *Cha Cha Cha* (1964) and *Street Singer* (1966).

[20] Rajendra Kumar, whom I (Bunny Reuben) labelled 'Jubilee Kumar' acted in noteworthy films such as *Mother India* (1957), *Dhool Ka Phool* (1959), *Dil Ek Mandir* (1963), *Sangam* (1964), *Arzoo* (1965), *Suraj* (1966), *Saathi* (1968) and *Geet* (1970).

in many 'silent' films, had no money to pay for his hospital expenses. And many now know of the difficult and tragic last days of one-time heroine and famous star of the 'silent' era, Sulochana,[21] who helped everyone in her heyday, but had no one to help her when she needed help the most. Therefore, in addition to what was being done through the association, Pran even individually helped many of these indigent artistes, including a small-time artiste Fazloo.

When Fazloo died, and the association increased its contribution to his widow and family, Pran correspondingly increased his contribution. When Pran felt that the amount the association was now giving Fazloo's family was sufficient, he stopped his personal contribution.

Interestingly, son Sunil said: 'He's been so quiet about this aspect that even the family didn't know about it, leave aside the outside world!'

However, Pran did not limit his generous giving to just film industry folk. His soft heart impelled him to stand by those who needed his help, whoever they may be.

What is the motivation behind Pran's acts of kindness, generosity and charity? When specifically asked about it for this biography, Pran replied: 'I was brought up in an atmosphere where giving was practised. My father was a very big-hearted man, very generous. And I observed the *pleasure* he got out of giving. This has been my experience too.'

5

Yet another fascinating aspect of Pran the man is that he has a passion for unusual things.

One of Pran's great passions was possessing exclusive cars. Vintage or new, they had to be different for Pran loved to make a style statement.

Although he cannot remember the make of the first car he bought in Lahore, there is no doubt that it must have been a car that nobody else had. His next car, which he bought in India, was a Hillman, which was totalled in a car accident just before the premiere of *Bahar* in 1951. He secretly admits that he had actually been wanting to get a new car, and just then his wife had had the accident! So he got himself a Chrysler.

---

[21] Real name: Ruby Myers.

Pran and Pinky in the MG Roadster.

After that he got an MG Roadster, which was a convertible and a Chevrolet. Eventually he bought a Volvo. Pran also bought two vintage Austin cars. Not one, but two! When asked how his taste in cars developed, Pran replied: 'I just had a love for them.' But his daughter Pinky added: '*I remember him saying once that he didn't want a car that everybody else had. In those days having a Mercedes was the ultimate but he wanted to be different. Whether it was cars, clothes or hobbies, my Dad wanted to stand out as different.*'

Pran also had a vast collection of pipes. His elder son, Arvind, said: 'He was not a pipe smoker as such, but occasionally he would smoke pipes or take tobacco. He was a great man for smoking cigarettes. He used

A young Pran sporting a pipe.

to go through about three packs (of twenty) a day. Of course, I don't think he actually smoked all those, since very often on the sets he would be puffing a cigarette and when the "take" started, he would probably throw it away or give it to somebody else.' Then when Pran gave up smoking, the pipes found their way into other people's collections.

It was the same with another item. Arvind recollected: 'He also had a fascinating collection of walking sticks…. Some of them had hidden swords, which are very popular in Kashmir, and intricately carved sticks. I don't know where they all are now. They just vanished! Regrettably, they weren't maintained as a collection.'

Pran's urge to collect unusual things extended to collecting glasses – all types of them. 'He also had a passion for collecting different types of beer glasses and goblets,' revealed Arvind. 'I remember some quite naughty ones…when you finished your drink and looked down, you could see some nude women at the bottom of the glass!'

6

A very fascinating facet of Pran the man is that he has always enjoyed the good life and has never been coy about it. 'My father was always a man of great taste and style,' declared Arvind Sikand.

Not many people know that Pran used to enjoy playing cards with his friends. Veteran actress Nadira revealed a little-known fact about Pran: 'Did you know that Pran *Saab* is one of the best cardsharps in India, and that he doesn't play cards any more because he doesn't want to lose his friends? Because even if he plays fairly and justly, and he doesn't cheat, who's going to stop people from suspecting that he did not move one card from here and put it somewhere else?'

Perhaps Nadira referred to the time when Pran saw firsthand the distress his friend Saadat Hasan Manto went through when he lost money in a game to Pran and his partner, and the partner refused to return Manto's money despite being told to by Pran.

Pran told Manto that he should take the money back. It was only when Manto protested that Pran should keep the money since he had won it from him that Pran revealed to him that he was the best cardsharp in town, but he would not cheat a friend. Whatever the reason, the fact remains that Pran stopped playing cards.

Veteran character actress, Shammi added: 'Pran's *Saab* is a font of *shairee*.[22] It resides in his [Pran's] heart.' (The late) Satish Bhalla remarked:[23] '[He] knows so much about Urdu poetry but *doesn't write it at all*! I've had the pleasure of sitting with him and listening to him recite; he doesn't sing, he recites them. Only a person with a deep understanding of Urdu poetry could recite so well.'

Pran's own knowledge of Urdu poetry and his ability to recite *shairee* are well known and have already been spoken about by most of his co-stars. Veteran actress Nadira said admiringly: 'The amount of poetry that's hidden in that man's heart, his soul, his mind, is absolutely amazing!'

Manoj Kumar too spoke admiringly of Pran's amazing gift of remembering countless numbers of *shers*:[24] 'Pran *Saab* has literature by heart, not just English literature but Urdu literature as well. He also has committed to memory the poetry of famous Urdu poets such as Asghar Gondvi, Faiz Ahmed Faiz, Firaq Gorakhpuri and Josh Malihabadi.

'He can recite the famous Punjabi poetess Amrita Pritam's verses with emotion and passion. I also know of the *shayars*[25] whom he has looked after. The world does not know about it, and he is too cultured a man to ever speak about it. But there are many families who have been looked after by Pran *Saab*. *I have seen actors who may be better than Pran* Saab, *but I have not seen a human being better than him in the film industry!*' exclaimed Manoj Kumar.

Although Pran used to regularly have his whisky every evening, he would never drink when on the sets. Commenting on his drinking habit, the veteran actor said: 'As a devotion to my art and craft, that is cinema, I never touch liquor when I have my make-up on. I do not even touch it when I am working.'

But after a hard day's work, once washed and cleaned up, Pran liked to relax with a drink and music. Some summer evenings, he would invite

---

[22] Urdu poetry.
[23] Unfortunately, Satish Bhalla passed away in 2003, while this biography was in the making.
[24] Couplets.
[25] Poets.

his friends over to his bungalow in Bandra, and over glasses of whisky and some delicious dinner, would recite some fabulous poetry for his guests.

Pran's love for his drink sometimes led to unexpected twists and turns. Pran recounts an episode when he ran afoul of the authorities. During Prohibition,[26] only those persons with permits could consume alcoholic drinks, that too, only in private places. Pran and close family friend and neighbour, Balraj Kohli,[27] both of whom had permits, came up with some ingenious ways to enjoy their regular evening pegs. One very original way was to travel up and down in a lift in their favourite haunt, the Cricket Club of India[28] guzzling their drinks, usually whisky. The police, however, were not amused and arrested them. They were later produced in court. The public prosecutor, however, had to withdraw the case as both individuals possessed the requisite permits and were drinking in 'a private place' as the CCI was not just a 'private club', it was also a second 'home' to them! When Pran and Balli turned up at the club after their brush with the law, all the members applauded and congratulated them on their 'release'.

Another time, the exuberant and unconventional Balli, who had a Scandinavian wife, decided to celebrate a very 'wet' Christmas eve during the height of the 'dry' days of Prohibition! Pran, recalling the episode with a twinkle in his eye, said· 'The party was in full swing and the liquor was flowing freely. Suddenly, he was informed that the police was about to raid his party. Balli moved fast! He promptly had all the liquor bottles put into my compound. Miraculously, the police did not peep over the compound wall!'

As much as Pran's deep-rooted passion for Urdu poetry and *shairee* is a part of his personality, so also literature, current affairs, politics and a wide perspective on international events are also very much part of Pran, the man. It is therefore no surprise that one finds out about another of Pran's loves — books!

---

[26] Prohibition was imposed by Chief Minister Morarji Desai during the 1950s.

[27] Balraj Kohli, or Balli, was very close to many luminaries in the film world, and, ironically, to Morarji Desai 's son, Kanti as well!

[28] Popularly known as the CCI, it is in Bombay.

Pran had one of the finest collection of books, all of which he read. If it had grown any larger, he would have had to buy a small apartment

just to house his library! Speaking about this hobby, Arvind turned nostalgic: 'His taste was far-ranging from fiction to the classics. He collected several volumes of books like *The Arabian Nights* and *The Encyclopedia Britannica*. I remember going through them for hours and hours as a youngster. I used to go through the adventures of Alexander the Great, and Greek and Roman mythology. My father's library was an interesting place to grow up in. There were lots of educative influences.'

Pran with a part of his book collection.

Pran managed to contain his huge library within manageable proportions by never saying 'no! to someone who wanted to borrow a book. The moment someone asked to borrow the latest fiction release (which Pran had bought), he would hand it over, saying: 'Take it! Read it – and keep it!' As a result, most of the books in the personal libraries of Pran's friends are those which Pran had asked them to keep!

7

Arvind Sikand recalled that another grand hobby of Pran's was gardening: 'There was an old gentleman; he must have been past seventy. He used to come by and consult with Dad and make sure that the garden was well maintained. He did it because he too loved gardening.'

Pran elaborated that the elderly gentleman, who used to attend to the garden because it was a passion with him, was a Parsee whose name was Minoo Patel. While the Sikands did have a regular gardener, who also worked for their neighbours, the Bajajs, Minoo Patel used to come by and oversee Pran's garden.

'We had a fabulous collection of roses which were a passion with my father,' said Arvind. 'I remember making trips to Poona [now Pune] to get roses for him from the nurseries there. Cacti were another great passion with him. He must have had well over three to four hundred different types – from the large ones, towering to about ten to twelve feet, to little miniatures ones of about two to three inches across.

'Our garden was a fascinating place for children,' recalled Arvind. 'We had all kinds of fruits too: *cheeku* (sapota), lemon, *sitaphal* (custard apple), sugarcane, coconuts and mango, even green chillies.... It was not quite self-sufficient but it gave you something to put on the table.'

Both Pran and Shukla love dogs passionately. Except for the time when they had no home in Bombay, the Sikands have always had dogs.

In Lahore they had an Alsatian and, after moving to Bandra, they had a golden retriever called Bonzo and several Alsatians, whom they named Bullet I, Bullet II and Jenny. They also had a jet black cocker spaniel whom they called Soda, and Whisky, which was a white Pomeranian. Another time they had Silky Sidneys called Laila and Majnu. Unfortunately somebody carried away Laila, and poor Majnu was left quite alone!

Arvind Sikand pointed out that Pran did not limit his love

Pran in the company of
Bullet I (1965)

of animals to just dogs: 'Dad used to bring some [other] animals back from the sets also.[29] One time he brought a parrot, another time a deer, one time a monkey, but that created havoc!

'This monkey was a real devil, quite prone to snapping at people.... He became a nuisance, so we kept him chained to the top of a castle-shaped kennel, which was occupied by the Alsatian.... The monkey and this dog didn't get on very well. He would tease the dog and the dog would bark and growl.... One day, during the monsoons, it was

---

[29] There were no strict laws then about the use of animals and birds in films.

pouring...and the monkey was sitting on top of the kennel all huddled up and shivering, getting totally soaked. Then he decided that this was no fun at all, so he swallowed his pride and went very quietly into the cage with the ferocious Alsatian. Amazingly, the dog didn't do anything to him.... When the rain stopped, the monkey crawled out and then they were back to being the best of enemies again!' smiled Arvind remembering the monkey's antics.

'Once this monkey ran away and all the residents of Pali Hill were chasing him. There were no skyscrapers in those days, only bungalows. We eventually managed to catch the monkey. That was it. We gave him back to the person from whom my father had brought him.'

Arvind also revealed that his father and his close friend Satish Bhalla, along with a few others, joined together to form a consortium to racehorses: 'One of the racehorses was called Never-Give-In, which was my old school's motto.[30] I think it did win one or two races. But raising racehorses was a hobby rather than a money-making thing.'

8

Yes, Pran has lived the good life and enjoyed every minute of it! Whether cars or clothes, animals or plants, Pran was not only different, he was stylishly different! His generosity and charity were as much a part of him as was his love of Urdu *shairee* and drink.

There were no haloes whatsoever.

Pran's interests were as diverse as diverse could be! And yet, these very interests had melded together in a way to make a unique, and exceptional person – Pran.

---

[30] Lawrence School, Sanawar (Himachal Pradesh).

THIRTY

In the Coolness of the Shadows

1

The villainy to which Pran had returned during the 1980s could not last. His advancing years would have made it difficult for him to display the same agility and vitality that he once had. Yet, apparently, Pran even now felt the need to move on and do something different, thereby revealing his entire attitude to life and his work.

And it was at this juncture that Pran got the offer to act in television serials.

Pran had earlier on emphatically declared that he would not like to work for the small screen because he did not like anything small. What made him change his views about acting on television? The explanation he gave will reveal some of the most interesting facets of Pran, the actor and the man.

He said: 'The small screen is no more small. It has grown to huge proportions — tending to surpass the "bigness" even of large-screen cinema. Times are changing and with them, I am also changing my views about television. A philosopher once said: "Those who don't change with time, get left behind." '

In the early 1990s, Pran announced that he had been signed up to work in three television serials. The first was titled *They Call Me Dangerous*, in which he was to play the role of an investigator, the kind of role seen in the *Commander* series.

The second was an unusual serial titled *Hum Matwale*, in which Pran was to play a retired *subedar*. This serial was to be based on the lives of real people who are in their twilight years. The story was to revolve around the experiences of several old people living in an old Parsee gentleman's building.

The third serial for which Pran started shooting was called *Baap Se Bada Rupaiyaa* in which he played a dual role: a CBI officer[1] and a dacoit.

The series had Pran playing a CBI officer called X3. During an encounter a vicious mafia criminal called Raaka (also played by Pran) is killed. Since his face is similar to that of the officer's, so X3 disguises himself as the dacoit and, along with another honest police officer, enters the world of criminals. How he brings the criminals to book is what that series was all about. Additionally, there was also the ubiquitous message for the modern generation and the inspiration to follow good morals.

Did these TV series see the light of day? Of the three television series in which Pran acted, only twenty-six episodes of *Baap Se Bada Rupaiyaa* were telecast on Doordarshan's Metro Channel.[2] Apparently, the other two remained in the cans.

During an interview in 2000 for the America-based newspaper, *India West*, Pran discussed one of the serials with the journalist Dr Rajiv Vijaykar: 'I did three episodes as a detective called Dangerous in *They Call Me Dangerous*. But I did not relish their style of working. The pace was very fast and they would even expect me to say my own lines instead of providing me with the dialogues!'

Pran was very aggrieved at being asked to also supply the dialogue for the series; indeed, it was an underhanded way of getting Pran, who

---

[1] Central Bureau of Investigation.
[2] Doordarshan is India's government-run nationwide satellite television intended to reach the masses.

had already shown his skill in coming up with impromptu dialogue for
Victoria No: 203, to do the same here!

2

During the sixth decade of an enviably long career, Pran himself, perhaps
in an unspoken pact made with advancing age, decided to accept fewer
roles.

Some of the films in which Pran acted during the 1990s were actually
signed much earlier but due to the vagaries of the film-making business
in Bombay, they were eventually released during this decade. These films
included *Azaad Desh Ke Ghulam*, *Lakshman Rekha*, directed by Pran's son

Sunil Sikand and two of
Saawan Kumar Tak's films:
Sanam Bewafa and *Bewafa Se
Wafa*.

Pran made special
mention of Rajan
Mukherjee's *Isi Ka Naam
Zindagi*, directed by Kalidas,
co-starring Aamir Khan,
Farah and Shakti Kapoor, a
film which was remade from
the Bengali version. This film
gave Pran much scope to
work on his get-ups,
depicting the transformation
from middle age to old age.
It was also one of the last
films in which his favourite
wig, beard and moustache
maker, Kabir, worked.

Pran in one more of his elaborate get-ups
in *Isa Ka Naam Zindagi*.

Among the films in which Pran acted during the 1990s was another
of Saawan Kumar Tak's films titled *Salma Pe Dil Aa Gaya*.

Veteran actress-vamp of a bygone era, Shashikala, referred to an
incident that took place on the sets this film, where she met Pran for

the first time in his get-up. He had chosen the get-up of a *pir* or holy man. Shashikala recalls the impression he gave as he walked on to the sets: '*It felt as if the whole set was filled with his presence and persona.... Further, it felt as if he was exuding a certain holiness; there were certain vibrations emanating from him.*'

For an actor who had played the wickedest of men, the vilest of characters, the most suave of conmen and the slimiest of villains to now play a saintly person and *to accomplish a merging of that persona with his own, and to also be able to convey such presence to those around him was indeed a rare feat,* an accomplishment to which few artistes can hope to lay claim.

The late Vinod Mehra's *Gurudev* starring Rishi Kapoor, Anil Kapoor, Sridevi and Danny finally saw the light of day in 1993. All the artistes who worked in this film cooperated to ensure that Vinod Mehra's dream be released. (Vinod had died due to the stress generated in making this film.)

Vidhu Vinod Chopra's 1942: *A Love Story,* starring Anil Kapoor, Jackie Shroff, Manisha Koirala, Anupam Kher and Danny, was one of the few films which did well during this decade. Pran played a significant role in this film.

One of the final films in which Pran acted was in Amitabh Bachchan Corporation Ltd.'s *Tere Mere Sapne* (1996), directed by Joy Augustine, starring Chandrachur Singh, Priya Gill, Arshad Warsi and Simran.

Reminiscing about the film, Jaya (Bhaduri) Bachchan said: 'I remember when we were making *Tere Mere Sapne* for ABCL. There was a role of a grandfather. I was very, very keen that Pran Uncle do it, because I just could visualize only him. And when the director Joy Augustine, went and spoke to him, he was very sweet about it. Pran Uncle readily agreed. He was very helpful to Joy Augustine.... I know this because Joy came and told me what a great help Pran Uncle was to him. Joy was a little disorganized at that time and Pran Uncle helped him out a lot.

'It was really sweet of Pran Uncle because he wasn't really in the best of his health at that time. *Tere Mere Sapne* was the story of two boys who change places, one was a rich boy, the other a poor one. They switch places and how they do it, that is the whole story. The role of the rich boy's grandfather was played by Pran Uncle.'

Pran also worked in a Telugu film, titled *Thandrapapa Raidu* (release date is not known), and in a Rajasthani film *Beti Hui Parai Re,* which was released in 1994.

Although art cinema or new-wave cinema film makers in Bollywood had tended to ignore Pran as a probable character actor for their films, Bengal's Gautam Ghosh did not.

Gautam picked a story by the eminent Bengali novelist Mahashweta Debi, titled *Johnny O Urvashi*, about the life of a ventriloquist. Made for Hindi-speaking audiences, the script was written by Ayn Rasheed Khan and its cast included Pran, Mithun Chakraborty, Nandana Deb Sen, Avtar Gill, Mohan Agashe, Masood Akhtar and Shubhendhu Chatterjee.

Released on 1 January 1997, the film won quite a few awards. And although it did not make too many waves in cinema theatres in India, it was the only Indian film selected for representation at the Cannes Film Festival that year.

3

Even as Pran began to work for television, his children decided that something needed to be done about the extraordinary milestone that Pran had crossed – fifty years in the film industry!

Pran's daughter, Pinky Bhalla, recalled the event: 'Arvind, Sunil and I had been talking about having a BIG celebration for Papa since he had worked for fifty years in the film industry. But Papa was not keen since he had a back problem those days. Then suddenly he agreed and Sunil and I had only a month to organize things.[3] We didn't even stop to consult Mummy about the party! It was such a rushed job that in the hurry we even forgot to put Arvind's name on the invitation cards! We really felt bad about that. Anyway, we decided to have a double celebration on his birthday on 12 February 1990. Sunil put together a very novel gift.'

What Sunil had done was to put together a short film which documented the journey of Pran's fifty years in cinema.

Sunil Sikand recounted how, in the short time he was given, he got the film ready: 'I had no idea how to go about things because video was so new in 1990. So I ran around and got whatever clippings I could and

---

[3] Arvind Sikand lives in the UK.

On Pran's seventieth birthday (12 February 1990). Standing (*left to right*): Sunil,
Vivek, Pinky and Arvind. Sitting (*left to right*): Arjun, Swati, Siddharth,
Pran, Shukla, Yuvraj and Sunaina.

put together a little documentary of his entire life.... Whatever I could
lay my hands on, some songs, some dialogues, some comic sequences,
I edited them and made a twenty-five-minute film, which we showed to
our guests at the party. I believe it was the first of its kind. After that,
everybody started doing similar things at their parties, showing songs
or whatever. Mine was a very amateurish job since I had no idea about
video. But when you view it in perspective, this film chronicled what
this man had done in his life.'

Pinky added that after the film had been shown at the party, there
was also a fireworks display. Pran was thrilled at this gift from his children
as part of the celebration of an event that comes to only a privileged
few. However, it is truly ironic that the film industry by and large did
not felicitate Pran on this great event which only a few can celebrate,
given the short spans of film careers today.

On the occasion of his completing fifty years in films, the *Telegraph
Magazine* (15 April 1990) did a cover story on Pran. When Sanjay Sayani
(of the *Telegraph*) asked Pran what half a century in the film industry had
given him, Pran quoted a couplet that he remembered:

Khuda taufeek deta hai jinhe, voh yeh samajhte hain
Ke khud apne hi haathon se banaa karti hain taqdeeren.[4]

Through this couplet, Pran acknowledged that the blessings he had received from his Maker as well as the help given by his colleagues and the love and affection of his fans had all contributed to his having had such a long career.

4

Although Pran did not know it then, difficult times lay ahead. While the difficulties were not financial in nature, every human had to cope with them – the difficulties that accompany old age.

After years and years of being offered the same type of roles, the beginning of the year 1998 saw Pran being offered a role by the Nadiadwalas in a film to be directed by Priyadarshan, a young new director whose recent films were being talked about and noticed by both audiences and critics.

Now, after a long time, Pran had become enthused with the role he was to do. He had been given his advance and had committed dates for the film until the month of June 1998. Then, suddenly, he got another good offer.

Raj Kapoor's son Randhir Kapoor approached Pran with the offer to do the grandfather's role in his brother Rishi Kapoor's *Aa Ab Laut Chalen*. Although the dates asked for by Randhir and Rishi were clashing with those he had allotted to Priyadarshan, Pran did not want to turn down this offer not only because the role was interesting, but also because the film was going to be made under the R.K. Films banner.

'I've worked with four generations of Kapoors – from the patriarch Prithviraj Kapoor to sons Raj, Shammi and Shashi; then from Randhir, Rishi and Rajiv, as well as with their daughters-in-law Babita [Randhir's wife] and Neetu [Rishi's wife] to little Karisma [Randhir and Babita's daughter],' Pran elaborated.

---

4   Loosely translated it means: 'Those who have been gifted by the Lord with great talent think/They have attained their good fortune through their own merit.'

So Pran called Priyadarshan and told him of the situation. Priyadarshan agreed to adjust the dates in such a way that Pran could fly to New Delhi for a couple of days in March 1998 and shoot his portions for the film.

Everything seemed to be falling into place with regard to the two films when, suddenly, for the first time in his seventy-eight years, Pran landed in hospital – he had suffered a heart attack, which had mimicked the symptoms of indigestion. It was only later that it was discovered that he had a blocked artery and that he would have to undergo surgery.

Pran was disappointed. 'Everything was working out just fine when this attack happened and put me out of action,' he said, later adding, 'it's destiny. "*Que sera sera*, whatever will be, will be." '

Although at the time Pran adopted a fatalistic attitude, the fact remains that the heart attack left Pran feeling shaken to the core of his being, especially since, all through the years, he had always maintained good health and had cared about his fitness. Yet, he retained his fighting spirit, saying: 'I've assured Priyadarshan that I won't quit the world without doing at least one film with him.'

Rishi Kapoor remembers the time he wanted to start his first directorial venture, *Aa Ab Laut Chalen* (released in 1999). 'There was a very important role – though not a very major role – of the grandfather of Akshay Khanna [the hero]. We took an appointment with Pran*jee*. He wasn't keeping the best of health those days.

'*Dabboo* [Randhir Kapoor] and myself went to him and narrated the role to him. He said: "You are like my children. I am very happy of course," blessing me like I was his son. After a few days, he called *Dabboo* and me over and said: "I'll not be able to do the film." I got a big shock! I said: "I've started my acting career with you.[5] Now I'd also like to start my directorial career with you. And I have a very good cameo role for you." He really liked that role.

'But look at the man's decency! He promptly said: "I'll not be able to do the role because I am not keeping well these days and if anything happens to me during the making of the film, I'll never be able to forgive myself."

---

[5]   *Bobby*, 1973.

'How many actors today think in these terms for the benefit of the producer? He had some heart problem. I said: "Nothing will happen Pran *Saab*." But he said: "No, I will not be able to forgive myself if something happens to me during the continuity of the film." This was the goodness of the man! He didn't do that film! He was more worried about my picture! He sacrificed his personal interest to do the role in favour of my interests! So I...eventually took Alok Nath for that role.'

Pran's setback as far as his health was concerned, sadly, resulted in his temporarily losing the confidence he had before the heart attack. This reaction to a sudden health problem was natural; it happens to anyone who appears to be in vibrant health all through his or her life and then, suddenly, one fine day, is laid low by a sudden rush of events.

Speaking to *Screen* in April 1998, Pran said: 'Today, I'm so afraid to step out of the house. This illness has resulted in a phobia which is so hard to shake off.'

The heart attack couldn't have come at a worse time – it had robbed him of the two roles which he really wanted to do, in addition to making him feel physically weak and taking away some of that confidence which was the hallmark of his personality both in real life and reel life.

Yes, just as Pran had told Vijay Anand, he *did* need to take things a bit easy.

5

The year 2000 was an especially good one for Pran, when he scored a hat-trick by winning *three* Lifetime Achievement Awards in the same year!

In January 2000, Hero Honda-*Stardust* – Salute to Indian Cinema (Millennium Honours) – chose him to be the 'Villain of the Millennium', a trophy which Pran especially cherishes among the hundreds that he has won over the decades.

Just a month earlier, in December 1999, Pran was chosen to be the recipient of the Lux-Zee Lifetime Achievement Award. At the Lux-Zee Cine Awards Show held on 11 March 2000, which was telecast live all over the world, Pran succeeded in moving everyone to tears. Already admired and loved worldwide as a good artiste and a fine human being, Pran made the most beautiful and spur-of-the-moment speech, bringing a lump to every throat among the audience members at the function and in every home that had its television set switched on that night. Pran physically came down to his knees and, crediting his fans and audiences through the years for his success, said: 'I bow before you all.'

The thunderous applause from the audience at the awards ceremony indicated the feelings that Pran's simple, unassuming speech had aroused.

Speaking for this biography, Pinky said: 'That programme was being telecast live — and millions of people saw it. We were inundated with telephone calls, letters and emails from friends as well as strangers saying how moved they had been by that programme.

'And do you know? My father wasn't even ready to go for that function! He said: "What will I do there? What will I say?" We had to push him to go there!'

At this point Pran spoke. He spoke slowly as though marshalling his thoughts, casting a cinematic long shot backwards over the entire panorama of a fascinating life and career. And he said:

'God has been much too kind to me, throughout my entire life. God has helped me and the public has appreciated me. Millions of them have appreciated me. I have thanked them in public at a function where several thousand people were present. My head bowed down before the people at that function and my fans worldwide and they were also very touched.'

In the year 2000, Pran was also awarded the Sansui-*Screen* Lifetime Achievement Award for his contribution to mainstream cinema.

Filmfare had already awarded Pran the Special Veteran's Award in 1997 itself, and that too was an honour. However, these three Lifetime Achievement Awards, coming one after the other in the eightieth year of his life and on the completion of sixty years in cinema, were especially meaningful.

Then in March 2001, the Government of India finally honoured Pran with the Padma Bhushan. As most of his fans and admirers said: '*Der aaye, durust aaye.*'[6]

And as recently as July 2004, when the Government of Maharashtra presented him the Raj Kapoor Award for his contribution to Hindi cinema, which carried with it a cash prize of one lakh rupees, Pran

---

6   Means: 'Better late than never!'

immediately donated the entire money back to the government to be used for the welfare of the handicapped artistes.

6

Now, in the twenty-first century, Pran has made every effort to finish his pending assignments so that his producers and directors are not inconvenienced.

Apart from some age-related problems like cataract and slight forgetfulness, Pran has continued to maintain fair health.

Even today, if somebody asks him to recite a *sher*[7] or any other poetry, he remembers each word. Even when asked about certain scenes from his most memorable films, Pran is able to recite his dialogue or catch phrases and even demonstrate the mannerism that he had adopted in a particular film.

For someone who loves the movies and his job so much, retiring from acting must have meant quite an adjustment. However, his daughter Pinky says that Pran himself tells people that he was feeling relieved!

Pran himself has never been one to look behind. He feels '*jo khatam ho gayaae toh khatam ho gayee.*'[8] Speaking for this biography in 2003, Pran revealed that he never thought very far back, nor has he felt regret and said: 'Oh, I wish I had done that!'

Retirement for Pran, however, does not mean vegetation. No. Pran still retains his youthful zest for cricket, and till today even if he has visitors at home, he will quietly allow wife Shukla to provide them company while he steals away to another part of his living room to watch an on-going cricket match on television!

Having spent so much of his life in the glare of the arc lights, it is almost as if Pran were saying that he would now like to enjoy the coolness of the shadows.

---

[7] Couplet.
[8] Means: 'What is over, is over.'

Epilogue

I am an actor.
And proud to be one.

The film industry gave me far more than what I could ever have imagined.

It gave me the respect of the people I worked with – the technicians, the actors, the workers and all I came in contact with. And it gave me the love and adoration of the fans.

I salute the film industry.

I am a Bombaywallah (now a Mumbaikar).
And proud to be one.
The city took me in after Partition and looked after me, nurtured me, gave me and my family a home.
I made friendships here, fleeting ones and others that lasted a lifetime.
I am ever grateful to the city.

I am an Indian.
And proud to be one.

Colonized, divided, battered and bruised, my country has weathered all storms, even sheltering people displaced by other storms – natural and man-made.

My country has my undying love.

> *Guzre hue zamaane ka ab tazkaraa hi kya,*
> *Achcha guzar gayaa, bahut achcha guzar gayaa.*

— Anon

Filmography

FILMS DONE IN LAHORE
(PRE-PARTITION)

Yamla Jat (1940)
P: Pancholi Art Pictures
D: Moti B. Gidwani
M: Ghulam Haider
C: Anjana, Noorjehan, M. Ismail and Pran

Chaudhry (1941)
P: Pancholi Art Pictures.
D: Niranjan
M: Ghulam Haider
C: M. Ismail, Noorjehan, Ramola and Pran

Khazanchi (1941)
P: Pancholi Art Pictures
D: Moti B. Gidwani
M: Ghulam Haider
C: M. Ismail, Ramola, S.D. Narang,
Manorama, Jankidas, Durga Mota, Ajmal
and Pran

Khandaan (1942)
P: Pancholi Art Pictures
D: Syed Shaukat Hussein Rizvi

M: Ghulam Haider
C: Noorjehan, Ghulam Mohammed,
Manorama, Ajmal, Durga Mota, Baby
Akhtar, Ibrahim and Pran

Sahara (1943)
P: Vaswani Art Productions
D: J.P. Advani
M: Gobindram
C: Renuka Devi, S.D. Narang, Sharda, Razia,
Meena, Irshad and Pran

Dasi (1944)
P: Pradhan Pictures
D: Hiren Bose
M: Pandit Amarnath
C: Ragini, Najam, Gyani, Om Prakash,
Khairati, Kalavati and Pran

Kaise Kahun? (1945)
P: Pancholi Art Pictures
D: Moti B. Gidwani
M: Pandit Amarnath
C: Ragini, Jagirdar, Najmal Hussein, Ajmal,
Durga Mota, Butt, Baby Akhtar, Akhtar
and Pran

P: producer; D: director; M: music director/s; C: cast

Ragini (1945)
P: Maheshwari Pictures.
D: Shanker Mehta
M: Pandit Amarnath
C: Smriti, Najam, Mumtaz, Aruna, Gyani, Ramesh, Shahnaz, Sajjan and Pran

Pardesi Balam (1945–46)
P: Dr Anand Prakash Parkar
Other details not available

Badnami (1946)
P: Shorey Films
D: Majnu
M: Anupam Ghatak and Lacchiram
C: Manorama, Zubeida, Asha Posle, Majnu, Leela and Pran

Khamosh Nigahen (1946)
P: Shorey Films
D: Moti B. Gidwani
M: Vinod
C: Manorama, Al Nasir, Subhasini and Pran

Paraye Bas Mein (1946)
P: India United Pictures.
D: Dawood Chand
M: Niaz Hussein Shadji
C: Asha Posle, Zubeida, Kandla, Ramlal, Mala, Zahur Shah and Pran

Rehana (1946)
P: Girdhar Bahar Productions
D: Harbans
M: Lal Mohammed
C: Manorama, Salim Raza, Ramesh, Farida, Asha, Leela and Pran

Guptraj (194?)
Other details not available.

Shahi Lutera (194?)
Other details not available.

Do Saudagar (194?)
P: A. M. Gupta
D: Millo Mehra
M: Ghulam Haider
C: Kalavati, Salim Raza, Majnu, Cuckoo and Pran

Arsi (1947)
P: Jeevan Pictures
D: Dawood Chand
M: Lacchiram and Shyam Sunder
C: Meena, Al Nasir, Cuckoo, Ajmal, Asha Posle, Chandrashekhar and Pran

Mohini (1947)
P: Mahindra Pictures
D: Mahindra Gill
M: Lachhiram and Bhailal
C: Chand, Mahapatra, Roofi, Nazar, Vishal, Niranjan and Pran

But Taraash (1947)
P: Butkadah Pictures
D: J.P. Advani
M: Ghulam Haider
C: Not available, except for Pran.

Barsaat Ki Ek Raat (1948)
P: Raja Brothers
D: G. Singh
M: Ghulam Haider
C: Amarnath, Begum Parveen, Asha Posle, Durga Mota, G.N. Butt, Shehzadi, Baby Lata and Pran

Birhan (1948)
P: National Film Productions
D: K. Bhandari
M: Lacchiram
C: Roopa, Begum Parveen, Cuckoo, Shanti Madhok and Pran

Chunaria (1948)
P: Kuldip Pictures
D: R. Dave
M: Hansraj Behl
C: Manorama, Wasti, Randhir, Sofia, Cuckoo, Chand Burque, Ramesh, Sarita, Baij Sharma and Pran

Nek Dil (1948)
P: Lighthouse Productions
D: S.R. Desai
M: Asghar
C: Amrit, Begum Parveen, Zubeida, Nazar, Smriti Biswas and Pran

FILMS DONE IN BOMBAY (POST-PARTITION)

Ziddi (1948)
P: Bombay Talkies
D: Shahid Lateef
M: Khemchand Prakash
C: Dev Anand, Kamini Kaushal, Veera, Nawab, Kuldip Kaur, Pratima Devi, Indu, Moshin, Chandabai, Amir Banu, Shivraj and Pran

Grahasti (1948)
P: Aina Pictures
D: S.M. Yusuf
M: Ghulam Mohammed
C: Sulochana Chatterjee, Kuldip Kaur, Masood Parvez, Lalita Pawar, Sharda, Yakub, Shyama, Mirza Musharraf, Faizi and Pran

Apradhi (1949)
P: Prabhat Pictures
D: Yashwant Pethkar
M: Sudhir Phadke
C: Madhubala, Leela Pande, Ram Singh and Pran

Badi Bahen (1949)
P: Famous Pictures
D: D.D. Kashyap
M: Husnlal Bhagatram
C: Suraiya, Rehman, Geeta Bali, Ulhas, Gulab, Roop Kamal, Baby Tabassum, Shanti Madhok, Niranjan Sharma, Ram Avtar, Pappoo and Pran

Roshni (1949)
P: Standard Pictures
D: Ramanlal Desai
M: C. Ramchandra
C: Rehana, Nihal, V.H. Desai, Mumtaz Ali, Sofia, Benjamin, Chand Burque, Kesari, Shyama, Sita Bose and Pran

Janmapatri (1949)
P: Popular Productions
D: K.P. Shanti

M: Gulshan Sufi
C: Sudha Rao, Hamid, Zebu, Vijay, Leela Gupte and Pran

Rakhi (1949)
P: Prakash Pictures
D: Shanti Kumar
M: Husnlal Bhagatram
C: Kamini Kaushal, Ulhas, Karan Dewan, Gope, Kuldip Kaur, Yashodhra Katju, Urvashi, Raj Adeeb, T. Sinha and Pran

Biwi (1950)
P: Paristan Pictures
D: Kishore Sharma
M: Aziz Hindi
C: Veena, Mumtaz Shanti, Madhuri, Al Nasir, Ramlal and Pran

Putli (1950)
P: Punjab Film Corporation
D: Wali Mohammed Wali
M: Aziz Hindi and Ghulam Haider
C: Mumtaz Shanti, Yakub, Husn Banu, Sheela Shrinath, Majnu, Prem Dhawan, Sheela Naik, Cuckoo and Pran

Lajawab (1950)
P: Variety Productions
D: J.P. Advani
M: Anil Biswas
C: Sohan, Rehana, Kuldip Kaur, Randhir, Prem Dhawan, Iftekhar, David, Kaveeta and Pran

Sangeeta (1950)
P: Sudha Pictures
D: Ramanlal Desai
M: C. Ramchandra
C: Nigar Sultana, Shyam, Suraiya Choudhry, Mumtaz Ali, Ram Singh, Radhakishen and Pran

Sheesh Mahal (1950)
P: Minerva Movietone
D: Sohrab Modi
M: Vasant Desai
C: Sohrab Modi, Naseem Banu, Pushpa Hans, Nigar Sultana, Mubarak, Amarnath, Leela Misra, A.Shah, Jawahar Kaul and Pran

Afsana (1951)
P: Sri Gopal Pictures
D: B.R. Chopra
M: Husnlal Bhagatram
C: Ashok Kumar, Veena, Jeevan, Kuldip Kaur, Cuckoo, Baby Tabassum, Ratan Kumar, Chaman Puri and Pran

Bahar (1951)
P: AVM Productions
D: M.V. Raman
M: S.D. Burman and N. Dutta
C: Vyjayanthimala, Karan Dewan, Pandari Bai, Leela Misra, Om Prakash, Baby Tabassum, Sunder, Gope, Shyamlal, Chaman Puri and Pran

Daman (1951)
P: Madhukar Pictures
D: Nanabhai Bhat
M: K. Dutta
C: Ajit, Nigar Sultana, Agha, Hiralal, Yashodhara Katju and Pran

Sabz Baagh (1951)
P: Nirmal Pictures
D: Aziz Kashmiri
M: Vinod and Gulshan Sufi
C: Nimmi, Shekhar, Om Prakash, Suraiya Choudhry, Kamal Kapoor, Majnu, Cuckoo, Khanjar, Rashid Khan, Chand Burque and Pran

Pyar Ki Baaten (1951)
P: Nargis Art Concern
D: Akhtar Hussain
M: Bhola, Sharmaji and Bulo C. Rani
C: Nargis, Trilok Kapoor, Cuckoo, Neelam, Rashid, Nissar, Nazir, Khurshid, Maruti, H. Prakash and Pran

Bewafa (1952)
P: Nargis Art Concern
D: M.L. Anand
M: A.R. Qureshi
C: Nargis, Ashok Kumar, Raj Kapoor, Neelam, Siddiqui, Anwar Hussain and Pran

Chham Chhama Chham (1952)
P: Mohan Pictures
D: P.L. Santoshi

M: O.P. Nayyar
C: Rehana, Kishore Kumar, Mohana, Radhakishen and Pran

Sanskar (1952)
P: Sunrise Pictures
D: V.M.Vyas
M: Roshan
C: Mumtaz Shanti, Ishwar Lal, Shashi Kapoor, Veera, Purnima, Razi, Murad, Sapru, Kalyani, Baby Naaz, Mirza Musharraf, Pappoo and Pran

Sindbad the Sailor (1952)
P: Deepak Pictures
D: Nanabhai Bhat
M: Chitragupt
C: Naseem, Nirupa Roy, Ranjan, Bhagwan, Yashodhara Katju, Jayant, Samson, Shakila and Pran

Zamane Ki Hawa (1952)
P: Punjab Film Corporation
D: Wali Mohammed Wali
M: Z. Sherman, G. Shafi, Khan Mastana and Aziz
C: Mumtaz Shanti, Suresh, Majnu, Husn Banu, Kesari, Neerja, Sharifa, Sita Bose, Murad, Kanu and Pran

Moti Mahal (1952)
P: Nigaristan Films
D: R. Dave
M: Hansraj Behl
C: Ajit, Suraiya, Veera, Jeevan, Baby Tabassum, Satish, Shrinath and Pran

Aah (1953)
P: R.K Films
D: Raja Nawathe
M: Shankar Jaikishan
C: Nargis, Raj Kapoor, Vijayalaxmi, Mukesh, Ramesh Sinha, Bhupendra Kapoor, Leela Misra and Pran

Aleef Laila (1953)
P: K. Amarnath Productions
D: K. Amarnath
M: Shyam Sunder
C: Nimmi, Asha Mathur, Vijay Kumar, Murad, Gope, Maya Devi and Pran

Aansoo (1953)
P: Famous Pictures
D: Shanti Kumar
M: Husnlal Bhagatram
C: Kamini Kaushal, Shekhar, Amirbhai Karnataki, Nawab, Kumkum, Chaman Puri, Madan Mohan and Pran

Baghi (1953)
P: Time Films
D: Anant Thakur
M: Madan Mohan
C: Naseem Banu, Ranjan, Shammi, Mukri, Anwar Hussain, B.M.Vyas and Pran

Farmaish (1953)
P: Majestic Films
D: B.K. Sagar
M: Husnlal Bhagatram
C: Bharat Bhushan, Vijayalaxmi, Kuldip Kaur, Gope, Maruti, Gulab, Chandrashekhar and Pran

Malkin (1953)
P: Gope Productions
D: O.P. Dutta
M: Roshan
C: Nutan, Sajjan, Purnima, Gope, Durga Khote, Raj Mehra, Yakub and Pran

Rahbar (1953–54)
P: New Art Theatres
D: Arun Mitra
M: Timir Baran
C: Balraj Sahni, Shakuntala, Sulochana, Nawab, Shammi, Nazar, Durga Khote and Pran

Biraj Bahu (1954)
P: Hiten Chaudhary Productions
D: Bimal Roy
M: Salil Chaudhary
C: Kamini Kaushal, Abhi Bhattacharya, Shakuntala, Randhir, Bikram Kapoor, Manorama, Kammoo, Baby Chand, Iftekhar, Moni Chatterji, Ravikant and Pran

Pehli Jhalak (1954)
P: Jagat Pictures
D: M.V. Raman

M: C. Ramchandra
C: Vyjayanthimala, Kishore Kumar, Om Prakash, Dara Singh, Shammi, Kamal Kant, Roopa Varman, Anil, Jawahar Kaul, Shivraj and Pran

Pilpili Saheb (1954)
P: Kwatra Films
D: H.S. Kwatra
M: Sardul Kwatra
C: Shyama, Agha, Sunder, Lalita, Lalita Kumari, Mumtaz, Mehmood, Rajan Kapoor, Madan Panditji, Devkishen and Pran

Sheeshe Ki Deewar (1954)
P: Manmohan Films
D: Manmohan Sabir
M: Shankar Das Gupta
C: Veena, Veera, Manmohan Krishna, Shammi, Cuckoo, Rashid, Sulochana and Pran

Angaray (1954)
P: Akash Chitra
D: K.B. Lal
M: S.D. Burman
C: Nasir Khan, Nargis, Ratan Kumar, Jeevan, Paro, K.N. Singh, Jagirdar, Sunalini Devi, Vanmala, Jawahar Kaul, Baby Nanda and Pran

Lakeeren (1954)
P: Sushil Pictures
D: Harbans
M: Hafeez Khan
C: Ashok Kumar, Nalini Jaywant, Tiwari, Durga Khote, Sulochana Chatterjee, Bela, Kamal, Yakub, Cuckoo and Pran

Meenar (1954)
P: Vishwbharti Films
D: Hemen Gupta
M: C. Ramchandra
C: Bina Rai, Bharat Bhushan, Sheila Ramani, Pratima Devi, Chandrashekhar, S.Nazir and Pran

Toofan (1954)
P: Starlight Pictures
D: Ram Prakash

M: S.D. Batish
C: Munawwar Sultana, Sajjan, Vijayalaxmi, Amarnath, Tiwari, Pratima Devi and Pran

Aab-e-Hayat (1955)
P: Filmistan
D: Ramanlal Desai
M: Sardar Malik
C: Premnath. Shashikala, Smriti Biswas, Ameeta, Mubarak, S.L. Puri, P. Kailash, Helen and Pran

Amanat (1955)
P: Bimal Roy Productions
D: Arabind Sen
M: Salil Chaudhary
C: Bharat Bhushan, Chand Usmani, Asha Mathur, Nazir Hussain, Asit Sen, Kanhaiyalal, Achala Sachdev, Ashim Kumar and Pran

Azaad (1955)
P: Pakshiraja Studios
D: S.M.S. Naidu
M: C. Ramchandra
C: Dilip Kumar, Meena Kumari, Om Prakash, S. Nazir, Badri Prasad, Raj Mehra, Randhir, Achala Sachdev, Murad, Shammi, Deepa Sahi, Subbulaxmi and Pran

Bara Dari (1955)
P: K. Amarnath Productions
D: K. Amarnath
M: Naashad
C: Ajit, Geeta Bali, Chandrashekhar, Gope, Murad, Tiwari and Pran

Chingari (1955)
P: Co-Operative Pictures
D: S. Srivastava
M: Manohar
C: Nalini Jaywant, Shekhar, Leela Misra, Sunalini Devi and Pran

Bahu (1955)
P: P.R. Films
D: Shakti Samanta
M: Hemant Kumar
C: Usha Kiron, Karan Dewan, Shashikala, Johnny Walker, Bipin Gupta, Mumtaz Begum, Kundan, Mehmood and Pran

Jashan (1955)
P: Hindustan Art Productions
D: S. Shamsuddin
M: Roshan
C: Vyjayanthimala, Karan Dewan, Agha, Kuldip Kaur, Johnny Walker, Randhir, Murad and Pran

Kundan (1955)
P: Minerva Movietone
D: Sohrab Modi.
M: Ghulam Mohammed
C: Sohrab Modi, Nimmi, Ulhas, Sunil Dutt, Baby Naaz, Om Prakash, Manorama, Roopmala, Murad, Dar Kashmiri and Pran

Munimji (1955)
P: Filmistan
D: Subodh Mukerji
M: S.D. Burman
C: Nalini Jaywant, Dev Anand, Nirupa Roy, Pran, Ameeta, S.L. Puri, Kanu Roy, Prabhu Dayal, Samar Chatterji and Pran

Devdas (1956)
P: Bimal Roy Productions
D: Bimal Roy
M: S.D Burman
C: Dilip Kumar, Vyjayanthimala, Suchitra Sen, Motilal, Nazir Hussain, Johnny Walker and Pran

Aan Baan (1956)
P: Kashyap Productions
D: D.D. Kashyap
M: Husnlal Bhagatram
C: Ajit, Nalini Jaywant, Usha Kiron, Mahipal, Ulhas, Manmohan Krishna, Niranjan Sharma, Baij Sharma and Pran

Chori Chori (1956)
P: AVM Productions
D: Anant Thakur
M: Shankar Jaikishan
C: Nargis, Raj Kapoor, Johnny Walker, Gope, Raj Mehra, Amir Banu, Bhagwan, David, Sai, Mukri, Raja, Sulochana and Pran

Hum Sab Chor Hai (1956)
P: Filmistan
D: I.S. Johar

M: O.P. Nayyar
C: Nalini Jaywant, Shammi Kapoor, I.S. Johar, Majnu, Ameeta, Badri Prasad, Ram Avtar, Ramesh Sinha, Rajendranath, Shakuntala, Mumtaz Begum and Pran

Hotel (1956)
P: Manmohan Sabir Productions
D: Manmohan Sabir
M: Suresh and Talwar
C: Geeta Bali, Jaswant, Shammi, Jairaj, Achala Sachdev and Pran

Halaku (1956)
P: All India Pictures
D: D.D. Kashyap
M: Shankar Jaikishan
C: Meena Kumari, Ajit, Veena, Niranjan Sharma, Minoo Mumtaz, Sunder, Shammi, Raj Mehra, Helen and Pran

Kar Bhala (1956)
P: Bhagwan Brothers
D: Bhagwan
M: Nissar and Chic Chocolate
C: Shashikala, Nasir Khan, Begum Para, Malika, Bhagwan, Baburao and Pran

Inspector (1956)
P: Pushpa Pictures
D: Shakti Samanta
M: Hemant Kumar
C: Ashok Kumar, Geeta Bali, K.N. Singh, Maruti, Nazir Hussain, Pratima Devi, Achala Sachdev, Mehmood and Pran

Naya Andaz (1956)
P: K. Amarnath Productions
D: K. Amarnath
M: O.P. Nayyar
C: Meena Kumari, Kishore Kumar, Gope, Johnny Walker, Kumkum, Murad, Jayant and Pran

Tankhah (1956)
P: Filmzar
D: M. Changezi
M: Bhola Shreshtha
C: Nigar Sultana, Ajit, Naina, Radhakishen and Pran

Jagte Raho (1956)
P: R. K. Films
D: Shambhu Mitra and Amit Mitra
M: Salil Chaudhary
C: Raj Kapoor, Pradeep Kumar, Sumitra Devi, Smriti Biswas, Pahari Sanyal, Nemo, Sulochana Chatterjee, Motilal, Daisy Irani, Nana Palsikar, Iftekhar, Bikram Kapoor, Moni Chatterji, Bhupendra Kapoor, Bhudo Advani, Rashid Khan, Nargis and Pran

Ek Jhalak (1957)
P: Deep and Pradeep Productions
D: Kalidas
M: Hemant Kumar
C: Vyjayanthimala, Pradeep Kumar, Rajendra Kumar, Anita Guha, Lalita Pawar, Mubarak, Om Prakash and Pran

Miss India (1957)
P: Rawal Films
D: I.S. Johar
M: S.D. Burman
C: Nargis, Pradeep Kumar, Nishi, Shammi, I.S. Johar, Tuntun, Minoo Mumtaz, Sheela Vaz and Pran

Asha (1957)
P: Raman Productions
D: M.V. Raman
M: C. Ramchandra
C: Kishore Kumar, Vyjayanthimala, Naina, Raj Mehra, Lalita Pawar, Om Prakash, Shivraj, Uma Dutt, Minoo Mumtaz, Randhir, Sunder, Asha Parekh (*as a child artiste*), Chaman Puri, Dhumal, Rajen Kapoor, Pravin Paul, Patanjali Sethi and Pran

Champakali (1957)
P: Filmistan
D: Nandlal Jaswantlal
M: Hemant Kumar
C: Suchitra Sen, Bharat Bhushan, Shubha Khote, S.L. Puri, Mumtaz Begum, Mubarak, Ram Avtar and Pran

Tumsa Nahin Dekha (1957)
P: Filmistan
D: Nasir Hussain

M: O.P. Nayyar
C: Shammi Kapoor, Ameeta, Raj Mehra, B.M. Vyas, Kanu Roy, Anjali Devi, Sheela Vaz, Ram Avtar and Pran

Mr X (1957)
P: Sippy Productions
D: Nanabhai Bhat
M: N. Dutta
C: Ashok Kumar, Nalini Jaywant, Johnny Walker, Nishi, Hari Shivdasani, Rajen Kapoor, Leela Misra, Amirbhai Karnataki, Sheela Vaz, Helen and Pran

Chandu (1958)
P: Chitra Niketan's N.R.Productions
D: Majnu
M: Bipin Babul
C: Meena, Begum Para, Majnu, Gope, Om Prakash, Shammi, Shashikala, Daljeet, Gulab, Raj Puri, Sunder, Mehmood, Bhudo Advani, Ameeta and Pran

Adalat (1958)
P: Kwatra Films
D: Kalidas
M: Madan Mohan
C: Pradeep Kumar, Nargis, Yakub, Achala Sachdev, Rashid Khan and Pran

Amardeep (1958)
P: Shivaji Productions
D: T. Prakash Rao
M: C. Ramchandra
C: Dev Anand, Vyjayanthimala, Padmini, Ragini, Johnny Walker and Pran

Daughter of Sindbad (1958)
P: Starland Productions
D: Rati Lal
M: Chitragupt
C: Nadira, Jairaj, Maruti, Tiwari, Kamal, S.N. Tripathi and Pran

Madhumati (1958)
P: Bimal Roy Productions
D: Bimal Roy
M: Salil Chaudhary
C: Dilip Kumar, Vyjayanthimala, Johnny Walker, Jayant, Tarun Bose, Tiwari, Misra, Bhudo Advani, Baij Sharma and Pran

Raj Tilak (1958)
P: Gemini
D: S.S.Vasan
M: C. Ramchandra
C: Vyjayanthimala, Padmini, Gemini Ganesan, Bipin Gupta, Lalita Pawar, Durga Khote, Agha, Shammi, Kumar, Jagirdar, Manmohan Krishna, Master Romi and Pran

Chandan (1958)
P: Dossi Films
D: M.V. Raman
M: Madan Mohan
C: Nutan, Shyama, Kishore Kumar, Mala Sinha, Johnny Walker, Karan Dewan, David, K.N. Singh, Kamala Laxman and Pran

Bedard Zamana Kya Jaane (1959)
P: Subhash Pictures
D: Babubhai Mistry
M: Kalyanji Virji Anandji
C: Ashok Kumar, Nirupa Roy, Jabeen Jalil, Sudesh Kumar, Neelam, Helen, Ratnamala, Sheikh, Amirbhai Karnataki, Master Chickoo, Iftekhar and Pran

Daaka (1959)
P: Starland Productions
D: Nanabhai Bhat
M: Chitragupt
C: Ashok Kumar, Nirupa Roy, Smriti Biswas, Jugnu, Maruti and Pran

Do Gunde (1959)
P: Minerva
D: V.M. Vyas
M: Ghulam Mohammed
C: Ajit, Kumkum, Jayashri Gadkar, Raaj Kumar and Pran

Guesthouse (1959)
P: Golden Movies
D: Ravindra Dave
M: Chitragupt
C: Shakila, Ajit, Tiwari , Lalita Pawar, Maruti, Vimla Kumari and Pran

Madam XYZ (1959)
P: Neolite
D: Nanabhai Bhat
M: Chitragupt

C: Shakila, Suresh, Nalini Chonker, Shammi, David, Sudesh, Purnima, Kumar, Majnu, Bhagwan and Pran

Pyar Ki Rahen (1959)
P: Thakur (Brothers) Pictures
D: Lekhraj Bhakri
M: Kanu Ghosh
C: Pradeep Kumar, Anita Guha, Helen, Jeevan, Tiwari, Om Prakash, Sunder, Kuldip Kaur and Pran

Jaalsaaz (1959)
P: Lalit Kala Mandir
D: Arabind Sen
M: N. Dutta
C: Kishore Kumar, Mala Sinha, Asit Sen, Achala Sachdev, Nana Palsikar, Shyama, Helen and Pran

Basant (1960)
P: M.P. Productions
D: Bibhuti Mitra
M: O.P. Nayyar
C: Shammi Kapoor, Nutan, Johnny Walker, Minoo Mumtaz, Kammo, Cuckoo and Pran

Bewaqoof (1960)
P: Johar Films
D: I.S. Johar
M: S.D. Burman
C: Kishore Kumar, Mala Sinha, I.S. Johar, Sabita Chatterji and Pran

Chhalia (1960)
P: Subhash Pictures
D: Manmohan Desai
M: Kalyanji Anandji
C: Raj Kapoor, Nutan, Rehman, Shobhana Samarth, Moppet Raja and Pran

Delhi Junction (1960)
P: Nigaristan Films
D: Mohammed Hussain
M: Kalyanji Virji
C: Shakila, Ajit, Nishi, Maruti, Pratima Devi, Cuckoo and Pran

Gambler (1960)
P: Vikas Productions

D: Dwarka Khosla
M: Chitragupt
C: Premnath, Shakila, K.N. Singh, Shammi, Madan Puri, Cuckoo, Agha and Pran

Jis Desh Mein Ganga Behti Hai (1960)
P: R.K. Films
D: Radhu Karmakar (and Raj Kapoor)
M: Shankar Jaikishan
C: Raj Kapoor, Padmini, Tiwari, Nayampally, Chanchal, Raj Mehra, Lalita Pawar, Sulochana Chatterjee, Nana Palsikar, Vishwa Mehra, Amar and Pran

Maa Baap (1960)
P: Ratnadeep Pictures
D: V.M. Vyas
M: Chitragupt
C: Rajendra Kumar, Kamini Kadam, Anwar, Kumar, Naaz, Leela Chitnis, Kuldip Kaur, Peace Kanwal, Bipin Gupta, Sunder, Romi, Leela Misra and Pran

Trunk Call (1960)
P: Mayfair Films
D: Balraj Mehta
M: Ravi
C: Shyama, Abhi Bhattacharya, Helen, Shammi, Randhir, Rajen Haksar and Pran

Mehlon Ke Khwab (1960)
P: Madhubala Films
D: Hyder
M: S. Mohinder
C: Madhubala, Kishore Kumar, Pradeep Kumar, K.N. Singh, Chanchal, Sulochana Chatterjee, Leela Chitnis, Cuckoo and Pran

Jab Pyar Kisise Hota Hai (1961)
P: Nasir Hussain Films
D: Nasir Hussain
M: Shankar Jaikishan
C: Dev Anand, Asha Parekh, Mubarak, Raj Mehra, Sulochana, Wasti, Rajendranath, Tahir Hussain, Dulari, Ram Avtar, Bhishan Khanna and Pran

Dil Tera Diwana (1962)
P: Padmini Pictures
D: B.R. Panthalu

M: Shankar Jaikishan
C: Shammi Kapoor, Mala Sinha, Mehmood, Shobha Khote, Om Prakash, Ulhas, Mohan Choti, Kathana, Puranik, Mumtaz Begum and Pran

Half Ticket (1962)
P: Cine Technicians
D: Kalidas
M: Salil Chaudhary
C: Madhubala, Kishore Kumar, Om Prakash, Helen, Shammi, Manorama, Tuntun, Anil Ganguly and Pran

Manmauji (1962)
P: AVM Productions
D: Krishnan Panju
M: Madan Mohan
C: Kishore Kumar, Sadhana, Naaz, Achala Sachdev, Om Prakash, Mohan Choti, Anwar, Durga Khote, Mukri, Ashim Kumar, Sulochana Chatterjee, Leela Chitnis, Sunder, Jayalalitha, Johnny Whisky and Pran

Jhoola (1962)
P: N. Vasudeva Menon
D: K. Shankar
M: Salil Chaudhary
C: Vyjayanthimala, Sunil Dutt, Sulochana, Achala Sachdev, Manmohan Krishna, Leela Misra, Rajendranath, Raj Mehra, Mohan Choti, Tuntun, Randhir, Kusum Thakkur and Pran

Bluff Master (1963)
P: Subhash Pictures
D: Manmohan Desai
M: Kalyanji Anandji
C: Shammi Kapoor, Saira Banu, Lalita Pawar, Tuntun, Mohan Choti, Rashid Khan, Niranjan Sharma, Santosh Kumar, Ramlal, Shyamlal, Jugal Kishore, Charlie Walker and Pran

Phir Wohi Dil Laya Hoon (1963)
P: Nazir Hussain Films
D: Nazir Hussain Films
M: O.P. Nayyar
C: Joy Mukerji, Asha Parekh, Rajendranath, Veena, Wasti, Tabassum, Krishan Dhawan, Ram Avtar, Amar and Pran

Ek Raaz (1963)
P: A.G. Films
D: Shakti Samanta
M: Chitragupt
C: Kishore Kumar, Jamuna, Lalita Pawar, Agha, Mumtaz, Madan Puri, Tuntun and Pran

Mere Arman, Mere Sapne (1963)
P: Lalit Kala Mandir
D: Arabind Sen
M: N. Dutta
C: Pradeep Kumar, Naaz, Sumitra Devi, Agha, Jayshri Gadkar, Asit Sen, Manmohan Krishna, Badri Prasad, Paul Mahendra, Asim Kumar, Johnny Whisky and Pran

Dil Hi To Hai (1963)
P: Rawal Films
D: P.L. Santoshi and C.L. Rawal
M: Roshan
C: Raj Kapoor, Nutan, Agha, Sabita Chatterjee, Nazir Hussain, Leela Chitnis, Manorama and Pran

Pyar Kiya To Darna Kya (1963)
P: Vikram Productions
D: B.S. Ranga
M: Ravi
C: Shammi Kapoor, B. Saroja Devi, Prithviraj Kapoor, Om Prakash, Nazir Hussain, Agha, Helen, Shubha Khote, Pushpavalli and Pran

Mere Mehboob (1963)
P: Rahul Theatre
D: H. S. Rawail
M: Naushad
C: Ashok Kumar, Rajendra Kumar, Sadhana, Nimmi, Ameeta, Rehman, Johnny Walker and Pran

Door Ki Awaaz (1964)
P: Goel Cine Corporation
D: Devendra Goel
M: Ravi
C: Joy Mukerji, Saira Banu, Om Prakash, Durga Khote, Johnny Walker, Malika, Rajoo, Gogia Pasha, Manorama, Prem Sagar and Pran

Ishara (1964)
P: Amarnath Productions
D: K. Amarnath
M: Kalyanji Anandji
C: Joy Mukerji, Vyjayanthimala, Agha, Azra, Subiraj, Jayant, Pratima Devi, Sajjan, Shammi, Murad and Pran

Kashmir Ki Kali (1964)
P: Shakti Films
D: Shakti Samanta
M: O. P. Nayyar
C: Shammi Kapoor, Sharmila Tagore, Anoop Kumar, Dhumal, Nazir Hussain, Sunder, Madan Puri, Padma Devi, Mridula and Pran

Pooja Ke Phool (1964)
P: AV.M Productions
D: A. Bhim Singh
M: Madan Mohan
C: Ashok Kumar, Mala Sinha, Dharmendra, Nimmi, Sandhya Roy, Nana Palsikar, Mohan Choti, Shivraj, Mukri, Sulochana Chatterjee, Leela Chitnis and Pran

Rajkumar (1964)
P: Saravana Films
D: K. Shankar
M: Shankar Jaikishan
C: Shammi Kapoor, Sadhana, Prithviraj Kapoor, Om Prakash, Rajendranath, Shivraj, Hari Shivdasani, Achala Sachdev, Manorama, Shanti and Pran

Do Dil (1965)
P: Uttam Chitra
D: Hrishikesh Mukherjee
M: Hemant Kumar
C: Rajshree, Biswajeet, Mehmood, Asit Sen, Durga Khote, Mumtaz, Indira, Kamal Kapoor and Pran

Khandaan (1965)
P: Vasu Films
D: A .Bhim Singh
M: Ravi
C: Sunil Dutt, Nutan, Mumtaz, Sudesh Kumar, Lalita Pawar, Om Prakash, Helen, Mohan Choti, Sulochana Chatterjee, Manmohan Krishna and Pran

Gumnaam (1965)
P: Prithvi Pictures
D: Raja Nawathe
M: Shankar Jaikishan
C: Nanda, Manoj Kumar, Mehmood, Helen, Madan Puri, Dhumal, Hiralal, Tarun Bose, Naina, Manmohan, Laxmi Chhaya and Pran

Mere Sanam (1965)
P: Sippy Films
D: Amar Kumar
M: O. P. Nayyar
C: Asha Parekh, Biswajeet, Rajendranath, Mumtaz, Dhumal, Achala Sachdev, Nazir Hussain, Asit Sen and Pran

Shaheed (1965)
P: K. P. K. Movies
D: S. Ram Sharma
M: Prem Dhawan
C: Manoj Kumar, Nirupa Roy, Kamini Kaushal, Sarita, Prem Chopra, Madan Puri, Asit Sen, Manmohan, Sailesh Kumar, Kamal Kapoor, Sapru, Indrani Mukherjee, Iftekhar, Anwar Hussain and Pran

Teesra Kaun (1965)
P: Bindu Kala Mandir
D: Mohammed Hussain
M: R. D. Burman
C: Feroz Khan, Kalpana, Shashikala, Shyam Kumar, Rajen Haksar, Kamal Mehra and Pran

Biradari (1966)
P: Gope Productions
D: Ram Kamlani
M: Chitragupt
C: Shashi Kapoor, Faryal, Mehmood, David, Lalita Pawar, Kanhaiyalal, Nana Palsikar, Helen and Pran

Dus Lakh (1966)
P: Goel Cine Corporation
D: Devendra Goel
M: Ravi
C: Sanjay Khan, Babita, Helen, Om Prakash, Manorama, Ramesh Deo, Seema Deo, Hari Shivdasani, Brahmchari and Pran

Do Badan (1966)
P: J. B. Productions
D: Raj Khosla
M: Ravi
C: Asha Parekh, Manoj Kumar, Simi, Wasti, Huda Bihari, Manmohan Krishna, Dhumal, Mohan Choti and Pran

Dil Diya Dard Liya (1966)
P: Kay Productions
D: A. R. Kardar
M: Naushad
C: Dilip Kumar, Waheeda Rehman, Rehman, Shyama, Rani, Sajjan, Sapru, Johnny Walker, Shah Agha, Murad and Pran

Love in Tokyo (1966)
P: Pramod Films
D: Pramod Chakraborty
M: Shankar Jaikishan
C: Joy Mukerji, Asha Parekh, Mehmood, Lalita Pawar, Shubha Khote, Dhumal, Ullhas, Asit Sen, Mohan Choti, Madan Puri, Tarun Bose, Murad and Pran

Sawan Ki Ghata (1966)
P: Shakti Films
D: Shakti Samanta
M: O.P. Nayyar
C: Manoj Kumar, Sharmila Tagore, Mumtaz, Jeevan, Sajjan, Madan Puri, Sunder, Mohan Choti, Padma Kumari, S. N. Banerji, Mridula, Kundan and Pran

An Evening in Paris (1967)
P: Shakti Films
D: Shakti Samanta
M: Shankar Jaikishan
C: Shammi Kapoor, Sharmila Tagore, Rajendranath, Sarita, K. N. Singh, David, Shetty, Madan Puri, Surendranath and Pran

Around the World (1967)
P: P. S. Pictures
D: Pachhi
M: Shankar Jaikishan
C: Raj Kapoor, Rajshri, Ameeta, Raj Mehra, Mehmood, Om Prakash, Achala Sachdev, Vishwa Mehra, Pachhi and Pran

Aurat (1967)
P: Gemini Combines
D: S.S. Vasan and S.S. Balan
M: Ravi
C: Padmini, Rajesh Khanna, Feroz Khan, Lalita Pawar, O.P. Ralhan, Nazima, Kanhaiyalal, Leela Chitnis, Achala Sachdev, David, Nana Palsikar and Pran

Milan (1967)
P: Prasad Productions
D: A. Subba Rao
M: Laxmikant Pyarelal
C: Sunil Dutt, Nutan, Jamuna, Shyama, Deven Verma, Surendra, Leela Misra, Vinod Sharma, Mukri, David, Aruna Irani and Pran

Patthar Ke Sanam (1967)
P: A. G. Films
D: Raja Nawathe
M: Laxmikant Pyarelal
C: Waheeda Rehman, Manoj Kumar, Mumtaz, Mehmood, Raj Mehra, Lalita Pawar, Tiwari, Mumtaz Begum, Aruna Irani and Pran

Ram Aur Shyam (1967)
P: Vijaya International
D: Chanakya
M: Naushad
C: Dilip Kumar, Waheeda Rehman, Mumtaz, Nirupa Roy, Kanhaiyalal, Nazir Hussain, Sajjan, Mukri, Amar, Leela Misra, Zebunissa, Baby Farida and Pran

Upkar (1967)
P: Vishal Pictures
D: Manoj Kumar
M: Kalyanji Anandji
C: Asha Parekh, Manoj Kumar, Madan Puri, Kamini Kaushal, Prem Chopra, Kanhaiyalal, Asit Sen, Manmohan Krishna, David, Manmohan, Sunder, Mohan Choti, Aruna Irani, Shammi, Krishan Dhawan, Gulshan Bawra, Caroline King and Pran

Safar (1967–68?)
P: Kewal Art Productions
D: Kewal Misra

M: Sapan Jagmohan
C: Naqvi Jahan, Devendra Kumar and Pran

Aadmi (1968)
P: S. V. Films
D: A. Bhim Singh
M: Naushad
C: Dilip Kumar, Waheeda Rehman, Manoj Kumar, Simi, Agha, Sulochana, Ullhas, Padma Chavan, Mohan Choti, Shivraj and Pran

Brahmachari (1968)
P: Sippy Films
D: Bhappi Sonie
M: Shankar Jaikishan
C: Shammi Kapoor, Rajshree, Mumtaz, Asit Sen, Dhumal, Jagdeep, Mohan Choti, Manmohan, Madhavi, Baby Farida, Master Sachin, Master Shahid, Mehmood Jr., Guddi and Pran

Kahin Din Kahin Raat (1968)
P: Shree Krishna Films
D: Darshan
M: O.P. Nayyar
C: Biswajeet, Sapna, Helen, Nadira, Malika, Johnny Walker, Asit Sen, Mohan Choti, Habib and Pran

Sadhu Aur Shaitan (1968)
P: Bhim Singh and Mehmood Productions
D: A. Bhim Singh
M: Laxmikant Pyarelal
C: Mehmood, Bharati, Kishore Kumar, Om Prakash, Nazir Hussain, Anwar, Master Shahid, Baby Farida, Mukri, Manju, Raj Kishore, Vijayalalitha, Keshto Mukherji, Dulari, Sunder, Ram Avtar, Tuntun, Jankidas, Dilip Kumar (*guest appearance*) and Pran

Muskurahat (1968–69)
P: Mali Pictures
Other details not available.

Anjaana (1969)
P: Emkay Productions
D: Mohan Kumar

M: Laxmikant Pyarelal
C: Rajendra Kumar, Babita, Nazima, Prem Chopra, Sunder, Nirupa Roy, Mohan Choti, Tuntun, Mehmood Jr. and Pran

Aansoo Ban Gaye Phool (1969)
P: Anoop Kumar Productions
D: Satyen Bose
M: Laxmikant Pyarelal
C: Ashok Kumar, Deb Mukerji, Alka, Nirupa Roy, Raj Mehra, Anoop Kumar, Rakesh, Helen, Kumud Tripathi and Pran

Bhai Bahen (1969)
P: Vikram Productions
D: A. Bhim Singh
M: Shankar Jaikishan
C: Ashok Kumar, Sunil Dutt, Nutan, Padmini, Sulochana, Helen, Divakar, Mukri, Bhalla, Shivraj, Babanlal, Sheikh and Pran

Madhvi (1969)
P: Shree Ganesh Prasad M.
D: Chanakya
M: Laxmikant Pyarelal
C: Sanjay Khan, Deepa, Padmini, Mehmood, Nazir Hussain, Murad, Roopesh Kumar, Mukri, Raj Kishore, Master Shahid, Aruna Irani and Pran

Nanha Farishta (1969)
P: Vijaya International
D: T. Prakash Rao.
M: Kalyanji Anandji
C: Baby Rani, Ajit, Anwar Hussain, Padmini, Balraj Sahni, Suresh, Raj Mehra, Maruti, Mukri, Sunder, Johnny Walker, Prem Kumar, Pandari Bai and Pran

Tumse Achcha Kaun Hai (1969)
P: Pramod Films
D: Pramod Chakraborty
M: Shankar Jaikishan
C: Shammi Kapoor, Babita, Mehmood, Lalita Pawar, Manmohan, Shubha Khote, Aruna Irani, Madan Puri, Snehlata, Indira Bansal, Lata Sinha, Leela Misra, Jayanthi, Mohan Choti, Dhumal, Murad, Ullhas, Asit Sen, Hari Shivdasani and Pran

Pyar Hi Pyar (1969)
P: R. S. Productions
D: Bhappi Sonie
M: Shankar Jaikishan
C: Vyjayanthimala, Dharmendra, Helen, Madan Puri, Dhumal, Mehmood, Mehmood Jr., Raj Mehra, Manmohan, Sulochana, Sapru, Sulochana Chatterjee, Paro and Pran

Sachhai (1969)
P: Em. Ce. R. Films
D: K. Shankar
M: Shankar Jaikishan
C: Shammi Kapoor, Sadhana, Sanjeev Kumar, Johnny Walker, Helen, Sulochana, Raj Mehra, Anwar, Dhumal, Shivraj, Jagdev, Ratnamala, Rajen Kapoor and Pran

Bhai Bhai (1970)
P: Ratan Mohan
D: Raja Nawathe
M: Shankar Jaikishan
C: Sunil Dutt, Asha Parekh, Mumtaz, Leela Chitnis, Mehmood, Manmohan, Krishna, Madan Puri, Raj Mehra, Jeevan, Iftekhar, Aruna Irani, Mukri, Mohan Choti, Rashid Khan, Asit Sen and Pran

Ganwaar (1970)
P: Naresh Kumar
D: Naresh Kumar
M: Naushad
C: Rajendra Kumar, Vyjayanthimala, Nishi, Jeevan, Tarun Bose, Sunder, David, Pratima, Ram Mohan, Nikita, Shefali, Randhir, Gulshan Bawra, Tabassum and Pran

Tum Haseen Mein Jawan (1970)
P: Bhappi Sonie
D: Bhappi Sonie
M: Shankar Jaikishan
C: Dharmendra, Hema Malini, Helen, Anwar Hussain, Rajendranath, Shabnam, Anjali, Dhumal, Sulochana, Krishan Dhawan, Brahm Bhardwaj, Lata Sinha, Mohan Choti, Lolita Chatterji and Pran

Gopi (1970)
P: T. S. Muthuswamy and S. S. Palaniappan
D: A. Bhim Singh

M: Kalyanji Anandji
C: Dilip Kumar, Saira Banu, Om Prakash, Johnny Walker, Lalita Pawar, Nirupa Roy, Farida Jalal, Sudesh Kumar, Durga Khote, Mukri, Tiwari, Aruna Irani, Shyamlal and Pran

Heer Ranjha (1970)
P: Chetan Anand
D: Chetan Anand
M: Madan Mohan
C: Raaj Kumar, Priya Rajvansh, Ajit, Jayant, Prithviraj Kapoor, Nana Palsikar, Jeevan, Veena, Kamini Kaushal, Sonia Sahni, Achala Sachdev, Zeb Rehman, Tuntun, Ullhas, Sapru, Sujata, Lata Sinha, Niranjan Sharma, Jagdish Raj, Tabassum, Padma, Rani, Kammo, Shefali Choudhari, Daisy Irani and Pran

Humjoli (1970)
P: Prakash Kapoor
D: Ramanna
M: Laxmikant Pyarelal
C: Jeetendra, Leena Chandavarkar, Shashikala, Nazir Hussain, Aruna Irani, Manmohan, Sapru, Dubey, Swaraj, Geeta Banker, Mehmood, Prem Kumar and Pran

Johny Mera Naam (1970)
P: Trimurti Films
D: Vijay Anand
M: Kalyanji Anandji
C: Dev Anand, Hema Malini, I. S. Johar, Jeevan, Iftekhar, Sulochana, Padma Khanna, Sajjan, Premnath, Jagdish Raj and Pran

Kab, Kyon Aur Kahan? (1970)
P: Arjun Hingorani
D: Arjun Hingorani
M: Kalyanji Anandji
C: Dharmendra, Babita, Helen, Asit Sen, Ashoo, Dhumal, Mohan Choti, Shetty and Pran

Nanak Dukhiya Sab Sansar (1970)
P: Dara Singh
D: Dara Singh
M: Prem Dhawan

C: Prithviraj Kapoor, Balraj Sahni, Achala Sachdev, Dara Singh, Mohan Ram and Pran

Purab Aur Paschim (1970)
P: Manoj Kumar
D: Manoj Kumar
M: Kalyanji Anandji
C: Ashok Kumar, Saira Banu, Manoj Kumar, Prem Chopra, Nirupa Roy, Vinod Khanna, Kamini Kaushal, Asit Sen, Bharati, Madan Puri, Manmohan, Shammi, Krishan Dhawan, Kuljit, Rajendranath, Leela Misra, Ram Mohan, V. Z. Sokti, Barbara Lindsey and Pran

Samaj Ko Badal Dalo (1970)
P: Gemini Studio
D: V. Madhusudana Rao
M: Ravi
C: Sharda, Ajay (Parikshit) Sahni, Kanchana, Prem Chopra, Mehmood, Aruna Irani, Shammi, Kanhaiyalal, Praveen Paul, Dubey, Dhumal, Mukri, Jayshree T., Naqi Mohan and Pran

Yaadgaar (1970)
P: S. Ram Films
D: S. Ram Sharma
M: Kalyanji Anandji
C: Nutan, Manoj Kumar, Prem Chopra, Kamini Kaushal, Mehmood Jr., Madan Puri, Asit Sen, Mohan Choti, Tiwari, Lolita Chatterji, Laxmi Chhaya, Shammi, Manmohan and Pran

Guddi (1971)
P: N. C. Sippy and Hrishikesh Mukherjee
D: Hrishikesh Mukherjee
M: Vasant Desai
C: Dharmendra, Jaya Bhaduri, Sameet Bhanja, Sumita Sanyal, Vijay Sharma, Utpal Dutt, A. K. Hangal, Chandra, Keshto Mukherji, Lalita Kumari, Bhagwan and Asrani. (*In guest appearances:* Ashok Kumar, Dilip Kumar, Rajesh Khanna, Om Prakash and Pran.)

Johar Mehmood in Hong Kong (1971)
P: Madan Chopra and K. Z. Sheth
D: S. A. Akbar

M: Kalyanji Anandji
C: Mehmood, I. S. Johar, Sonia Sahni, Aruna Irani, Tiwari, Kamal Kapoor, Tuntun, Haroon, Agha, Manorama, Madhumati, Murad, Mukri, Mehmood Jr., Polson, Raj Kishore and Pran

Jawan Mohabbat (1971)
P: Hardeep Chatrath and Krishen
D: Bhappi Sonie
M: Shankar Jaikishan
C: Shammi Kapoor, Asha Parekh, Balraj Sahni, Nirupa Roy, Dhumal, Shashikala, Rajendranath, Madhumati, Raj Mehra, Sarika and Pran

Jwala (1971)
P: M. V. Raman
D: M. V. Raman
M: Shankar Jaikishan
C: Sohrab Modi, Sunil Dutt, Madhubala, Lalita Pawar, Ullhas, David, Jagirdar, Raj Mehra, Asha Parekh, Kamla Laxman, Vijayalaxmi, Naaz, Daisy Irani and Pran

Lakhon Mein Ek (1971)
P: Gemini
D: S. S. Balan
M: R. D. Burman
C: Mehmood, Radha Saluja, Aruna Irani, Ramesh Deo, Kanhaiyalal, Nazir Hussain, David, Mohan Choti, Viju Khote, Mukri, Jalal Agha, Polson, Keshto Mukherji, Anwar, Birbal, Brahmchari, Bhalla, Madan Puri, Lalita Pawar, Shubha Khote, Praveen Paul, Sulochana Chatterjee and Pran

Naya Zamana (1971)
P: Pramod Chakraborty
D: Pramod Chakraborty
M: S. D. Burman
C: Dharmendra, Hema Malini, Lalita Pawar, Mehmood, Aruna Irani, Manmohan, V. Gopal, Indrani Mukherjee, Shabnam, Dhumal, Guddy, Roopali, Jankidas, Kanu Roy and Pran. (*In a guest appearance:* Ashok Kumar.)

Maryada (1971)
P: Arabind Sen
D: Arabind Sen

M: Kalyanji Anandji
C: Mala Sinha, Raaj Kumar, Rajesh Khanna, Asit Sen, Bipin Gupta, Helen, Abhi Bhattacharya, Gurnam Singh, Abhimanyu Sharma, Dulari, Jankidas, Rajendranath and Pran

Adhikar (1971)
P: S. Noor
D: S. M. Sagar
M: R. D. Burman
C: Ashok Kumar, Nanda, Deb Mukerji, Helen, Raj Mehra, Shammi, Rajnish, Kishan Mehta, Ratnamala, Tabassum, Brahmchari, Sumati Gupte, Indira Bansal, Kundan, Nazima and Pran

Pardey Ke Peechhe (1971)
P: M. G. R. Films
D: K. Shankar
M: Shankar Jaikishan
C: Yogita Bali, Vinod Mehra, Jagdeep, Bindu, Padma Khanna and Pran

Ganga Tera Pani Amrit (1971)
P: Virendra Sinha
D: Virendra Sinha
M: Ravi
C: Ashok Kumar, Rehman, Navin Nischol, Yogita Bali, Shatrughan Sinha, Nirupa Roy, Jayshree T., Achala Sachdev, Pandari Bai, Nana Palsikar, Tiwari, Ramesh Deo, Jagdeep, Narendranath and Pran

Preetam (1972)
P: Bhappi Sonie
D: Bhappi Sonie
M: Shankar Jaikishan
C: Shammi Kapoor, Leena Chandavarkar, Vinod Khanna, Mehmood, Helen, Sulochana, Raj Mehra, Tiwari, Anwar Hussain, Siddhu, Brahm Bhardwaj, Malika, Manmohan and Pran

Aan Baan (1972)
P: Malik Chand Kochar
D: Prakash Mehra
M: Shankar Jaikishan
C: Rajendra Kumar, Rakhee, Kumkum, Som Dutt, David, Kanhaiyalal, Anwar Hussain, Sunder, Tabassum, Jagdeep, Sharad Kumar and Pran

Aankhon Aankhon Mein (1972)
P: J. Om Prakash
D: Raghunath Jhalani
M: Shankar Jaikishan
C: Rakhee, Rakesh Roshan, Achala Sachdev, Tarun Bose, Raj Mehra, Pankaj, Tuntun, Jayshree T., Dara Singh and Pran

Be-imaan (1972)
P: Sohanlal Kanwar
D: Sohanlal Kanwar
M: Shankar Jaikishan
C: Manoj Kumar, Rakhee, Nazima, Snehlata, Prem Chopra, Raj Mehra, Premnath, Sulochana, Brahm Bhardwaj, Murad, Lata Bose, Tuntun and Pran

Buniyaad (1972)
P: Virendra Sinha
D: Virendra Sinha
M: Laxmikant Pyarelal
C: Shatrughan Sinha, Rakesh Roshan, Yogita Bali, Farida Jalal, Bindu, Faryal, Sajjan, Jankidas and Pran

Ek Bechara (1972)
P: B. N. Ghosh
D: S. M. Abbas
M: Laxmikant Pyarelal
C: Jeetendra, Rekha, Vinod Khanna, Kalpana, Bindu, Salomi, Johnny Walker, Anwar Hussain and Pran

Jangal Mein Mangal (1972)
P: Rajendra Bhatia
D: Rajendra Bhatia
M: Shankar Jaikishan
C: Kiran Kumar, Reena Roy, Balraj Sahni, Sonia Sahni, Jayshree T., Meena T., Paintal and Pran

Parichay (1972)
P: V. K. Sobati
D: Gulzar
M: R. D. Burman
C: Jeetendra, Jaya Bhaduri, Asrani, Veena, Dev Kishan, A. K. Hangal, Leela Misra, Keshto Mukherji, Paintal and Pran. (*In guest appearances*: Sanjeev Kumar, Gita Siddharth and Vinod Khanna.)

Roop Tera Mastana (1972)
P: M.M. Malhotra, Baldev and Mohan Bali
D: Khalid Akhtar
M: Laxmikant Pyarelal
C: Jeetendra, Mumtaz, I. S. Johar, Malika, Leela Misra, Brahm Bhardwaj, Jankidas, V. Gopal, Mirza Musharraf and Pran

Victoria No: 203 (1972)
P: Brij
D: Brij
M: Kalyanji Anandji
C: Ashok Kumar, Saira Banu, Navin Nischol, Anwar Hussain, Mohan Choti, Ranjeet, Meena Roy, Lalita Chatterjee, Anoop Kumar and Pran

Sazaa (1972)
P: S K Kapoor
D: Chand
M: Sonik Omi
C: Ashok Kumar, Yogita Bali, Kabir Bedi, Helen, Rajendranath, Mehmood Jr., Jeetendra, Rekha, Sonia Soni, Faryal, Madan Puri Kamaldeep and Pran

Yeh Gulistan Hamara (1972)
P: Atmaram
D: Atmaram
M: S. D. Burman
C: Dev Anand, Sharmila Tagore, Sujit Kumar, Kanan Kaushal, Lalita Pawar, Ramesh Deo, Raj Mehra, Sapru, Keshto Mukherji, Iftekhar, Johnny Walker, Jayshree T., Asrani and Pran

Zanjeer (1973)
P: Prakash Mehra Productions
D: Prakash Mehra
M: Kalyanji Anandji
C: Amitabh Bachchan, Jaya Bhaduri, Ajit, Bindu, Randhir, Om Prakash, Iftekhar, Gulshan Bawra, Ram Mohan, Yunus Pervez, Purnima, Bhushan Tiwari, Sanjana, Keshto Mukherji and Pran

Bobby (1973)
P: Raj Kapoor
D: Raj Kapoor
M: Laxmikant Pyarelal
C: Rishi Kapoor, Dimple Kapadia, Premnath, Sonia Sahni, Durga Khote, Aruna Irani, Pillu Wadia, Prem Chopra and Pran

Ek Kunwari Ek Kunwara (1973)
P: Jasbir Singh Khurana
D: Prakash Mehra
M: Kalyanji Anandji
C: Leena Chandavarkar, Rakesh Roshan, Kumkum, Rajendranath, Zeb Rehman, Jayshree T., Raj Mehra, Yunus Pervez, Jankidas and Pran

Ek Mutthi Aasmaan (1973)
P: Virendra Singh
D: Virendra Singh
M: Madan Mohan
C: Radha Saluja, Vijay Arora, Kamini Kaushal, Yogita Bali, Kamal Kapoor, Aruna Irani, Gulshan Arora, I. S. Johar, Mehmood and (*in a special appearance*) Pran

Dharma (1973)
P: S.K. Kapoor
D: Chand
M: Sonik Omi
C: Navin Nischol, Rekha, Ramesh Deo, Bindu, Madan Puri, Mohan Choti, Anjali Kadam, Ajit, Jayshree T. and Pran

Jugnu (1973)
P: Pramod Chakraborty
D: Pramod Chakraborty
M: S.D. Burman
C: Dharmendra, Hema Malini, Prem Chopra, Manmohan, Mehmood, Lalita Pawar, Ajit, Nazir Hussain, Sujit Kumar, Sonia Sahni, Jayshree T., Dhumal, Kamal Kapoor and Pran

Gaddaar (1973)
P: Harmesh Malhotra
D: Harmesh Malhotra
M: Laxmikant Pyarelal
C: Vinod Khanna, Yogita Bali, Padma Khanna, Anwar Hussain, Iftekhar, Manmohan, Madan Puri, Ranjeet, Satyen Kappu, V. Gopal, Jankidas, Ajit and Pran

Insaaf (1973)
P: S. Krishnamurti
D: Subba Rao

M: Laxmikant Pyarelal
C: Waheeda Rehman, Tanuja, Vijay Arora, Ravindra Kapoor, Meena T., Manmohan Krishna, Madhumati, Aruna Irani and Pran

Jeevan Rahasya (Bengali) (1973)
P: Not known
D: Salil Ray
M: Not known
C: Tarun Kumar, Madhabi (Chakraborty) Mukherjee and Pran

Jheel Ke Us Paar (1973)
P: Bhappi Sonie
D: Bhappi Sonie
M: R.D. Burman
C: Dharmendra, Mumtaz, Yogita Bali, Prem Chopra, Mehmood Jr., Ranjeet, Faryal, Veena, Kumar, Anwar Hussain, Iftekhar, Jagdish Raj, Urmila Bhat and Pran

Rickshawala (1973)
P: RMV
D: K. Shankar
M: R.D. Burman
C: Randhir Kapoor, Neetu Singh, Anwar Hussain, Mala Sinha and Pran

Joshila (1973)
P: Gulshan Rai
D: Yash Chopra
M: R.D. Burman
C: Dev Anand, Hema Malini, Rakhee, Bindu, Mahendra Sandhu, Madan Puri, Sulochana, Laxmi Chhaya, Sudhir, Iftekhar, Jagdish Raj, Roopesh Kumar, A. K. Hangal, I. S. Johar and Pran

Panch Dushman (1973)
P: Manu Narang
D: Bimal S. Rawal
M: R.D. Burman
C: Manu Narang, Rajee, Prem Chopra, Durga Khote, Vinod Khanna, Manmohan, Shatrughan Sinha, Nazir Hussain, Mukri, Jagdish Raj, Mohan Choti, Helen, Aruna Irani, Mehmood and Pran

Kasauti (1974)
P: Arabind Sen

D: Arabind Sen
M: Kalyanji Anandji
C: Amitabh Bachchan, Hema Malini, Bharat Bhushan, Abhi Bhattacharya, Ramesh Deo, Satyen Kappu, Jankidas, Viju Khote, Sonia Sahni, Vijay Sharma, Macmohan, Shobha Khote and Pran

Jeevan Rekha (1974)
P: Parsuram J. Devnani
D: Nanabhai Bhat
M: Sumanraj and Jagdish J.
C: Farida Jalal, Tabrez, Jalal Agha, Keshto Mukherji, Chandrashekhar, Asit Sen, K. N. Singh, Ajit, Manmohan and Pran

Majboor (1974)
P: Premji
D: Ravi Tandon
M: Laxmikant Pyarelal
C: Amitabh Bachchan, Parveen Babi, , Farida Jalal, Satyen Kappu, Sulochana, Iftekhar, Sapru, K.N. Singh, Sajjan, Murad, Macmohan, Jagdish Raj, Tiwari, Madan Puri, Anoop Kumar, Sudhir, Rehman, Master Alankar, Ravindra Kapoor and Pran

Zehreela Insan (1974)
P: Virendra Sinha
D: S.R. Puttanna Kanagal
M: R.D. Burman
C: Rishi Kapoor, Moushumi Chatterjee, Neetu Singh, Dara Singh, Paintal, Nirupa Roy, Madan Puri, Iftekhar, Manorama, Raj Mehra, Sajjan, Asit Sen, Dulari, Jagdish Raj and Pran

Chori Mera Kaam (1975)
P: Chander Sadanah
D: Brij
M: Kalyanji Anandji
C: Ashok Kumar, Shashi Kapoor, Zeenat Aman, Anwar Hussain, David, Deven Verma, Iftekhar, Raza Murad, Shetty, Maruti, Asha Potdar, Komila Virk, Urmila Bhat, Anoop Kumar, Chaman Puri and Pran

Do Jhoot (1975)
P: Sohanlal Kanwar
D: Jitu Thakur

M: Shankar Jaikishan
C: Vinod Mehra, Moushumi Chatterjee, Prem Chopra, Kamini Kaushal, Ajit, Aruna Irani, Alka, Sulochana, Naaz and Pran

Lafange (1975)
P: Harmesh Malhotra
D: Harmesh Malhotra
M: Laxmikant Pyarelal
C: Mumtaz, Randhir Kapoor, Anwar Hussain, Randhir Sr., Gulshan Bawra, Asha Sachdev, Sapru, Rajen Haksar, Sujit Kumar and Pran

Sanyasi (1975)
P: Sohanlal Kanwar
D: Sohanlal Kanwar
M: Shankar Jaikishan
C: Manoj Kumar, Hema Malini, Premnath, Prem Chopra, Aruna Irani, Prema Narayan, Helen, Nazima, Indrani Mukherjee, Sulochana, Kamini Kaushal, Raj Mehra, Chandrashekhar, Tuntun, Sailesh Kumar, Jayshree T., V. Gopal, Aparna Choudhary, Hari Shivdasani, C.S. Dubey, Yunus Pervez and Pran

Zinda Dil (1975)
P: K. Shorey and K. L. Bhatia
D: Sikandar Khanna
M: Laxmikant Pyarelal
C: Rishi Kapoor, Neetu Singh, Rajesh Lahr, Zahira, I. S. Johar, Roopesh Kumar, Raj Mehra, Pinchoo Kapoor, C.S. Dubey and Pran

Warrant (1975)
P: N. P. Singh
D: Pramod Chakraborty
M: R. D. Burman
C: Dev Anand, Zeenat Aman, Dara Singh, Satish Kaul, Ajit, Bunty, Madan Puri, Joginder, Jankidas, Sulochana, Jagdish Raj, V. Gopal, Habib and Pran

Dus Numbri (1976)
P: Madan Mohla
D: Madan Mohla
M: Laxmikant Pyarelal
C: Manoj Kumar, Hema Malini, Premnath, Bindu, Om Shivpuri, Kamini Kaushal, David, Sajjan, Ram Mohan, Shivraj,

V. Gopal, C.S. Dubey, Abhi Bhattacharya, Imtiaz and Pran

Khalifa (1976)
P: Jeetendra Luthra
D: Prakash Mehra
M: R. D. Burman
C: Randhir Kapoor, Rekha, I. S. Johar, Sonia Sahni, Arpana Choudhary, Urmila Bhat, Madan Puri, Alka, Lalita Pawar, Jankidas, Mohan Choti, Hari Shivadasani, Yunus Pervez and Pran

Shankar Dada (1976)
P: S. K. Kapoor
D: Shibu Mitra
M: Sonik Omi
C: Ashok Kumar, Shashi Kapoor, Neetu Singh, Anwar Hussain, Bindu, Roopesh Kumar, Anjali Kadam, Sonia Sahni, Chandrashekhar, Mohan Choti, Helen, Jankidas, Asit Sen and Pran

Amar Akbar Anthony (1977)
P: Manmohan Desai
D: Manmohan Desai
M: Laxmikant Pyarelal
C: Vinod Khanna, Rishi Kapoor, Amitabh Bachchan, Neetu Singh, Shabana Azmi, Parveen Babi, Nirupa Roy, Jeevan, Mukri, Ranjeet, Nadira, Helen and Pran

Chandi Sona (1977)
P: Sanjay Khan
D: Sanjay Khan
M: R. D. Burman
C: Sanjay Khan, Parveen Babi, Premnath, Raj Kapoor, Danny, Ranjeet, Paintal, Kamini Kaushal, Asrani, Achala Sachdev, Mukri, Iftekhar and Pran

Chakkar Pe Chakkar (1977)
P: S. Jagdish Chandar
D: Ashok Roy
M: Kalyanji Anandji
C: Shashi Kapoor, Rekha, Amjad Khan, Bindu, Madan Puri, Lalita Pawar, Raza Murad, Asrani, Tarun Ghosh, Rajesh Behl, Naaz, Viju Khote, Bhagwan, Bhushan Tiwari, Ram Mohan and Pran

Dharam Veer (1977)
P: Subhash Desai
D: Manmohan Desai
M: Laxmikant Pyarelal
C: Dharmendra, Jeetendra, Zeenat Aman, Neetu Singh, Ranjeet, Indrani Mukherjee, Jeevan, Dev Kumar, Pradeep Kumar, Sujit Kumar, Chand Usmani, Hercules, Azad, B. M. Vyas, Sapru and Pran

Hatyara (1977)
P: Sunil Sharma
D: Surendra Mohan
M: Kalyanji Anandji
C: Vinod Khanna, Moushumi Chatterjee, Rakesh Roshan, Abhi Bhattacharya, Pradeep Kumar, Nirupa Roy, Chand Usmani, Priyadarshani, Shahu Modak, Manmohan, Kanhaiyalal, Dev Kumar, Raj Mehra, Laxmi Chhaya and Pran

Apna Khoon (1978)
P: S. K. Kapoor
D: B. Subhash
M: Sonik Omi
C: Ashok Kumar, Shashi Kapoor, Hema Malini, Amjad Khan, Anwar Hussain, Bindu, Helen, Chandrashekhar, Murad, Mohan Choti, Jankidas and Pran

Chor Ho To Aisa (1978)
P: N. P. Singh
D: Ravi Tandon
M: R. D. Burman
C: Shatrughan Sinha, Reena Roy, Anwar Hussain, Sulochana, Bindu, Madan Puri, Macmohan, Jagdish Raj, Raza Murad, Rajendranath and Pran

Chor Ke Ghar Chor (1978)
P: Chander Sadanah
D: Vijay Sadanah
M: Kalyanji Anandji
C: Ashok Kumar, Randhir Kapoor, Zeenat Aman, Deven Verma, Helen, Anwar Hussain, Sulochana, Sajjan, Sapru, Anoop Kumar, Chaman Puri, Bindu and Pran

Des Pardes (1978)
P: Navketan Films
D: Dev Anand

M: Rajesh Roshan
C: Dev Anand, Tina Munim, Indrani Mukherjee, Mehmood, Ajit, Prem Chopra, Bindu, Amjad Khan, A. K. Hangal, Shreeram Lagu, Paintal, Tom Alter, Gufi Paintal, Bharat Kapoor, Raj Mehra and Pran

Do Musafir (1978)
P: R. N. Kumar and Anwar Hussain
D: Devendra Goel
M: Kalyanji Anandji
C: Ashok Kumar, Shashi Kapoor, Rekha, Prem Chopra, Jagdeep, Chandrashekhar and Pran

Don (1978)
P: Nariman Irani
D: Chandra Barot
M: Kalyanji Anandji
C: Amitabh Bachchan, Zeenat Aman, Iftekhar, Om Shivpuri, Helen, Satyen Kappu, Jairaj, Kamal Kapoor, Macmohan, Jagdish Raj, Shetty, Azad and Pran

Ganga Ki Saugandh (1978)
P: Sultan Productions
D: Sultan Ahmed
M: Kalyanji Anandji
C: Amitabh Bachchan, Rekha, Amjad Khan, Bindu, I. S. Johar, Jeevan, Nana Palsikar, Satyen Kappu, Sulochana, Tiwari, Macmohan, Jagdeep, Mukri, Anju Mahendru, Anwar Hussain, Iftekhar, Farida Jalal and Pran

Kala Aadmi (1978)
P: G.S. Poddar and K. M. Poddar
D: Ramesh Lakhanpal
M: Laxmikant Pyarelal
C: Sunil Dutt, Saira Banu, Ranjeet, Sonia Sahani, Tom Alter, Satyen Kappu, Helen and Pran. (*In guest appearances*: Premnath, Zahira, Anwar Hussain, Jagdish Raj and Parikshit Sahni.)

Khoon Ki Pukar (1978)
P: Tahir Hussain
D: Ramesh Ahuja
M: Bappi Lahiri
C: Vinod Khanna, Shabana Azmi, Aruna Irani,

Iftekhar, Amjad Khan, Reeta Bhaduri, Roopesh Kumar, Chandrashekhar and Pran

Phaansi (1978)
P: Harmesh Malhotra
D: Harmesh Malhotra
M: Laxmikant Pyarelal
C: Shashi Kapoor, Sulakshna Pandit, Ranjeet, Asrani, Iftekhar, Sapru, Mohan Choti, Urmila Bhat, Ram Mohan, Dev Kumar and Pran

Rahu Ketu (1978)
P: B. Pandey
D: B. R. Ishara
M: Kalyanji Anandji
C: Shashi Kapoor, Rekha, Bindu, Monty, Aruna Irani, Keshto Mukherji, Kamini Kaushal, Asit Sen, Jayshree T., Premnath and Pran

Vishwanath (1978)
P: Pawan Kumar
D: Subhash Ghai
M: Rajesh Roshan
C: Shatrughan Sinha, Reena Roy, Premnath, Reeta Bhaduri, Iftekhar, Jagdish Raj, Madan Puri, Viju Khote, Sapru and Pran. (*In guest appearances*: Lalita Pawar, Parikshit Sahni, Mukri, Satyen Kappu and Ranjeet.)

Atmaram (1979)
P: Sohanlal Kanwar
D: Sohanlal Kanwar
M: Shankar Jaikishan
C: Shatrughan Sinha, Vidya Sinha, Bindya Goswami, Farida Jalal, Aruna Irani, Sulochana, Amjad Khan and Pran

Teen Chehrey (1979)
P: S.A. Patel and Deepak Kapoor
D: Y.N. Kapoor
M: Shyamji Ghanshyamji
C: Anjana, Sujit Kumar, Jayshree T., Meena T., Raviraj, Ravindra Mahajan, Leela Patel, Mohan Choti, Birbal, Nana Palsikar and Pran

Sonal Dighe (1970s)
P: Not known
D: Ashim Bannerjee

M: Not known
C: Joy Mukerji, Pran and others

Aap Ke Dewane (1980)
P: Vimal Kumar
D: Surendra Mohan
M: Rajesh Roshan
C: Ashok Kumar, Rishi Kapoor, Rakesh Roshan, Tina Munim, Deven Verma, Ranjeet and Pran

Bombay 405 Miles (1980)
P: Brij
D: Brij
M: Kalyanji Anandji
C: Shatrughan Sinha, Zeenat Aman, Vinod Khanna, Amjad Khan, Deven Verma, Helen, Birbal and Pran

Desh Drohi (1980)
P: Bhagwant Singh and G. L. Khanna
D: Prakash Mehra
M: Kalyanji Anandji
C: Saira Banu, Navin Nischol, Ranjeet, Asrani, Jairaj, Madan Puri, Padma Khanna, Dev Kumar, Yunus Pervez, Rajen Haksar, Keshto Mukherji and Pran

Dhan Daulat (1980)
P: Vinod Shah
D: Harish Shah
M: R. D. Burman
C: Rajendra Kumar, Mala Sinha, Rishi Kapoor, Neetu Singh, Prem Chopra, Premnath, Sujit Kumar, Madan Puri, Agha, Kader Khan, Asit Sen, Sajjan and Pran

Dostana (1980)
P: Yash Johar
D: Raj Khosla
M: Laxmikant Pyarelal
C: Amitabh Bachchan, Shatrughan Sinha, Zeenat Aman, Prem Chopra, K.N. Singh, Macmohan, Helen, Amrish Puri, Sudhir, Jagirdar, Sudha Chopra, Iftekhar, Jagdish Raj, Sharat Saxena, Trilok Kapoor, Paintal, Yunus Pervez and Pran

Jwalamukhi (1980)
P: Baboo Mehra
D: Prakash Mehra

M: Kalyanji Anandji
C: Waheeda Rehman, Shatrughan Sinha, Reena Roy, Vinod Mehra, Shabana Azmi and Pran

Jal Mahal (1980)
P: R.K. Soral
D: Raghunath Jhalani
M: R.D. Burman
C: Jeetendra, Rekha, Deven Verma, Jagdeep, Jayshree T., Chand Usmani, Sunder, Jankidas, Viju Khote, Rajesh Behl and Pran

Karz (1980)
P: Jagjeet Khorana and Akhtar Farooqui
D: Subhash Ghai
M: Laxmikant Pyarelal
C: Rishi Kapoor, Tina Munim, Simi, Raj Kiran, Premnath, Pinchoo Kapoor, Durga Khote, Jalal Agha and Pran

Patthar Se Takkar (1980)
P: Gulab Mehta
D: Gulab Mehta
M: Laxmikant Pyarelal
C: Sanjeev Kumar, Neeta Mehta, Jeevan, Satyen Kappu, Farida Jalal, Amrish Puri, Urmila Bhat, Macmohan, Bhagwan, Birbal, Leela Misra, Javed Khan and Pran

Khuda Kasam (1980)
P: Baldev Pushkarna
D: Lekh Tandon
M: Laxmikant Pyarelal
C: Vinod Khanna, Tina Munim, Ajit, Nazneen, Zahira, Jalal Agha, Shakti Kapoor and Pran

Zaalim (1980)
P: Ram Singh
D: B. Subhash
M: Laxmikant Pyarelal
C: Vinod Khanna, Leena Chandavarkar, Nirupa Roy, Iftekhar, Rehman, Madan Puri, Jayshree T., V. Gopal, Keshto Mukherji and Pran

Kaalia (1981)
P: Iqbal Singh
D: Tinnu Anand
M: R.D. Burman

C: Amitabh Bachchan, Parveen Babi, Amjad Khan, Asha Parekh, K. N. Singh, Sajjan, Anwar, Kader Khan and Pran

Khoon Ka Rishta (1981)
P: Siraj Darpan, Amar Roy and Harila Thakkar
D: Sameer Ganguli
M: Kalyanji Anandji
C: Jeetendra, Neetu Singh, Amjad Khan, Jagdeep and Pran

Krodhi (1981)
P: Ranjit Virk
D: Subhash Ghai
M: Laxmikant Pyarelal
C: Dharmendra, Shashi Kapoor, Premnath, Zeenat Aman, Sachin, Ranjeeta and Pran. (*In a special appearance*: Hema Malini.)

Ladies' Tailor (1981)
P: Khalid Akhtar
D: Khalid Akhtar
M: Laxmikant Pyarelal
C: Sanjeev Kumar, Reena Roy, Deven Verma, Amjad Khan, Urmila Bhat, Manju Singh and Pran. (*In a special appearance*: Bindu.)

Maan Gaye Ustad (1981)
P: S. K. Kapoor
D: Shibu Mitra
M: Sonik Omi
C: Ashok Kumar, Shashi Kapoor, Hema Malini, Ajit, Bindu, Amjad Khan and Pran

Naseeb (1981)
P: Manmohan Desai
D: Manmohan Desai
M: Laxmikant Pyarelal
C: Amitabh Bachchan, Shatrughan Sinha, Rishi Kapoor, Hema Malini, Reena Roy, Kim, Prem Chopra, Shakti Kapoor, Jeevan, Lalita Pawar, Amjad Khan and Pran

Waqt Ki Deewar (1981)
P: T. C. Diwan
D: Ravi Tandon
M: Laxmikant Pyarelal
C: Sanjeev Kumar, Jeetendra, Neetu Singh, Sulakshna Pandit, Amjad Khan, Kader Khan and Pran

Jeeo Aur Jeene Do (1982)
P: Ratan Mohan
D: Shyam Ralhan
M: Laxmikant Pyarelal
C: Nutan, Jeetendra, Reena Roy, Danny, Vijayendra, Kajal Kiran, Kader Khan, Om Shivpuri and Pran

Taqdeer Ka Badshah (1982)
P: Ram Dayal
D: B. Subhash
M: Bappi Lahiri
C: Ranjeeta, Mithun Chakraborty, Suresh Oberoi, Tamanna, Vijay Arora, Amjad Khan and Pran

Partner (1982)
P: Anil Tejani
D: Anil Tejani
M: Vijay Singh
C: Kanwaljit, Deepti Naval, Shakti Kapoor and Pran

Taaqat (1982)
P: Raaj Grover and Shabranjan Majumdar
D: Narinder Bedi
M: Laxmikant Pyarelal
C: Rakhee, Vinod Khanna, Parveen Babi, Nadira, Bharat Bhushan, Bharat Kapoor, Chandrashekhar, Rajendranath, Shammi and Pran

Andha Kanoon (1983)
P: A. Puranchandra Rao
D: T. Rama Rao
M: Laxmikant Pyarelal
C: Hema Malini, Reena Roy, Madhavi, Rajnikant, Prem Chopra, Danny, Madan Puri and Pran. (*In special appearances:* Amitabh Bachchan and Amrish Puri.)

Daulat Ke Dushman (1983)
P: Manu Narang
D: Bimal Rawal
M: R.D. Burman
C: Shatrughan Sinha, Manjushree, Vinod Khanna, Ajit, Paintal and Pran

Ek Jaan Hai Hum (1983)
P: Parvesh Mehra

D: Rajiv Mehra
M: Anu Malik
C: Shammi Kapoor, Rajiv Kapoor, Divya Rana, Gulshan Grover, Rakesh Bedi and Pran

Film Hi Film (1983)
P: Shahab Ahmed
D: Hiren Nag
M: Bappi Lahiri
C: Bipin, Beena, Ramesh Deo, Farquan, Sonit and Pran

Janwar (1983)
P: Pardyuman Mohla
D: Ali Raza
M: Laxmikant Pyarelal
C: Rajesh Khanna, Zeenat Aman, Yogita Bali and Pran

Lalach (1983)
P: Prem Bedi
D: Shankar Nag
M: Bappi Lahiri
C: Vinod Mehra, Bindya Goswami, Ranjeet, Anant Nag, Kajal Kiran and Pran

Nauker Biwi Ka (1983)
P: Nishi Kohli
D: Raj Kumar Kohli
M: Bappi Lahiri
C: Dharmendra, Reena Roy, Raj Babbar, Rajeev Anand, Om Prakash, Kader Khan, Anita Raj and Pran. (*In guest appearances:* Rishi Kapoor, Vinod Mehra and Neeta Mehta.)

Souten (1983)
P: Saawan Kumar Tak
D: Saawan Kumar Tak
M: Usha Khanna
C: Rajesh Khanna, Tina Munim, Padmini Kolhapure, Shreeram Lagu, Prem Chopra, Shashikala and Pran

Woh Jo Hasina (1983)
P: C.P. Sharma
D: Deepak Bahry
M: Ram Laxman
C: Ranjeeta, Mithun Chakraborty, Prema Narayan, Madan Puri, Kader Khan,

Rajendranath, Chander, Satyen Kappu and Pran

Nastik (1983)
P: Vinod Doshi
D: Pramod Chakraborty
M: Kalyanji Anandji
C: Amitabh Bachchan, Hema Malini, Amjad Khan, Deven Verma and Pran

Bade Dilwala (1984)
P: Bhappi Sonie
D: Bhappi Sonie
M: R. D. Burman
C: Rishi Kapoor, Tina Munim, Sarjka, Aruna Irani, Jagdeep, Madan Puri, Kalpana Iyer, Roopesh Kumar, Bharat Bhushan, Amjad Khan and Pran

Farishta (1984)
P: Sunil Sikand
D: Sunil Sikand
M: R.D. Burman
C: Ashok Kumar, Kanwaljit and Smita Patil. (*In special appearances*: Master Raju, Master Rajiv Bhatia, Ambika Shourie, Bharat Bhushan, Danny and Pran.)

Haisiyat (1984)
P: Srikant Nahata
D: Narayana Rao
M: Bappi Lahiri
C: Jeetendra, Jayaprada, Shakti Kapoor, Rohini Hattangadi, Kader Khan, Jayshree T., Viju Khote, Raza Murad and Pran

Jagir (1984)
P: Pramod Chakraborty
D: Pramod Chakraborty
M: R. D. Burman
C: Dharmendra, Zeenat Aman, Mithun Chakraborty, Shoma Anand, Danny, Beena, Iftekhar, Sujit Kumar, Ranjeet, Amrish Puri and Pran

Laila (1984)
P: Saawan Kumar Tak
D: Saawan Kumar Tak
M: Usha Khanna
C: Sunil Dutt, Poonam Dhillon, Anil Kapoor,

Yogita Bali, Seema Deo, Ramesh Deo, Satyen Kappu and Pran

Mera Faisla (1984)
P: Ranjit Virk
D: S. V. Rajendra Singh
M: Laxmikant Pyarelal
C: Sanjay Dutt, Rati Agnihotri, Jayaprada, Nirupa Roy, Shakti Kapoor, Kader Khan and Pran

Raja Aur Rana (1984)
P: S. K. Kapoor
D: Shibu Mitra
M: Bappi Lahiri
C: Ashok Kumar, Puneet Issar, Aloka Soundh, Ajit, Shakti Kapoor, Madan Puri, Chandrashekhar, Rajen Haksar, Chand Usmani, Madhu Malhotra, Om Prakash and Pran

Raj Tilak (1984)
P: Anil Suri
D: Raj Kumar Kohli
M: Kalyanji Anandji
C: Sunil Dutt, Raaj Kumar, Dharmendra, Hema Malini, Kamal Hasan, Reena Roy, Raj Kiran, Ranjeeta, Sarika, Yogita Bali, S.A. Vikram, Ajit, Jamuna, Rajeev Anand, Om Prakash and Pran

Duniya (1984)
P: Yash Johar
D: Ramesh Talwar
M: R. D. Burman
C: Ashok Kumar, Dilip Kumar, Saira Banu, Rishi Kapoor, Amrita Singh, Prem Chopra, Amrish Puri and Pran

Sohni Mahiwal (1984)
P: F. C. Mehra
D: Umesh Mehra
M: Anu Malik
C: Sunny Deol, Poonam Dhillon, Zeenat Aman, Tanuja, Gulshan Grover, Rakesh Bedi, Mehar Mittal and Pran. (*In guest appearances*: Shammi Kapoor and Mazhar Khan.)

Sharabi (1984)
P: Satyendra Pal

D: Prakash Mehra
M: Bappi Lahiri
C: Amitabh Bachchan, Jayaprada, Om Prakash, Ranjeet, Satyen Kappu and Pran

Inquilab (1984)
P: N. Veeraswamy
D: T. Rama Rao
M: Laxmikant Pyaralal
C: Amitabh Bachchan, Sridevi, Utpal Dutt, Kader Khan, Ranjeet and Pran

Durga (1985)
P: S. K. Kapoor
D: Shibu Mitra
M: Sonik Omi
C: Ashok Kumar, Hema Malini, Raj Babbar, Aruna Irani and Pran. (*In a special appearance:* Rajesh Khanna.)

Hoshiyar (1985)
P: G. A. Seshagiri Rao
D: K. Raghvendra Rao
M: Bappi Lahiri
C: Jeetendra, Shatrughan Sinha, Jayaprada, Asrani, Meenakshi Sheshadri, Kader Khan, Shakti Kapoor, Purnima, Ranjeet and Pran

Bewafai (1985)
P: C. Dhan Dayuthapani
D: R. Thayagarajan
M: Bappi Lahiri
C: Rajesh Khanna, Rajnikant, Tina Munim, Padmini Kolhapure, Meenakshi Sheshadri and Pran

Karamyudh (1985)
P: Dimppy
D: Swaroop Kumar
M: Bappi Lahiri
C: Mithun Chakraborty, Anita Raj, Amrish Puri, Bharat Kapoor, Asha Sachdev and Pran

Maa Kasam (1985)
P: Vikas and Veena Sharma
D: Shibu Mitra
M: Bappi Lahiri
C: Mithun Chakraborty, Divya Rana, Ranjeet and Pran

Sarfarosh (1985)
P: Prasan Kapoor
D: Dasari Narayan Rao
M: Laxmikant Pyarelal
C: Jeetendra, Sridevi, Leena Chandavarkar, Kader Khan, Prem Chopra, Ranjeet, Asrani and Pran

Yudh (1985)
P: Gulshan Rai
D: Rajiv Rai
M: Kalyanji Anandji
C: Jackie Shroff, Anil Kapoor, Tina Munim, Nutan, Danny, Deven Verma and Pran. (*In special appearances:* Hema Malini, Shatrughan Sinha and Suresh Oberoi.)

Pataal Bhairavi (1985)
P: G. Hanumantha Rao
D: K. Bapaiah
M: Bappi Lahiri
C: Jeetendra, Jayaprada, Amjad Khan, Kader Khan, Shakti Kapoor, Asrani, Nirupa Roy, Bindu, Prema Narayan, Dimple Kapadia, Shoma Anand and Pran

Dosti Dushmani (1986)
P: T. Rama Rao
D: T. Rama Rao
M: Laxmikant Pyarelal
C: Jeetendra, Rishi Kapoor, Rajnikant, Bhanu Priya, Kimi Katkar, Poonam Dhillon, Shafi Inamdar, Kader Khan, Shakti Kapoor, Asrani, Amrish Puri and Pran

Dilwala (1986)
P: D. Rama Naidu
D: A. Murli Mohan Rao
M: Bappi Lahiri
C: Mithun Chakraborty, Smita Patil, Meenakshi Sheshadri, Kader Khan, Shakti Kapoor, Sarika, Suresh Oberoi, Shreeram Lagu, Arun Govil, Asrani, Gulshan Grover, Raza Murad, Paintal, Supriya Pathak, Bandini Mishra and Pran

Dharam Adhikari (1986)
P: U.V. Suryanarayan Rao
D: K. Raghvendra Rao
M: Bappi Lahiri

C: Dilip Kumar, Jeetendra, Sridevi, Anuradha Patel, Kader Khan, Shakti Kapoor, Asrani, Rakesh Bedi, Sujit Kumar, Rohini Hattangadi, Preeti Sapru, Gita Siddharth, Mayur and Pran

Jeeva (1986)
P: Romu Sippy
D: Raj N. Sippy
M: R.D. Burman
C: Sanjay Dutt, Mandakini, Amjad Khan, Shreeram Lagu, Sachin, Shakti Kapoor, Gulshan Grover, Beena, Vidya Sinha, Anupam Kher.and Pran

Love and God (1986)
P: Akhtar Asif
D: K. Asif
M: Naushad
C: Sanjeev Kumar, Nimmi, Nazir Hussain, Jayant, Lalita Pawar, Amjad Khan, Achala Sachdev, Asha, Murad, Nazima, Randhir and Pran

Ricky (1986)
P: Chotu Bihari
D: Ashok Bhushan
M: Jagdish Uttam
C: Meenakshi Sheshadri, Kunal Goswami, Nutan, Sharmila Tagore, Amrish Puri, Prem Chopra and Pran

Suhaagan (1986)
P: V. Kanaka Raju
D: K. Raghvendra Rao
M: Bappi Lahiri
C: Jeetendra, Sridevi, Padmini Kolhapure, Tanuja, Shakti Kapoor, Asrani, Kader Khan, Aruna Irani, Baby Zeenat, Chandrashekhar and Pran. (*In a special appearance:* Raj Babbar.)

Dilruba Tangewali (1987)
P: Devi Films
D: S.R. Pratap
M: Anwar Usman
C: Hemant Birje, Sriprada, Deva, Krishna Devi, Chand Usmani, Rajendranath and Pran

Goraa (1987)
P: R.K. Mehta
D: Desh Gautam
M: Sonik Omi
C: Rajesh Khanna, Sulakshna Pandit, Raj Kiran, Preeti Sapru, Om Puri, Ramesh Deo, Seema Deo and Pran

Insaaf Kaun Karega (1987)
P: Suresh Bokadia
D: Sudershan Naag
M: Laxmikant Pyarelal
C: Dharmendra, Rajnikant, Madhavi, Jayaprada, Gulshan Grover, Rohini Hattangadi, Bindu, Amrish Puri, Shakti Kapoor and Pran

Kudrat Ka Kanoon (1987)
P: Suresh Bokadia
D: K. C. Bokadia
M: Laxmikant Pyarelal
C: Hema Malini, Jackie Shroff, Kiran Kumar, Radhika, Charanraj, Asrani, Satyen Kappu, Shafi Inamdar, Ramesh Deo and Pran

Imaandaar (1987)
P: Surendra Pal Choudhry
D: Sushil Malik
M: Kalyanji Anandji
C: Sanjay Dutt, Farah, Sumeet Saigal, Mehmood, Om Prakash, Ranjeet, Satyen Kappu and Pran

Hifazat (1987)
P: A. Suryanarayan
D: Prayag Raj
M: R.D. Burman
C: Ashok Kumar, Nutan, Anil Kapoor, Madhuri Dixit, Bindu, Kader Khan, Shakti Kapoor, Gulshan Grover, Shubha Khote, Lalita Pawar and Pran

Muqaddar Ka Faisla (1987)
P: Yash Johar
D: Prakash Mehra
M: Bappi Lahiri
C: Raj Babbar, Raaj Kumar, Rakhee, Akbar Khan, Meenakshi Sheshadri, Tina Munim, Bindu, Om Prakash, Ranjeet, Kajal Kiran, Vijayendra and Pran

Maa Beti (1987)
P: Radhika Films
D: Kalpataru
M: Anand Milind
C: Shashi Kapoor, Sharmila Tagore, Meenakshi Sheshadri, Sachin, Ashok Saraf, Kader Khan, Tanuja and Pran

Sitapur Ki Geeta (1987)
P: S.K. Kapoor
D: Shibu Mitra
M: Sonik Omi
C: Hema Malini, Rajesh Khanna, Rajan Sippy, Shoma Anand, Amjad Khan, Shakti Kapoor, Raza Murad, Chandrashekhar and Pran

Dharam Shatru (1988)
P: A.V. Mohan
D: Harmesh Malhotra
M: Hemant Bhonsle
C: Shatrughan Sinha, Reena Roy, Amjad Khan, Mahesh Anand, Nirupa Roy and Pran

Paap Ki Duniya (1988)
P: Pahlaj Nihalani
D: Shibu Mitra
M: Bappi Lahiri
C: Sunny Deol, Chunkey Pandey, Neelam, Danny, Shakti Kapoor, Rubina, Paintal, Gita Siddharth, Sarla Yeolekar, Seema Deo, Renu Joshi, Pinchoo Kapoor, Macmohan, Sudhir, Birbal, Manmaujee and Pran

Sherni (1988)
P: Ramayan Chitra
D: Harmesh Malhotra
M: Kalyanji Anandji
C: Sridevi, Shatrughan Sinha, Kader Khan, Ranjeet, Sudhir, Lalita Pawar, Jagdeep, Tej Sapru, Ram Mohan and Pran

Aurat Teri Yehi Kahani (1988)
P: Mohanji Prasad, S. K. Jain and B. K. Jaiswal
D: Mohanji Prasad
M: Anand Milind
C: Meenakshi Sheshadri, Raj Kiran, Shreeram Lagu, Sushma Seth, Aruna Irani, Nilu Phule, Nirupa Roy, Shoma Anand,

Kader Khan, Ashok Saraf and Pran. (*In a special appearance*: Raj Babbar.)

Dharam Yudh (1988)
P: Pawan Kumar
D: Sudershan Naag
M: Rajesh Roshan
C: Sunil Dutt, Shatrughan Sinha, Kimi Katkar, Aditya Pancholi, Suresh Oberoi, Saaniya, Sushma Seth, Ranjeet, Disco Shanti and Pran

Gunahon Ka Faisla (1988)
P: Pahlaj Nihalani
D: Shibu Mitra
M: Bappi Lahiri
C: Shatrughan Sinha, Dimple Kapadia, Chunkey Pandey, Prem Chopra, Gulshan Grover, Danny, Ranjeet, Shakti Kapoor, Aruna Irani, Anjana Mumtaz, Satish Kaul, Rajesh Puri and Pran

Kasam (1988)
P: Indra Kumar and Ashok Thakeria
D: Umesh Mehra
M: Bappi Lahiri
C: Anil Kapoor, Poonam Dhillon, Amrit Pal, Gulshan Grover, Kader Khan, Aruna Irani, Guddi Maruti, Johnny Lever, Satyen Kappu, Adi Irani, Puneet Issar, Viju Khote, Master Bunty and Pran

Mohabbat Ke Dushman (1988)
P: Prakash Mehra
D: Prakash Mehra
M: Kalyanji Anandji
C: Raaj Kumar, Hema Malini, Sanjay Dutt, Farah, Amrish Puri, Dina Pathak, Satyen Kappu, Vijayendra, Ram Sethi, Mehmood Jr., Alka Nupoor, Vikas Anand, Sudhir, Parveen, Gurbachan, Manjeet Kaur and Pran

Shahenshah (1988)
P: Tinnu Anand, Bittu Anand and Naresh Malhotra
D: Tinnu Anand
M: Amar Utpal
C: Amitabh Bachchan, Meenakshi Sheshadri, Amrish Puri, Kader Khan, Aruna Irani, Prem Chopra, Jagdeep, Rohini

Hattangadi, Supriya Pathak, Vijayendra, Sudhir, Dan Dhanoa, Bandini Mishra and Pran

Rama-O-Rama (1988)
P: Humayun, Shahrukh and Mahrukh Mirza (Mirza Brothers)
D: Mirza Brothers
M: R.D. Burman
C: Raj Babbar, Kimi Katkar, Aasif Shaikh, Gulshan Grover, Kiran Kumar, Raza Murad, Shiva and Pran

Bade Ghar Ki Beti (1989)
P: M. Prasad Jain and Jaiswal
D: Kalpataru
M: Laxmikant Pyarelal
C: Rishi Kapoor, Meenakshi Sheshadri, Shammi Kapoor, Sushma Seth, Satish Shah, Raj Kiran, Gulshan Grover, Aruna Irani, Shoma Anand, Jayshree T., Ashok Saraf, Kader Khan, Asrani and Pran

Chingari (1989)
P: Kalpanalok
D: Ram Maheshwari
M: Shafi M. Nagari
C: Sanjay Khan, Leena Chandavarkar and Pran

Jadugar (1989)
P: Prakash Mehra Productions
D: Prakash Mehra
M: Kalyanji Anandji
C: Amitabh Bachchan, Jayaprada, Aditya Pancholi, Amrita Singh, Amrish Puri, Raza Murad, Vikas Anand, Ram Sethi, Bharat Bhushan and Pran

Mitti Aur Sona (1989)
P: Pahlaj Nihalani
D: Shiv Kumar
M: Bappi Lahiri
C: Chunkey Pandey, Sonam, Gulshan Grover, Anjana Mumtaz, Om Shivpuri, Sushma Seth, Tej Sapru, Macmohan, Paintal and Pran. (In a special appearance: Neelam and in a guest appearance: Vinod Mehra.)

Nigahen (1989) (Nagina – Part 2)
P: Harmesh Malhotra

D: Harmesh Malhotra
M: Laxmikant Pyarelal
C: Sridevi, Sunny Deol, Anupam Kher, Gulshan Grover, Jagdeep, Anjana Mumtaz, Aruna Irani and Pran

Shukriyaa (1989)
P: Kailash Chopra
D: A.C. Trilokchander
M: Anu Malik
C: Rajiv Kapoor, Amrita Singh, Asrani, Prem Chopra, Rohini Hattangadi, Beena, Shiva, Jugnu, Chandrashekhar, Ashalata, Birbal, Chhotu Ustad and Pran

Toofan (1989)
P: Manmohan Desai
D: Ketan Desai
M: Anu Malik
C: Amitabh Bachchan, Meenakshi Sheshadri, Amrita Singh, Goga Kapoor, Farooque Shaikh, Zarina Wahab, Raza Murad, Sushma Seth, Kamal Kapoor, Master Makarand, Jack Gaud, Mahesh Anand, Sudhir Dalvi, Chhotu Dada, Chandrashekhar, Bharat Bhushan, Maneck Irani, Bob Christo, Ramesh Deo and Pran

Zooni (1989–90)
P: Muzaffar Ali
D: Muzaffar Ali
M: Khayyam
C: Dimple Kapadia, Sushma Seth, Master Farouq, Shabi Abbas, V. K. Kaul, Mohanlal Aima, Shaukat Kafi, Dilip Tahil and Pran

Azaad Desh Ke Ghulam (1990)
P: Suresh Bhagat
D: S.A. Chandrashekhar
M: Laxmikant Pyarelal
C: Rekha, Rishi Kapoor, Jackie Shroff, Prem Chopra, Suresh Bhagwat and Pran

Pyar Ka Toofan (1990)
P: S. M. Iqbal
D: D.M. Iqbal
M: Kalyanji Anandji
C: Aditya Pancholi, Jamuna, Gulshan Grover, Aruna Irani, Kulbhushan Kharbanda, Ashalata and Pran

Roti Ki Keemat (1990)
P: Suresh Grover
D: Ramesh Ahuja
M: Bappi Lahiri
C: Mithun Chakraborty, Kimi Katkar, Sadashiv Amrapurkar, Puneet Issar, Jagdish Raj, Anjana Mumtaz and Pran

Sanam Bewafa (1991)
P: Saawan Kumar Tak
D: Saawan Kumar Tak
M: Mahesh Kishore
C: Salman Khan, Chandni, Danny, Kanchan, Vijayendra, Dan Dhanoa, Dina, Puneet Issar, Master Alok, Mahajan, Jugnu, Tahir Khan and Pran

Lakshman Rekha (1991)
P: Satyendra Pal
D: Sunil Sikand
M: Laxmikant Pyarelal
C: Jackie Shroff, Naseeruddin Shah, Sangeeta Bijlani, Shilpa Shirodkar, Danny, Shammi Kapoor, Om Prakash, Rohini Hattangadi, Raza Murad, Anjan Srivastava, Mangal Dhillon, Girija Shankar, Avtar Gill, Amrit Pal, Karan Razdan and Pran

Banjaran (1991)
P: Om Prakash Mittal/Ram Singh
D: Harmesh Malhotra
M: Laxmikant Pyarelal
C: Rishi Kapoor, Sridevi, Gulshan Grover, Kulbhushan Kharbanda, Raza Murad, Rakesh Bedi, Sudhir Pandey, Anjana Mumtaz, Renu Arya, Madhu Malhotra, Sharat Saxena and Pran

Jigarwala (1991)
P: Surinder Kaur Jerath
D: Swaroop Kumar
M: Nadeem Shravan
C: Anil Kapoor, Tina Munim, Gulshan Grover, Amrish Puri, Sanjay Jog, Kanan Kaushal, Jagdeep and Pran

Mashooq (1992)
P: Humayun, Shahrukh and Mahrukh Mirza
D: Mirza Brothers
M: Shyam Sunder

C: Ayub Khan, Ayesha Jhulka, Kiran Kumar, Beena, Raza Murad and Pran

Meera Ka Mohan (1992)
P: Super Cassettes Industries
D: K. Ravi Shankar
M: Arun Paudwal
C: Avinash Wadhawan, Ashwini Bhave, Deepak Saraf, Alok Nath, A.K. Hangal, Ashok Saraf, Rakesh Bedi, Kunika, Vikas Anand, Brando Bakshi and Pran

Do Hanson Ka Joda (1992)
P: Barkha Silky and Combines
D: G. D. Talwar
M: Dilip and Sameer Sen
C: Anupam Kher, Kiran Kumar, Reema Lagu, Kanchan, Mohan Kumar, Sulabha Deshpande, Beena, Rajendranath and Pran

Bewafa Se Wafa (1992)
P: Saawan Kumar Tak
D: Saawan Kumar Tak
M: Usha Khanna
C: Juhi Chawla, Vivek Mushran, Naghma, Aruna Irani, Lalit Tiwari, Mehmood and Pran

Panaah (1992)
P: Lawrence D'Souza and Mahendra Pandya
D: Krishnakant Pandya
M: Nadeem Shravan
C: Naseeruddin Shah, Siddharth, Jeet Upendra, Pallavi Joshi, Kiran Kumar, Shrisht, Mohsin, Harish Patel, Amrit Patel, Ram Mohan and Pran

Isi Ka Naam Zindagi (1992)
P: Rajan Mukherjee
D: Kalidas
M: Bappi Lahiri
C: Aamir Khan, Farah, Shakti Kapoor, Asrani, Beena, Anjan Srivastava, Tej Sapru, Rajesh Puri, Shiva, Babloo Mukherjee, Bharat Kapoor and Pran

Chandramukhi (1993)
P: Karishma International
D: Debaloy Dey

M: Anand Milind
C: Sridevi, Salman Khan, Mohnish Bahl, Tinnu Anand, Gulshan Grover, Kunika, Puneet Issar, Tej Sapru, Asha Sachdev, Avtar Gill and Pran

Dosti Ki Saugandh (1993)
P: Nisha Manish Arts
D: Mohanji Prasad
M: Surinder Kohli
C: Shammi Kapoor, Chandni, Upasana Singh, Ronit Roy, Shakti Kapoor, Kader Khan, Pankaj Dheer, Sujit Kumar, Sushma Seth, Ajinkya Deo, Ram Singh, Sudha Chandran, Urmila Bhat, Paintal, Aparajita, Jayshree T., Shashi Puri and Pran

Gurudev (1993)
P: V. M. Productions
D: Vinod Mehra
M: R.D. Burman
C: Rishi Kapoor, Anil Kapoor, Sridevi, Danny, Kader Khan, Kiran Kumar, Asrani, Seema Deo, Satyen Kappu, Shammi, Macmohan, Tej Sapru, Mahavir Shah, Harish Patel and Pran

Kohra (1993)
P: Heera International
D: Partho Ghosh
M: Charanjeet Ahuja
C: Armaan Kohli, Ayesha Jhulka, Tinnu Anand, Deepak Saraf, Kiran Kumar, Sadashiv Amrapurkar, Gulshan Grover and Pran

Aaja Meri Jaan (1993)
P: Super Cassettes Industries
D: Ketan Anand
M: Amar Utpal
C: Krishan Kumar, Tanya Singh, Girish Malik, Shammi Kapoor, Prem Chopra, Deven Verma, Manohar Singh and Pran

Bhagyawan (1993)
P: Upendra Jha
D: S. Subhash
M: Anand Milind
C: Asha Parekh, Govinda, Juhi Chawla, Sriprada, Ranjeet, Johnny Lever, Aruna Irani, Suraj Chaddha, Reshma Singh, Kirti Kumar, Disco Shanti and Pran

1942 – A Love Story (1994)
P: Vidhu Vinod Chopra
D: Vidhu Vinod Chopra
M: R.D. Burman
C: Anil Kapoor, Jackie Shroff, Manisha Koirala, Anupam Kher, Danny, Chandni and Pran

Hum Hai Bemisal (1994)
P: Geeta Gupta
D: Deepak Bahry
M: Anu Malik
C: Akshay Kumar, Suniel Shetty, Shilpa Shirodkar, Madhoo Rangnathan, Jagdeep, Arun Bakshi and Pran

Sajan Ki Bahon Mein (1995)
P: Dinesh Patel
D: Jayprakash
M: Nadeem Shravan
C: Rishi Kapoor, Tabu, Raveena Tandon, Sumeet Saigal, Vijeta Pandit and Pran

Vaapsi Sajan Ki (1995)
P: Atiq Rehman
D: Grev Bedwal
M: Anand Milind
C: Shoaib Khan, Shoma Sircar, Ashwini Bhave, Gulshan Grover, Parikshit Sahni and Pran

Lalchee (1996)
P: Amit Khanna and Mukesh Bhatt
D: Raj N. Sippy
M: Dilip and Sameer Sen
C: Rohit Roy, Anil Dhawan, Kareena Grover and Pran

Dadagiri (1997)
P: Not known
D: Not known
M: Not known
C: Mithun Chakraborty, Ayub Khan, Simran, Raza Murad, Shakti Kapoor, Kader Khan and Pran

Gudia (1997)
P: Not known
D: Gautam Ghosh
M: Not known
C: Mithun Chakraborty, Nabneeta Deb Sen, Shubhendhu Chatterjee and Pran

Lakha (1997)
P: R.S. Sodhani
D: Not known
M: Jugal Kishore Tilakraj
C: Arun Govil, Sahila Chaddha, Seema Vij and Pran

Luv Kush (1997)
P: Dilip Kankaria
D: V. Madhusudan
M: Ram Laxman
C: Jeetendra, Jayaprada, Dara Singh, Arun Govil, Beena, Jayashri Gadkar, Tiku Talsania and Pran

Kaun Rokega Mujhe (1997)
P: Kamal Raj International
D: Kamal Raj Bhasin
M: Laxmikant Pyarelal
C: Govinda, Chunky Pandey, Naghma, Gulshan Grover, Ranjeet, Prem Chopra and Pran

Mrityudaataa (1997)
P: Amitabh Bachchan Corporation Ltd.
D: Mehul Kumar
M: Anand Milind
C: Amitabh Bachchan, Dimple Kapadia, Karishma, Arbaz Ali Khan, Paresh Rawal, Ashish and Pran

Salma Pe Dil Aa Gaya (1997)
P: Saawan Kumar Tak
D: Saawan Kumar Tak
M: Adesh Shrivastava
C: Ayub Khan, Sadhika, Milind Gunaji, Mukesh Khanna, Shashikala and Pran

Badmash (1998)
P: Anis Sabri
D: Goutam
M: Shyam Sunder
C: Jackie Shroff, Shilpa Shirodkar, Paresh Rawal, Tej Sapru and Pran

Tere Mere Sapne (1999)
P: Amitabh Bachchan Corporation Ltd.
D: Joy Augustine
M: Viju Shah
C: Chandrachur Singh, Priya Gill, Arshad Warsi, Simran and Pran

Jai Hind (1999)
P: Manoj Kumar
D: Manoj Kumar
M: Laxmikant Pyarelal
C: Rishi Kapoor, Kunal Goswami, Shilpa Shirodkar, Manisha Koirala, Raveena Tandon, Prem Chopra and Pran

OTHER FILMS OF PRAN IN THE 1990s

Buddha Mil Gaya
Dharam
Raghuvanshi
Yeh Ishq Ishq Hai
Ek Hi Manzil

FILMS OF PRAN IN THE NEW MILLENNIUM

Dosh (2002)
P: Golden Productions
D: Pappu Phalvinder
M: Manoj Gajendra and Paresh Parekh
C: Roopali, Puru Raaj Kumar, Govind Namdeo, Sadashiv Amrapurkar, Sonu Ghotra, Om Puri and Pran

Ek Hindustani (2002)
P: R.K. Nayyar
D: Tinnu Anand
M: Anand Raj Anand
C: Suniel Shetty, Raveena Tandon, Shahbaaz Khan, Mohnish Bahl, Danny, Mohan Joshi and Pran

Mohabbat Pehli Nazar Mein (2002)
P: Noor Films
D: Gautam
M: Siddhartha
C: Munawwar Ali, Aish Kanwal, Akshay Anand, Sangeeta Ghosh, Amjad Khan, Anupam Kher and Pran. (*In a guest appearance*: Amrish Puri.)

Suryakant (2002)
P: Waris Ali Rizvi
D: Inayat H. Sheikh
M: Mahesh Kishore
C: Dharmendra, Madhoo, Sonu Walia, Arjun, Kiran Kumar, Mohan Joshi, Arif Khan, Jagdeep and Pran

Tum Jiyo Hazaron Saal (2002)
P: Pragati Pictures
D: Ramnesh
M: Jatin Lalit
C: Sandeep Khosla, Raageshwari, Tanuja and Pran

OTHER FILMS OF PRAN IN THE NEW MILLENNIUM

Deewana Tere Pyar Ka (2003)
Kiska Dosh? (2003)

SOME OF PRAN'S SHELVED FILMS

Vasantsena
Lal Qila
Talaa Chabi

Awards Won by Pran

YEAR	AWARD	AWARDED BY
1960	Best Villain	Andhra Pradesh Film Journalists' Association
1961	Best Villain	Andhra Pradesh Film Journalists' Association
1963	Best Villain	Uttar Pradesh Film Journalists' Association
1967	Best Villain	Andhra Pradesh Film Journalists' Association
1967	Best Supporting Actor for *Upkar*	*Filmfare*
1967	Special Award for *Upkar*	Uttar Pradesh Film Journalists' Association
1969	Best Supporting Actor for *Aansoo Ban Gaye Phool*	*Filmfare*
1970	Top Awards Winner	Andhra Pradesh Film Journalists' Association
1970	Best Supporting Actor for *Johny Mera Naam*	All-India Filmgoers' Association
1970	Lenin Centenary Award (for services in the fields of art and culture)	Lenin Centenary Committee, Uttar Pradesh
1970	The Nizam's Gold Medal	Andhra Urdu Periodicals' Association
1970	For his Supporting Portrayal in *Aansoo Ban Gaye Phool*	Andhra Pradesh Film Journalists' Association
1970	For his Supporting Portrayal in *Aansoo Ban Gaye Phool*	Social and Cultural Bureau (Bombay)
1970–71	Best Supporting Actor for *Johny Mera Naam*	Maharashtra Film Fan Club
1970–71	Best Supporting Actor for *Ganwaar*	Bhavnagar Cine Circle
1971	Best Supporting Actor for *Adhikar*	Filmgoers' Association
1972	Best Supporting Actor for *Victoria No: 203*	Filmgoers' Association

(cont.)

YEAR	AWARD	AWARDED BY
1972	Best Supporting Actor for *Be-imaan*	*Shama-Sushma*
1971	Most Outstanding Supporting Actor of 1972	Lion's Club of Bombay (Colaba)
1972	Best Supporting Actor Trophy for *Be-imaan*	Crystal Association
1972	Best Supporting Actor for *Be-imaan* (Pran refused to accept this award)	*Filmfare*
1972–73	Best Character Artiste Award	Chitralok Cine Circle (Ahmedabad)
1973	Best Supporting Actor	Lion's Club of Bombay (Cumballa Hill)
1973	Actor of the Year – Everest Award	Filmgoers' Association
1973	Best Supporting Actor for *Zanjeer*	*Shama-Sushma*
1973	Trophy for *Zanjeer*	Crystal Association
1973	Outstanding Supporting Actor	Lion's Film Awards Committee
1973	Best Performance in *Zanjeer*	Bengal Film Journalists' Association (Calcutta)
1973	Best Actor of the Decade for *Zanjeer*	Uttar Pradesh Film Journalists' Association
1974	A Perfect Actor	Filmgoers' Association
1974	Best Supporting Actor for *Dharma*	*Shama-Sushma*
1974	Outstanding Supporting Actor	Lion's Film Awards Committee
1975	Outstanding Supporting Actor	Lion's Film Awards Committee
1975	Best Supporting Actor	*Mehndi* (Gujarati monthly)
1975–76	Most Versatile Actor	Bombay Film Awards Committee
1976	Outstanding Supporting Actor	Lion's Film Awards Committee
1977–78	Most Versatile Actor	Bombay Film Awards Committee
1978	Best Character Actor	North Bombay Jaycees
1980	Outstanding Motion Picture Performances (presented by the vice president of India)	Shiromani Award Committee
1983–84	Best Character Actor for *Lalach*	Punjabi Kala Sangam (New Delhi)
1984	Abhinay Samrat (king of acting)	All-India Filmgoers' Association
1984	Extraordinary Special Award as Wizard of Acting	Bombay Film Awards Committee
1985	Kala Bhushan	Punjabi Kala Sangam
1987	Outstanding Performance of the Decade	North Bombay Jaycees
Not known	Vijayshree Award (for enriching human life and outstanding attainments)	India International Friendship Society
Not known	Excellence in emotive art	'Ars Gratia Artis' Award
1990	For fifty years in the industry	Punjab Association
1990	Kala Rattan Award (for completing fifty glorious years in cinema)	Punjabi Kala Sangam
1990	In recognition of invaluable services to charity at the celebration of the golden jubilee of his services to the film industry	Southhall Lion's Club, London
1990	Honoured for outsanding achievement in cinema	Slough Borough Council (UK)

(cont.)

YEAR	AWARD	AWARDED BY
1991	Abhinay Samrat (for contribution to Indian cinema for fifty years)	Indian Cinegoers' Academy
1992	Outstanding contribution to Indian film industry	IMPPA (Indian Motion Pictures Producers' Association)
1997	Special Veteran's Award (this award is not the same as the Lifetime Achievement Awards, which incidentally were awarded to Dharmendra and Mumtaz that year)	*Filmfare*
2000	Villain of the Millennium	Hero Honda-*Stardust*
2000	Icon of the Millennium – Pran the Versatile Actor	Rupa Filmgoers' Millennium Awards
2000	Lifetime Achievement Award for Excellence in Cinema	Lux-ZEE Cine Awards
2000	Lifetime Achievement Award	*Screen*
2001	Padma Bhushan	The Government of India
2001	Felicitation (on winning the Padma Bhushan)	The Cine Artistes' Association
2001	Felicitation (on the occasion of the forty-third Baisakhi celebrations in Mumbai)	Punjab Association

Index